DEPARTURE;

OR,

Selections from the Jottings

OF

TWENTY YEARS.

BY THOMAS JEFFERSON RICE.

TOLEDO:
BLADE PRINTING AND PAPER CO.
1875.

PREFACE.

In laying before the public a production of this character, it may not be amiss very briefly to give the history of its origin.

In the spring of '53, we commenced jotting down, as briefly as possible, the substance of such thoughts upon man, his nature, destiny, etc., also upon God, his character, government, etc., as to us seemed valuable; and, after adding the proper date, of laying the same aside for further consideration at some more leisure time. The winter of '58, with the exception of attending to the usual farm-chores, we devoted wholly to looking over the fragmentary mass of papers which had thus accumulated in our drawer, making additions to such ideas as then seemed to us sound, altering those that were adjudged to be partly right and partly wrong, and destroying, as worthless, all such as we had already outgrown and left behind; it being ever a rule with us to speak and to act, upon any and all subjects, in accordance with the light we have at the time, no matter what may chance to have been our former opinions thereupon.

With that winter's labor, we were so well pleased and satisfied, that we have made it a practice from that time up to this present date, 1875, not only to keep on thus jotting during the more busy portions of the year, and overhauling the same the ensuing winter, but of carefully reviewing and altering to our then liking, else of destroying, as the case might require, all such of our former writings as had been previously examined and pronounced good, no matter how many times over that thing might have been done; in this way, ever keeping such of them as were thus annually approved, and hence laid by for still further future examinations and amendments, currently up to our steadily advancing views.

And it is out of such disconnected and fragmentary, but well-considered and carefully selected writings, that has finally come this little volume.

In making public this work, upon which we have spent so many happy days, it is not our aim to create division, or wound the feelings of such as may chance to differ with us upon religious subjects in either opinion or practice, but to awaken thought, stimulate inquiry, and excite discussion upon the different subjects whereof it thus briefly and imperfectly treats; consequently to enlighten, elevate, and bless a large and worthy class of persons who are believed to be to-day, the same as once were we, palsied in their affections, palsied in their sympathies, and palsied in their energies by doubts and uncertainty as to what is their true character and mission in the world; and hence, through such existing class, to a greater or less extent, all coming generations of men.—From thinking, and not from refusing or neglecting to think, cometh knowledge; from knowledge, goodness; and from goodness, happiness.

To say nothing of its want of method, and other kindred imperfections, that this volume is exempt from errors of fact we have not the vanity to suppose; and yet, that it contains numerous real truths that are not to be met with in any existing publication, and some which are of a fundamental character, we must and do believe. *Those*, the errors of fact, having no foundation upon which to rest, are certain to fall, as fall they should; but *these*, the real truths, each and all, having God for their supporter and defender, no matter how fiercely they may be assailed, will assuredly stand and ultimately come to be welcomed by an enlightened world.

With this brief description of its origin, character, and aim, this little book goes forth to the public under the hope that it may, in some small degree at least, accomplish the mission whereupon it is sent.

T. J. RICE.

HAMBURG, MICH., May, 1875.

CONTENTS:

DEPARTURE.

CHAPTER I.

TRUTH.

"Truth crushed to earth shall rise again,—
The eternal years of God are hers;
But Error, wounded, writhes in pain,
And dies amid her worshipers."

Of truth there are evidently two kinds; the one real, and the other merely mental, or moral. Real truth we shall define to be fact, to be conformity to what is, or was, or is to come; to be such truth as is consonant to some fact, past, present, or future, no matter whether it accords with the opinion of any man that ever did, now does, or ever shall exist, or not. Moral truth we shall define to be belief; to be such truth as was or is consonant to somebody's opinion, no matter whether it accords with any fact that ever was, now is, or ever shall be, or not.

Or thus: Just as long as does an idea, no matter what, hold the place of a fact in any man's head, just so long, and no longer, is such idea to that individual a moral truth; no matter whether such idea is consonant to any fact or not, or to any other human being's opinion or not, nor how in his head it came to have existence. Wherefore, to the extent that a man's opinions are consonant to fact, to that extent, in such individual's head, are the two kinds of truth harmoniously united in one; and to the extent that his opinions are dissonant from fact, to that extent are the two kinds as separate and unlike in both their character and consequences, as are fact and falsehood. And wherefore, to the extent that a man's words are consonant to his opinions and also to facts, to that extent doth he speak both moral and real truth ; and to the extent that his words are consonant to his opinions but dissonant from facts, to that extent doth he speak moral truth, but not real truth. Such being the case, it follows that to the extent a man's words are intentionally dissonant from his opinions, notwithstanding they may chance to coincide with facts, to that extent, and no further, is he guilty of uttering moral falsehood, and hence to that same extent, and no further, is he accountable for such utterance, either to his own conscience or to his fellow men.

Illustrative examples:—When a man says the Sun rose in the east eighteen hundred years ago, believing such to have been the fact, he speaks both a moral truth and a past real truth ; when he says the Sun rose in the east to-day, believing such to be the fact, he speaks both a moral truth and a present real truth; and when he says it will rise in the east eighteen hundred years hence, believing that such will be the fact, he speaks both a moral truth and a real truth to come. When a man says the Sun travels around the Earth every twenty-four hours, thus causing day and night, believing such to be the fact, he states a moral truth ;—a moral truth to him and all such as thus believe, whether few or many, notwithstanding it is in reality a falsehood ; and when he says (because beginning to feel ashamed of being suspected of thinking otherwise,) that the Earth revolves upon its axis every twenty-four hours, thus causing day and night, and at the same time does not believe such to be the fact, he states a moral falsehood ;—a moral falsehood to him and all such as believe with him, notwithstanding he utters a real truth. When men speak out in words what they believe to be fact, (as doubtless did the people of Salem when, upon their Bible oaths, they accused sundry innocent persons among them of the crime of witchcraft,) they speak moral truth, and when they go further and speak out their opinions in action, that is, go on and do what they sincerely think it is right and proper that they should perform, (as doubtless did the public functionaries who executed such of the aforesaid innocent Salemites as were judicially convicted of the crime thus charged against them, and hence condemned to die therefor,) the action is morally right,—morally right to them and all such as think with them; no matter what the thing done, what its effect, nor what may be the opinion of some other set or division of men concerning it. In the same manner, when Paul verily thought within himself *that he ought to do many things contrary to the name of Jesus of Nazareth*, that thought was to him and to all who believed with him, a moral truth; and hence, when, acting in accordance with such thought, he persecuted the saints, shut them up in prison, and gave his voice against them when they were being put to death, he was acting morally right and not morally wrong, notwithstanding in truth and in fact, the thing done was both foolish and wrong. And when, a short time thereafter, he came to change his opinion upon the subject, and hence just as verily to think he ought to preach Jesus of Nazareth, and so be himself a saint, he was, in like manner, acting morally right and not morally wrong, notwithstanding he was now acting directly contrary to what he had just as conscientiously and morally right been doing, only a few days before. And thus on, of every human being, whether ancient or modern, Jew or Christian, and of their beliefs and doings, to the full chapter's end.

What a great and glorious thing, then, is moral truth! And yet, even in this most enlightened and highly Christian land, it is the very kind that is, for the most part, being sought after, studied, taught, and believed. Yea, from the day on which Pontius Pilate made the inquiry, "*What is truth?*" down to the present hour, there is, perhaps, no one subject about which so much has been said, on which so much has been written, over which men have wrangled so much, and upon which so little light has been shed, as upon this; and Why? As seems to us, it is mainly because between real truth and moral truth, or more plainly, between such truths as are consonant to facts and such as are dissonant therefrom, but consonant to the opinions of men, and especially between such as are dissonant from facts, but consonant to the opinions of those certain ancient individuals who wrote the Bible, no line of distinction was made or attempted.

And the moral character of a man, What is it either more or less than the character which, from hereditary causes, educational influences, the force of habit, or of all these things combined, his brain doth stamp upon him? In other words, Is it not a man's daily walk and conversation which constitute his moral character? And, of this walk and conversation from beginning to end, notwithstanding spoken into outward existence by the tongue and other appropriate muscular organs, Is not the brain the parent cause? Self-evidently, as seems to us, this must be the case, since not a muscle of the tongue or any other part can ever move, except it be, by that organ, authorized and empowered so to do.

Also moral power, moral force, &c., What are they, each and all, but the influence which the brains of some certain individual or class of persons, either directly, by such brain's presence, or indirectly, through the works to which they stand parent cause, exert upon the brains, and hence upon the opinions and conduct, of some other person or class? Obviously enough, to a correct decision of questions of this kind, it is wholly immaterial whether the influence thus exerted be great or small, or whether the effect of such influence is good or bad.

And now, in view of all this, we appeal, Can it be possible that real truth, notwithstanding

"The eternal years of God are hers,"

is so meagre in quantity, feeble in quality, and uncertain in its mode of operation, that it will not answer a much better purpose as a guide to enlightened man upon any and all subjects, religion included, than will or can merely moral truth, *alias* error, the very thing which,

"—— wounded, writhes in pain,
And dies amid her worshipers?"

We repeat the question, "Can it be possible?" For others, of course, we cannot speak, but, as for ourself, we must answer no; it is not possible. Wherefore we must think it about time that an attempt was made not only to distinguish between such truths as are real, and hence have existence in the broad realm of facts, and such as are merely moral, and hence, except within the narrow heads of men, not anywhere existence have, but to arrest the further, and still further, spread and multiplication of error, by ceasing longer to speak and to teach just as though all the numerous acts and things, to which the word *moral* chanced to become prefixed before the natural sciences were born, were, in some special manner, connected with Almighty God, his character, and government, and consequently were, each and all, just so many permanent realities, and sacredly binding, instead of being, everywhere and ever, just as feeble and vacillating as are the heads of men, their fountain-source.

CHAPTER II.

BREVITIES.

Men may be belied, reviled, and persecuted when not in fault, but they can never be put down unless they put themselves down.

It is alike impossible for the vile and selfish to be happy, or the pure and unselfish to be miserable.

Many a man has a splended house, but no home; spacious rooms and costly furniture, but nowhere a warm, quiet place, and cozy cot on which to stretch his weary limbs when tired, or lay his aching head when sick; and hence, into dissolute habits and an untimely grave, he not unlikely falls.

"The way of the transgressor is hard," and self-condemning; that of the willing and obedient, easy, and self-approving.

The more men become enlightened, the more they become impressed with the necessity of praying by acts appropriate to bring about desired results, and the less are they disposed, by mere words, to petition therefor.

Overworking, overeating, and undersleeping are the three great sins of the age.

Meats that have been blessed in the raising, blessed in the preserving, and blessed in the cooking, have no need of any further blessing, except to be eaten in moderation and their nourishment expended in the promotion of good.

The chief end of man is to enjoy life. And, in order to enjoy that first and greatest of all blessings to the highest extent, it is not only necessary to live in obedience to the laws of health and those of the State, but so far to conform to the usages of that society in which we are placed, no matter of what kind it may chance to be, as not to render ourselves specially obnoxious thereto.

It is not a kind and merciful Providence that inflicts upon the children of men those numerous sicknesses and distresses which render life a burden, or that kindles those filthy plagues, hateful pestilences, and devastating wars, which fill the earth with mourning for the untimely dead; but it is we who bring them upon ourselves, in spite of all his severe and yet kindly warnings to shield us therefrom.

As it is the faculty of reason which pre-eminently distinguishes man from the monkey and other kindred animals; so, to the extent that men do purposely neglect or refuse to exercise such noble faculty, to a like extent are they guilty of narrowing down that God-ordained distinction between themselves and mere brutes.

At some time in the future, there will doubtless spring up a great and terrible war of ideas, based not upon a mere difference of opinion as to the propriety of making menials by law, as well as in practice, of this, that, or the other less favored people, but upon a difference as to the necessity of ridding the Earth of any and all such inferior races, as shall be judged to stand in the way of the further spread and multiplication of the highest and strongest race of all.

Many are the men who are able to out argue their friends and associates upon various subjects of common interest; but small is the number possessed of so persuasively presenting their views as to convince them of their error, however wrong they may chance to be, and thus set them right.

Ignorant and self-conceited disputants are ever prone to think the subject exhausted and the question won, just as soon as thereupon the bottom of their feeble sense is reached.

As enemies, the habitually hasty and indiscreet are little to be feared; as friends, they are ever dangerous.

For the young to be obliged to wait, economize, and labor for what they have, is to be blessed of Heaven; for them to be allowed to grow up in idleness, with their every want supplied, is to be cursed by their parents, guardians, or somebody else.

Not penance, but enjoyment, within the limit of abuse to ourselves or anybody else, is the best preparation for heaven; or more properly, enjoyment, within such limit, of whatsoever our natures crave, is heaven itself.

God blesses such as do in action bless themselves, and such as thus do curse themselves, he just so often curses.

Genuine sincerity is never at discount; feigned sincerity, seldom at par.

Such faults in children and youth as do naturally grow stronger with years should be closely watched, without seeming to do so, and carefully checked; but such as time is certain to work their cure, it is better not to see, or at least not to make many comments upon.

Because a man succeeds in proving the opinions of this, that, or the other set of men erroneous, it does not follow that the views by him entertained upon those same subjects are sound.—Ability to annihilate the most beautiful picture is no proof of capacity to execute even a tolerable daub.

Often as it has been tried, the number who have succeeded in gaining for themselves an enviable notoriety, by traducing the characters of their friends and associates, is exceedingly small.

He is not the richest man who has the most material wealth, but he who has the fewest of unsatisfied desires. The boy with his first top is better filled and satisfied than the banker with his gold, notwithstanding counted by millions.

Some men do raise themselves to eminence by the mere gift of gab; but more by the faculty of looking wise and keeping silent when they don't know what to say.

No matter how untiring may be the efforts of the advocates of the Mosaic theory of creation to perpetuate the idea of the Earth's youthfulness, not much longer, by an enlightened world, will the evidence presented by those silent time-measurers, the stalactites and stalagmites, continue to be believed down.

In a social point of view, that is not the most perfect man who has in his nature the fewest faults to struggle against, nor yet the one who commits the fewest errors; but the man who commits the fewest of that class whose consequences end not with himself, but extend to society.

To Nature's laws there are no exceptions, every seeming departure from uniformity of operation being the legitimate result, not in any change of the law itself, nor yet in its mode of operation, but of the modifying effect of the presence and action of some other law, by us unobserved. And hence, notwithstanding the numerous apparent clashings and seeming inconsistencies, Order, throughout all vast Nature's realm, eternally doth reign.

Few things are more hateful than a sour, selfish, fault-finding person; and yet such individuals are not without their beneficial uses in society. Such persons! why, what are they but so many faithful, mirror warnings, bidding us beware how we ourselves behave and do?

Cheery, sunny persons, just like bright, sunny weather, impart life and pleasure to all who come within their influence; whereas those of a sour, gloomy, and desponding cast of mind, just like sour, gloomy, and inclement weather, exert a withering, blasting influence wheresoever they go. Blessed are the children who have cheerful and happy parents, nurses, and teachers; whilst blighted and cursed are those who have of these the reverse.

The big fish can swallow the little ones; and they do it.—How selfish and cruel! The little fish cannot swallow the big ones; and they never attempt it.—How very kind and considerate!

Because both freedom of speech and of the press are guaranteed by the Constitution, it does not follow that a man is bound to talk like a fool, or write himself down an ass.

For the reason that men are not all organized and balanced alike, for that reason what one man may practice daily for years without injury to himself, it may be *a sin unto death* for some other to perform a single time.

Do justice to the absent man, and defend the character of the absent friend; for so would you have both the one and the other do by you.

Under the operation of rigid collection laws, both fraudulent debtors and fraudulent creditors are ever found to increase; under the operation of laws exempting almost everything from execution for debt, both are found to diminish. Corollary: — The credit system tends to make men rogues, the pay-down one to make them honest.

As from the cradle to the grave our connection is with the living and not with the dead, so there is little danger of our thinking too much of the former and not enough about the latter.

If men would think more, and examine more, they would know more, and believe less; consequently they would be less wise in their own conceit, put forth their views less dogmatically, and hence be better friends.

It is a great mistake to measure others by ourselves,—a gross error to suppose that everybody must needs look, feel, think, believe, and act, just as we do, in order to be free from the pains of hell, or enjoy the pleasures of heaven.

As the man who is uniformly successful in his business, no matter what, cannot reasonably be suspected of acting in violation of the laws which regulate and govern the same; so the man who is uniformly healthy and happy cannot reasonably be accused of sinning against the laws of health and happiness, as the same are organically enstamped upon him, no matter what effect the doing of those same things by others may have upon them.

The most acceptable service we can render unto God is faithfully to do our duty to ourselves, our fellows and our country. In other words, if a man does his duty to himself, his country, and his fellow-men, he has no good reason to fear either to live or to die.

It is better to be something than nothing,—better to decide in some way such things as must be decided and go ahead wrong, than be eternally hesitating and so never do anything. The most unenviable of all conditions, not actually criminal, is a state of chronic betweenity.

Almost without exception, great men bequeath to the world their great thoughts in words that are simple and appropriate; small men their small thoughts in those which are large and high-sounding, whether appropriate or not.

The more men come to understand Nature and her laws, the wider the field in which they are privileged to pluck the flowers of pleasure, and the more actively kind, unselfish, and useful they are, the greater the sum of their enjoyments.

Civility is ever a cheap article; incivility, not unfrequently a costly one.

Time is a blank estate. Time is an estate which can be turned into gold only by its use.—Labor is the parent of wealth. Labor is KING.

It is doubtless a great blessing to be born into life a human being; but the greatest of all blessings is to be descended from sound, intelligent, well-mated, and happy parents of the same high race.

Those who give the largest parties, drive the fastest horses, and cut the biggest swell, are generally such as would not have a shilling, had all their different creditors their fair and honest dues.

Would we be loved, we must try to be lovable; would we have people civil and obliging to us, we must be so to them. It is only by being neighborly ourselves that we can secure good neighbors, and without the sympathy of his neighbors, when in trouble and distress, who would care to live?

So nearly omnipotent is the force of habit, that we should make it a rule not to do once what we know it would be unsafe for us many times to repeat, and which we are certain might quite as well never be done at all.

All men are liable to error, but it is only the great who great errors can commit.

Broad charity for our fellow-men, notwithstanding their numerous failings and besetments, is not the fruit of any narrow sectarian faith, but the legitimate product of broad inquiry into variant human nature, and the numerous different springs of human action.

Faith in God is faith in man, and love toward God, love toward our fellow-men.—"If a man say, I love God, and hateth his brother, he is a liar." So taught John; and no doubt he was right. First General Epistle of John, 4, 20.

Men glorify God the most when they most do glorify themselves by glorifying their occupation, be it whatsoever legitimate one it may.

To borrow money when needed may be good policy, but to borrow trouble which we do not want, must be the height of folly.

Everybody knows, and can tell exactly, how to manage a bad wife, undutiful child, &c., except the man who is so unfortunate as to have one. He, poor, stupid soul! does not know how to do it; nor is he able to learn from all the wisdom that is being showered upon him by his more astute neighbors.

The Earth was undoubtedly here, revolving upon its axis, making its journeys around the Sun, and bearing upon its bosom plants, flowers, shrubs, trees, and various kinds of animals of low order, long ages before proud man a being had; and not unlikely it will continue thus to revolve, and make its journeys, long ages after its surface shall have become too cold and shrunken for human habitation.

For men to become as supremely good and happy as it is possible for them ever to be, it is not necessary that any portion of their original nature should be expunged, but only that their strong animal propensities should be elevated, and brought to bow obedience to the moral sentiments, and the moral sentiments elevated, and brought to bow obedience to the teachings of sober intellect.

Could wisdom and goodness be flogged into children, then, indeed, had most of us old men been brimful of these things. Inasmuch, however, as we are none of us thus overflowing, and inasmuch as it is almost invariably in those children who are thus most liberally dealt with, that these virtues are found to exist in the least abundance, Would it not be well for our successors to conclude that, of these delicate fruits, the stern, unfeeling rod is not the parent tree?

In some few cases it may be impolitic, if not wholly unjustifiable, to give assistance to the nearest relative; but, as a rule, it is both manly and proper to stand by our friends when in trouble or assailed, whether we regard them as being right, or whether wrong

The real gentleman, be he Turk or be he Christian, is ever polite and affable in his manner, notwithstanding he may be unyielding in his course of action; and ever yielding in his course of action, except in matters of consequence, or upon questions wherein some principle is involved. Even favors of magnitude may be so ungraciously granted as to be offensive to the recipients; and they may also be so graciously refused as to afford quite as much pleasure as pain.

Those who to the intellect do speak address the few; those who to the passions and prejudices appeal, the many.

Goods upon the shelf are a better representative of cash than second class credits, consequently they will buy more bread, clothe more backs, and pay off more debts.

Credit, at best, is but a poor substitute for capital. Wherefore, to avoid all danger of falling into bankruptcy, let dealers pay when they buy, and take pay when they sell. A canoe all our own is better than a ship in which we have only a nominal interest.

Aside from feeling more independent, when we meet our fellow-men in the street or elsewhere, it is better to suffer some little inconvenience from want of a larger house, fresher furniture, more changes of clothing, &c., and have a few spare dollars at interest, than to have a roomy mansion, with furniture, wardrobe, &c., to match, and be troublously in debt therefor. Indeed, it may be laid down as a rule, that a mortgage upon a man's farm, except to secure a portion of the purchase-money, is, to a greater or less extent, an incumbrance upon his independence of feeling, and hence upon his manhood.

A sly, insinuating enemy, however weak, is ever more to be dreaded than a bold and out-spoken one, no matter how strong.

The constitutional grumbletonian, whoever he may be, is greatly to be pitied, being too miserable to be envied, and too hateful to be loved.

NOTE.—The foregoing remarks, whether really true or not, being all moral truths to us, as such we state them.

CHAPTER III.

MAN'S NATURE AND AGENCY.

It has come to be believed by some, and by our humble self among the number, that the Science of Man, or the knowledge of man's mental nature, advances in proportion as its key-branches, Physiology, Phrenology, and Magnetism, are unfolded. Men act magnetically one upon another, each exerting an influence upon his associate, thereby rendering him in taste, character, and habits more like himself, whereby they mutually become more attached, else more unlike each other, and hence mutually more hateful and repulsive.

Each individual member of an association, the same as each ordinary magnet in a bundle, exerts a certain amount of influence upon all the rest, they in return doing the same thing upon him; the law being that each must act and keep acting to the extent of his own inherent power. Two magnets, within the proper proximity, act upon each other, each exerting upon the other an equal amount of force, but affecting each other equally or unequally, according to the equality or inequality of their respective powers. The same thing holds good of a magnet and a piece of iron not technically magnetic; whereby not only magnets of equal weight, but a magnet and a piece of iron of the same weight, being within the proper attracting distance and alike free to move, mutually approach each other with equal speed; and those of unequal weights the same, only with correspondingly unequal velocities.

When the difference in power between two bodies thus mutually acting is very great, although both are acted upon to an amount which is equal, they are quite unequally affected, owing to the vast inequality of their inherent powers. In this way, the Sun is only slightly made to move, while the earth is constantly compelled to wheel herself around him.

As "All are but parts of one stupendous Whole," and as this principle, in some form, doth more or less pervade everything in Nature, so it becomes important to bear in memory these most common and yet everywhere-governing laws.

It has also come to be believed that circumstances and things other than human beings, when in close proximity, and between which and men there exists some mutual relation, ever exert a greater or a lesser influence upon them; the same, in principle, as does a bit of iron upon the magnet. In this way, do circumstances and things more potent than man rule him, in spite of all his powers of opposition, whilst those less potential he bends to his purpose; the weaker, be it him, or be it them, ever modifying the dominion of the stronger in proportion to its own inherent might.

And now, reader, for the purpose of illustrating this point, permit us to present, to your mind's eye, the well-known pocket compass. How beautifully and steadfastly doth this little magnetic-needle, obedient to the law of its nature, indicate the direction of the polar star. It appears to be as stable in its nature and as well settled in its modes of action as any man we ever saw, wherefore we cannot doubt it is; but, to test its stability a little, let us introduce into its immediate neighborhood this one external circumstance, this small bit of iron, between which and it there exists a mutual relation. See! in its course of action it begins to hesitate and waver, as if undetermined what to do. A little nearer goes the bit of iron, and its influence becomes so irresistible, that to the tempter it now tremblingly yields,—tremblingly bows submission thereunto, as unto fate, and no longer between two opinions seems to halt. Indeed, it would now seem to be converted to a different faith, so to speak, and to have its mind made up that, henceforth, not at right angles to the equator, but parallel therewith, shall its body lie. Well, let us see; first this way, then that, and then round and round it goes, like a dog in pursuit of his tail, as moves this more potent circumstance, this bit of iron, to whose superior power it blindly bows submission, the same to all appearance as if it was not in accordance with its individual nature, when influenced by external circumstances, steadfastly in the direction of the polar star to point. Not only this, but the longer the needle is left to pursue its wonted course, so to speak, and constantly at right angles with the equator to remain, the more powerful and seemingly set in its way it becomes; and the more it is interfered with by circumstances, and the longer it is made parallel with the equator to remain, the weaker and less stable it is found to be.

Just so to the natural magnet, man. When influenced by external circumstances and things, he seems to be a tower of strength, and so indeed he is, but let difficulties, darkness, and dangers, undefinable, come to multiply, thicken, and press upon him on every side, then what and where is he? Then, just like the needle, he hesitates, wavers, yields, and moves with the current of circumstances which, like a resistless stream, whirl him forward, backward, and around, he knows not how nor whither, much the same as if inherent nature and opinions of his own, he never had any. And sure enough, the longer this state of things continues, and the more this class of facts and circumstances come to multiply and press upon him, the less of these does he possess; until, finally, contrary to his own spontaneous desires, he is overpowered and led captive thereby. And all this, notwithstanding seemingly inconsistent, is nevertheless natural; and hence must needs be, upon the whole, both good and right.

We say, all this must needs be, upon the whole, both good and right, because, directly in consequence of his highly complex and hence greatly variant nature, man is neither an independent nor an isolated thing; consequently, instead of his being able to act independently, he is ever compelled to conform to such other circumstances and things, as between which and him mutual relations exist, to the extent that his own inherent powers are unequal to the task of bending the same, and bringing them to be in harmony with himself. In other words, such is the law which rules in man's nature, and such his relation to other things and of these to him, that he is just as much compelled to yield obedience to such proximately surrounding circumstances and things as are to him superior in point of activity and power, as is the needle to the bit of iron; and hence, in thus yielding obedience, he must needs be acting right, and not wrong.

Obedient to these same unbending laws are the Sun and planets all, and harmony the most perfect is the legitimate result. And what is true, in this respect, of those vast worlds of substance, must needs be true, not only of the different atoms of which they are composed, but of that little, self-important aggregate of atoms, known as man. In view of all these things, the conviction is forced upon us that if we would ever come to know what is man's true character and mission in the world, we must leave off idle speculation, and attend to sober facts.

When we wish to learn what is the nature, or real character, of any inorganic substance or organic remains, What do we do? Why, we analyze and examine the same in every possible way. When we wish to learn what is the nature of any ordinary animal, do we not carefully observe its every movement and note its every act? And having oft done this upon many of the same species, and always obtaining substantially the same results, do we not conclude that its nature is in a line of accordance with those results, be they what they may?

Take, for example, the domestic cat. How came she to be pronounced a beast of prey? And how a prowling, treacherous creature, which suddenly falls upon and kills her unsuspecting victim? Plainly enough, it is because she is ever found to be such in practice. In other words, we have allowed her to speak for herself—have allowed her to speak out her nature by and through her acts; and, having so allowed her, have concluded that as she does, so she is; as is the fruit, so is the tree that bears it. Accordingly, when we see old Puss prowling about seeking what she may devour, we never suspect that in so doing, she is not acting out the nature which was enstamped upon her by her Creator,—never suspect that in so doing, she is not fulfilling the law of her being; and never that she is specially instigated thus to be and do by any other serpent or destroying angel than her own inherent nature, by God organically enstamped. And when, an hour thereafter, we behold her all docility and playfulness—she being now satiated with blood—we naturally conclude that this is only her other side,—is only another phase of her variant nature; never once dreaming that she is specially moved thus to be and do, by any other divine spirit than her own complex nature.

In all this, we act like rational beings; but, when we come to ascend a little in the scale and inquire, What is the nature which God impressed upon the animal called man? our good sense seems suddenly to leave us. Then, instead of letting that higher animal answer the question himself by and through the emphatic language of his doings, and concluding that he, too, acts out his real nature, the nature by God organically enstamped upon him, and hence fulfills the law of his being, the very reverse is inferred. In other words, it is first modestly admitted that God made him, and then it is assumed, not only without proof, but contrary to the very plainest evidence, as seems to us, that he did not enstamp upon him any permanent organic nature at all; or, what amounts to the same thing, that he stamped it upon him so slightly and fitted it to him so loosely that, whilst yet in his leading strings, he shook it all off, and substituted another of his own manufacture; and which other is all wrong, corrupt, and rotten, from beginning to end.

An all-wise, all-good, and all-powerful God create man, and enstamp upon him an organic nature which is so fragile and loose-fitting, that, in his very infancy, he slips out of it, and tramples it under his puny feet? Strange conclusion, this! In this way is man clothed, not only with creative power, but with self-creative power; a power which not even the eternal God himself has ever been supposed to possess. How individual man who from the cradle to the grave is upon all sides round hemmed in and pressed upon by circumstances and things which are to him superior, can reasonably be supposed to be the creator of his own nature, and the author of his own destiny, we are at a loss to discover.

Allowing man to have been created by an omnipotent, Spirit God, of infinite wisdom and goodness possessed, we can see no evidence that it was not his intention when he made him, that he should manifest in action the nature which he in his wisdom and goodness saw fit to enstamp upon him, the same as do the lower animals. And not only this, but if it was his intention, when he created man, that he should live out in practice the nature which he was at the trouble of organically enstamping upon him, then we must think it is his intention still; and hence that his designs have not been frustrated, and never can be by any power in earth or heaven, much less by feeble individual man. Self-evidently, man is not a lump of insipid, homogeneous elements, but is endowed with a highly complicated organic structure, through and by means of which he must necessarily manifest correspondingly variant and complicated functions, provided no part of that structure was made in vain. How, then, can he be expected to possess and manifest a monotonous sameness of thought, feeling, or of action? When he is seen exhibiting the sterner qualities of his complex nature, How can it be inferred that he is not acting out the nature by God organically impressed upon him; and consequently that he is not, upon the whole, acting right and acceptably, instead of wrong and unacceptably? And how that he is moved and instigated thus to be and do by any other devil than his own God-enstamped complex, and hence variant nature? And when he exhibits the gentler qualities of that same diverse nature, (he being all smiles and goodness now,) Why the inference that he is moved thus to be and to do by any other divine spirit than the one which legitimately resides within that same complex organic nature? In short, how came man to be invested with power so great and strong that he is able to set the laws of his omnipotent Maker at defiance, and strike out a course of action for himself?

Man, a battle-ground between the two contending parties, God and the Devil, and the Devil generally win the field? Why, if God really is an infinitely great, wise, omnipresent, and omnipotent Being, consequently not only all his created works doth fill, but all the vast immensity of space as well; who, then, can be this more than omnipotent Devil which not anywhere a dwelling place can have, since every spot and place and thing, not with his Satanic Majesty, but with the presence of the everlasting God, is filled?

If it be admitted that God, the GREAT FIRST CAUSE, and Author of all other causes that are, of his own spontaneous accord, created the secondary cause, man, and enstamped upon him such an organic structure, and hence such a nature, as he saw fit, then it cannot be supposed that the course pursued by his said secondary cause, man, was unexpected, and hence dissonant from his desires, without imputing unto him short-sightedness in planning his creation, else carelessness in executing it, or both. To suppose that an all-wise and all-powerful God created man is equivalent to supposing that he created him as he wanted him; and to suppose that he commanded him to do certain things, and not to do certain others, is equivalent to supposing that he wanted *those* done, and *these* not done. Wherefore, as surely as is God all-wise to plan and all-powerful to execute, just so surely will such things as he wants done be done, and such as he does not want done cannot be done by mortal man, or any other of his created works. His commandments to man, the same as to all things else, unless we are greatly mistaken, he gives not by mere words, which are liable to be misunderstood or forgotten, but enstamps them upon his organic structure, and ingrains them into his nature; wherefore, understood, remembered and obeyed, to the living letter, they must necessarily be and are.

Or, to present the idea in a little different form, From that FOUNTAIN of causes, the GREAT FIRST CAUSE, God, legitimately flow all other causes, great and small, inanimate and animated, that are. And since a cause unfollowed by a corresponding effect, or an effect unpreceded by a corresponding producing cause, can never be; therefore, to suppose that it was in accordance with God's nature, and hence was his intention, that man, one of his created secondary causes, should do a certain act, no matter what, is equivalent to supposing that so did he organically adapt and relate him to such action, as that he is thereby and therethrough commanded to do it, and hence do it he must; otherwise, in the case of man, there is a secondary cause failing to produce into existence its corresponding effect. And to suppose that it was contrary to God's nature, and hence contrary to his intention, that his said secondary cause, man, should do some certain act, no matter what, is equivalent to supposing that he could not and did not confer upon him the requisite organic adaptations and relations thereto to enable him to do it, and consequently he can never perform it; otherwise there is here an effect produced into existence without being preceded by any corresponding producing cause. A cause, and no corresponding effect following it, an effect, and no corresponding producing cause preceding it;—strange things, these!

That man, the passively created secondary cause, through which, as his fit instrument, the GREAT FIRST doth act, is ostensibly the prime actor is not denied and cannot be, since it is ever he, and not the GREAT, INVISIBLE FIRST, that is seen to perform the action. And yet, as surely as did God, the GREAT FIRST CAUSE, create man, just so certain is it that man is only the secondary cause, or fit instrument, through and by means of which the GREAT FIRST, that created and constituted him such instrument, himself, unseen, doth operate to produce into existence the different results, each and all, which unto man, the visible actor, we are wont to ascribe. In other words, it is in reality God, the GREAT FIRST CAUSE of all other causes, and not man, his mere secondary cause, or fit instrument, that acts; and hence it is God, the Creator and Principal, and not passively created man, his mere agent or instrument, that is supremely responsible therefor, if any supreme responsibility there be. We repeat, it is not denied and cannot be that man, as such created secondary cause and fit instrument, possesses power and hence acts; but, then, the question which just now concerns us is, How came man by this power to act? Did he upon himself confer it, or did he from God, the source of all power, steal it? In short, How came individual man to be, how of power possessed, and to what or whom is he responsible for its exercise, except unto himself and such of his fellow-men as are affected thereby?

Plainly enough, according to the Bible account of the matter, God created Cain, the murderer of Abel, by and through the agency of Adam and Eve, his created secondary causes and fit instruments to produce him into being; otherwise he did not create Cain at all. And if through them, as his secondary causes and fit instruments, he created the man Cain, then, by unavoidable consequence, as seems to us, it is he, the all-wise and all-powerful God, the Being who thus created him, and not the poor, feeble man Cain, by him thus passively created, who is responsible not only for his coming into existence, but for his being the kind of man he was, and his doing as he did.—It is not upon an imperfect machine, nor yet upon its productions, but upon its inventor and maker, that responsibility doth rest.—In like manner, God created us, one and all, by and through the agency of his said created fit instruments, Adam and Eve, and their lineal descendants in an unbroken chain all the way down to our immediate parents according to the flesh, who as his thus far remotely created fit instruments, produced us into being; otherwise, with the exception of Adam and Eve, he never created a single human being in all the world.

It is undoubtedly thought by large numbers of men of

good endowments, not only that God created man all at once, and full-sized, out of "the dust of the ground," but that he then and there clothed him, in kind, character, and amount, with all and singular the feelings, emotions, passions, propensities, and powers which he to-day possesses. And, in substance and effect, it is doubtless just about as extensively believed, that he then and there commanded him by word of mouth, and long years thereafter in writing, to manifest his said feelings, emotions, passions, propensities, and powers in a certain way, and not to manifest them in a certain other way; and then left him at liberty to manifest them in accordance with such commandments, or contrary thereto, or not at all, as he himself might choose. Such are undoubtedly, in substance and effect, the opinions which are honestly entertained by a large majority of professed Christians to-day; and yet, strangely absurd as it may seem to this wide class of persons, we are compelled to think differently,—are compelled to think that God's uniform way of giving his commandments to the higher animal man, the same as to all the different orders below him, is by organically enstamping them upon him;—is by so organically adapting and relating him to the required action, that all the option he has in the matter is merely seeming, and not real; and hence that every individual, unless therefrom prevented by the pressure of influence which is too strong to be by him resisted, must and doth obey.

And now, for the purpose of shedding what little light we can upon this point, we propose to invest a certain portion of the aqueous fluid, a giant oak, the wolf, and the lamb with such faculties as are common to man, and then refer the same to each in turn, and see what will be their respective testimonies thereupon.

God made the Waters which compose this noble River, and enstamped upon them not only fluidity of form, but such properties and relations to the Earth's mass, as give them inherent weight ; and which conjoint conditions we regard as being neither more nor less than a positive, ingrained command to run down hill at all times, when not therefrom prevented by some power too strong to be by them resisted.

Thus far all seems to be plain work; and to this the Waters as they constantly roll past do murmur their assent. —Let it now be supposed that when God created those Waters, and commanded them thus down hill to run, he verbally instructed them that they were at liberty to do as they might choose about yielding obedience to said ingrained commandment, and hence about thus uniformly running down hill.

And what, to said verbal instructions, doth the River say by her constantly onward-moving waters?—Plainly this: "In spite of all mere verbal instructions or permits, run down hill, as by the law of my nature I am commanded, I forever must continue to do, unless therefrom prevented by some overpowering circumstance outside myself."

God created yon giant Oak, and organically enstamped him with such a nature, and conferred upon him such adaptations and relations to surrounding things, as constitute his tendency to grow, to bear acorns at the proper times, to fall heavily to the ground when severed at the root, and to crush all such trifling things as shall offer resistance to its descent.

"All right!" responds the staunch old Tree, as slightly he bows his aged head to the fierce northern blast.—Let it now be supposed that when God created that giant Vegetable, and organically enstamped the oak's nature, adaptations, and relations upon him, he verbally instructed him that he was at liberty to do as he might choose about falling heavily to the ground, when severed at the root, also that he might bear figs instead of acorns, if it should be his choice.—"Impossible!" ejaculates the staunch old Tree, by a shower of acorns from his bushy top; "my organic nature constitutes me an oak, and not a fig-tree. Wherefore, disobey the laws which are thus organically impressed upon me, I cannot; and wherefore, to bear any other fruit than acorns, I am powerless, all verbal instructions or written commandments to the contrary notwithstanding."

God created the Wolf, and organically enstamped him

with such a nature as causes him to be hungry, very hungry, after long-continued fasting. He also conferred upon him such adaptations and relations to lambs, and other kindred things, that, to satisfy the gnawings of hunger, and thus prevent his own dear self from wasting away, he will kill and devour them with real savage gusto.—Let it now be supposed that, when God created the Wolf, and organically enstamped his savage nature upon him, he verbally instructed him that he was at liberty to do as he pleased about being hungry after long-continued fasting; also that he was at liberty, when famishing from the effects of such a fast, to spare the lamb within his grasp and starve to death himself, if it should be his choice so to do. Whoever doubts what, under such circumstances, would be the Wolf's uniform reply in practice, let him occasionally present him with a lamb, and see.

Let it now be supposed that when God created the Lamb, and organically enstamped upon him such a nature as legitimately constitutes him a very feeble, timid creature, he verbally exhorted him to be plucky,—verbally instructed him that he was at liberty to do as he pleased about fearing the ravenous wolf; also that he might boldly attack, kill and eat the ferocious brute, if it should be his choice so to do, instead of being himself thereby killed and eaten.

And to this, what is the Lamb's invariable answer, as spoken out in the emphatic language of his constantly timid and non-carniverous practice?

As water, by virtue of its inherent nature, is ever commanded, and hence compelled, to plunge down the precipice, and has no power to refuse obedience, as the wolf is organically commanded to feed upon lambs, etc., and hence has not the power to choose to die of hunger and let such feeble quadrupeds go free; in short, since the wolf and lamb are each enstamped, not only with its own peculiar organic form, texture, adaptations, etc., but with a character which with these conditions invariably accords, whereby the former is denied the power to be and act the latter, and the latter, the former, each being organically commanded, and hence compelled, to be the thing it is, and to live out in practice the traits of character which it does, we must think that the higher animal man, who is in like manner enstamped, not only with peculiar organic form, texture, adaptations, and relations, but with a character which is in harmony therewith, is also commanded, and hence compelled, by and through his said peculiar organic form, etc., to be what he is, and to act as he does; and consequently that he is just as powerless to do otherwise or, at bottom, to choose to act differently, as are those animals of lower order.

Of course, we may have fallen into error's broad channel, but, whether so or not, we must not only confess our inability to see how man can be exempt from the operation of what certainly seems to be a universal law, but to understand for what purpose, other than for use, his different organic feelings, emotions, passions, propensities, and powers were conferred upon him; and especially are we unable to see in what way extrinsic commandments, whether positive or permissive, oral or written, can ever annul such as are organically enstamped, and hence permanently, part and parcel of man himself.

And now, reader, as a last resort, let us put a few questions to man himself, as he is known to exist in actual practice, to the end that we may see how far the real, breathing man of Earth doth correspond with this said hypothetic one by Orthodoxy created, and constantly held up to view.

Here, then, is our neighbor, Deacon S., one of the best of men practically, him will we interrogate as to the cause of his uniform good conduct, and let his acts, both general and particular, as spoken out in practice during a long series of years, give answer. Fine-grained, tall, erect, narrow between the ears, forehead full and lofty, high in the coronal region, and occiput small; all this we know by having seen him perhaps a thousand times, and, by running the mind's eye back over his past life, we can see how beautifully his character, as lived out in practice, doth correspond with the organic commandments which are thus enstamped upon him.

If it be a fact that, notwithstanding these said organically enstamped commandments to the contrary, he is left at liberty to be and act the bully, blackguard, knave, and villain, How comes it to pass that he never speaks out any of these things in practice? Why is it that, throughout the whole course of his life, he has acted the dove, and never once the tiger or hyena? Indeed, is not the fact that his course of action, just like that of the wolf and lamb, has ever been in a line of accordance with the commandments which are organically enstamped upon him, pregnant with meaning? We repeat, if it be a fact that, notwithstanding his organic adaptations and relations to the contrary, he possesses the power, and hence is at liberty, to quarrel, fight, lie, cheat, steal, rob, and murder, Is it not exceedingly strange that he should never live out in practice any of these things?—How feelingly at the prayer-meetings held in the dear, old schoolhouse does he urge upon the young the necessity of dedicating their lives to the practice of sobriety and virtue! How kindly and affectionately doth he warn them against the many snares and temptations with which their pathway is beset! And yet he was never known to split the old pine table with his fist in endeavoring to pound heaven into them, or hell out of them.—Never!

And here also is Mr. D., the butcher, a man not of the rabbit but of the bull-dog stamp, a descendant of a practical butcher, reared in the shambles, educated in the slaughter-house, and always delighting in broils and blood. Look at him! and note how coarse and animal his whole manner and appearance, even to the deep gutteral tone of voice. What an amount of back-head; what breadth between the ears; and the coronal region, how villainously flat and low!

And now, we appeal, upon that man, Is not "blood and thunder" just as plainly stamped, as is power upon the iron horse? Can it be that, notwithstanding his organic adaptations and relations to the contrary, he possesses the power, and hence is at liberty, to be timid, gentle, and lamb-like? Can it be that he possesses the power, and hence is at liberty, to faint at the sight of a drop of blood, like the extremely delicate and nervous Mrs. B.? And if so, why is it that he doth not accasionally live out these things in practice, instead of uniformly delighting to plunge deep the fatal knife into every hog, sheep, and bullock, that looks sleek and happy?—Why?

From all this, what is the inference?—As seems to us it is that every man of every class and grade possesses his own peculiar characteristics, both physical and mental; and so possesses them, not by virtue of any free-will choice of his own, but because they are so organically enstamped upon him and engraved into him by those certain branches of the great Parent, known as hereditary causes, educational influences, and other surrounding circumstances not within his control, as that they are legitimately part and parcel of him, consequently constitute him what he is, and hence distinguish him from everybody else. Wherefore it is but natural that the deacon, the butcher, and every other class and grade of men should feel as they do, think as they do, act as they do, love what they love, and hate what they hate. And wherefore, whenever deacon or butcher or anybody else assumes that others who are differently organized and balanced, as well as differently circumstanced, should feel, think, love, hate, and practice the same things which he himself does, and no other, and hence imputes unto them the sin of disobedience to the laws of God because they do not, he is not to blame, but simply errs in judgment from want of knowledge. Whoever lives in obedience with the normal requirements of his own individual nature lives in obedience with what is of him required by his Maker, no matter what by the same rule may be demanded of his differently constituted neighbor; and whoever not thus in obedience doth live, both sins against himself and the laws of his Creator.

Summary of conclusions:—God made man, wolf, lamb,

etc., and enstamped each with such organic form, texture, adaptations, etc., as he saw fit, or more properly, as he needs must. In this way, by and through their respective physical organizations, they are each endowed with all and singular the feelings, capacities, propensities, etc., which they possess, and hence do manifest. In this way, and no other, as seems to us, is the wolf commanded to be and act the wolf, the lamb, to be and act the lamb, the man of the bull-dog stamp, to possess and manifest the bull-dog characteristics, the lamb-like man, to possess and manifest the traits of the lamb; and thus on of all the different kinds and grades of men. The lamb-like character possessed by Deacon S., being organically enstamped upon him, and ingrained into him, he has no alternative, but is compelled to manifest it; is compelled to manifest it, and can no more manifest any other, than can the lamb manifest the character of the wolf, or the wolf that of the lamb.

As surely as is Nature *bound fast in fate*, or governed by fixed laws, just so surely is that product of Nature, *the human will*, not left free, but *bound fast in fate*, or governed by fixed laws. Or thus: As certainly as is the mental man dependent upon the physical man for manifestation, just so certainly is the mental man ever compelled to be in conformity with the physical man that manifests it; and hence, just as certainly as is the physical man the creature of natural law, and not of free-will choice, just so certainly is the mental man the creature of natural law, and not of free-will choice.

If like begets like and cannot beget unlike, then it is simply impossible for God, THE GREAT FIRST CAUSE of all effects, and hence of all other causes that are, to stand *parent cause* to the pushing into existence of any effect or secondary cause, inanimate or animated, which is unlike himself; that is, any whose nature, from beginning to end, doth not accord with some branch or department of his own vast and vastly complex nature. In fine, were it not simply impossible for law-governed causes to produce into existence any other than law-governed effects, then might the law-governed oak, for example, chance to push into existence non-law-governed acorns instead of law-governed ones,—might chance to push into existence acorns from which pines, or any other kind of tree, would be as likely to grow as oaks; and hence, throughout all created Nature, inanimate and animated, dread uncertainty and confusion come to take the place of certainty and order.

CHAPTER IV.

MISCELLANEOUS SUBJECTS.

LOVE AND HATRED.

That we all love some persons and objects, all hate some persons and objects, and toward some persons and objects feel indifferent, every one knows; and yet, probably, not one in a hundred has ever seriously reflected upon the cause thereof. As we have come to see it, we thus do simply because these feelings, instead of being optional with us, as generally supposed, are the subjects of law; and because the law by which they are created, regulated, and governed, is just as much part and parcel of our several natures, as is that of gravitation which chains us to the Earth; consequently it is equally mandatory and binding upon us in all its different parts; and hence it is no more a special virtue, in an individual, to love such persons and things as he does love, or a sin to hate such as he does hate, than it is for him to weigh more when he is fleshy than he does when he is lean;—not any more.

The law in reference to this matter, or rather its operation, may be briefly stated thus: Whatever person or thing affects us, upon the whole, agreeably, we love some; whatever person or thing affects us, upon the whole, more agreeably, we love more; and whatever person or thing affects us, upon the whole, most agreeably, we love most; and we cannot help it. Whatever person or thing affects us, upon the whole, disagreeably, we hate some; whatever person or thing affects us, upon the whole, more disagreeably, we hate more; and whatever person or thing affects us, upon the whole, most disagreeably, we hate most; and, reason as we may, and profess to think differently who will, we are powerless to do otherwise. Such being the case, it follows, that, toward such persons and objects as affect us neither way, we are obliged to feel indifferent; and such as affect us just about as much the one way as the other, we are compelled to hate just about as much as we love, and to love just about as much as we hate. All this being understood, it is needless to go further and explain why it is that when a friend, or anybody else, affects us quite agreeably, we like him, or why, when as decidedly disagreeably he affects us, we hate him; why, with the same individual, by turns we quarrel and by turns make love, or why by turns we push from us, as offensive, our brothers, sisters, and even our bosom companions, and by turns do pull them back.

Some men and women are so very unique in their mental taste and balance, that a truly congenial mate they cannot easily find; and then there are others who are so very like every fifth person they meet, that, age and caste aside, almost any one of the opposite sex will sufficiently well answer them for a life companion. This class of persons, if they do not live any too happily together in the marriage state, are seldom known seriously to fall out; wherefore they are apt to conclude there must be some great wrong somewhere, at sight and hearing of those domestic quarrels which not unfrequently take place between such men and women as are not only quite positive in their characters, but who, unfortunately, are badly paired. As it is no sort of evidence, however, that both oil and water are not pure and good, because they can never be brought permanently to coalesce, but simply proof that they are to each other uncongenial; so, from these disagreements between husbands and wives of opposite tastes and dispositions, it must not be too hastily concluded that either is essentially wanting in the elements of happiness, or that each is not desirous of rendering the other happy. Indeed, so greatly variant is human nature that, in ninety-nine cases out of every hundred, all that is established by such domestic disagreements is the fact, that both parties are neither oil nor water. Or, to state the idea a little more at length, by the frequent occurrence of such domestic disagreements, it is rendered painfully apparent to the more thoughtful observer, if not to the parties themselves, that they are not—as they doubtless honestly but quite too hastily concluded they were—the stray halves of the same unit; and hence, notwithstanding with all due solemnity they were matrimonially made one, still two they do remain. We say, as they doubtless honestly but quite too hastily concluded they were, etc., because the serious matter of courtship, whose consequences are not only life-long, but posterity-long, is, for the most part, so conducted, as to be little else than a delusive farce;—is, for the most part, so conducted, that passions and feelings, mostly factitious, have vastly more influence in the choice of our life-companions, than do the promptings of the moral sentiments and the teachings of sober intellect. And what is the consequence?—Why, just as soon as these blind incentives to union become frittered away, (as frittered away they surely will be, when brought into contact with the many stern realities with which life's rugged path is checkered,) and when reason and right feeling come to assume their lawful sway, then, too late, we find that the sum of permanent, mutual attractions, existing between us, is far too evenly balanced, if not outweighed, by the sum of repulsions, now no longer latent. All this, however, forms no solid objection against the marriage institution, but only against the thus almost criminally overlooking, in the choice of a life companion, of those dominant mental tastes, feelings, and likenesses, by whose influence alone it is possible for two individuals ever to become permanently blended, and lost in one.

So much for the evils of those courtships whose tendency, we will not say object, is to deceive the lady addressed, consequently the gentleman addressing her, and hence both. Now a few words concerning the remedy, and we leave the subject. Dear, then, as ever is the school of experience, and painful as are not unfrequently her lessons, nevertheless so are we organized and balanced, that, to become truly wise, we have got to see, feel, and handle things for ourselves. And as no man can gain light and knowledge upon a subject from his own observation and experience, until he has seen and tasted in practice more or less of the things which pertain thereto, so we would say to the sensible young man, who is beginning to look about him for a partner to enact with him the great drama of wedded life, you must create for yourself the requisite occasions for the use of your mental, as well as physical, eyes. Or, more plainly, do not always put on your Sunday hat and coat whenever you suppose it possible you may be brought into contact with the gentler sex; and never in your intercourse with them, affect the simpering, opinionless dandy. By a few such non-acts, you will not unlikely see, hear, and learn many things, the which, if you heed, will be of lasting benefit to you. Never in female society affect to be in appearance what you are not in character; and never in character what you neither are nor ever intend to be. By so doing, or rather by so not doing, upon the principle that like begets like and nothing begets nothing, you will neither greatly deceive others, nor be yourself in consequence quite as badly taken in. In short, in all your intercourse with her whom you are beginning to think of making bone of your bone and flesh of your flesh, not only always appear to be what you are, but let your courtship thenceforward, until closed by marriage or otherwise, be as thoroughly seasoned with the every-day aims and incidents of real life as conveniently you can; to the end that you may learn both from observation and experience, before it is too late, whether you are paying your addresses to a mere butterfly in human form, or to a whole-souled woman, who, endowed with the capacity of adapting herself to the varied circumstances that do checker human life, would be to you an helpmate. Brains are of no account, remember, unless they are used; and surely their use is never more imperatively demanded than when selecting a partner for life.

A young man go a wooing in a plain, every-day kind of

dress? Yes; provided he is a plain, every-day kind of a man, wants a plain, every-day kind of a wife, and expects, when married, to make a plain, every-day kind of a husband; for, depend upon it, young man, and young woman, it is not of Sundays nor of holidays, but of plain, every-days, that real life is ever, principally, made up.

A charming and beautiful young lady receive the addresses of the lords of creation, in her usual comely, every-day habiliments? Certainly, provided it be upon some one of the numerous every-days, that her suitor happens to drop in upon her for a little chat; unless, indeed, she expects always to be and appear in full company costume, after she shall have abandoned the maid and assumed the matron.

And young ladies and gentlemen have views, wishes, and opinions of their own, during that most tender and endearing season, the season of courtship? Yes; most assuredly they should then both have, and manifest, all these things, else they should not have any of them after they are married.

And now, to such of our dear young lady friends as are, and ever intend to be, something more than mere parlor toys, we would say, forget not that the exquisite thing in pants called a young man is just no man at all, until, in some appropriate way, he has himself begun to enact the man. In other words, remember it is not saying pretty things, nor wearing fine clothes, nor riding in father's carriage, nor spending father's money which constitutes a man, but the putting forth of efforts, in some legitimate calling or pursuit, to gain something for himself, that does it. Wherefore, as you value a prosperous and happy future, look ye, each, well to it, that you do not hastily reject the real man, and accept instead some over-indulgent father's brainless spendthrift. And yet one thing more:—If at any time, whilst being attentively courted and flattered, you feel instinctively rising up within you misgivings as to the propriety of yielding your hand to the man, who is thus ostensibly seeking to obtain it, delay such yielding, and seriously reflect. And if you find that the longer you thus delay, and the more you reflect, the stronger and more definite in shape those misgivings become; then, at the risk of being left to live and die an old maid, heed the timely warning of thy guardian angel, and, with that individual, make the delay eternal.

SUDDEN CONVERSIONS.

It is almost invariably such as are not past the volatile and giddy stage of life, else those who are constitutionally excitable, and hence to rowdyism naturally inclined, and not the habitually sober and discreet, who constitute the harvest that is gathered at protracted meetings, and other kindred gatherings of great religious furor and excitement, where not sober reason, but great noise, and still greater confusion, bear rule. To gatherings of this character, whether religious or theatrical, it is perfectly natural that this class of persons should dearly love to go, when once they have gotten a taste thereof, for here they are at home. And when in such a place they are fairly seated, with heads filled with nothing, or rather with vague and undefinable fun and frolic full, they are then within the vortex; and hence, just like the noisy, blustering blackguard in a real fight, they are sure to be the first to cave. All this is not only well understood by revivalists, but is systematically being acted upon all over the land; it having long since passed into a proverb with them, That there is more hope of the young than of the old, and of the desperately wicked and ungodly, than of the self-consistent and strictly moral man.

And why have they more hope of those merely moral ciphers in the social column, than of these stern, significant figures therein?—Because they understand full well, that, for the reason empty barrels make the most noise, for that same reason are they more easily upset and moved about. In other words, they know that such, the world over, are more easily wrought upon by surrounding circumstances, and hence are correspondingly more easily made any kind of somerset to turn.—Such, as we understand the matter, is a brief explanation of the cause of constitutional rowdies becoming suddenly changed,—not in their organic nature, but simply in their views, and hence in the mode of manifesting that nature in practice,—from bar-room rowdies, making night hideous with their bacchanalian songs, to religious rowdies, boisterously shouting and singing the praises of the Lamb.—Mushrooms are the growth of an hour; trees the product of time.

BLESSINGS IN DISGUISE.

The numerous difficulties and obstructions, or evils, so-called, by which from the cradle to the grave we are constantly surrounded, undoubtedly tend to develop Combativeness, or the resistive principle that is organically implanted in man, by exciting him to action,—by exciting him unto the putting forth of opposing efforts, great, and still greater, to overcome them; and hence do legitimately tend to elevate and bless the race. When weary and worn with trials and difficulties, it is pleasant to think and to talk about the coming of an imaginary period, when there shall be perfect freedom from everything that is hurtful or annoying; but then, beyond a rational doubt, much less than a thousand years of such millennial, monotonous sameness from all disturbance, trouble and care, would have the effect to sink the world of mankind into the miserable condition of milk-and-water sops.—Beds of down and balmy ease, although good in their place, are never the parents of either greatness or goodness.

PRAYER.

Once upon a time, as the story goes, just as Deacon A., a thrifty old farmer, in the town of N., had concluded his morning's devotions, in which, as was invariably his custom, he thanked God he was not like other men, and with outstretched arms and trembling accents, besought the Giver of all good to remember the poor and the needy, to feed the hungry, clothe the naked, and relieve the destitute, the sick, and distressed, everywhere, it so happened that a poor man, who for years had been a day-laborer in the neighborhood, was seen approaching his door with a bag on his arm. A few moments after, as the two neighbors were sitting in opposite corners by the large open fire, Mr. C. modestly proceeded to lay his necessities before the Deacon, ending with an urgent request to be trusted for a bushel of wheat, until his sick wife should so far recover from her recent confinement as to allow him to leave her and the little ones, when he would go to work, earn the money, and pay him.

The old farmer, who had been nervously listening to the poor man's tale of woes and needs, after delivering himself of a goodly number of a–hems! proceeded in a very kind and soothing manner to express his sorrow for his neighbor's misfortunes, his grief at the destitute and suffering condition of his family, and finally wound up by saying, "I am very sorry, but, really, I do not see how I can spare you any." As is not unusual however in such cases, just as the poor man was about to leave, he graciously advised him to call on neighbor M., who, he seemed to feel quite sure, would be able to accommodate him. And thus this poor day-laborer, in the heart of winter, and with a sick wife and starving children at home, from this so-called house of prayer, went empty and sorrowing away.

Scarcely had the sound of his footsteps died upon the Deacon's ear, however, when little Harry, who had been an attentive listener, and who as yet was nature's own unsophisticated child, thus accosted his pious parent: "Father, did you not just now pray God that he would feed the hungry, clothe the naked, and relieve the destitute, the sick, and distressed everywhere?"—"Why, to be sure," responded the somewhat confused and astonished parent, "I always so pray. But what makes you ask so strange a question, my son?"—"Because," said the simple-hearted, noble-minded little fellow, looking first toward the slowly retreating form of Mr. C. with the empty bag upon his arm, and then into the face of his parent with a mixture of doubt and surprise depicted upon his countenance,—"because, father, I cannot help thinking that if I had been in your place, and had your big bin of wheat, I would have answered a part of that prayer myself."

And now we appeal, in that brief sentence, Does there not reside a sermon with an idea in it;—an idea that will live as long as civilized man shall tenant the Earth, notwithstanding the little preacher may have long since passed away, and his name become forgotten? The empty, formal practice of looking up to an imaginary God with our eyes shut, and asking him with our lips to do *in general* what we ourselves will not begin to do *in particular*, although blessed with the necessary means, and notwithstanding thereunto besought with tears, cannot, we think, be particularly pleasing to our great Parent; and most assuredly it can never be productive of any very beneficial results either to ourselves or anybody else.

We would not be understood as saying it is not good for us ardently to desire that the hungry should be supplied with food, the naked clothed, etc.; nor yet that it is not our duty, as well as privilege, earnestly to beseech God to do all these things, and numerous others of a kindred nature, for poor, weak, sinful mortals, like ourselves, as well as to ask him to *forgive us our debts, as we forgive our debtors.* Far from it! Praying for good things, just like the practice of thinking of things that are good, or of acts which are generous and noble, legitimately tends to render us better; and praying for things that are bad, just like thinking of evil things, or of acts which are coarse, arbitrary and cruel, to make us worse. But then we must be permitted to think that it would be wisdom in such of us as are in the habit of shutting our eyes and stopping our ears to the wails and woes of poor, suffering humanity,—such of us as never surrender a demand so long as a chance remains for its enforcement by the law's strong aid,—Such of us are so slow to forgive even fancied offenses committed against our darling selves, and yet so fast to advocate, not the reformation of the erring brother upon ameliorated plan, but his speedy punishment as an outlawed wretch in tyrant jail, gloomy prison, or halter's fatal noose,—to pause and consider what it really is for which we thus do pray. Yea, and thoughtfully reflect upon what would be our condition, were that God, who we thus in solemn mockery address, so far to take us at our word as to grant us just one tithe of these our thoughtless, soulless petitions, which in mere empty sound and idle show their beginning have, and there, their worthless end.

St. James says, "The effectual fervent prayer of a righteous man availeth much." And, to us, it is clear that no prayer is *fervent and effectual*, which in mere words begins and ends, but only such as are spoken out in works meet to bring about the asked-for result either by the petitioner himself, or by those upon whom it shall act as a sufficiently exciting cause, to induce them to put forth the necessary efforts to make it a thing effectual and availing. Nor do we claim the merit of originating these views, or of being the first to put them forth. Upon the contrary, years ago, the learned Dr. Blair, in a sermon on the unchangeableness of the Divine Nature, discoursed as follows: "It will be proper to begin this head of discourse, by removing an objection which the doctrine I have illustrated may appear to form against religious services, and, in particular, against the duty of prayer. To what purpose, it may be urged, is homage addressed to a Being whose purpose is unalterably fixed; to whom *our righteousness extendeth not;* whom by no arguments we can persuade, and by no supplications we can mollify?" "The objection," he continues, "would have weight, if our religious addresses were designed to work any alteration on God; either by giving Him information of what He did not know, or by exciting affections which he did not possess; or by inducing Him to change measures which He had previously formed. But they are only crude and imperfect notions of religion which can suggest such ideas. The change which our devotions are intended to make, is upon ourselves, not upon the Almighty. Their chief efficacy is derived from the good dispositions which they raise and cherish, in the human soul. By pouring out pious sentiments and desires before God, by adoring his perfection and confessing our own unworthiness, by expressing our dependence on his aid, our gratitude for past favors, our submission to his present will, our trust in his future mercy, we cultivate such affections as suit our place and station in the universe, and are thereby prepared for becoming objects of divine grace." To the same effect taught the student and philosopher, Lord Kames, when he said: "The Being that made the world governs it by laws that are enflexible, because they are best, and to imagine that He can be moved by prayers, oblations, or sacrifices, to vary his plan of government, is an impious thought, degrading the Deity to a level with ourselves."—Such, upon this point, is the common-sense testimony of these eminent men. In conclusion thereupon, we will merely add, that the only prayer which either from our own observation, or from credible authority, we have ever known to be sufficiently *effectual, fervent and availing*, to dig a well, excavate a cellar, or tunnel a mountain, was that which was put forth by the shoulder and elbow of the laborer, with implement in hand.

That "faith without works is dead," we have the testimony of this same witness James; and, with all the light and knowledge now in the world, it cannot need either testimony or argument to prove, that an erroneous faith, with all its corresponding works, is quite as bad as dead, if not a little worse. And as it is not possible for any more than one of all the numerous and different conflicting faiths that are in the world to be true to great Nature, and hence an eternal *verity*, so it needs must follow that all, save one, together with the vast amount of diverse works unto which they have stood parent cause, are a greater or a lesser hindrance to the spread of real and abiding truth, and hence to the upward progress of the race.

Unquestionably,

> "There is a divinity that shapes our ends,
> Rough-hew them as we will,"

And that divinity, as we see it, is the resistless operation of natural law.

LUCK.

It may be laid down as a rule, to which there are but few exceptions, that, of good luck, good management is the parent cause, and, of bad luck, bad management. It is unsafe to have any sort of business connection with such as are constitutionally unlucky, no matter how honest, intelligent, or agreeable as companions they may be. Nor would it be prudence in a personal friend of such a man to consent to give him counsel, since, should he do so, and his unlucky friend attempt to follow it, the chances are ten to one that he would leave a screw loose somewhere, consequently fail, and hence lay the blame at the door of his adviser. In a word, if a man possesses, within himself, the elements of success, no matter who he is, where he came from, or what he undertakes, he is almost certain to succeed; and if stamped all over with the elements of failure, though descended from a line of kings, he is just about certain to fail, attempt what he may.

DIFFERENT INDIVIDUALS, DIFFERENTLY AFFECTED.

There are not only innate virtues of different kinds, but faults and weaknesses as well. Some persons are so organized and balanced that they naturally firm and upright stand, whilst others are so constituted that they are ever quite easily upset. To some the cup is a temptation too strong to be by them withstood; to others tea, tobacco, and thus on. Then, again, there are those whom none of this class of things has power to tempt beyond their bearings, but which the love of sensual indulgence with the opposite sex, or something else may. The few who are so fortunate as to possess an organization and mental balance which render them, in reference to all the different appetites, passions, and besetments, a living law unto themselves, should not only be thankful therefor, but exceedingly charitable and forbearing toward such as are thus constitutionally powerless, in certain directions. Indeed, it would be well, not only for such, but for all the more favored classes to remember, that we did none of us very extensively make ourselves; consequently, that not so much to us, as to parents, education, and other causes over which we had no control, is due the credit of our being what we are. In other words, we are proof against this, that, and the other allurement, and hence the kind of persons we are, just because these things, to us, instead of being temptations deep and strong, are very nearly indifferent, if not actually distasteful.

To be tempted and not sin may be regarded as a personal virtue, but not to sin because not thereunto tempted, notwithstanding the same thing may be a strong temptation to somebody else, is simply so much hereditary, educational, or other good fortune, for which we have good cause to be thankful, but none for the putting on of personal airs. We say, to be tempted and not sin may be regarded as a personal virtue, because, the more an individual is tempted and withstands the temptation, the stronger he legitimately becomes; and hence just so much the more certain is he not to sin. In other words, the multiplication of surrounding temptations ever legitimately improves, and strengthens in virtue, all such as are sufficiently resolute to withstand their influence, whilst it is only by the most careful avoidance of temptation, that the safety of those less firm is assured. Children that are naturally bold, determined, and self-reliant, hence not inclined to see, think, or believe by proxy, are in little danger of being led into erroneous opinions and practices by the influence of others, go where they may; whilst those that are naturally timid, obsequious, and confiding, however bright and quick to learn they may chance to be, are in imminent danger of being misled, stay where they will.

POLITICIANS.

There are not only two political parties always in the country, but two classes of politicians belonging to each; namely, the representative and non-representative. The former are ever ready to think, say, and do whatever the voting masses may chance to desire to have them think, say, and do; consequently, not from inherent weight of personal character, but the want thereof, these tricksters rise to the surface, float upon some one or more of the popular planks that are periodically placed in those cunningly wrought skimmers, denominated platforms, and thus, when happening to belong to the stronger party, straight into office they are quite sure to ride. Not so with the latter class. The opinions of these men not being thus manufactured to order, but their own, so they are always bent upon representing themselves, whether they ever anybody else do represent or not. And of this the consequence is, that not often are they honored with even a nomination to office, and, when they are, they are almost certain to be elected to stay at home; where, by their superior talents, persevering industry, and consequent general influence over those same masses with whom, during the canvass and at the polls, they are thus seemingly unpopular, they dictate to and rule the nominal rulers. In this way is the governmental practice ever made quite nearly to comport with the views and wishes of those more bold, active, and outspoken, but at-home-staying politicians; thus mainly obviating the danger, not only of insurrections against the government, but of any great and long-continued usurpation of power by any one of its different co-ordinate branches. In a word, the nation is, for the most part, ruled by brains; but not, for the most part, by the brains of the so-called rulers.

CRIMES AND THEIR PUNISHMENT.

Aside from the teachings of phrenology, we should be false to the light of our own personal observation and experience,—as well as to the charity and good will we bear toward all human kind,—did we not respectfully urge the propriety of such an alteration in our criminal code, as shall make it discriminate between offenses committed against human nature, as the same exists in the great body of society, and offenses not so much against general human nature as against the rights of property, and such other enactments as are designed to restrict individual action within certain, arbitrary limits. In other words, we must think the good of society imperatively demands such a modification of the penal system, as shall abolish from among us no small class of crimes, punishable in the penitentiary, by sinking them into misdemeanors, punishable through the pocket for the benefit of the party injured; and hence obviate, in no small degree, not only the demoralizing effects of the prison, but the trouble and expense consequent thereupon. We say, such a modification of the penal system, as shall abolish from among us no small class of crimes, etc., because, as really seems to us, a majority of all the acts which are, to-day, denominated crimes, and punishable by the prison with all its degrading and manhood-annihilating consequences, are the legitimate result of an over-ardent desire to obtain property. Wherefore to punish the possessors of such inordinate desire through their property, by fine, is to punish them through the very God they worship. And hence, such punishment, without essentially impairing the delinquent's usefulness in society, or materially disgracing his friends, would do much more toward curing him of his unfortunate defect, (and being begotten, born, and educated under the influence exerted by this wealth-worshiping and poverty-despising age, this is the only appropriate name for both over-large and over-active acquisitiveness,) than is it possible for confinement in a penitentiary to do. Not only this, but as it is punishment inflicted, and not punishment merely threatened, that tends to prevent crime, so this being much more reasonable and just, it would be much more certain to be executed. In short, as we have come to see it, in order to render the world a great deal better and happier than it now is, it is only necessary that a large share of its inconsiderate severity should be exchanged for an equal amount of considerate kindness. And, in order to effect such an exchange, the reformation must begin at the top of the social column,—must begin up among the leaders in both church and state; and not away down at the bottom among the uninfluential, and unfortunate erring.

FAITH VS. INVESTIGATION.

According to the latest authorities upon the subject, there are now in the world about 340,000,000 of Boodhists, 160,000,000 of Mohammedans, 195,000,000 of Roman Catholics, and 97,000,000 of Protestants. Hence, allowing numbers to be evidence of the correctness of religious faith, we Protestants are only about two-thirds as likely to be right, as are the Mohammedans; about one-half as likely to so, as are the Roman Catholics; and about one-fourth as likely, as are the poor, despised Boodhists, whose fourth deity died a long time before our Christ was born, and whose fifth is not expected to make his appearance upon the Earth for many centuries to come.

Corollary:—Not early borrowed faith of any kind, however universal, but close investigation, irrespective of who may be thereunto opposed, is the best evidence of sound opinions, as well upon the subject of religion, as upon every other.—Straight and narrow is the way that leads to real truth; and yet it is broad enough for all mankind to walk therein to a much greater extent than they now do, were they only thus supremely inclined.

PROGRESSIONISTS AND NON-PROGRESSIONISTS.

A Progressionist is one who makes it a rule, as far forth as possible, not only to look and think for himself, but to speak and act in accordance with the light which he, at the time, possesses upon the subject, no matter what may chance to have been his prior opinions thereupon, or what his former course of action. Consequently, in looking over the different chapters into which the life of such a man doth naturally divide itself, there will be many things discoverable, which, although bearing evidence upon their face of having been deliberately said and done, are nevertheless irreconcilably at variance, the one with the other.

A non-progressionist is one who makes it a point, not only not to look or think for himself, any more than he cannot help, but to speak and to act just as did his venerable father before him, and because his father did thus speak and act, no matter what the subject, nor how much such speech or action may chance to be at variance with the little personal observation and experience, that have been forced upon him. Of course, in the life of such a man, there will be found but one chapter; and that, whether right, or whether wrong, a self-consistent one from beginning to end.

Or, to state the case a little more fully, large Causality and Comparison, joined with small Veneration and Firmness, ever dispose their possessors to look carefully into the sayings and doings of contemporaries for guidance and instruction,—ever dispose them to scan well the facts and circumstances connected with the more advanced present in search of light; and consequently, in both thought and action, they are ever onward-moving. Upon the other hand, large Veneration and Firmness, joined with small Causality and Comparison, ever dispose their possessors to look to the ancients for guidance and instruction,—ever dispose them to look back into the past for light and knowledge; and consequently, whatsoever things were chanced to be said and done by certain of the ancient Fathers, those same are they disposed to say and do forever on. In other words, there is a class of persons who are so organized and balanced, that they are always ready and willing, not only to learn what is real truth upon every subject of interest to man, but to confess by their actions as well as in words, that they are wiser to-day than they were yesterday, and hope to be still wiser to-morrow. Such, wherever found, naturally look forward, and not backward, consequently are progressive in their character and yearnings; and hence, between their opinions and practice, past and present, there will ever be found to exist discrepancies, more or less glaring. And then there is another class whose organization and mental balance is such that they are strongly predisposed, if not irresistibly inclined, forever to be and remain of the same traditional opinions and narrow practice, that were their revered ancestors. These, irrespective of caste or profession, ever, naturally, look backward, and not forward; consequently they are sure to remain just about stationary in both opinions and practice; and hence, whether right or whether wrong, and whether weighty or whether weightless, they are never guilty of being inconsistent with themselves.

Consistency is doubtless a *jewel;* but not that kind of consistency which requires that a man should purposely go wrong *to-day*, because, from ignorance or inadvertence, he chanced to go wrong *yesterday;* but the kind which currently determines him to avoid, as far forth as possible, the errors of yesterday, and to pursue the right to-day, as the same to him shall appear.

TEACHERS.

Good book-learning, although a very desirable thing in a teacher, is by no means the only qualification that is needed to insure success in teaching. Indeed, a teacher that is considerably deficient in scholarship, but possessed of native tact, and a brain of the positive stamp, is ever to be preferred to one of good book-learning, but devoid of tact and force of character. The presence of the former in the schoolroom, notwithstanding his deficiency in scholarship, ever exerts a strengthening, upbuilding influence; that of the latter, notwithstanding his fine scholastic acquirements, a weakening, downward-dragging one; and especially upon such of his pupils as are themselves lacking in these same elements. In the schoolroom, the same as everywhere else, like begets like. In other words, positive influences impart power, and negative influences detract therefrom.

CHAPTER V.

CHARACTER OF THE BIBLE'S GOD.

Such is our confidence in the goodness and justice of our great Parent, call we him God, Nature, or by whatever name we may, that we can never believe him guilty of having conducted himself toward us, his children, in a way which would stamp with undying infamy the earthly parent who should evidence a like character, by behaving toward his offspring in a manner precisely similar. Not only this, but such is our desire to see respect for the Bible placed upon some more fitting basis, than is a blind, presumptuous faith in its superhuman origin, bordering upon idolatry, that we can never yield our assent to such a construction of its pages as must tend to sink it in the estimation of all right-minded, generous-hearted, thinking men and women who, from Nature's volume, are convinced that the God of all the Earth doth right. Or, to state our position a little differently, because not only the miraculous portion of the Bible, but much of the so-called historic, will not admit of a literal construction without weakening the reader's confidence in, and lessening his respect for, the character and government of that God of whom its pages treat, therefore, as long as shall it continue to be made the rule of human faith and the measure of its practice, so long must we continue to object to any such construction being put thereupon. And to prove that such is the case, even with the most fundamental Bible narrations, we propose to take the first one which presents itself, and admit the account of the course pursued by God toward man, as chronicled by Moses in the first three chapters of Genesis, to be literally correct, and then proceed to illustrate the same by an assumed example.

As a foundation, then, we will assume that somewhere within the United States, there resides a very wealthy man of fifty years, who, at the age of thirty, was left a widower with two infant children, a promising little son, the image of himself, and a beautiful little daughter, the picture of her mother. This much being assumed as a fact, let it now be supposed as hereinafter follows:—Immediately after his wife's decease, and ostensibly for the purpose of favoring these motherless innocents, this millionaire proceeded to lay out a garden, wherein he planted a great variety of trees that are pleasant to the sight and good for food. In addition to these, and in the midst of the garden, he planted a kind of tree, the fruit of which, although pleasant to look upon, was nevertheless a deadly poison; also another, whose fruit was by him known to be, unto such poison, an effectual antidote.

A few years thereafter, and when the different trees were covered with fruit, this parent took the two confiding, little innocents by the hand, led them into this paradise, and said, "Behold, all this richness and beauty, out of the abundance of my paternal love, have I prepared and spread out as an agreeable surprise before you; and now, to your care and keeping, I commit it. Here you are at liberty to roam and regale yourselves, and of every tree of the garden you may freely eat: *but of the tree of knowledge of good and evil*, pointing thereto, you must not eat of it: for in the day you eat thereof you shall surely die." This all done in true paternal style, he smiled upon them a parting blessing and withdrew, leaving the innocent and happy pair alone to dress the garden, eat of its goodly fruits, and enjoy its pleasures.

In true child-like style and simplicity, thoughtless and happy as the birds that were singing their love notes on the boughs o'er their heads, or the fishes that were sporting their short lives in the stream at their feet, these juveniles at once proceeded to ransack every nook and corner, upsetting this and overturning that; here in ecstacies at sight of this new object, and there wondering at some other; under this tree stuffing themselves with its delicious fruit, and beside that, in boisterous merriment, rolling upon the green grass carpet, not knowing what to do next. In this way the hours flew by, until, at length, they found themselves under the interdicted tree; the sight of which not only reminded little Eva of what her father said about it, but greatly excited her feminine curiosity to know what there could be so very peculiar about this tree, whose strange name, *knowledge of good and evil,* created in her mind only a blank idea of its nature, she having never yet tasted the quality by the latter part of the name denoted. These things all conspired to excite her curiosity to the highest pitch; and when she saw *that the tree was good for food, and that it was pleasant to the eyes, and a tree to be desired to make one wise,* she not only took of the fruit thereof herself and ate, but gave also unto her little brother that was with her, and he ate. No sooner was this done, however, than sad experience made them wiser, for then they knew not only good, but also evil by its gnawings and fatal effects. Just at that moment too their father was heard coming, and so they ran and hid themselves from his presence among the trees of the garden. This childish expedient was of no avail however, as he immediately called to them in an imperative tone, demanding to know where they were. Upon this little Adin, who was a fraction older than his twin sister Eva, frankly made answer thus: "I heard you coming into the garden, father, and being afraid, *I hid myself.*" The father suspecting what they had been about immediately inquired, "Have you eaten of the tree whereof I commanded you not to eat?"—Whereupon the ingenuous little Adin, without waiting to have the question repeated, proceeded straightforwardly to acknowledge his error by saying: "My little sister whom you left with me in the garden, *she gave me of the tree, and I did eat.*" Upon this the father turned to Eva and said, "*What is this that thou hast done?*"—And she, too, unlike a child steeped in falsehood, but like a very good little girl as she had ever been, made full confession thus: "What you said, about the tree, father, when you called our attention to it, together with its pleasant look, tempted me, *and I did eat.*" The parent thus understanding not only what they had done, but their consequent perillous condition, immediately turned to some one—we cannot tell whom—and said, "Behold, these children have each become as one of us, *to know good and evil;* and now, lest they put forth their hands and take also of the tree whose fruit is an antidote to the poison which contrary to my injunctions they have swallowed, and so become healed, I will drive them out of the garden, and place a guard about it that will effectually prevent them." Such being his decision, he at once proceeded to carry it into execution by summarily ejecting them from the garden, and placing before the entrance *a flaming sword which turned every way to keep the way* which led into the garden, and hence to the antidotal tree, effectually guarded. This done, he sat himself down and calmly awaited the result, which, it is needless to say, was just what he well knew it would be; namely, before the Sun's last rays had faded in the west, little Adin and Eva, his only children, were both lying cold in death upon the ground before him. Thus were these little, motherless innocents, for this their first false step, and for the taking of which they were so much indebted to a train of circumstances purposely spread as a temptation and snare in their path by the hand of him who, from the high and holy relation in which he stood to them, should have been their nurse when sick, the protector of their persons when well, and the shield of their innocence from every foreseen temptation and danger, left to sicken, suffer, and die before his eyes.

And now, in all sincerity, we ask, Does not every considerate person, acquainted with the careless, inquisitive, and confiding nature of inexperienced children, see and know that what befell these unfortunates, if not certain to take place, will at least be liable to happen just about as often as shall such an unnatural, inhuman, and wicked experiment be repeated? We repeat the question, Does not every considerate person see and know this?—But whether they do or not, and be the answer given what it may, this much is certain; the experiment has not been repeated, and never will be by any sane parent, rich or poor, black or white. But, to bring the matter as near home to our reader's own doors, as should we be pardonable in doing even by supposition, what think ye would have been and still be your feelings, and especially such of you as are parents, had this unnatural father chanced to be a resident of your own quiet, little neighborhood; had this event but last week taken place; had you been present at their funeral; and had you all the while supposed them to have been thus suddenly stricken down by some unaccountable accident, until, at the conclusion of the solemn services, and with hearts overflowing with kindly sympathy for the bereaved parent, you were suddenly undeceived by hearing that father boastingly proclaim aloud, as a model paternal example, the exact cause and manner of their death? Aye, and what the judgment,—when, by a faithful press, the unvarnished tale shall have been trumpeted to the remotest nook tenanted by civilized man,—which an astonished and indignant world would be compelled to pronounce upon that father, whose superior wisdom and forecast are known to be such as to render it certain, not only that he fully comprehended the imminence of the hazard to which he was thus wantonly exposing his inexperienced and hitherto innocent children, but that this fatal and fatally tempting danger was, by him, deliberately planned, and placed before them? To say nothing of the emotions that would heave the fond bosoms of tender mothers and doting fathers, would not the following be, in substance and effect, the thoughts and the feelings which would swell every other kind and manly breast?—The sane parent who can thus deliberately go and plant, in grounds set apart for the use and improvement of his innocent offsprings, a tree whose fruit is pleasant to the eye, but a deadly poison, and then trust to threatened punishment of any kind to shield them from the impending danger, however carefully pointed out, is a *wretch*. The father who can stand by and see his children sicken, suffer, and die from the effects of disobediently eating a known deadly poisonous fruit, which, in spite of all his efforts to prevent, will ever, more or less plentifully, grow about his door; and neglect to force down their throats, if force be requisite, a known antidote which is at hand, and thus relieve their sufferings and save their lives, is either a MAD MAN or a FOOL. And the parent whose feelings are so callous that he can find it in his heart deliberately to say, of his thus offending, suffering, and dying children, "And now, lest they put forth their feeble hands and take also of the tree whose fruit is an antidote to the poison which contrary to my injunctions they have tasted, and so find relief therefrom and live, I will drive them from it;" and not only can find it in his heart deliberately to say so terribly unnatural and inhuman a thing, but to put the same into full execution; and then, with the self-satisfied air of a man who feels that he has washed his paternal hands of all responsibility in the matter, sit himself down and unmoved look on, and see them suffer and die before him, is not a man, but a MONSTER.

It cannot be necessary to go further and show, that these our assumed children, not only in point of age, but of knowledge and experience, much more nearly approach a state of equality with their supposed earthly parent, than do the oldest and wisest of us, fathers and mothers, to that eternal Being, whom a literal rendering of the Bible's language would make to be the Creator and Parent of us all. Not only this, but it must be obvious to every one that we have been compelled to represent said children as then and there, physically, expiring, such being the worst punishment which, by any fair supposition, we could represent as being inflicted; whereas the death contemplated in said Mosaic account, as authoritatively interpreted and taught in the schools, did not cease to be a *power* when it had slain the persons of our first parents, nor yet doth its dread mission come to an end with the cessation of bodily life in their numerous posterity; but, instead, extends its baleful influence unceasingly on in the form of an endless misery-creating, misery-extending, and misery-entailing influence, or a *death that never dies.*

And now, kind readers, to you, as candid perusers of the Bible, we appeal, Is not the illustration, although feeble and limited, at least a fair one; allowing said Mosaic account is not to be so interpreted as to make it accord with the lights of reason and of nature, but is to be understood either as by a living clergy it is explained, or as in black and white it reads? Also, whether or not our position is thus far sustained by the record, and whether we have treated the subject with that fairness and candor which become an inquirer after real truth, or whether we have not, you are the judges.

We will next take up the character of God as evidenced not only by the summary method he is said to have adopted, at quite an early day, to rid the Earth of sinful men, but also of the way he is reported to have contrived, long years thereafter, for bringing about a state of reconciliation between himself and the creatures whom he, unasked, had made; and whom, it would seem, he considered as being already dead to him, because so contaminated by the sins of their great first parents next after himself, that there was left no soundness in them. As a starting point, we will admit the different chapters and parts of chapters, passages and parts of passages, having reference to either of said events, no matter in which Testament found, to be, each and all, just so many plain historic narrations of facts which, in manner and form therein set forth, took place; and then proceed, as before, to illustrate each by an assumed example.

In some remote sea, then, and not within the jurisdiction of any state or country, we will assume there exists a solitary and spacious, but somewhat low and basin-shaped island, unto which a certain enterprising young man, long since, privately withdrew, taking with him not only a wife, but a reasonable supply of the different kinds of domestic animals; and where, "the world forgetting and by the world forgot," he still resides. This much being assumed as a fact, let it further be supposed as hereinafter set forth:—
In process of time, in this secluded spot, this man came to

be surrounded by an immense number of children, grandchildren, great-grandchildren, great-great-grandchildren, etc., all of whom, both male and female, had disobeyed and offended him in various ways; wherefore, with them all, he was sore displeased. The old adage, *Like father, like son*, seems here to have been most strikingly verified, not only in the character of his immediate children, but in that of his grandchildren, great-grandchildren, etc., who, witnessing their immediate parents' habits of rudeness and contempt of restraint, failed not in their turn to enact the same things, not only toward their fathers and mothers from whom they learned them, but also toward him who was the common parent of them all. In this way, and not because wheat, when timely sown upon ground that is suitable, will not take root and grow as well as tares, the thing naturally extended itself downward in an unbroken chain to the great-great-great-grandchildren, old enough to lisp and ape those older than themselves. Wherefore this clear-headed old parent and patriarchal governor, instead of looking complacently upon even the helpless infant in the cradle, seemed disposed to remember against such the sins of their parents, grandparents, etc., backward through a certain number of generations, always being careful to stop, however, just before it all centered in himself as the great head and starting-point. As already remarked, he was not upon terms of good feeling with even the smallest of his great-great-great-great grandchildren, but regarded them as being tainted by the sins of their immediate parents, else suffered himself to be displeased with them in advance for offenses he felt certain they would commit, just as soon as they should become possessed of the ability to do so. Thus did matters for a long time stand upon this beautiful island, where, strange and unaccountable as it may seem, all this misconduct of his progeny was suffered to go on, take place, and be, notwithstanding he was supreme governor there, or might at all times have been, had he chosen to assert his rightful authority, and exercise his power. Indeed, from the very nature of things, such was ever his power and authority there, that he had but to will it to have the strictest obedience to his every mandate rendered, and so had harmony and order taken the place of all this confusion and disorder. But all this disobedience and disorder, from the beginning down to the time under consideration, he suffered to be practiced by the clay over which he was potter, not, as said, because he could not at any time have put a stop thereto, had he chosen to do so, nor yet for the reason that he did not know beforehand that all these things would come to take place among his children and subjects, when thus left without governmental restraint, (save the little that resides in mere verbal threats of punishment at some indefinite future period,) but because it was his determination at the beginning, and all along, to hold them, and not himself, responsible for their being and doing the very reverse of what he their progenitor and untrammelled governor wanted they should be and do, and of what it was clearly within his province to have made them been and done. For this reason, and for no other that we can see, was all this mischief suffered to be afoot, and to take whatever course it would up to a certain time, when, as appears from the book of records there kept, he began to reflect upon its character and consequences. And it repented the old gentleman that he had begotten any children, and it grieved him at his heart. And he said, "I will destroy the children whom I have begotten, from the face of the island, both man and beast; for it repenteth me that I have begotten any children, or brought beasts upon the island." Notwithstanding all this, however, it seems that one of his sons, called Nor, found grace in the eyes of his father; and so he finally concluded not to make a clean sweep of the thing, but to save Nor and his household. He proceeded at once to inform his said son of his terrible determination, and instructed him to make ready a boat for the salvation of himself and family, together with a sufficient number of beasts of the different kinds, to preserve the seed thereof. Nor immediately set about making ready the craft as by his father directed, into which, when finished, he entered with his family and other appointed freight. And then, to bring about the work of destruction aforementioned and determined upon, the old gentleman opened the gates of a great sluice in the levee, of which he alone had knowledge and control, and so let the water flow in upon the face of the island, some forty days and forty nights; thereby soaking, chilling, starving, and drowning, indiscriminately, the men, women, children, and beasts of every kind. The more robust and active of his numerous posterity, suffered long and intensely from wet, cold, hunger, and fright, as from covert to covert and hillock to hillock they fled to escape the terrible and constantly-rising waters, until, at last, they were swallowed up in death;—until, at last, all in whose nostrils was the breath of life, of all that was in the island, died.

Such, in brief, was the nature of the difficulties complained of, such the causes which had led thereto, such the remedy determined upon therefor, and such its awfully devastating effects when into execution carried. And now, without a word of comment, we submit the broad question, Does not this whole transaction, from beginning to end, look much more like the work of a demon, than it does like the deliberate doings of a kind and indulgent parent, acting under the guidance of wisdom and justice?—But whether the dictate of wisdom and justice, or whether of folly and madness, the great work of death has been done, and the gates again closed.

And such in character and practice, according to the Mosaic account, was the God of the ancients: a Deity unto whom they were constantly sacrificing the first-fruits of the land, the firstlings of their flocks, the firstlings of their herds, and numerous other rich and savory things, not from feelings of love, but those of slavish fear; hoping, by thus ministering to the gratification of his appetite, to mollify his anger, turn aside his jealousy, and, if possible, to propitiate him into bearable good humor.

But to return from this digression: After many days, according to an entry found in the book of records, dry land again made its appearance upon the face of the island;

and Nor and his family gladly exchanged their pent-up quarters for its more ample and inviting surface. And Nor builded an altar unto his father, and took of every clean beast, and every clean fowl, and offered burnt-offerings on the altar. And his father smelled a sweet savor, and said in his heart, I will not again curse the ground any more for my children's sake, for the imaginations of my children's hearts are evil from their youth; neither will I again smite any more everything living as I have done. And the old patriarch blessed Nor and his sons, and said unto them, "Be fruitful, and multiply, and replenish the island;" a command just like the one he gave to each of his immediate children before he drowned them, likewise to all that vast multitude of human beings that had been brought into existence in obedience thereto. And the old gentleman spake unto Nor, and to his sons with him, saying, "And I, behold, I establish my covenant with you, and with your seed after you; and with every living creature that is with you; and I will establish my covenant with you; neither shall all flesh be cut off any more by the waters of a flood; neither shall there any more be a flood to destroy the island. And, as a token of this my said covenant, I will set my bow in the sluice by the gates, and the bow shall be in the sluice by the gates, and I will look upon the bow, that I may remember the everlasting covenant between me and every living creature that is upon the island."

A good understanding having been thus secured between himself and these his few remaining children, multiplication, marrying, and giving in marriage again began and went on, until there again came to be not only quite a numerous posterity of his upon the island, but until things were getting to be in just about the same entangled and disorderly state as before.

And so the yet hale old patriarch of Samsonian muscle, and more than Methuselahn longevity, again begins to look about him and consider. Plainly enough he discovers it is of little use to repent himself that he ever begot any children, since that being a thing done can never be recalled;

and besides he sees the bow quite too oft and plainly to allow him to forget that he has bound himself, by solemn covenant, not to drown them any more by the waters of a flood. So, upon a careful review of the whole matter, he finally comes to see just what he perfectly well knew from the beginning; namely, that by thus permitting the mass of his children and subjects, (for, as appears by the book of records, most of the time, since that terrible drowning affair, a few favorites and an occasional pet among his children he seems to have had,) to run on and do the very things he does not want done, and to leave undone those which he is desirous they should do, he is but repeating his former experiment, and hence must needs reap the same dissatisfactory results. All this, as said, he knew from the beginning; wherefore it can never with any show of reason be urged that he was taken by surprise, or in the least disappointed by their occurrence. And yet, strange and unaccountable as it may appear, the old patriarchical governor seems now, for the first time, to see and appreciate the obvious fact, that the high and holy relation of parent ever, naturally, brings along with it certain other imperative duties beside that of simply giving unto those, upon whom is thus forced a living existence, a place whereon to stand and to grow. And seeing this, he seems to have come to the only conclusion that can ever, logically, be drawn from the premises; namely, That this state of things, however long permitted to continue, must needs be and remain just as disagreeable and unprofitable to him, as it is injurious and fatal to them. Indeed, it would seem, to all appearance, but just now to have occurred to the old gentleman, that such a course of procedure could no more contribute to his good and happiness than to theirs, since, by an unalterable decree of his own, or of somebody else, their interest must needs be his interest, their joys, his joys, and their sorrows, his sorrows. Such being the state of affairs, such the tenor of his reflections, such the failure of the great drowning experiment, and such his covenant never again to repeat it, he now begins to cast about him to discover, if possible, some more effectual remedy. Plainly enough he sees that somebody has done wrong; wherefore he is determined that somebody shall suffer. Yea, blood must be shed before he can so much as think of abating his fury, or suffering his fierce anger to be appeased. And yet the idea of chastising each for his own personal transgressions, as he justly deserves, does not seem to strike him favorably, since, by such a course, he would be obliged to punish the whole of his remaining posterity, except one certain good and noble son who, it would seem, had never sinned. Tacitly admit that he had himself been a little remiss in the discharge of his duties as parent and governor, by extending to all unconditional pardon for past offenses, without punishing a single individual any further than has each already been by the natural effects of wrong-doing, he is determined he will not; notwithstanding he knows there is not a tongue in all the island that would object, or a hand that would be raised in opposition thereto.

No; for angry he is, and angry he will be; and his fierce anger he will not suffer one jot to be appeased without blood. And so he finally determines—ah! and what does he finally determine? That he will chastise each and all according to their several deserts?—No. That he will make an example of certain ringleaders, and offer a conditional pardon to all the rest?—No; not this: but that he will punish in a most cruel and ignominious manner the only innocent child he has, the very one who has merited naught from him, save love, kindness, and protection.—Strange determination, this! And stranger still that it should be called by the name of either Mercy or Justice!

But the plan being now determined upon in his own mind, he proceeds to lay the same before this generous and noble hearted son who, not for the novelty of the thing, nor yet for the empty eclat, but for the great and noble purpose of permanently benefiting his ignorantly erring and greatly beloved kindred, magnanimously assents to be made for them a vicarious sacrifice. And mark it! this strange and strangely unnatural father does not step kindly forward, and, with his own feeling hand, himself inflict the dreadful blow, (thereby extracting as much as possible the sting therefrom,) but sends him forth unprotected and alone among his enraged and cruel sons, grandsons, great-grandsons, etc., who are themselves the guilty wretches, and whose hatred toward this his defenceless child and bosom confidant is just about as deep and unrelenting, as toward himself, the common head and parent of them all. Thus are these miscreants, who it would certainly seem were already sufficiently dyed with crime, purposely permitted to add still another to their already dark catalogue of offenses,—that of glutting their savage cruelties, even unto the death, upon the head of a kind and generous-hearted relative, who has never injured either him or them.

But, to make a long, horrid, and strangely unnatural story as short as possible, this innocent victim of folly, treachery, and hate, with the magnanimity and self-possession which had ever characterized his noble and generous nature, strengthened now by an ardent desire to appease his father's anger, and thus confer a lasting benefit upon his erring kindred, meekly bore their cruel taunts and buffetings: and yet, when the diabolical punishment, to which their malicious hate had doomed him, came to stare him fully in the face, he staggered under it. Wherefore he besought his father to be spared *this cup*, if consistently with his will it could be done. This appeal, it would seem, touched somewhat his father's feelings; and yet, judging from what immediately followed, as appears from the book of records, it is manifest the unhappy child obtained no encouragement that this his most reasonable request should be granted. For, being in an agony, he prayed the more earnestly: *and his sweat was as it were great drops of blood falling down to the ground.* But the agonizing prayer of this his unhappy son, the stern father grants not. The cup, the bitter cup, of a slow, cruel, and ignominious death, he is not only made to taste, but to drink to the very dregs: for, by his enraged kindred, he is pursued as a criminal, taken, tried, condemned, and executed. We say, he was tried, because a sort of hearing he seems to have had; notwithstanding the infamous farce was most unceremoniously interrupted and cut short by repeated cries of crucify him, crucify him. Accordingly, without form or order, he is led away from the judgment-hall, nailed to the barbarous cross, placed between two thieves, the more pointedly to signify that he was the soul and center of their hate; and there, stretched between the heavens and earth as if unfit for either, amid shouts, revilings, and senseless ribaldry, he lingers, suffers, and dies; the stern father all the while looking on, that his angry vengeance, not toward him, but toward the inhuman perpetrators, might be satisfied.—When in this terribly ignominious and suffering condition he found himself, no more did he petition to be spared that cup: for then all hope thereof had fled. In the midst of all this gloom and anguish, however, his native kindness did not seem to desert him, but shone out—"The ruling passion, strong in death." Wherefore, here it was that love, strengthened by fear that even this his most tragical end might prove insufficient to appease his father's anger, and thus reconcile him to his ignorantly erring kindred, forced upon him his recollection and constrained him to repeat that pure, unselfish, and never-to-be-forgotten prayer of the man of Nazareth, "*Father, forgive them: for they know not what they do.*"

Thus did the pure, the innocent, and unoffending suffer, not by unfortunate mistake, but was purposely made to bleed and die, for and instead of the known impure and guilty. And hence the plan of reconciliation between this offended parent and his disobedient children has now become a perfected thing. We say, it has now become a perfected thing; because, after having thus permitted the already deeply criminal to add, unto past criminality, this one more deep and damning blood-stained crime, the old gentleman finds himself so much better pleased with the vile perpetrators than before, that he is now ready, willing, and anxious, upon terms both simple and easy, to extend unto all forgiveness, not only for this, but for all past offenses. Or, to present the different philosophical beauties of this so-called salvation's plan in one brief sentence, because vengeance, dire and bloody, has been executed upon the head of the undoubtedly pure and unoffending, therefore have the known deeply criminal become so nearly innocent as to be fit subjects, not only of a cold, formal pardon, if they will accept of it, but of reception into favor, if they shall desire it.—And such in character and practice, according to Moses and the evangelists, is the God of orthodox moderns: a Deity whom it is impossible to love, or not to dread; and one from whose impending wrath they hope to make their escape, by shouting and singing the praises, not of *him*, but of that excellent and most grossly wronged *man*, who bore the name of Christ; and whose philanthropic spirit, amiable character, and unselfish teachings, it is both natural and easy to love and revere.

That savage barbarians do sometimes shock the moral sense of the world by inhumanly butchering a friend or associate of the offending party, in place of the transgressor who has eluded their grasp, is not denied; but wherever the blessed lights of science and civilization have dawned, except, possibly, during deep and damning war, it is never done. And why not?—Policy forbids it! justice forbids it! every finer feeling of the human heart forbids it! O thou Father of mercies, God of all grace, and Author of light, knowledge, and civilization among men! forgive us the thus laying at thy door motives, feelings, and barbarities, which, if seriously laid to ours, would kill us of very shame. Yea, forgive us: for, verily, such are the blinding effects of early-made impressions and after-associations, that, touching many things naturally plain, *we know not what we do*.

And yet again, kind readers, are we obliged to admit the want of perfect parallelism between the supposed case, and the real one; since, in this, the same as in the first, it is not within the scope of our feeble imaginative powers to lay before you an exact likeness of the original, in all its immensely unnatural and inhuman length and breadth. Wherefore, be pleased to consider the following suggestive questions:—1. Do not all and singular the deviations from parallelism which, from the nature of things, we have been compelled to make, operate in favor of the character of the Bible's God, and not against it, allowing that its pages are not to be so interpreted as to make them harmonize with the lights of reason and nature, but are to be understood either as by the schools they are explained, or as in black and white they read? 2. Notwithstanding you could not fail to admire the unselfish generosity and kindness of the single man who should modestly step from the ranks, and offer himself as a target in place of his brother, who is sentenced to death for ignobly deserting the army of his country, and who has a wife and children to mourn his loss; still would you not be compelled to look down with contempt upon that wretch of a commanding officer who, even momentarily, could so far forget his duty as a soldier and his dignity as a man, as to nod his assent to the exchange; and thus permit the brave and the innocent to be shot down like a beast, whilst prayerfully knelt upon the coffin designed for his offending brother? 3. Was a neighbor of yours, before starting upon a journey, to lay down a chart of rules for the guidance of his six minor sons during his absence, and was one of them in all things to obey his instructions, whilst the other five laugh at both him and his requirements, and so go on behaving and doing contrary thereto; and should that man upon his return, after being informed of what had been done, who were the ones that did it, and which the individual that took no part therein, refuse to forgive his five offending children upon any terms, until they had first seized, stripped, and cowhided in a most brutal manner, the one who had been thus obedient; and was that man then to turn to said five and say, And now, upon the strength of what your innocent brother has been made to suffer, I will forgive your disobedience, if you will but confess your faults, and ask pardon therefor; and should that parent the next morning, when you his near neighbors, in a peaceful manner, present yourselves before him to labor with him upon the subject, undertake to inflict upon you a long rigmarole, not only about the necessity of punishing somebody, since he had promised them all a flogging, if they did not obey, but about the *wisdom, justice and mercy* of thus indirectly, but brutally, punishing this one good and dutiful child, instead of decently chastising the five delinquents, or one or two of the leading rebels;—law-abiding, as you doubtless are, Do you think anything short of well-grounded doubts of his sanity would save him from the smell of pitch, and a realizing sense of the proper *et cetera's?* 4. And how came you in possession of a nature which thus instinctively revolts at the idea of adopting any such unreasonable course toward your own children, or of seeing it adopted toward those of a neighbor, unless it was organically enstamped upon you by that God, in whose image and likeness you are created? —How? 5. Admitting the taking of the life of Christ by violence, to have been, in the mind of Almighty God, an essential plank in the platform of man's salvation; and also admitting that all who were upon the Earth, at the time Christ was here, had believed in him, that is, had believed his story about his being the Son of God, etc., consequently had been his followers, the same as were Peter, James, and John, and hence had treated with gentleness and respect; then is it not plain that God would have been obliged to have slain him directly, and with his own hand, instead of indirectly, through the unbelieving Jews, as his fit instrument; else that the entire plan of human salvation would have been a dead failure? 6. Allowing the death of Christ by violence, to have been originally, in the mind of God, a part of salvation's perfected plan, or rather one of the essential links in the chain of prederminate causes which brought the plan of salvation to a state of perfection; and also allowing that God would not himself have laid violent hands upon Christ, and thus have been his murderer, then is not the inference irresistible, that we are just as much indebted to the awfully wicked Jews for killing him, as we are to the Holy Ghost for begetting him, the Virgin Mary for bearing him, or to God the Father for raising him from the dead? In other words, if, for bearing Christ,—whose mission it was to save the world, not by his birth alone, but by his birth and death,

—Mary is worthy to be sainted; then why are not the Jews for killing him, and thus rendering his said mission a thing complete?—That they honestly thought they were doing a service to society, if not to the world, by killing him, as seems to us, there can be no doubt; and consequently none that they were acting morally right;—were acting just as morally right, when they did it, as was Mary, when unresistingly submitting herself to be overshadowed by the Holy Ghost; and thus brought into a condition, whereby, in due course of time, she was compelled to give birth to the babe called Jesus.—7. And does not the bare suggestion of punishing those who do not deserve it, and letting go unpunished such as have richly merited it, just because the innocent have undeservedly been made to suffer, involuntarily carry your thoughts back to those days of heathenish darkness, when wisdom and justice were the exceptions, and folly, favoritism, and revenge the rule, instead of up to a wise, just, and impartial God?

Of course, we may wrong, but, as we have come to see it, such is human nature, and such the Bible account of God and of Christ, that men have no option, but are compelled, by the nature that is in them, to detest the character of the former, and to admire that of the latter; in other words, they are irresistably led to love and deify the *man*, and to hate the *God*. Wherefore, again we repeat, so long as shall the Bible continue to be made the rule of our religious faith and the measure of its practice, just so long must its every chapter, verse, and sentence be so construed as not to make its teachings pander to our grosser animal passions, or shock the higher and better portion of our nature. For, manifestly enough, just what we need is, that the animal man within us should be dragged upward, and still upward, until it shall come harmoniously to stand upon the same high plane, legitimately occupied by the greatly advanced intellectual and moral man; and not that the intellectual and moral man within us should be debased down, and still down, to a level with the animal man, as the same existed within the human tabernacle some two or three thousand years ago. On a word, that religious standard, and that only, tends to better us, whose precepts and examples are more noble and exalted than are our own spontaneous promptings, and yet not so much above the level of our natures, be that level high or be it low, as to render at all attempts at successful imitation hopeless.

CHAPTER VI.

AN UNLOVELY GOD CANNOT BE LOVED.

It may be a misfortune, but whether so or not, such is our organic structure and such our mental balance, that it is not possible for us to believe what to us appears incredible, or to love what to us doth seem both hateful and unjust. Although we might greatly fear a Being who should demean himself toward his offspring in the manner we are told that God did toward our first parents, and, through them, toward all human kind, the same as we doubtless should a great and powerful, but cruel and vindictive human tyrant, (should it ever be our fortune to fall into the hands of such an earthly curse,) still we can no more truly respect such a Personage, than could we a self-wise, self-willed, and self-righteous neighbor who, instead of trying to devise ways and means for so far abridging the freedom of choice and of action in his innocent offspring, as to prevent them, without injury to themselves or anybody else, from doing such things as he does not want done, should first pompously command them, upon pain of punishment, not to do it, and then sit himself complacently down in his large easy-chair, and, from that stand-point, look doggedly on, and see and hear, his and their, implacable enemy, approach, pursue, and instigate them into the doing of that same thing, which he knows will have the effect to blast their reputations, and destroy their happiness forever;—not any more.—Unto love, pity bears some slight resemblance, but fear none at all.

Strange as it may appear to many timorous, trembling, well-meaning souls, in whom love of self and fear of personal harm bear rule, we sincerely hope we may never sink so low in the scale of what to us doth seem to be genuine manliness and self-respect, as that we could come to feel ourself at home in the presence of any *potentate*, just because he should vouchsafe to pamper us and a few other individuals with an undeserved paradise of ease and plenty, when, at the same time, by the eye of faith we could see him busily engaged in heaping upon the mass of his subjects, our friends and neighbors among the rest, toil and reproaches, famine and torture without intermission, and without end. Indeed, if we know ourself, we do not covet a seat in any such narrow, half-filled heaven, as is the Calvanistic one; and that in sight of such an overflowing hell, with kindred, friends, and fellow-travellers, filled. And, unless we greatly err, to be obliged to be in the place commonly described as heaven, in the presence of such a God, and in sight of such an awful set of endless-misery surroundings, all of his contriving and creation, would be, unto vast numbers of the race, *the very hell of hells*. If in this we are correct, (which we must think we are,) then, as certainly as there doth ever exist a sure relation between effects and their parent causes, just so certainly must these unnatural views of the character of God and his government have a tendency to render men more unfeeling, selfish, and oppressive;—have a tendency to render men more like the God they worship, and hence worse instead of better. Indeed, we are constrained to think the reason why men are no worse, than experience proves them to be, is not because the irreverent dogma of man's totally depraved nature has been so plentifully interwoven into their sectarian creeds, but because their blind faith therein is greatly modified by their rational doubts of its truthfulness; and because that same inherent nature, which is so much inveighed against, is too deep-rooted and strong to be ever wholly covered up, or smothered out of the human tabernacle, by this or any other docrine, no matter how highly it may be eulogized nor what its reputed origin.—As the matter stands out revealed to us, whether right or whether wrong, not uninterruptedly, but, as a whole and upon the whole, the animal called man, since his first creation upon this earthly ball, has fallen greatly upward and not downward; and is still falling, quite as fast as ever, in that same direction.

If, therefore, from either principle or policy, we are unwilling to accelerate the Bible's doom, we must so construe its pages, read as they may, as not to bring its teachings in collision with such facts and principles as stand out revealed in any portion of great Nature's volume: for, manifestly enough, between this great and constantly-growing revelation, and that said narrow former, there must ever exist the most perfect harmony; else, not *this*, the living testimony, but *that*, the one in artificial language penned, must fall. Indeed it behooves us, each and all, to see to it that our highly valued boxes of religious faith and practice are so arranged and packed as that they shall be rightside up, which ever side is up, otherwise they may be seriously damaged by that general search after facts and overhaul of principles which on board the world's great ship, by the aids of natural science, are everywhere being made. Or, to present the idea in a little different form, strongly fortified by antiquity and endeared by early remembrances as is that cherished Volume, nevertheless the time has arrived, when it can no longer successfully wage and carry on a war against facts and principles that are demonstrably true. Unless we mistake causes and misinterpret effects, it is not so much the action of its enemies, as want of attention on the part of its friends and defenders to this plain fact, which stands bottom cause of that Bible skepticism now lurking in the heads, not of rowdies, nor men of copper whose consciences reside within the bond, but of such sober, thinking men and women, as are firm believers in a fixed-law government of a God superior to popular opinion, place, or favor, higher, and more to be regarded, than are all the barren dogmas prescribed by convocations or by synods; and whose constantly improving condition, both physical and mental, daily intercourse with equals, kindness to inferiors, forbearance toward the unfortunate erring, and practical charity toward all, bear unmistakable evidence that their faith cannot be greatly wrong, since their lives, its only true exponent, are clearly in the right.

As a barren dogma is good for nothing and dead faith no better, so the only faith which is worth anything is that which is active and practical,—is that which produces fruit; and, of this kind, that must needs be most valuable which yields the best fruit, and the most of it. Christ undoubtedly spoke a real truth, as well as moral one, when he said, "For every tree is known by his own fruit: for of thorns men do not gather figs, nor of a bramble-bush gather they grapes." If, therefore, the tree of our religious faith which we are so zealously endeavoring to propagate, and upon which we so confidently rely to remove darkness by its presence, remedy evil by its sap, and elevate the race by its fruit, be a mere mass of empty forms, barren theories, and impracticable beliefs, then, most assuredly, it can never produce any greatly beneficial results,—can never yield any truly valuable fruit; even though by dint of industry, and patient perseverance in its culture, its branches should come to cover the whole earth, and, at mention of its name every knee was to bow and every tongue pronounce its praise. *A living dog is better than a dead lion.* And better for the reason that being possessed of vital force, he is able to remove his good-for-nothing carcass out of the way; whereas that defunct monarch of the forest, notwithstanding his kingly proportions, is not only powerless to do positive good, but to restrain the passive evil of annoying the neighborhood by his own noisome effluvia. Inasmuch, then, as it is not the form of our faith, however high-sounding and popular, nor the amount, however great and imposing, but the quality, as evidenced by the fruit it bears, which constitutes the test of its worth; and inasmuch as we have been instant in season and out of season in adding line upon line and leaven after leaven, and still the body of our hearers, instead of manifesting a more elevated state of religious fermentation, give unmistakable signs of becoming more sour, soggy, and averse to swallowing our prescriptions; would it not be well to conclude that the leaven with which we have thus been laboring to elevate the human lump, instead of being of the active and practical sort, and hence to the wants of humanity adapted, is of that lifeless, Pharisaic order, which is impotent to do more than nauseate and drive away, by its offensive odor? It would really seem that the want of success attendant upon the practice of teaching the present established religious dogmas and their kindred lifeless ceremonies ought of itself to be sufficient to suggest to our spiritual guides the idea, that possibly some other doctrine or mode of procedure might be better calculated to bring about the result at which they are aiming; namely, the bettering of mankind, without eternally waiting to be dragged and driven, inch by inch, into a change of programme by the growing intelligence of that world in charge, which they are essaying to instruct and lead. Surely nothing in heaven or earth can be plainer than that, if we are upon the wrong track, although greatly beaten, and notwithstanding once pressed by the feet of our ancestors, the sooner we find it out and abandon it the better, not only for us, and such of contemporaries as are following in our wake, but for that posterity in whom not a few of our thoughts and practices are certain, onward, more or less long to live.

As surely as does the Governor of the world work systematically, and so makes use of appropriate means to bring about desired results, and as surely as are effects forever true to their parent causes, just so certain is it that the tree of our olden religious faith which produces that apathy and skepticism, over which we so long and dolorously do mourn, is not fit to cumber the ground, but should be hewn down to make room for a better. We do not say that it should be hewn down, because we have the slightest doubt of the sincerity of the mass of its worshipers, but because we cannot deem it possible for reason and knowledge, the antipodes of blind faith, ever to become and be to *pure and undefiled religion* opposed, and because, self-evidently, as seems to us, in their sentiments and feelings, the more enlightened portion of the race have so far outgrown, and left behind them, the mass of that ancient, inelastic, semi-Jewish, semi-Christian, and hence semi-neither-one-nor-'tother system, that it can no longer fill and satisfy the yearnings of their higher nature. And, to prove that such is the case, what better evidence can the different sectarian leaders desire than that furnished by their own stereotyped complaints and admissions; namely, That notwithstanding all the means which are constantly being devised and put forth by an industrious clergy to excite the feelings, arouse the passions, and enlist the judgment of universal civilized man in favor of those certain forms of faith and ceremonial observances, which they are wont to call religion, although nothing but its outer shell; still the mass of enlightened human kind, everywhere, and especially the more thinking portion thereof, are daily becoming more and more indifferent and even skeptical thereto?—A personal God, and a personal Devil; a fiery hell, and a local heaven paved with gold; such things will do to help make up a fancy sketch, but, as sober realities, their day is nearly past.

Religion, it must be borne in mind, is a term of extensive import, and embraces not only Christianity, but Judaism, Hindoism, Mohammedism, Rationalism, etc., as well. Feeble, then, as was originally the base of Christianity, it has constantly been splitting up, changing front, and otherwise diluting itself, until, finally, there is manifest danger of its becoming swallowed up and lost in mere churchanity. Christianity, as for the most part it to-day exists in sectarian practice, why, what is it either more or less than the numerous, narrow, and bigoted efforts which are being put forth, not to inculcate charity and good-will toward such as upon some mere speculative point of doctrine may chance to differ with us in opinion, but to build up *this our particular ism*, and pull down every *other?*

Plainly as we are wont to talk, it is not our intention to speak disrespectfully of that legitimate branch of human nature, called Religion; nor would we speak in terms of needless severity of any of the different forms and ceremonies by which it is the pleasure of our fellow-men, Jew or Gentile, Turk or Christian, to manifest their reverence for such objects, whether real or imaginary, as they adjudge to be unto themselves superior. But it is our aim to do all that we can to prevent the numerous mistaken devotees of religion from exalting said branch of human nature, in dignity and importance, above the station legitimately occupied by its parent tree; and especially to prevent them from investing such branch, or any of its sanctions, with supremacy over the teachings of that certain other and superior branch thereof, known as sober intellect. In the absence of known facts to direct his steps, Reason is man's only safe guide, the same as is the compass that of the mariner, when there is neither Sun nor Moon nor stars in sight. Unenlightened religion is superstition, bigotry, and intolerance; enlightened religion, charity, forbearance, and good-will toward all mankind.

Of course, we may be wrong, but whether so or not, we can never believe an all-wise, all-good, and all-truthful God would ever create, or for one moment suffer to exist, (if in some other way he should chance to creep into being,) an all-foolish, all-evil, all-lying Devil. Nor can we believe that a wise, just, and merciful God is ever going to do so unwise, unjust, and cruel a thing, as to punish any of the creatures whom he, unasked, has made, with an endlessly long and bitter punishment after they are physically dead, for offenses committed during a short physical lifetime. In short, as we can see no good reason for believing that a God of superior light, knowledge, and civilization will ever inflict upon his children punishment, either long or short, severe or light, from any motive, except that of rendering them, as a whole, more obedient to his laws, and hence, upon the whole, more blest and happy in consequence of its infliction, so we are unable to believe that he ever will.

CHAPTER VII.

THE COAT TOO SMALL.

That the Hindoos hold to some strange dogmas, the Parsees to many ridiculous notions, and the Mohammedans to religious opinions which are sadly in contrast with their practical good sense upon other subjects must be admitted; and yet we incline to think there does not exist in any of those systems, a single point of doctrine which is more directly at variance with the every-day phenomena of living and of life, and hence more grossly absurd, than is our own Bible story of the Holy Ghost and the Virgin Mary. And so long as we continue to sing and to preach as a fact, this strangely unreasonable dogma, just so long will the transition therefrom to belief in spirit-rappings, table-tippings, and every other species of ghostly humbug be so natural and easy, that we shall continue to see and hear to our fill of the workings of this same old, superlative credulity-inspiring leaven.

As the numerous and different real truths, that are in the world, do not all belong to the same high class, so the numerous and different moral truths, which are actual errors, every one, do not all belong to the same low grade. Wherefore the Bible system of religion is doubtless a long step in advance of the purely Jewish, or any other extensively adopted system. And wherefore, outgrown as we deem the mass of the Bible's teachings to be in this and other highly enlightened Christian countries of the world, we are not sorry to see that book going forward, breaking the chains, undoing the fetters, and removing the rubbish by other and greatly inferior religious systems imposed. Indeed, we regard the Bible system, notwithstanding its multitude of errors and numerous impracticable teachings, as offering just about as convenient a stepping-stone from ancient paganism to a still more elevated state of religious sentiment and feeling, as did Dilworth's very imperfect Spelling-book from a more faulty predecessor to a much better subsequent, elementary treatise. Excellently well-calculated as is the Spelling-book, at the proper time and place, to advance in learning every human born, still it must be admitted that its teachings fall much short of reaching that grand eminence in literature, unto which it is possible for men to attain; consequently, just as soon as by any class of pupils its inferior grade of teachings shall have been mastered, just so soon should it be treated as a thing, by that particular class of learners, sufficiently outgrown to give place to teachings of a higher order. And now, whether right or whether wrong in these our feeble views, if we have not made ourself understood upon the point of deeming the mass of the Bible's teachings as being outgrown and left behind, in this and other olden Christian countries where light and knowledge are greatest, and, at the same time, as not being yet grown up to in those heathenish lands where as pioneer and schoolmaster it has never gone, or only a comparatively short time been, then, indeed, are we unfortunate.

But again; as we see it, the reason why the Bible system of religion is, as a whole and upon the whole, better than the purely Jewish, or any other extensively adopted system, is not because it is, in any special sense, a revelation from Almighty God, but because it is based less upon the animal passions and propensities, and more upon the moral sentiments. And the reason why it needs to be thoroughly revised, and largely amended, in order to prevent it from becoming and being a hindrance instead of a helper to the cause of progression with man, in his present state of advancement, is not so much upon account of its being mainly based upon the moral sentiments, as the same existed in the heads of men long centuries ago, as because it almost wholly repudiates the teachings of sober intellect;—the very department of the brain which confers upon the animal called man his manhood, and consequently prevents him from sinking into a mere brute of superior order. Indeed, it is doubtful whether a more effectual method could be devised for retarding human progress, and hence of rendering perpetual the errors of the past, than from generation to generation to impress it upon the young and tender brain, that, to the teachings of sober intellect, not the slightest credence is due, whenever such teachings shall chance to be at variance with the promptings of the strong, blind, moral sentiments, and their ever ready coadjutors, Combativeness and Destructiveness. In short, as it is only by the aid of intellect that men can ever be brought to see, until by experience they have first been made to feel; so, upon the subject of religion, the same as every other, it is unto the higher revelations by the dispassionate teachings of intellect made known, and not to the impassioned promptings of the strong, blind, moral sentiments, that men should look for light to guide them in forming their opinions, and by which to shape their lives. Illustrative example:—At the breaking out of the late rebellion, Intellect saw clearly that unless secession was crushed, division would soon succeed division, and hence that, at no very distant day, weakness and anarchy, with all their attendant evils, would come to take the place of union, prosperity, and strength. And of this act of foresight, What was the consequence?—Why, soon was large Benevolence, acting under the guidance of sober Intellect, brought to see and acknowledge that to strike, and strike hard, would be merciful and not cruel; and as Combativeness and Destructiveness had no objections to dealing the blows, they were accordingly dealt. But, after the great and terrible, and yet merciful blows had been struck and repeated until the gigantic rebellion was finally crushed to earth, that same large Benevolence, acting now—so far as acting at all—under the stern leadership of Firmness, backed by the promptings of highly aroused Combativeness and Destructiveness, instead of continuing to act, as in the beginning, under the gentle guidance of Intellect, failed to see that the now humble and prostrate States were occupied by men of like passions with us; and hence that it was not only impolitic, but cruel, to remember against them their past honest errors of opinion and accordant action, any more forever. And, of this act of shortsightedness, the probable consequence is that at least one full generation of men will have to pass away, before its ill-effects will have become effaced.

But to return:—Unless the Bible, by the great and good men of the Earth, shall be thoroughly overhauled and amended, or, from the materials selected from the best authorities both ancient and modern, a new rule of religious faith and practice shall be compiled and adopted, every really thinking man will be measurably obliged to shape his religious course by the light of his own judgment.

Had not some progressive Luther solemnly protested and kept on protesting against certain decrees, doctrines, and practices of the stand-still Romish Church, it is plain that the whole Christian world would still have been Papists, and Protestantism remained unborn. Wherefore, we appeal, Is it not about time that some other progressive Luther should enter another solemn protest against certain barren dogmas and formal practices of stand-still Protestantism; to the end that a yet higher, nobler, and more liberal grade of religious faith and practice may come to take root and grow? Can it be possible that of religious progression, any more than of progression in the arts and sciences, the end is come? In other words, by unavoidable consequence, must not the coat of the boy be too small for the man?

That the writings of Moses and several other less ancient manuscripts, which have a place in the Christian Bible, were, in their own proper day, masterly productions, consequently greatly in advance of the general intelligence of the age in which they were penned, and hence operated as a sort of ample, stimulating band, thrown around mind to quicken and protect it in its upward shoot, we doubt not; and yet, when we reflect that this said Bible band is not composed of india rubber, but of words and phrases which, notwithstanding the much they may be varied by ingenious construction, must nevertheless have some limit set to their meaning, which the good sense of mankind and the usages of language can never suffer them to pass; also that whenever this point is reached, that moment it becomes an inelastic hoop; also that the mind of man is not a thing which is stationary, but is ever legitimately expansive, and hence progressive in its character and yearnings, we are not surprised that such should have been the mental growth of the vanguard of the race, since the date of that book, as that there should now be very many minds which must burst the narrow limits of this once loose-fitting band, else be cramped, chafed, and girdled on all sides round thereby. We say, *the vanguard of the race*, because there undoubtedly exists, even in this most free and generally enlightened country, a large class of persons who not from motives of policy, nor yet from a mistaken sense of duty merely pretend to believe, but who sincerely think the Bible is the word of Almighty God to mortal man in artificial language given, for his special guidance and instruction in all things which it is good for him to know. Beyond a question such are perfectly honest in their endeavors to convict and convert the world of mankind into the belief, that they can never possibly come up to the measure of the Bible's boundless wisdom, much less outgrow and leave behind them any of its teachings. Indeed, it is painfully apparent that there are still lingering among us very many such laggards and buriers of talents; and these we by no means consider in any immediate danger of being crippled in their tardy growth thereby.

And here, perhaps, it may be well to say, that, after long years of reflection upon the subject, we have at last become satisfied that our rejecting the Bible as the rule of our faith and the measure of its practice, as well in matters of religion, as upon other subjects, (for the reason that we deem so large a portion of its sayings erroneous, and so many of its truthful teachings outgrown, that it is, now and here, upon the whole, a hindrance instead of a helper to the cause of progression,) and stepping upon the much broader platform of facts and principles already known, and such others as observation, reason, and experience shall currently reveal, will no more have the dreaded effect to weaken its restraints upon the aforementioned class of persons, than has the past growth in light and knowledge of their friends and neighbors, full before their eyes, been the cause of their breaking those degrading shackles of general ignorance, superstition, and bigotry, by which they are to-day fast bound;—not any more. To the anxious and oft-repeated inquiry of friends, "Are you not afraid the reasons by you assigned for believing the Bible to be the production of ancient human brains, and hence, just like all other things of human origin, subject to become outgrown and left behind by an advancing world, will have the effect to weaken the restraints which a belief in an avenging God, an endless hell, and a consious personal existence after death throw around the lower orders of society?" we make answer as follows:—Know ye not, men and brethren, that it is no easy matter to convert this class of persons from the Catholic to the Protestant faith, or from Protestantism to Romanism, notwithstanding they are but different branches of the same common system?—Most certainly you do. How slight then must be the danger that such will ever become converted from either of these narrow, formal branches of the same common faith, to a religion which is as broad and comprehensive as is all real truth, whether between the lids of the Bible found, or whether outside thereof in great Nature's volume? Do you not see that there are right here among us, to-day, large numbers of men who, in spitè of all the arguments which you or we or anybody else can present, will still continue to carry a stone in one end of the bag, the same as their fathers;—will still remain in the very alphabet not only of religious growth, but of every other kind and grade of improvement, until death shall finally wipe them out of existence? And, seeing this, are you not ready to conclude with us, that not all the arguments which can be adduced will ever annul God's governing facts,—will ever reverse great Nature's wheels; or for the better or worse, materially change the *living dead?* To suppose this class of persons to be in danger of taking in light upon this subject is equivalent to supposing them capable of taking it in upon other subjects; and to suppose them capable of taking it in, not only upon this, but upon others, is equivalent to supposing that, with them, the time has arrived when the stronger and more wholesome restraints imposed by light and knowledge should be substituted for those feeble ones imposed by darkness. We say, *the stronger and more wholesome restraints imposed by light and knowledge,* because, manifestly enough, to feel and to know that, as surely as we sin, just so surely shall we be obliged to suffer the penalty therefor, will do much more toward keeping us, each and all, straight upon the course of endeavoring to lead lives of virtue and obedience, than will a mere blind, traditionary belief in a future hell for the punishment of present sins, coupled with another belief equally blind, traditionary and strong, that, by casting those sins all upon Christ, we shall not only be able to escape their consequences, but to secure a seat in heaven. Surely such a theory of escape from the consequences of unlimited self-indulgence and crime must be a very feeble incentive to the practice of self-denial and virtue, no matter how laudable may be the intentions of its advocates. There is not only a class of persons who will cheat, steal, rob, murder, etc., notwithstanding they know full well there are laws forbidding these things, and prisons to punish such as do them, but also another class who never commit any of these acts, notwithstanding upon penal codes and penitentiary walls they never bestow a single thought. The conclusion therefore would seem to be irresistible, that the fear of an avenging God and dread of an endless hell have little restraining influence upon such as had the misfortune to be hell-begotten, hell-born, hell-bred, and hence hell-constituted and balanced; and none at all upon those whose good fortune it was to be heaven-begotten, heaven-born, heaven-bred, and hence so heavenly constituted and balanced, as that they are a living law unto themselves.

But it may not unlikely be asked, "Why cannot the naturally weak minded, hence greatly fearing, and hence strongly superstitious, by the presentation of arguments, be materially changed in either belief or practice?"—To this we answer: It is because, by a sure law of nature, the mental eye, just like the orb of outward vision, ever so contracts and adjusts its curtains as to shut out all such kinds and qualities of light, as are for it too great and strong. Wherefore, notwithstanding the avidity with which the strange, the marvellous, and utterly impossible are seized upon and swallowed by such as are young in wisdom, no matter what the number of their years, there is no danger of their gulping down what is entirely beyond the compass of their throats to admit;—no danger that arguments to sober intellect addressed, and not appeals to the strong blind passions made, will ever injure anybody. And not only this, but, as we have finally come to see it, it is the righteous right and bounden duty of the vanguard of the race, irrespective of such human ciphers, to have, teach, and enjoy just such a religion as is best adapted to their paramount needs.

When the great, the good, and the wise consent to play the hypocrite, thinking thereby to bless the ignorant, the low, and the vile, they not only mistake their true character and mission, but miserably fail in their object; the laws of Nature being inexorable.

CHAPTER VIII.

MARY, HER BIRTH, PARENTAGE, ETC.

From Mary's account of the way and manner in which she was brought into the condition of being with child, as detailed by St. Luke, and so handed down to us in the New Testament, it would seem that the Holy Ghost, or the angel Gabriel, as his representative upon that occasion, was nothing loth to push the advantage by him gained over that young, innocent, and unsuspecting girl to such a state of completion, as should secure to him the gratification of his fleshy desires. We say, *it would so seem from Mary's account of the way, etc.*, because it would be an unpardonable insult to the innate modesty of the sex to suppose, that a bashful young virgin, in the presence of witnesses, would ever willingly submit to be thus come upon and overshadowed even by a ghost, no matter how high and holy he might be. And we say, *it would so seem from Mary's account, etc., as detailed by St. Luke, etc.*, because he is the only writer in all the Bible proper, who makes any attempt at going into particulars in reference to that transaction, and because he nowhere pretends that anybody saw the act performed, or that he himself ever heard Mary say a word about it; but simply claims to narrate unto his friend Theophilus, what was the current belief in the neighborhood in reference thereto at the time of his writing, which was not until several years after the man Christ had been laid in his grave. As we see it, then, this great question—and great only because so very much doth hinge thereupon—may be fairly considered as narrowed down to this: Was Mary brought into the condition of being with child in a miraculous manner and by superhuman agency; or was she simply mistaken upon that point? In other words, Was she in a miraculous manner brought into that condition; or was the young, the innocent, and unsuspecting girl pursued, misled, and grossly imposed upon by some unscrupulous man, claiming to be, not only an angel and a ghost, but the Holy Ghost?—

Strange as it may seem, the following is, in substance and effect, all the testimony furnished by the Bible proper, bearing upon this point:—"And in the sixth month the angel Gabriel was sent from God unto a city of Galilee, named Nazareth, to a virgin espoused to a man whose name was Joseph, of the House of David; and the virgin's name was Mary. And the angel came in unto her, and said, Hail, thou that art highly favored, the Lord is with thee: blessed art thou among women. And when she saw him, she was troubled at his saying, and cast in her mind what manner of salutation this should be. And the angel said unto her, Fear not, Mary: for thou hast found favor with God. And behold, thou shall conceive in thy womb, and bring forth a son, and shalt call his name JESUS. He shall be great, and shall be called the Son of the Highest; and the Lord God shall give unto him the throne of his father David. And he shall reign over the house of Jacob forever; and of his kingdom there shall be no end.—Then said Mary unto the angel, How shall this be, seeing I know not a man?—And the angel answered and said unto her, The Holy Ghost shall come upon thee, and the power of the Highest shall overshadow thee: therefore also that holy thing which shall be born of thee, shall be called the Son of God. And behold, thy cousin Elizabeth, she hath also conceived a son in her old age; and this is the sixth month with her who was called barren: for with God nothing shall be impossible.—And Mary said, Behold the handmaid of the Lord, be it unto me according to thy word.—And the angel departed from her."—Luke, I. 26—38.

Now, from this mere heresay testimony of the single individual Luke, as by him narrated to his friend Theophilus a number of years after the event took place, and by others overhauled, re-overhauled, placed in the New Testament, and so handed down to us, it quite plainly appears that an angel intruded himself into the presence of this young and unsuspecting female, that he saluted her in a most flattering manner, and that he most graciously applied himself to allaying the fears in her excited by his unexpected visit and singular language; also that he proceeded in a most condescending manner to explain the way in which she should be brought to conceive, and thus come to be the honored mother of a wonderfully great and extraordinary babe. It also, further, quite plainly appears therefrom, that this young and unsophisticated girl swallowed the gilded bait thus temptingly held out before her; and so, in the simple but modest language, "Behold the handmaid of the Lord, be it unto me according to thy word," consented that the Holy Ghost might come upon her as by the angel thus bewitchingly explained.

As the foregoing succinct quotation from Luke contains, in substance and effect, all the testimony bearing upon this point, that is anywhere to be found between the lids of the Bible proper, and since it is desirable to obtain all the light possible thereupon, we will now proceed to quote from the apocryphal book, called "The GOSPEL of the BIRTH of MARY;" a book which is ascribed to St. Matthew, and one that very properly occupies the first place in the Apocryphal New Testament.—

"The blessed and ever glorious Virgin Mary, sprung from the royal race and family of David, was born in the city of Nazareth, and educated at Jerusalem, in the temple of the Lord. Her father's name was Joachim, and her mother's Anna. The family of her father was of Galilee and the city of Nazareth. The family of her mother was of Bethlehem. Their lives were plain and right in the sight of the Lord, pious and faultless before men. For they divided all their substance into three parts: one of which they devoted to the temple and officers of the temple; another they distributed among strangers, and persons in poor circumstances; and the third they reserved for themselves and the uses of their own family. In this manner they lived for about twenty years chastely, in the favor of God, and the esteem of man, without any children. But they vowed, if God should favor them with any issue, they would devote it to the service of the Lord; on which account they went at every feast in the year to the temple of the Lord. And it came to pass, that when the feast of the dedication drew near, Joachim, with some others of his tribe, went up to Jerusalem, and, at that time, Issachar was high-priest; who, when he saw Joachim along with the rest of his neighbors, bringing his offerings, despised both him and his offerings, and asked him, why he, who had no children, would presume to appear among those who had? Adding, that his offerings could never be acceptable to God, who was judged by him unworthy to have children; the Scripture having said, Cursed is every one who shall not beget a male child in Israel. He further said, that he ought first to be free from that curse by begetting some issue, and then come with his offerings into the presence of God.

"But Joachim, being much confounded with the shame of such reproach, retired to the shepherds who were with the cattle in their pastures; for he was not inclined to return home, least his neighbors, who were present and heard all this from the high-priest, should publicly reproach him in the same manner.

"But when he had been there for some time, on a certain day, when he was alone, the angel of the Lord stood by him with a prodigious light, to whom, being troubled at the appearance, the angel who had appeared to him, endeavoring to compose him, said, Be not afraid, Joachim, nor troubled at the sight of me, for I am an angel of the Lord, sent by him to you, that I might inform you, that your prayers are heard, and your alms ascended in the sight of God. For he hath surely seen your shame, and heard you unjustly reproached for not having children; for God is the avenger of sin, and not of nature; and so, when he shuts the womb of any person, he does it for this reason, that he may in a more wonderful manner again open it, and that which is born appear to be not the product of lust, but the gift of God. For the first mother of your nation, Sarah, was she not barren even till her eightieth year, and yet, even in the end of her old age, brought forth Isaac, in whom the promise was made of a blessing to all nations. Rachel also, so much in favor with God, and beloved so much by holy Jacob, continued barren for a long time, yet afterwards was the mother of Joseph, who was not only governor of Egypt, but delivered many nations from perishing with hunger. Who, among the judges, was more valiant than Samson, or more holy than Samuel? And yet both their mothers were barren.

"But if reason will not convince you of the truth of my words, that there are frequent conceptions in advanced years, and that those who were barren have brought forth to their great surprise; therefore Anna your wife shall bring you a daughter, and you shall call her name Mary; she shall, according to your vow, be devoted to the Lord from her infancy, and be filled with the Holy Ghost from her mother's womb, she shall neither eat nor drink anything which is unclean, nor shall her conversation be without among the common people, but in the temple of the Lord; that so she may not fall under any slander or suspicion of what is bad. So in the process of her years, as she shall be in a miraculous manner born of one that was barren, so she shall, while yet a virgin, in a way unparalleled, bring forth the Son of the most High God, who shall be called Jesus, and, according to the signification of his name, be the Savior of all nations. And this shall be a sign to you of the things which I declare, namely, when you come to the golden gate of Jerusalem, you shall there meet your wife Anna, who, being very much troubled that you return no sooner, shall then rejoice to see you.—When the angel had said this, he departed from him.

"Afterwards the angel appeared to Anna his wife, saying, Fear not, neither think that which you see is a spirit; for I am that angel who hath offered up your prayers and alms before God, and am now sent to you, that I may inform you, that a daughter will be born unto you, who shall be called

Mary, and shall be blessed above all women. She shall be, immediately upon her birth, full of the grace of the Lord, and shall continue during the three years of her weaning in her father's house, and afterwards, being devoted to the service of the Lord, shall not depart from the temple, till she arrives to years of discretion. In a word, she shall there serve the Lord night and day in fasting and prayer, shall abstain from every unclean thing, and never know any man; but, being an unparalleled instance, without any pollution or defilement, and a virgin not knowing any man, shall bring forth a son, and a maid shall bring forth the Lord, who, both by his grace and name and works, shall be the Savior of the world. Arise therefore, and go up to Jerusalem, and you shall come to that which is called the golden gate, (because it is gilt with gold), as a sign of what I have told you, you shall meet your husband, for whose safety you have been so much concerned. When therefore you find these things thus accomplished, believe that all the rest which I have told you, shall also undoubtedly be accomplished.

"According therefore to the command of the angel, both of them left the places where they were, and when they came to the place specified in the angel's prediction, they met each other. Then, rejoicing at each other's vision, and being fully satisfied in the promise of a child, they gave due thanks unto the Lord, who exalts the humble. After having praised the Lord, they returned home, and lived in a cheerful and assured expectation of the promise of God.

"So Anna conceived, and brought forth a daughter; and, according to the angel's command, the parents did call her name Mary. And when three years were expired, and the time of her weaning complete, they brought the Virgin to the temple of the Lord with offerings. And there were about the temple, according to the fifteen Psalms of Degrees, fifteen stairs to ascend. For, the temple being built in a mountain, the altar of burnt-offering, which was without, could not be come near but by stairs. The parents of the blessed Virgin and infant Mary put her upon one of these stairs; but while they were putting off their clothes, in which they had traveled, and according to custom putting on some that were more neat and clean, in the meantime, the Virgin of the Lord in such a manner went up all the stairs one after another, without the help of any to lead her or lift her, that any one would have judged from hence, that she was of perfect age. Thus the Lord did, in the infancy of his Virgin, work this extraordinary work, and evidenced by this miracle how great she was like to be hereafter. But the parents, having offered up their sacrifice, according to the custom of the law, and perfected their vow, left the Virgin with other virgins in the apartments of the temple, who were to be brought up there, and they returned home.

"But the Virgin of the Lord, as she advanced in years, increased also in perfections, and according to the saying of the Psalmist, her father and mother forsook her, but the Lord took care of her. For she every day had the conversation of angels, and every day received visions from God, which preserved her from all sorts of evil, and caused her to abound with all good things; so that when at length she arrived to her fourteenth year, as the wicked could not lay anything to her charge worthy of reproof, so all good persons, who were acquainted with her, admired her life and conversation.

"At that time the high-priest made a public order, That all the virgins who had public settlements in the temple, and were come to this age, should return home, and, as they were now of a proper maturity, should, according to the custom of their country, endeavor to be married. To which command, though all the other virgins readily yielded obedience, Mary the Virgin of the Lord alone answered, that she could not comply with it, assigning these reasons, that both she and her parents had devoted her to the service of the Lord; and besides, that she had vowed virginity to the Lord, which vow she was resolved never to break through by lying with a man. The high-priest being hereby brought into a difficulty, seeing he durst neither on the one hand dissolve the vow, and disobey the Scripture, which says, Vow and pray, nor on the other hand introduce a new custom, to which the people were strangers, commanded, that at the approaching feast all the principal persons both of Jerusalem and the neighboring places should meet together, that he might have their advice, how he had best proceed in so difficult a case. When they were accordingly met, they unanimously agreed to seek the Lord, and ask counsel from him on this matter. And when they were all engaged in prayer, the high-priest, according to the usual way, went to consult God, and immediately there was a voice from the ark, and the mercy-seat, which all present heard, that it must be inquired or sought out by a prophecy of Isaiah, to whom the Virgin should be given and betrothed; for Isaiah saith, There shall come forth a rod out of the stem of Jesse, and a flower shall spring out of its root, and the Spirit of the Lord shall rest upon him, the Spirit of Wisdom and understanding, the Spirit of Counsel and Might, the Spirit of Knowledge and Piety, and the Spirit of the fear of the Lord shall fill him.

"Then, according to this prophecy, he appointed, that all the men of the house and family of David, who were marriageable and not married, should bring their several rods to the altar, and out of whatsoever person's rod after it was brought, a flower should bud forth, and on the top of it the spirit of the Lord should sit in the appearance of a dove, he should be the man to whom the Virgin should be given and be betrothed. Among the rest there was a man named Joseph, of the house and family of David, and a person very far advanced in years, who drew back his rod, when everyone besides presented his. So that when nothing appeared agreeable to the heavenly voice, the high-priest judged it proper to consult God again, who answered, that he to whom the Virgin was to be betrothed was the only person of those who were brought together, who had not brought his rod. Joseph therefore, was betrayed. For when he did bring his rod, and a dove, coming from Heaven, pitched upon the top of it, every one plainly saw, that the Virgin was to be betrothed to him: accordingly, the usual ceremonies of betrothing being over, he returned to his own city of Bethlehem, to set his house in order, and make the needful provisions for the marriage. But the Virgin of the Lord, Mary, with some other virgins of the same age, who had been weaned at the same time, and who had been appointed to attend her by the priest, returned to her parent's house in Galilee.

"Now at this time of her first coming into Galilee, the angel Gabriel was sent to her from God, to declare to her the conception of our Savior, and the manner and way of her conceiving him. Accordingly going in to her, he filled the chamber where she was with a prodigious light, and in a most courteous manner saluting her, he said, Hail, Mary! Virgin of the Lord most acceptable! Oh Virgin full of grace! The Lord is with you, you are blessed above all women, you are blessed above all men, that have been hitherto born. But the Virgin, who had before been well acquainted with the countenances of angels, and to whom such light from heaven was no uncommon thing, was neither terrified with the vision of the angel, nor astonished at the greatness of the light, but only troubled about the angel's words: and began to consider what so extraordinary a salutation should mean, what it did portend, or what sort of end it would have. To this thought the angel, divinely inspired, replies: Fear not, Mary, as though I intended any thing inconsistent with your chastity in this salutation: for you have found favor with the Lord, because you made virginity your choice. Therefore while you are a virgin, you shall conceive without sin, and bring forth a son. He shall be great, because he shall reign from sea to sea, and from the rivers even to the ends of the earth. And he shall be called the Son of the Highest; for he who is born in a mean state on earth, reigns in an exhaulted one in heaven. And the Lord shall give him the throne of his father David, and he shall reign over the house of Jacob forever, and of his kingdom there shall be no end. For he is the King of Kings, and Lord of Lords, and his throne is forever and ever.

"To this discourse of the angel the Virgin replied, not as though she were unbelieving, but willing to know the manner of it: she said, How can that be? For seeing, according to my vow, I never have known any man, how can I bear a child without the addition of a man's seed?

"To this the angel replied and said, Think not, Mary, that you shall conceive in the ordinary way. For, without lying with a man, while a Virgin, you shall conceive; while a Virgin, you shall bring forth; and while a Virgin, shall give suck: for the Holy Ghost shall come upon you, and the power of the Most High shall overshadow you, without any of the heats of lust. So that which shall be born of you shall be only holy, because it only is conceived without sin, and being born shall be called the Son of God.

"Then Mary, stretching forth her hands, and lifting her eyes to heaven, said, Behold the handmaid of the Lord! Let it be unto me according to thy word."—

Now, from this quotation, which is quite full upon the point, it will be seen that angels and ghosts were quite plenty in those days; that Anna, the mother of Mary, was honored with their attention; and consequently that her daughter Mary was, by birthright, no ordinary person. Also that Mary was brought up from childhood in the temple of the Lord, where the angels were so numerous that she was daily favored with their presence, and conversation, as well as with visions from the Lord. Also that, at the early age of fourteen, the angels began quite unceremoniously to intrude themselves upon her privacies. Also that, having been all along accustomed to seeing them and hearing them converse, she was neither terrified nor astonished at the entrance of the angel Gabriel into her chamber, but only troubled at his extraordinary salutation, and the strangeness of his words; the which, the angel at once perceiving, he very considerately proceeded to lull her suspicions and calm her fears by explaining to her in a most winning way, that nothing inconsistent with her chastity was intended; but only that, inasmuch as she was a favorite virgin of the Lord, the Holy Ghost would condescend to come upon her and overshadow her, without any of the heats of lust; to the end that, whilst yet a virgin, she might conceive without sin; and so become the honored mother of a most blessed and extraordinary babe, that should be "called the Son of God." Also that, by this most lucid and flattering explanation, the angel so far succeeded in soothing her feelings and quieting her girlish fears, as to gain her consent to let the Holy Ghost come upon her and overshadow her, as by him so persuasively described. And, finally, that it was by virtue of the Holy Ghost's so coming upon her and overshadowing her, that she came to be with child, and hence, in all due time thereafter, the honored mother of the babe called JESUS.

At the time when the Old Testament was written, it must be borne in mind, that belief in the personal existence of individual man, after the death of the body, had by no means come to be either strong or general; wherefore, in those days, there were no such beings or things as ghosts, good or bad, holy or unholy, putting in their appearance either by day or by night; and wherefore there is no mention made of the existence of any such beings in all that wonder-narrating Volume. We repeat, in so far as can be gathered from the Old Testament records, there were no such beings as Ghosts in existence in those days, good or bad, real or imaginary. And it is hardly supposable that there would ever have been any, had not the idea somehow chanced to take root and grow, that the animal called man does not die when, to all appearance, he seems to,—does not die when he finally ceases to breathe; but, instead, doth continue to live on, in spirit form, to all eternity. Indeed, it is only upon the supposition that men do thus continue to live personally on, after they are dead, that spirits and ghosts stand any chance for existence at all.

At a later day, however, and when the New Testament was written, there seems to have been in existence such beings as ghosts; and the first time in all that volume proper, that we hear of any such being as a holy ghost, or *the* Holy Ghost, we hear him spoken of in connection with a certain fourteen-years-old girl, called the Virgin Mary. From this circumstance, and the further historical fact that some half a century thereafter, and several years after Christ's death, quite a number of recent converts to the Christian faith, upon being interrogated by Paul as to whether they had received the Holy Ghost, since they became believers, made answer, "*We have not so much as heard whether there be any Holy Ghost*,"[a] we are led to infer that the great reign of ghosts, and especially of that particular one which had somehow come to be called *the Holy* Ghost, had its beginning about the time Anna, the mother of Mary, came upon the stage of action; and suffered its first and most severe shock when it came to be generally noised abroad in the land, that said Ghost had so far assumed to exercise man's special prerogative, as himself to become the father of a real flesh-and-blood child.

In so far as can be gleaned from the pages of the Bible proper, What do we learn about the mother of that distinguished personage called Christ, the Son of God?—Just this, and nothing more: *That she was a virgin; and her name was Mary.*

And why in all human probability did the men who, from the multifarious writings of the Christian Father's, compiled the New Testament, reject therefrom, as non-canonical, the historical book ascribed to St. Matthew, called the "GOSPEL of the BIRTH of Mary;" and which book, had it been vouchsafed a place therein, would have informed the millions upon millions of New Testament readers, all about the birth, parentage, education, and early life of that most singularly fortunate of all grossly deceived and imposed-upon maidens? Was it for the reason that they supposed the numerous believers in Christ and his teachings would feel no sort of interest in knowing anything about the origin and personal antecedents of the woman that bore him; or was it because they were afraid that such historic account might prove a little too much?—Which?

Upon taking into consideration what the Bible proper does say upon the subject, what the Apocryphal Scriptures

---

a Acts, 19, 2.

have to say about it, also what the great book of Natural revelation teaches in reference thereto, we are irresistibly led to the conclusion, whether right or whether wrong, that the angel who thus worked his way into Mary's chamber, who thus courteously saluted that young and inexperienced girl of only fourteen summers, and who so very wooingly proceeded to explain, and mystically to argue the point with her, was none other than the high-priest himself. Consequently that the Holy Ghost who, at the close of the interview, so graciously condescended to come upon her, was that very same functionary, no matter how disguised he may have been. And hence that Christ, instead of being in any special sense the Son of God, was the offspring of a young girl of pure, womanly desires, and the son of a man who, in addition to having brains, was no unwilling observer of the great Mosaic multiplication commandment. Indeed, who at this late day and age of the world is not aware, that large numbers of young and unsuspecting girls, as pure, as lovely, and well-descended as Mary, are constantly being pursued, flattered, and led on to ruin, by men of full age, gentlemanly appearance, winning manners, and occupying high social position both in the church and out? Yea, and who does not know that all this is manipulated and brought about by aid and operation of the perverted use of natural law, instead of by miracle?—Who?

CHAPTER IX.

KNOWLEDGE AND IGNORANCE.

> "Ignorance is the curse of God,
> Knowledge the wing wherewith we fly to heaven."

Knowledge is power; ignorance, its diametrically element, is weakness. Knowledge, which is only another name for mental riches, is ever to be desired for the good she brings; ignorance, or mental poverty, is ever more to be dreaded than destitution in any other form, since in it nearly every other kind of poverty has its seat. To sins committed against our organisms, because profoundly ignorant of the mutual relations existing between us and surrounding nature, is the physician mainly indebted for his living and superior social position among men; want of understanding our own individual rights and interests renders the services of the lawyer necessary, hence gives life and strength to the legal profession; and ignorance of our true character and mission in the world, not only opens wide the door of existence to the clergy, but affords them an ample theater for operations. Naturally enough, this latter class of men, the same as the two preceding ones, ever readily avail themselves of opportunities thus gratuitously offered, and so down upon us, their ignorant benefactors, in the direction of our blind side fear, belching forth fire and sulphur, they come. Else, which is more agreeable, adroitly and with good address they make sure their approaches through the broad avenue by our weak side, vanity, presented, and so up to gods do puff us with undefinable expectations of living and reigning as kings and princes, in some far-off floating heaven, when we are dead.

Mistake us not. It is not our intention to speak disrespectfully of any set or division of men; but simply to call attention to a class of facts that are quite well understood by the different learned professions, but which we the common people, whom they equally concern, are slow to comprehend. Thus, the really scientific physician knows full well that the various ills, from which we suffer, are none of them inflicted upon us by a revengeful Providence, but are, for the most part, the legitimate result of our own folly and improvidence. When, therefore, it is he that is sick, he first consults Hygiene; that failing, he calls to his aid abstinence and the healing virtues of a naturally good constitution, uncontaminated by drugs; thus in self-practice proclaiming, as from the house-top, Not for me is *materia medica*, but for those who are unwise enough to neglect nature and her teachings. The lawyer, also, of expanded intellect, too highly appreciates the blessings which naturally flow from studying peace with all men, and minding well his own business, to let them lightly slip through his fingers; wherefore, in self-practice, he lays before us the why and the wherefore it is, that, in the intricate meshes of the law, he is never found entangled; that is, why law-suits of his own he never has any. Nor does the learned and venerable priest need be reminded that obedience is better than sacrifices offered for sin; wherefore, in his own behalf, it is not often he attempts to bribe the Lord in that way. Health, upon his own head, he is seldom heard to invoke, always preferring fomentations to the Prayer-cure, when it is *he* who has the colic. As a matter of course, professionally, and as God's chosen embassador, his concern is the salvation of the souls and not the bodies of men; wherefore, with line upon line and precept upon precept, he warns his flock against the vanity of this world's goods; and wherefore, with upturned eye and elevated hand, he as often points them to those more durable riches that are laid up in heaven. And yet, in self-practice, the most emphatic of all language, he may be said to live out constant proclamation, in form and substance nearly as follows: Within the sacerdotal robe which you see, resides a man of flesh and blood, possessed of like passions and desires with other men; who, with eye intent upon the main chance, so contrives and manages the thing, as not only to render the professional garment an honorable appendage, but to make its wearer's sojourn, in this present and non-fictitious world, quite easy and comfortable.

That the foregoing picture is quite life-like cannot be denied; and yet we are happy to know that it is not as much so to-day, as it once was, nor as much so here, as it still is in other and less enlightened lands. Wherefore we are constrained to think that these things, when taken in connection with the apathy for real knowledge which prevails among us the common people, as compared with our inordinate respect for ancient usage and love of lucre, have been, and still are, upon the whole, both good and right. In other words, we must think that, to the extent which these things continue to exist among us, to that extent they must needs be so existing among us legitimately; and hence that physician, lawyer, and priest are, each and all, just so many *human-nature appointed instruments* to convict, convert, elevate, and save the race, in the only way that it can be done consonant to the workings of natural law; namely, by frittering away, little by little, the shackles imposed by ignorance, bigotry, and superstition, through and by means of the effective appeals which they are constantly making to that most sensitive part, our breeches pockets.

Viewed from this standpoint, in the midst of all this seeming inconsistency and apparent chaos, Order is seen to preside. And, viewed from this standpoint, there is not only little to discourage, but much to gladden and stimulate to action every enlightened philanthropist, professional and non-professional. We say, there is much to gladden and stimulate to action this class of persons, because it is not every well-wisher of the race that with clear and comprehensive intellect is blessed; and because, notwithstanding the most vulgar eye can see and stupid tongue complain that the times are not now, as they used to be, it is only given to the more observing and deeply philosophic to deduce therefrom the soul-cheering fact, Nor are the times nor men nor human opinions nor the practices of men, to-day, what in a few brief years they will come to be, when the eternal law of progression shall have still further wrought her legitimately enlightening and elevating work.

For the reason that ignorance is the parent of bigotry, the mother of superstition, the author of all our devils, and the bottom cause of sin, for that reason is it the *curse of God;* and, for the reason that knowledge is the only power which, from all these things, can ever set men free,—can ever elevate and save the world, for that reason is it *the wing wherewith we fly to heaven.*

Work and work on is a command inherently residing in the nature of every element and thing under the whole heaven; and progression is the legitimate result. Would we of any talent committed to our charge, more properly transmitted to us by parentage, make two, that is, double its activity and power, we must exercise it, and keep on doing so, within the limit of abuse; this being the only condition upon which normal increase of power, either muscular or mental, is ever attainable. Wherefore, to growth in knowledge, increase of study, and not increase of faith, must forever constitute the key.

CHAPTER X.

EXPEDIENCY THE CRITERION OF RIGHT.

The Christian nations of the old world no more derived their right from the Bible to dominate over the beasts of the field, and to eat their flesh, than did the unlettered inhabitants of the new, who never heard of any such book. Upon the contrary, they both, and both alike, derived such right from the patent fact that the animal called man is superior to the brute creation; hence is legitimately possessed of superior rights, and hence of the right to dominate over them, press them into his service, and to feed upon their flesh to the extent that he shall deem it expedient so to do. In other words, the men who wrote what is now the Bible, the same as the natives upon this side the water, not only saw and read the fact in animated nature's volume, lying open all around them, that man was superior to the beasts of the field, but, like the wild Indian, they felt the love of dominion rising high within them, together with a hankering after the flesh-pots too strong to be by them mistaken. Wherefore the men who wrote that volume, the same as the untutored savage, and the savage the same as they, from said plain data, inferred it to be the right of human beings to have dominion over the lower orders of animals, and to kill and eat such of them as they not only loved to feast upon, but adjudged to be wholesome food.

As the western natives could neither read nor write, so they were obliged to content themselves with teaching the discoveries, thus made, unto their children and children's children by their own daily practice and camp-fire traditions. And as certain leaders among the inhabitants of the old world could both read and write, so they were able to go a step further, wherefore a step further they went, and in the form of a permissive commandment wrote it down. And wherefore, in after years, another set of leaders being equally desirous of distinguishing themselves went a little further still, and, in a book called the Bible, placed it; and there it still remains. We say, all this was inferred from animated nature's open volume, as well by civilized man as by the savage, because we are abundantly satisfied, not only that it is from this same indubitable source that we of to-day derive our right to dominate over the brute creation, but that, in truth and in fact, the god, man, is all the god who ever wrote or said a word upon the subject.

Not from said artificial book, (for certainly all books, as well as written languages, are artificial things,) did we derive our right to dominate over our children under a certain age, and to appropriate their earnings to our use, but from this same pre-eminence which adults ever, naturally, possess over the young and immature. And the right to conduct ourselves in the same way toward such of the black race as, fortunately for them, but unfortunately for us, are situated among us, we gain not from that commandment which Moses represents as issuing directly from the mouth of the Lord, in the following words: "Both thy bond-men, and thy bond-maids, which thou shalt have, shall be of the heathen that are round about you; of them shall ye buy bond-men and bond-maids. Moreover, of the children of the strangers that do sojourn among you, of them shall ye buy, and of their families that are with you, which they begat in your land: and they shall be your possession. And ye shall take them as a inheritance for your children after you, to inherit them for a possession; they shall be your bond-men forever: but over your brethren the Children of Israel, ye shall not rule one over another with rigor."—Lev., 25. 44—46.—We repeat, not from this plain Scripture, which was merely from the book of human nature inferred, and hence declared to be the commandment of that God who, of both man and human nature, is the Author, did we derive the right to hold the negro in bondage, but from that same living book of human nature which declares such to be the natural superiority of the white race over the black, as legitimately confers upon the former paramount rights; and hence the right of dominion over the latter, to the extent which the superior race shall adjudge it expedient to exercise it. Nor does the law of paramount right, which grows out of natural supremacy, end here, but extends to the red man of the forest to the extent that are we to him superior. We say, to the extent that are we to him superior, because experience proves that, in point of power of will, personal independence of feeling, and settled determination to be free, he is at least our equal; and hence, to enslave his person and tax his muscles, we have not the right. As, however, we are, upon the whole, much his betters, and especially in skill to bargain and quarrel ourselves into difficulties, as well as to fight our way out of them, so we have the right to drive him back, out of the way, to make room for our superior settlements, just as often and just as far as shall it be, by us, adjudged necessary and expedient so to do. And even between adults of the same race, who under ordinary circumstances are equals and coequals, in extreme emergencies, and especially where life is at stake, this same rule will be found to hold.

Because a man possesses a sort of general, theoretic right to perform some certain act, no matter what, it does not follow that it would be expedient for him to do it, and hence that it would be right in fact. Upon the contrary, in all this wide class of cases, both the right and the wrong of men's actions are ever to be determined by their expediency or inexpediency; that is, by the effects which they will naturally produce, not upon society, to whom they are here assumed to be things of indifference, but upon the individuals themselves. The poor day-laborer, for example, possesses, theoretically, the personal right to kill and eat his only cow, notwithstanding she doth monthly furnish more of living for his family than would her entire body, if slaughtered. As it would, therefore, be bad policy for him, as provider, to kill and eat up in a single month a family favorite, which with trifling expense would furnish his wife and little ones half their living for years to come; so it would not be right, but wrong for him to do it. In like manner, because not forbidden by statute, in a quiet way, to kill the horses that draw for us the plow, the cattle which fill our stalls, the sheep that feed upon our pastures, etc., and so leave not a thing upon our farms to breathe, except ourselves and families; and because we are to them superior, hence have, by natural ordinance, the right of dominion over them, consequently the abstract right thus wantonly to slay them, it does not follow that it would be expedient for us thus to do, and hence that it would be right in fact.

From what has been said it will be seen, that, according to our understanding of the matter, of right and of wrong, the same as of good and bad, economy and extravagance, and numerous other things, there is not in reality any fixed standard; and hence that what is right under one set of circumstances may be wrong under another set, and *vice versa.* Thus, economy is not only admitted by everybody to be right, but all men everywhere mean to be and think they are economical; consequently the most extravagant are unable to see that they themselves are at all extravagant. Whatever may have been their past practice, they feel sure they do not *now* waste what they have, do not *now* run about more than is necessary or *buy* what they do not need. This is the feeling which exists all over the world, notwithstanding the prodigality which so extensively prevails; and it so exists, because neither economy nor extravagance is a fixed thing, but both dependent upon circumstances; and because the circumstances by which they are regulated and governed are far too little consulted. In other words, the same thing which it would be economical in C. to do, it may be extravagance in D. to ape. Thus, for instance, it would be both wisdom and economy in C., however hale, with his net income of ten thousand a year, to hire a horse and buggy to ride half a dozen miles out of town, upon some verbal errand which he must needs execute in person; and yet it would be both folly and extravagance in D., an able bodied man having a family, with no capital but his hands, and hence no income, save half a dozen dollars a week, the recompense of his daily toil, to go and pay a dollar for that same horse and buggy to ride the same distance upon a similar errand. Folly and extravagance in him! and hence wrong; because such are his circumstances, both pecuniary and domestic, that he cannot thus afford to spend his scanty means; and because by riding the horse with which Dame Nature has provided him, he could save twice as much money in the same length of time for the benefit of himself and family, as he is able to earn in his usual, more laborious way. And thus on through all the different grades of society and various walks in life.

Of course, this view of right and wrong and their foundations will not meet the preconceived opinions of such as honestly regard the revealed will of God, as contained in the Bible, as being of these things both the rule and the measure. As, however, there are to-day vast numbers of different right acts and things, as well as wrong ones, and as there will be more to-morrow, unless we all at once to a Chinese stand-still come, so we are unable to see how we are going to determine what is, and what is not, the will of God in reference to this, that, and a thousand other things which are constantly coming up, and which by our acts, if not in words, we are compelled to sanction else condemn, unless we do consult expediency, which is but another name for the fitness of things under the circumstances of the case; and hence, with such, we are compelled to take issue.

According to our view, then, whether right or whether wrong, it will readily be seen that, of what is, and what is not, expedient for the living occupants of Earth to do, such living occupants are currently to judge and determine for themselves, from just such light as they at the time possess upon the subject; and that whatsoever thing shall be by them thus adjudged to be, upon the whole, expedient or inexpedient, is, for those same reasons and by the same act of the judgment, also determined to be right or wrong, as the case may be.

Now let us turn from this plain, practical theory which ever lets universal, living and progressive man be the universal living and advanced judge of all the different acts and things which it is, upon the whole, expedient, and hence right, for him to perform, to the one which wholly to the Bible looks for rules to point out, and arbitrarily settle, not only for to-day, but for to-morrow, and not only for to-day and to-morrow, but forever on, all these things of every kind, class, and grade.

It must be borne in memory, whilst viewing this subject, that what is now the Bible was once a confused mass of separate writings in foreign language penned, with word following word and sentence following sentence, without any pause or break between. It must also be kept in mind that those olden writings have all been overhauled and re-overhauled, translated and re-translated, not by God himself, but by mere men who, even allowing them to have no preconceived opinions of their own upon the subject, were nevertheless quite as liable to err in judgment as to what was, and what was not, the true intent and meaning of the writers, hence as to what is, and what is not, the correct rendering, as were they, as are we, and as will be those who shall come after us as to what is right, and what is wrong, in reference to the different subjects and things of which the Bible treats. And, to satisfy ourselves that the translators, trimmers, and assorters of those ancient manuscripts were not only liable to err in these respects; but that they did thus err, we have only to compare the different translations, not with the original manuscripts and parts of manuscripts, which were finally adjudged worthy of holding a place within that volume, but simply with each other. In other words, self-evidently, the men who wrote the different books and parts of books, which now compose the Bible, must have meant, when they were writing them, just what they did mean, and could not have meant anything more or less or different; consequently the fact that no two translations agree is proof that there is no reliance to be placed upon any of them as being true to the original manuscripts, and hence true to the intent and meaning of the men who penned them. Indeed, so different from each other are the two versions now in general use among us,—to say nothing of the still greater difference between these and the original manuscripts, before such manuscripts, by the different councils of men, were overhauled, assorted, and trimmed, the better to make them suit their tastes, and before, by the preconceived opinions of translators, they were here a little fulled and there a little stretched,—that the Catholic portion of Christians will not allow a Protestant version a place among them, nor will the Protestant wing use a copy of the Catholic Bible in the pulpit, or anywhere else;—not they. But this is not all nor the half of it; since it is certain that all who read the Bible, whether Catholic or Protestant, are but frail human beings; consequently, instead of being able to understand the same version alike, they are compelled to understand it so differently that we Protestants, who just a little for ourselves have dared to think, are to-day divided and subdivided into sects and parties as variant from each other in opinion, as to what is God's revealed will in reference to certain questions of fundamental importance, as is undying love toward all mankind, from eternal hatred toward full three-fourths of the human family.

With all these things staring us in the face, can we not see that even allowing God to have specially dictated every word that was written upon the original manuscripts, still the copies and copies of copies thereof, now in the Bibles before us, are so filled with errors from unintentional mistranslation, and such others as ignorance, superstition, and a blind devotion to Catholicism upon the one hand, and to Protestantism upon the other did cause to creep in, as that, when altogether taken, they must necessarily render the copies of that book, now in our possession, just about as reliable a standard of what is right and what is wrong in human actions, as would be an *India rubber string of the linear yard?*—Not only this, but allowing the Catholic and Protestant Bibles to read substantially alike, also allowing that both versions are substantially true to such of the original manuscripts and parts of manuscripts as were, by a majority of the men who composed the different councils, adjudged worthy to occupy a place therein; still is it not plain that we are obliged to use human art, human science, and human understanding in seeking out, comparing, and determining, not only the purport of the different passages, but their relevancy to the case in hand; and consequently that the decision is, after all, little else than a matter of current human judgment and discretion? Indeed, is it not plain as plain can be, that, in this land of human praying, human preaching, human Sabbath schools, etc., we do none of us come to the Bible blank sheets;—do none of us come there opinionless to find our opinions, but, instead, all of us with our heads filled with opinions from tradition's early fount, in search of something that will still further strengthen and confirm them? And who that is at all conversant with the matter does not know, that by selecting a passage here and a passage there, because with our preconceived opinions they chance to accord, and by stretching else by fulling up, as the case may seem to require, such other passages as shall be found upon their face with our said opinions to conflict, until they shall be made to correspond therewith, we can prove almost anything to be the will of God, and hence right, which we ourselves adjudge to be? In short, who that is not utterly blinded by prejudice cannot see that, in this way, we do ever make the India rubber measure agree in length with whatever thing, whether long or short, *we ourselves adjudge is just a yard?*

Plainly enough, as seems to us, to make the Bible to be the exponent of the will of God, and consequently the rule and measure of right and wrong in human actions, is just about equivalent to handing the matter all over to the clergy, who are certainly neither more nor less than human beings, and hence to every form of human influence and human frailty subject. Against this, then, we are obliged to enter our protest; not, however, because we deem them less competent or less disposed candidly to consider and determine those questions, than would be some other set or division of men, but because we would not leave any question, in which the whole human family have each an equal personal interest, wholly to the decision of any class of men; and because we can see no sort of use in us, the common people, being born with eyes and understanding, if we are not to use them in examining and determining, as far forth as possible, all such questions as do us, just as much as anybody else, concern. Besides we must think it tends more to advance mankind in knowledge, and also in the ways of virtue, to hold each individual personally responsible for his own misjudgments, consequently for his own wrong acts, than it does thus to exonerate the mass from all blame in the matter; and then so divide up the responsibility between an ancient, inanimate book, and a numerous living clergy, as that, for wrong actions between man and man, the same as between soulless corporations, there shall be nobody to be found unto whom a living Nathan can point his finger and say, *Thou art the man* who misjudged, consequently the man who committed the wrong act, and hence the man that is responsible therefor. For these reasons, if for no other, we can never yield our feeble assent to any theory or doctrine which declares in effect, that, in reference to a matter in which all are alike, personally, interested; namely, the important matter of judging as to what is right and what is wrong in human actions, the whole human family, with the exception of the clergy, would be just as well off without brains as with. Understand, we do not say or mean that we would any more reject whatever of light is shed upon the subject, either by the Bible or the clergy, than would we light derived from any other source; but, then, we would be understood as both saying and meaning, that we would, at all times, have the question stand wide-open to discussion and trial upon its merits; to the end that the character of men's acts may ever, currently, be determined by the effects which they shall currently produce; and not by any one set of men, or by any assumed, fixed standard, no matter what, nor when, nor by whom prescribed. So much for the Bible as the rule and measure of what is right and what is wrong in human actions, allowing its every word to have been written by men who were specially God-inspired, consequently to have originally contained nothing but real truth, and hence to have been and be fully self-consistent from beginning to end.

And now, for the purpose of seeing whether or not from beginning to end it is thus self-consistent, let us for a moment look between its covers.—In the paragraph standing between the 21st and 26th verses of the 21st chapter of Exodus, Moses represents the Lord as instructing him to command as follows: "If men strive and hurt a woman with child, so that her fruit depart from her, and yet no mischief follow, he shall be surely punished, according as the woman's husband will lay upon him; and he shall pay as the judges determine. And if any mischief follow, then thou shalt give life for life, eye for eye, tooth for tooth, hand for hand, foot for foot, burning for burning, wound for wound, stripe for stripe."—Some fifteen hundred years later, in his celebrated sermon on the mount, Christ is reported by Matthew as commanding thus: "Ye have heard that it hath been said, [referring to the above-quoted commandment of Moses] An eye for an eye, and a tooth for a tooth. But I say unto you, that ye resist not evil: but whosoever shall smite thee on thy right cheek, turn to him the other also. And if any man will sue thee at the law, and take away thy coat, let him have thy cloak also. And whosoever shall compel thee to go a mile, go with him twain."—Mat., 5. 38—41.

Now who doth not see that both the letter and the spirit of these two rules, which, by those different Bible writers, at such different periods of time, were laid down as guides for human action, instead of being in harmony, are with each other at variance direct? And who not that the teachings of the New Testament are, as a whole, as much in advance of those contained in the Old, as were the men who wrote the last testament in advance of those who penned the first, in point of general intelligence, civilization, and refinement? And further, Is not the fact, that in proportion as men became advanced in knowledge, civilization, and refinement, in that same proportion are the rules laid down, and doctrines taught, by the later Bible writers, found to be in advance of those of former periods, at least next-door neighbor to proof positive, that it was not an unchangeable God who, at these different eras, took such opposite views of the same subjects, but, instead, the differently advanced human fractions of the great HIM; precisely the same as do they now, and doubtless ever onward will?

Again, to the inquiry made by the Pharisees, "Is it lawful for a man to put away his wife for every cause?" Matthew reports Christ as answering thus: "Have ye not read that he which made them at the beginning, made them male and female, and said, For this cause shall a man leave father and mother, and shall cleave to his wife: and they twain shall be one flesh? Wherefore they are no more twain, but one flesh. What therefore God hath joined together, let no man put asunder." And to the further question by them immediately propounded, "Why did Moses then command to give a writing of divorcement, and to put her away?" he is by this same Matthew reported as replying as follows: "Moses, because of the hardness of your hearts, suffered you to put away your wives: but from the beginning it was not so. And I say unto you, Whosoever shall put away his wife, except it be for fornication, and shall marry another, committeth adultery: and whoso marrieth her which is put away, doth commit adultery."—Mat., 19. 3—9.

Now, from Matthew's report of this brief conversation between Christ and the Pharisees, we not only learn that this his said teaching is in flat contradiction to that of Moses, but also that they, the Pharisees, did not ask him why it was that *God* commanded to give a writing of divorcement, and to put her away nor why *God*, by the mouth of his servant Moses, so commanded but why Moses gave such commandment; thus clearly showing that of such commandment, according to their understanding of the matter, not God, but the great lawgiver *Moses* was both the author and the promulgator. Neither unto said inquiry did Christ make answer and say, It was not Moses but *God* who gave the commandment of which you speak, and hence it is right; nor that *God*, by the mouth of his servant Moses, gave it, and therefore it is right; nor yet that it was given by the great lawgiver Moses because it was by him adjudged to be just and equal, and hence right; but, instead, that "*Moses*, because of the hardness of your hearts, suffered you to put away your wives, but from the beginning it was not so." Thus clearly showing that Christ did not understand that even the man Moses regarded the doctrine in said commandment laid down, as being either intrinsically right, or in accordance with the judgment of the Almighty as pronounced from the beginning In fact, in and by his said answer, Christ just as good as tells the Pharisees that Moses, in consequence of the hardness of the Israelitish people's hearts, was under the necessity of suffering them thus to put away their wives; and hence, by way of making a virtue of such necessity, that in the form of a commandment he granted them permission to do it. And not only do we gather this from said brief answer of Christ, but, by fair implication, we therefrom further learn that Christ regarded it as being no uncommon thing with Moses to give unto that ignorant, superstitious, and idolatrous people, such commandments as he adjudged were imperately demanded by their peculiar circumstances and low condition, instead of such as have their foundation in a more enlightened justice. For if it be a fact that Moses, because of the hardness of their hearts, that is, because of their low moral and intellectual condition, was under the necessity of suffering them, under the sanction of a commandment, thus to put away their wives, contrary to enlightened justice, as well as contrary to the judgment of God as pronounced from the beginning; then is the inference irresistible that, directly in consequence of this same hardheartedness or savage condition, he was under the necessity of suffering them to do numerous other things under the sanction of numerous other commandments, positive and permissive, upon the pages of the Bible standing; and which other things it would not be proper for people whose hearts are much less hard, that is, for people who are morally and intellectually much more elevated and enlightened, to imitate and do. In short, from the general tenor of Christ's said answer, we cannot doubt but that he looked upon Moses as being a man, who was not only shrewd enough and politic enough to command that ignorant, turbulent, and rebellious people thus to put away their wives, but also to command them to do numerous other things, which he saw it would not be possible for him to restrain them from doing; to the end that they might thus be brought to think and to feel, whilst doing them, that were acting in obedience to his authority, and not in opposition thereto; and so, without their seeing the drift of the thing, gradually bring them to become and be a more law-loving, and hence a more law-abiding people.

NOTE.—The Mosaic commandment, which gave rise to the aforementioned conversation between Christ and the Pharisees, is contained in the first paragraph of the 24th chapter of Deuteronomy.

CHAPTER XI.

PANIC.

As the term Panic seems fast coming to occupy a conspicuous place in American history, so it may not be amiss very briefly to explain the rationale of the phenomenon which is thereby intended to be denoted.

As we understand the matter, then, the human brain is not a simple but a complex structure, embracing quite a number of different parts or organs, each of which performs its own proper function and no other. Some of those organs are always much larger than others, and every organ, whether large or small, draws unto itself more of stimulant, in the form of blood, when in a state of action, than when at rest. Hence, whenever the large organ called Cautiousness, whose business it is to act toward us the part of guardian angel, watching over us, warning us of the approach of danger, and prompting us to ward it off, else to make our escape therefrom, becomes unduly active, no matter from what cause, nor whether real or imaginary, it legitimately draws unto itself more than its usual quantity of this stimulating element; whereby, for the time being, the neighboring organs are more or less robbed of their usual healthy supply.

Unwilling, then, as we may be to acknowledge it even to ourselves, it is nevertheless a fact that under the accumulated pressure of untoward circumstances and a greatly depressed condition of spirits, superinduced upon the individual by the most sickening scenes, gloomy prospects, and a state of great physical exhaustion, the organ of Cautiousness is liable to become unduly active;—is liable suddenly to become and be so intensely active, even in the most prudent and well-balanced head, as temporarily to rob its neighboring organs, Combativeness and Destructiveness, of their proper supply of stimulus, and hence to leave them, for the time being, just about as good as dead. And upon the taking place of such an event, no matter when nor where, the possessor at once becomes so completely occupied by the one strong feeling of personal danger, as to be perhaps deprived of ability to move from the spot, and perhaps compelled to fly therefrom with all the power at his command.

Of course, it is not claimed that the organ of Cautiousness, when relatively large, is not more liable to become so engorged with blood as temporarily to produce, in its possessor, that certain form of insanity called *panic*, than is that same organ when relatively small; but only that such organ exists in sufficient volume in the head of every prudent and sound-minded man, even when relatively small, to paralyze his courage and erase his manhood to such an extent as to leave him, for the time being, little else than a living, breathing mass of imbecility, from overwhelming fear; provided that, at the fitting moment of great physical exhaustion and depression of spirits, the proper kind of fear-inspiring agony be piled upon him high enough. We say, provided that, at the fitting moment, etc., the proper kind of fear-inspiring agony be piled upon him high enough, because so nearly omnipotent is the power of habit, that a great natural coward may gradually be brought to become so familiar with some certain class of horrid scenes and threatening dangers, as that it shall finally be almost impossible for any amount or degree of this class of things to move him; and yet let the same scenes and dangers, in all their terribleness, be suddenly precipitated upon a man who is a stranger thereto, and he turns sick at heart and pale with fear, notwithstanding endowed by nature with the most undaunted courage. Not so much to any inborn skill in his fingers is the violinist indebted for his ability, thus dexterously, to touch the strings, as to the education they have received; and not so much to his native courage is the veteran soldier indebted for his ability, unmoved, to stand and face the cannon's mouth, as to the strength of that habit, into which, from the force of circumstances, his brain has finally fallen.

Let no man, therefore, who claims to be an American and a loyalist, plume himself too highly upon his untried courage; or too freely censure, as weak and timid, such of his patriotic brothers as, at the memorable battle of Bull Run, did falter, fall into disorder, and wildly fly before a superior, rebel enemy. Rather let him reflect that, upon that eventful day, these men were not leisurely discussing the state of the country at home, or severally partaking the comforts of some well-furnished table, in shady back-kitchen or more airy hall. Yea, and forever remember that long miles of rapid marching under heavy burdens, followed by long hours of hard fighting under the fierce rays of a high midsummer Sun, consuming thirst, the groans of the wounded, and sight of the dying, were none of them things that were very well calculated to nerve men up, firmly to stand, and boldly to face, indefinitely on, the fresh battalions that were swarming forward to the aid of an already outnumbering foe. Indeed, when are fairly taken into account all the untoward circumstances under which this eventful battle was fought, and lost to our arms, by these raw levies, fresh from the farm, the workshop, the counting-house, etc., we must think their courage, devotion to their country's flag, and even their powers of physical endurance, do not unfavorably compare with those same qualities possessed and manifested by any equally numerous body of unpracticed soldiers, that were ever marshaled in battle array.

NOTE.—The foregoing thoughts, suggested by the flight at Bull Run, were written out for a Lyceum Paper, in the fall of '61; but as their philosophy is not limited to time or place they are here inserted.

CHAPTER XII.

GOD, CREATION, ETC.

"Revere thyself——thou'rt near allied
To angels on thy better side:——"

Thus saith the poet. And revere thyself, O man! say we.—Not, however, because we think thee in part, merely, near allied to angels; but because, in whole, part and parcel of the eternal God.

As all created forms and things, small and great, less durable and more durable, with whose rise and progress it is our fortune to to be acquainted, do in some way grow or come up gradually from small beginnings, and not a thing, all at once, into ripe existence springs; so, as often as we take known facts for our data, and not assumed ones either ancient or modern, just so often is the conclusion forced upon us that the theory of creation, which this natural order of things reverses, at the wrong end begins, and hence bottom-upward stands. Yon giant oak, for example, the same as the feeble mushroom, we know was not sprung into being all at once and full-sized out of nothing, but that it gradually came up by growth or accretion of some sort out of the elements which now compose it; and yet so slowly and silently is the aggregating process carried on, that not once in all our lives did we ever see it grow, but only that it does. The solid rock also, we are satisfied from numerous indexes, did not always exhibit the same appearance that it does to-day; and yet so gradual is the metamorphic change brought about, that the life of a human being furnishes a period too short for the detection of any alteration. And, of old Earth, the same in principle, only in a greatly superior degree. For these and other reasons we are compelled to think that said oak is just as much the work of creation, as is the Earth itself; and consequently that it is, to-day, just as much part and parcel of this terrestrial globe, as were its different composing elements before they thus, by slow degrees, a monster oak became.

Anciently, there was not only much less of light and knowledge in the world than now, but the men of olden time were much less given to deep and studious inquiry than are the habitants of Earth to-day; wherefore they were correspondingly more prone to hanker after the strange and the marvelous, consequently to rely upon naked assertion, and hence to believe upon testimony that was weightless, if not wholly irrelevant.

The elements, and all the different worlds, being here, it is not only natural that the present generation of men should be anxious to understand how all these things came to be, but that they should yield their assent to such time-honored hypothesis as shall seem to account therefor; provided such hypothesis does not present, within itself, a second difficulty fully as great and inexplicable as is the first. As said however, anciently, there was much less of light and knowledge in the world than now, and, as a natural consequence thereof, a correspondingly greater amount of wonderment and faith. It is not strange, therefore, that, for the purpose of satisfying the growing curiosity of others, the more shrewd and aspiring Moses should have had resort to that most simple method of accounting for the Earth's being here; namely, by first creating hypothetically an invisible, intangible, pre-existent Being of unlimited power and skill possessed; and then letting him, of his own sovreign will and pleasure, create the Earth, the heavens, and all things else, just as they now are.

We say, it is not strange that the more shrewd and aspiring Moses should have had resort to that most simple method, etc.. for who at this late day and age of the world cannot see that it is just as easy as it is to sit and think, for any one to account satisfactorily to himself and everybody else for the creation of the Earth, or any other phenomenon under heaven or above it, by simply framing an hypothesis which shall reach and cover all the known facts in the case; provided he is able to bring himself and the rest of mankind to believe, that such hypothesis, notwithstanding dogmatically put forth, is really true? And who cannot see that the Mosaic hypothesis, whether correct or whether incorrect, by which the phenomenon called creation is explained, is excellently well calculated by its majestic brevity and boldness to inspire mankind with awe? And who not that it is admirably adapted by its unlimited breadth of sweep to reach and cover, not only all known facts in the case, but every other possible or impossible thing which the fancy of man can suggest? And hence who that is not blinded by prejudice cannot see that, from these two circumstances, it was excellently well calculated to gain the assent, not only of that ignorant, superstitious, and credulous people to whom it was specially addressed, but of subsequent generations of men, even were they allowed the opportunity, without bias, of forming their own opinions upon the subject? Upon this great question, however, which more or less underlies all genuine science, men are not permitted and have not been to think dispassionately or, without bias, to form their own opinions; and to prove this, we offer in evidence the unimpeachable fact that, ever since the day on which said Mosaic hypothesis first fell upon the ears of the astonished Israelites, this same idea has been pricked into the brains of every succeeding generation of children under the solemn sanction of religion, by those unto whom they naturally upward look for light with most implicit confidence. In this way, from then till now, upon this great foundation subject, to an extent which no human being can calculate, has bold, independent, and manly thought been crippled and the judgments of men forestalled.

As it has already been said that the hypothesis by which Moses essayed to account to the children of Israel for the Earth's being here, clothed with verdure, tenanted by beasts and men, furnished with its different lights, etc., was excellently well calculated by its majestic brevity and boldness to inspire that ignorant, superstitious, and miracle-loving people with profoundest awe, also that it was admirably adapted by its unlimited breadth of sweep to reach and cover all the different kinds and character of phenomena then known, and hence to cut off all chance for objection thereto upon the score of narrowness, so we will now add that, had he made it less broad and imposing, that is, had made his God to have been an immensely great, wise, and powerful material Being, instead of an immaterial and invisible one of infinite knowledge and power possessed, it is almost certain that some one or other of the more inquisitive and doubting of even this most stupid and credulous people would have been nervously anxious to see so august a Being, and impatiently desirous of knowing whereabouts upon the face of the Earth he kept himself, etc.; since this our feeble planet was then supposed by all, Moses included, to be the masterpiece of all creation, consequently would naturally have been selected by them as his abiding place. And failing in their efforts to catch a glimpse or discover the track of so prodigiously large a Being as they would naturally have supposed he needs must be, sooner or later an idea would have struck somebody, and been whispered around; whereby the general faith in his existence would have begun to wane, and the suspicion that it was all a myth to wax and continued waxing, until, finally, in such hypothesis, there would have been no believers left.

Anciently, however, and when the number of accurately ascertained facts of the most simple kind was comparatively quite small; when, among the lower order of society, reason had scarcely a seat in the brain; when miracles, or things directly at variance with the order of Nature, were all the rage—because supposed to be the only infallible tests of real truth; and when men were so profoundly ignorant and desperately eager to believe something and to fall down and worship something, that worship something they must and would, if it was nothing but a *molton calf*, it is not surprising that they should have been filled to overflowing with said Mosaic account of creation; but that the more sober, intelligent, and thinking portion of mankind should still remain so blinded by prejudice as seriously to think of looking back to those days of heathenish darkness for light, upon this or any other subject, seems a little strange. It has already been intimated and we now say distinctly that, according to our understanding of human nature, it is perfectly natural that every generation, both ancient and modern, should drink in like a sponge and continue to believe, not only in youth, but during early manhood, whatever doctrine, theory, or hypothesis is exclusively taught and impressed upon them as religious truth, in their tender and confiding years; also that they should continue on, until stopped by death, to cherish that same opinion, no matter what, nor how repugnant to reason and the every-day phenomena by which they are surrounded; provided that, upon such subject, they never allow themselves one jot to think and to reason. But, then, as heretofore said, it seems a little surprising how men can help thinking to some slight extent at least, upon every subject of general interest; since, in spite of the opposing decision of that council of cardinals, which reflected the views of nearly all Christendom at the time, the stubborn world did move,—moves on, and progression marks its track.

The present generation of adults which is made up of individuals who, a few short years ago, were tender, confiding children, listening with open mouths to catch instruction from a generation of men and women that were our immediate predecessors, and which children, or at least a larger proportion of them than ever before, notwithstanding all the vast array of means that were constantly being devised and put forth by such preceding generation to enstamp upon us their own image and likeness, by filling us to the brim with the same creational notions and other religious dogmas with which, from ancient fount, their heads were filled, and hence to make of us a stereotyped edition of themselves, the same as are they of those who them preceded, have so far outgrown and burst the shell which enclosed our revered parents and teachers, as to be, comparatively speaking, quite bold and vigorous thinkers upon all subjects, except only such as we are still deterred from approaching by our strong, blind veneration for the persons, views, and opinions of certain ancient individuals; and this notwithstanding our intellect tells us that those said ancient individuals were greatly our inferiors in point of research, consequently in point of knowledge, and hence in point of ability to see and judge correctly upon this or any other subject. We repeat, it is perfectly natural that men who, upon general subjects, are in the habit of thinking and judging for themselves, (as well as those who are never guilty of perpetrating an independent thought,) should continue on believing and teaching unto others this same ancient hypothesis by which the creation of the world, etc., is accounted for, and which, as religious truth, was so thoroughly pricked into their young and susceptible brains; provided it never occurs to them that such hypothesis, in addition to lacking proof, presents within itself a new difficulty quite as great and inexplicable, as does the phenomenon called creation for which it serves to account. And inasmuch as this is eminently the case with said Mosaic hypothesis, we must be permitted to think, and hence to give it as our opinion for what it may be worth, that it is the dictate of wisdom to cast it from us as so much hindering machinery, and to fall back upon the original facts preparatory to taking a new and more correct start. Indeed, there does not seem to be any other course left to such of us as are determined that we will, as far forth as possible, be governed by reason, and not by the promptings of our strong, blind feelings of veneration for ancient men and ancient modes of thought, but to discard all naked opinions, whether new or old, and plant ourselves upon what we know is solid ground; or at least upon what, from observation, experience, and the teachings of natural science, we have every reason for believing to be such. And what are the facts which, at this late day and age of the world, are known to be such to a reasonable certainty, and upon which we are to fall back in search of light, when we shall have taken our departure from the old Mosaic hypothesis? Permit us to enumerate just a few, to the end that they may be clearly seen and specifically objected to, if it shall be thought we are claiming too much.—

In the first place, then, stands boldly out Substance itself of every name and kind and form, since, obviously enough, all created things, small and great, inanimate and animated, are wholly composed of its different elements; and since it is perfectly manifest that it is their composing elements, and nothing else, which constitute them appreciable things; and hence that it is these same elements, and nothing else, which, by their blessed presence, prevent all created forms and things, our proud selves included, from shriveling down into just nothing at all. 2. Notwithstanding all the different created forms and things with which we have come to be intimately acquainted are both mutable and perishable, and many of them exceedingly so, still it may be regarded as an established fact that it is only their forms which perish and not their composing elements; since, with all the power that has yet been brought to bear upon them, not a single particle of elementary substance was ever known to be annihilated. 3. It is an undoubted fact that all which takes place when any of those different created forms of substance which help compose that important branch of creation, known as the Vegetable kingdom, are destroyed, or struck from the roll of existence, is simply this: Their composing elements fall back into their primary estate, or a state quite nearly approximating thereunto. 4. It is conceded by all who have carefully considered the subject, (and of course the adverse opinions of such as have never seriously reflected thereupon are weightless,) that the stock of elements fit to nourish and hence to enter into the composition of plants, although inconceivably vast, is not unlimited; also that the present, rich, vegetable garment, with which old Earth to-day is clothed, is principally made up, not only of the same kind of materials, but of the self-same elements, that were its different predecessors for countless ages past. 5. It is reasonably certain that *Substance all*, whether material or immaterial, and whether in primary or created form, doth possess certain inherent properties and powers which are never dormant, but constantly exerting all their force; also that it is these properties and powers of substance, which stand parent cause or creator of all the numerous unions and variant forms which, by growth or accretion, its different elements, all over the globe, do manage to work themselves into. 6. It has come to be understood by quite inferior brains, that the vegetable kingdom is a sort of half-way station between inorganic substance and the animal creation; in other words, that the existence of vegetables is an absolute prerequisite to the existence of animals; also that the vegetable kingdom, although possessed of an organized structure, is nevertheless wholly made up of elements which, in their primary estate, are purely inorganic. 7. It is quite well understood by men of intelligence, that vegetable life is not an entity of any kind; that is, that it is not a thing which anywhere exists independently of plants; but is simply a consequence of certain functions performed by vegetable organs, and which organs are wholly composed of inorganic substance. 8. It is generally understood by men of intelligence, that ordinary animal life is not an entity of any kind; that is, that it is not a thing which in the absence of physical animals doth anywhere exist; but is simply a consequence of organic function of a higher order than that performed by vegetable organs; consequently that whatever of low grade of thought, memory, and knowledge, ordinary animals do possess, they possess by virtue of certain functions performed by that complex organ or structure called the brain, and which brain is wholly composed of non-seeing, non-feeling, non-thinking, inanimate elements; or of elements which, in their uncombined estate, are purely inorganic, and hence of elements which are wholly devoid of any recognized order of life. 9. In private conversation with his confidential friends, every candid and well-informed man will admit that, in so far as he is able to see and determine by sense, human beings, in all these respects, do seem to be standing upon the same footing with other animals; and that the only evidence he has to the contrary is derived from certain ancient writings called the Bible, from the teachings of spiritualism, from ghost stories, and deductions drawn from nature by the faculty of reason, and hence that the whole combination of evidence, although sufficient to inspire hope and induce belief, doth nevertheless fall a number of degrees short of coming up to the standard of actual knowledge.

And now, in all sincerity, we ask, Is not here presented an ample field for thought to stretch her busy wings? Do not the above facts, although few and modest, furnish sufficient data to enable growing Reason to begin to indulge the hope, that she may ere long be able so far at least to unravel the mysteries of creation as to remove all doubt of its being the creature of natural law,—as to remove all doubt of its being the legitimate result of the ceaseless workings, co-workings, and antagonist workings of the undying properties and powers, inherently residing in Elementary Substance;—the very thing of which all created forms and things, high and low, great and small, inanimate and animated, with whose character and composition we have come to be acquainted, are found to be composed?

It is certain that every human being is born a child, born a blank sheet; and consequently, that it is locality, education, etc., which make of one set of persons Mohammedans, of another Christians, and thus on. Wherefore had Moses chanced to adjudge, and hence to have written it down in the first three chapters of Genesis, that the elements, one and all, of which the Earth is composed, eternally existed, only in scattered form throughout the realms of space; and that the Sun, Moon, and stars were the joint and eternal God who, or which, at a preconcerted signal given by the Sun, "created the heaven and the Earth," and all things therein and upon, out of said elements, in the twinkling of an eye; and had this extraordinary account, from then till now, been just as thoroughly pricked into the brains of every succeeding generation of children, youth, and men, as has the no less extraordinary account which in said chapter he did give; then does not every intelligent man see that we should, each and all, have been just as firmly wedded thereunto, as are we now to the one at the front end of the Bible standing?—As seems to us, every intelligent man must see this; and, seeing it, ought to regard it in the light of a commandment to look into the matter, as far forth as possible, for himself.

Again, since the phenomena invariably exhibited by the heavens can in no way be rationally accounted for, except by admitting that the Earth is spherical in form and, upon its axis, daily turns, else that the Sun, and yet more distant stars, do all revolve around our mundane sphere, and thus come to pass over us every twenty-four hours, it must therefore be obvious that the planets, one and all, primary, secondary, and cometary, were either full-sized created, started in their courses, and set spinning upon their axis by some Power, whether itself created or uncreated, present or remote, that was superior to all these mighty moving orbs combined; else that they were, each and all, (just like every other thing we ever in our lives do see,) gradually created by virtue of the workings legitimately consequent upon the undying properties and powers in ELEMENTARY SUBSTANCE contained; and set moving and in motion kept by virtue of those same undying properties and powers within such orbs, as a grand Whole, residing; and so resident therein, because part and parcel of the *eternal elements themselves* of which they are composed. And since it is not possible rationally to account either for their existence or their motions, except upon one or the other of these theories, so the following questions naturally present themselves: 1. Which of the two theories involves the greatest miracle or departure from what is known to be fixed law? 2. Which is the most beautifully consistent with the general appearance exhibited by their ordinary movements? 3. Which is the most consistent not only with their ordinarily regular movements, but with their perturbed motions?—This we ask, because, as seems to us, these irregularities in their motions do shed much light upon the subject; and especially since it has come to be admitted by all philosophers of any note, that these deviations from their usual regular courses are all of them caused to take place, not by any agency or power outside the general system, but by the influence which one celestial body ever exerts upon another, and consequently upon its movements, whenever any two or more of those mighty moving powers into the same vast neighborhood do come. 4. Which is the most rational as well as simple, and simple as well as best in keeping with what, upon all sides round us, we every day behold, this theory which assumes nothing, but takes things just as it finds them, (or at least as to our every sense they appear to be,) and so lets the cause of all the different vasty world's creation—the same as that of the feeble mushroom—and the cause of all their swift and varied movements—just like the gentle falling of an apple from its parent tree—forever be and remain a thing within their own conjoint Selves legitimately residing, and so resident therein, because of their every composing element eternal part and parcel; or the one which, contrary to all observation and experience, as well as to every known fact, starts off upon the assumption of the existence by chance, or somehow else, of an uncreated Spirit Being, infinite in extent, infinite in wisdom, and infinite in power, and hence possessed of power and skill sufficient to enable him to make all these mighty and substantial orbs out of nothing, and in harmonious motion set them going; and then, because the assumed premises are broad enough to cover the conclusion that he could so create them, and because they are here, and known to be one around another constantly revolving, infers therefrom as a fact which must never be called in question, that this said supposed Being did thus, out of nothing, create, fashion, and bring into full existence, all at once, these mighty moving powers, and bid them in this manner forever on to run?

According to Solomon's view of the case, as stated in the 17th verse, of the 11th chapter, of the Apocryphal book called the Wisdom of Solomon, *God made the world of matter without form.* And can it be possible it was because the idea was here advanced by Solomon, that *God made the world of matter without form*, that is, of matter which, in its primitive estate, was wide-scattered in the realms of space, and hence shapeless, instead of out of nothing, that this said book of his was denied a place among the canonical Scriptures, by the men who, in that branch of the matter at least, were acting the God?—That said production of Solomon, the same as all the different Apocryphal books of both the Old and New Testaments, was denied a place in the Sacred Volume by the men who compiled it, either because it contained teachings that were thought to be in themselves objectionable, else because it contained statements that were seen to be irreconcilably at variance with some other writing which, for reasons known only to themselves, it was determined must and should have a place in the Bible, cannot be doubted.—Surely that must be rather poor divine revelation which, by frail human beings, needs thus be overhauled, assorted, trimmed, and a portion rejected as of doubtful authority, in order to save it from impeaching itself by its own contradictions.

And now, for the purpose of carrying the mind back a few thousand years, permit us to suggest that there must have been a time, away back somewhere in the world's past history, when there existed no definite opinion upon the subject of creation; also a time when men first began to think and inquire within themselves, how all these great and wondrous things came to be. There was doubtless also a time when the pursuit of this train of thought finally led some one of the more thoughtful and inquiring of the race, to the then new and greatly advanced conclusion that all these overwhelmingly great and beautiful worlds were made,—made out of nothing, by some awfully great, wise, and powerful Being. Indeed, if we will but run our mind's eye back over the matter, it must be just as plain that this idea that the worlds were created, or made out of nothing, by a great, pre-existent, and hence extrinsic Maker, could not have been in full existence in the heads of men to-day, had it never in the head of mortal man a first beginning had, as it is that the worlds themselves could not have been here to-day, had their creation never been begun.

Or thus: Because, anciently, the same as now, this world and all the different orbs of light were here; because, in process of time, the animal called man became so far advanced that it was by feeble intellect adjudged, that the different worlds could not have been here, had they not been created and placed here; and because these things were seen to be so exceedingly great and numerous and mighty; therefore it was that somebody, at some time, away back in the past history of man, not only conceived the great thought , but gave it birth in language, that this immense world of ours, the plants and animals thereupon, its daily attendant Sun and nightly Moon and glittering stars, were all made,—made out of nothing and placed here by some awfully great, wise, and powerful, pre-existent Being. In this plain natural way, and not by miracle, was this great idea, this grand conclusion, at some time and somewhere by somebody, for the first time in all the world arrived at, and to others less bold and inquisitive told and taught. Wherefore, after being much wondered at and criticised by the early *savans*, it finally grew into a great moral truth in their heads, in form and substance nearly as follows: Some few centuries ago, reckoning back by human generations, a great self-existent Spirit Being in the form of a man and called God, for reasons known only to himself, went at it with a will and, in six days, out of nothing, made the heavens and the Earth, and all things therein and upon, together with the Sun, Moon, and stars to give light upon the Earth; and then betook himself to his former state of rest.—Wherefore, at some time, this said grand conclusion was by Moses, or somebody else, for the first time in all the world written down; consequently, long years thereafter, by a council of men it was placed in the front end of a book called the Bible as a sure foundation fact; and hence it is to-day quite generally believed, and not because the idea is sustained either by analogy or enlightened Reason. In other words, it is to-day believed by a large majority of both Jews and Christians, just because it was anciently by somebody so adjudged; just because it was anciently by somebody so written down; and just because anciently, by a council of men, it was placed in a book called the "Holy Bible;" and not for the reason that the present adult generation of either Jews or Christians have ever given the subject any careful consideration.

From the great patent fact that this our goodly Mother Earth, the radiant Sun, milder Moon, and glittering stars are here, was anciently drawn the conclusion that they could not possibly have been thus in existence, had they not been made out of nothing and placed here, by some pre-existent Being that is greater and more potent than are all these things together put; and, from the same great patent fact, else from some imaginary data, the diametrically opposite and greatly ascending conclusion was likewise anciently drawn; namely, that such greater and more potent, pre-existent Being not at all, himself, a maker needs. Can we not see and would not our less than half-grown children see, (did we not so early check the inquiry and prick it into their tender brains differently,) that this said supposed Maker of the ancients just as much stands in need of a yet greater and more potent, pre-pre-existent MAKER, in order to account for his being in existence, and clothed with such inconceivably wondrous power and skill as enabled him, out of stark naught, all these numerous and substantial worlds to make and set moving, as did these mighty orbs themselves before that he was thus hypothetically conjured up and brought to their relief?

Of course it is not supposed that all men are by nature deeply thinking and inquiring, and yet we have known quite a number of children who not only appeared thoughtful upon the subject, before the waves of thought within them by the banks of a false education were stayed, but who, in spite of all the hindrances which are thus purposely made to turn every way to keep the way of inquiry hereinto close shut, ventured to look up to their mothers and ask, Who made God? Where did he come from? Where did he live before he made the world, etc.? Thus clearly demonstrating, as seems to us, that of such innocent thoughts, feelings, and aspirations as little children do by nature possess, is the reign of happiness within, called the kingdom of heaven, composed; and not of those narrow, superstitious, and intolerant ones which seek to debar anybody, young or old, weak or wise, from inquiring into the composition, character, and whereabouts of the God that made them. And so we now ask, Not which is most in harmony with our early taught and hence preconceived opinions, but which is the most exalting in its tendency, this theory which needs no assumption upon which to stand, since it ever grows right out of the nature of things themselves, (if we will but permit them, in their own modest way, to reveal the story of their gradual creation out of the eternal Elements, by virtue of said Element's own incessant workings legitimately consequent upon their different, undying properties and powers,) or the one which, contrary to anything we ever, anywhere, in our lives do see, assumes that, extrinsic of all these Elements and endlessly before they were, there existed a Being possessed of such wondrous power and skill as enabled him to make all the different worlds, and numberless things thereupon, inanimate and animated, *not out of fitting portions of his own vast eternal Self*, nor yet out of the elements of which they are *seen and known to be composed*, but out of just *nothing at all?* And which lies most open to the charge of blind atheistic chance, this theory which assumes nothing, but simply lets the infinitude of Elements, and every property and power resident therein, eternally to have been in existence, consequently to have been eternally operating in just such a manner as they needs must operate, and so lets fixed law eternally in all things reign; or the one which makes the existence of all the different elements, consequently the existence of all their different properties and powers, and hence the existence of all created things that are of elementary substance composed, to depend upon its having somehow pre-happened, some six thousand years ago, to become and be the sovereign will and pleasure of an infinitely great, wise, and powerful Spirit Being, who chanced to be in full existence himself without ever having been created, to speak them into being, all at once and full-sized, out of naught?—Which?

But, to present the matter in a little different form, throughout universal Nature, all is cause and all effect, except the GREAT FIRST CAUSE of all. And what is this GREAT FIRST CAUSE of all other causes, and hence of all effects of every name and kind that are?—Since it is a fact that the entire range of vegetables and animals, with which we are acquainted, are composed of ELEMENTARY SUBSTANCE; since it is a fact that the entire vegetable and animal creation, in so far as we have any reliable knowledge of their rise and progress, do all have their feeble beginnings so far back in the vast ocean of elements, of one kind and another by which we are surrounded, as that they are finally lost to us therein; and since it is also a fact that it is ELEMENTARY SUBSTANCE, and this alone, which has proved itself to be indistructible, hence uncreated and eternal; therefore the conclusion seems to be irresistible that it can be neither more nor less than the eternal Elements themselves, which PARENT CAUSE do stand to all created forms and things that are. Or thus: As we are certain that some things do gradually and legitimately come up into a great, complicated, and powerful existence from very small beginnings, and as we do not certainly know that anything whatsoever has ever come into created existence in any other way; so, when reasoning from the little which we know instead of from the much which we do not, but merely imagine or believe upon trust, we are forced to the conclusion that it is these same eternal Elements, these same *innumerable particles of substance*, these same numberless *first causes* which, collectively taken, do constitute all the *causes* there really are; consequently that they are the GREAT FIRST CAUSE of all other *causes and their effects;* and hence that it is *these* which, by their own spontaneous and incessant workings, co-workings, and antagonist workings, have thus legitimately arranged, transformed, aggregated, and cemented themselves into all and singular the numberless different created forms and things, high and low, great and small, that do to-day exist.

As these undying elementary particles are always active in their nature, and hence have forever been operating and at work with all their feeble single and powerful combined might, so we have no option, but are compelled to think that the complex phenomenon, known as creation, is ever steadily going on by means of their unceasing labors. We say, when reasoning from the little we know, instead of from the much that we do not, etc., we are thus led to conclude, because we are not unmindful that the same organs which enable men to reason from the known to the unknown do also enable them to reason from the merely assumed-to-be-known, but actually unknown, to still deeper unknown, when at strange conclusions they not unfrequently arrive.—If men reason logically from premises which are false, they must inevitably arrive at false conclusions, but if illogically therefrom, then it is barely possible they may blunder upon such as are correct.

Again; as these undying elementary particles are ever in possession of all their different inherent properties and powers, and as they are eternally exerting their full strength, as well when in aggregation joined as when they are not, so it would seem to follow that in those immense aggregations of them, called worlds, there must ever be bound together an immense amount of the attracting force. And as this force is eternally active part and parcel of the elements themselves, and hence of the different orbs which they compose, so it would seem to follow that the different worlds ever do and forever must attract each other at immense distances, since they are themselves so very large, and hence their attracting force so very great and strong. Indeed, the more we reflect upon the subject, the more are we inclined to think it may be by virtue of the constant operation of this giant force in the different spheres legitimately residing, that the different planets are not only held in their respective places, and made to wheel themselves around that larger and more potent orb the Sun, but to revolve upon their axis in the manner which they do.

Our mundane sphere, with her single attendant *luna*, the

same as the mighty Jupiter, with his greater number, ever presents us with a very good miniature likeness of the Solar system; the Earth standing, in relation to her lone secondary, ruling center, and cause of its orbital and axial motion, the same as does old Sol to her. We say, the cause of the Moon's *axial motion*, because such seems to be the existing mutual relation between the Earth and her lone attendant, as ever compels it to present to her the same side, a thing which it could not do, did it not upon its axis turn in reference to the center of the system. In other words, that the Moon is prevented from revolving upon its axis with reference to this mundane sphere, and hence compelled to turn thereupon, with reference to the Sun, just as often as does it make its full progressive circuit around the Earth, by virtue of some influence that is legitimately exerted upon it by the Earth, its ruling center, we must regard as being at least probable. Wherefore, by parity of reason, we are led to think it probable that the Earth and other primaries are made to revolve upon their axis by virtue of some influence that is legitimately exerted upon them by the Sun, their ruling center. And it can hardly be necessary to add that we can see no possible way by which this terrestrial globe could exert any such influence upon the Moon, did not said influence a permanent residence have within the limits of the Earth's mass, by virtue of the nature of its composing elements; or that the Sun could put forth the necessary power to compel the Earth and other primaries around him to wheel, and upon their axis constantly to turn, was not said power one of the attributes of that shining orb; and so an attribute thereof, because, deep in the nature of its composing elements, it has its seat.

The reason why stress is laid upon the fact of the Moon's revolving upon its axis with reference to the Sun, just as often as does it make its full progressive circuit around the Earth, is this: To suppose the Sun or any other *power*, except this mundane sphere, to stand parent cause of the Moon's thus turning upon its axis with reference to the Solar system's center, consequently to its making its revolutions thereupon in the same length of time which it takes it to travel around the Earth, and hence to stand cause to compelling it, with reference to the Earth, not to have any axial motion at all, is to suppose the happening of a coincidence more remarkable than any we ever chanced to meet with upon historic record.—

With all the light and knowledge that are now in the world, whenever an act, whether transitory, like the dropping of an apple from its parent tree, or continuous, like the revolution of the Earth upon its axis, cannot be accounted for upon any known principle, nor by any hypothesis which does not, upon its face, just as much call for the assistance of a second hypothesis to account for the first one, as does the act under consideration for the aid of said first, and thus on; it may safely be taken for granted, as we think, that the cause of the act, not in whole, but in an essential part, legitimately resides within the agent or thing which performs the action.

CHAPTER XIII.

GOD, HIS COMPOSITION, AND CHARACTER.

As we cannot help feeling that the real difference of opinion which at bottom exists between the more observing and thinking portion of believers in the old Mosaic theory of God, creation, and his government thereof, and our humble self, is far less wide than at first glance would seem to appear, so we propose very briefly to state, not only our views upon those different points, but also what we incline to think are the inner views of this class of persons thereupon; to the end that the supposed difference, and hence the real one, if such supposed difference be correct, may the more readily be seen, and the merits of our respective opinions the more correctly judged. In the first place we will give a synopsis of what we are inclined to think are the views of this class of persons, as deep down within them they do to-day exist.

For sundry reasons, then, we are led to think they inwardly believe that spirit substance, or that kind of substance which is so very ethereal that it cannot reveal its existence directly to any human sense, is self-existent, and hence eternal; and that material substance, or that kind of substance of which the human senses are capable of taking direct cognizance, is not self-existent, consequently not eternal, and hence would never have been in existence, had it not by some POWER that is eternal been created, or brought into being out of naught. Also that they inwardly believe it was this same self-existent class of elements, called spirit substance, which performed the act of creating, or bringing into being out of naught, all that wide class of elements, known as material substance, of every name and kind that anywhere exists. Also that they believe it was this same infinitude of self-existent spirit substance, (anciently transformed by a bold figure of speech into an infinitely great, wise, and powerful Being, called God,) which performed the act of aggregating, arranging, and fashioning such created class of elements, called material substance, into all the numerous worlds and different created forms and things, inanimate and animated, that are. Yea, and that they further believe in their very inmost souls, that it is this same infinitude of self-existent spirit substance,—thus by figure of speech personified and called God,—which reigns in and rules over all created forms and things, high and low, great and small, in just such a manner as it needs must, because ever in accordance with the nature of its own undying properties and powers. Such, in brief, is the substance of the views which we incline to think are to-day entertained by this class of persons, at very bottom. We will now proceed to state, but in a somewhat argumentative form, our feeble opinion upon those same points.

As seems to us, then, the proofs are quite as numerous and strong that material substance is unchangeable in its nature and indestructible in its elements, hence self-existent and eternal, as they are that spiritual substance is. Consequently we can no more conclude that *spirit substance* created, or brought into being out of naught, material substance, than can we that *material substance* did spiritual; and especially can we not since both classes, in so far as it is possible to determine by the lights of reason, observation, and experience, do seem to be standing upon the same eternal basis. In other words, so far from being able to think that either one of said classes of elements stands parent cause to the pushing into existence of the other, and hence reigns in and rules over that other, we are forced to conclude they are both, and both alike, self-existent and eternal. Consequently that all created forms and things, high and low, great and small, inanimate animated, are but legitimate results of their continuous conjoint workings. Consequently that not in six days or years or decades of centuries were the worlds created, but that, for myriads of years, the process of their creation has been going on, and is still progressing. And consequently that it is by virtue of the conjoint presence and operation of the different undying properties and powers inherently residing in said two classes of elements, known as material and immaterial substance, that all created forms and things are ruled and governed. Such, in brief, being the substance of the views by us entertained upon those several points, it follows, as a matter of course, that it is neither material nor immaterial substance, but both combined in all their immensity, which constitute the great eternal WHOLE which it is our habit to personify, and call by the different appellations, Nature, God, great Nature, Nature's God, Elements All, etc., and to whose undying properties and powers, otherwise eternal laws, otherwise supreme decrees, no matter by which name designated, we desire to bow in humble submission. Great, glorious, and mighty, then, as legitimately is the infinitude of spirit substance which they are wont to personify, endow with human semblance, invest with such attributes as they themselves prefer, call by the name of God, and bow down before and worship, by unavoidable consequence, the God we adore is inconceivably greater, more glorious, and potent; since *he*, *she*, or *it* (no matter by which pronoun represented as the elements by each denoted are forever resident therein) embraces, not only all and singular the immense amount of elements of which their said spirit-substance God is composed, but all the inconceivably vast amount of material substance in every form and condition besides.

In all this, of course, we may be wrong; but, whether so or not, it will readily be seen that we not only look upon the Sum of all Substance, material, immaterial, and mixed, as constituting and being the eternal God, but that we regard creation, or more properly all currently existing created forms and things, high and low, great and small, inanimate and animated, man included, as being just as much and just as legitimately part and parcel of the great Creator, as were their different composing elements when in primary form existing.

Or thus: In a great dualistic Parent, or an eternal Father-and-Mother God, so to speak, in the shape of the eternal Elements All, material, immaterial, and mixed, we firmly believe; also in a constantly changing, and hence, upon the whole, ever advancing God in the shape of the numberless forms and things, high and low, great and small, inanimate and animated, that are ever currently being pushed into created existence by such elemental Father-and-Mother God, not out of nothing, but out of certain fitting portions of his and her own vast Parent Self; but in the existence of an eternal personal God, or a plurality of eternal Gods all of the same sex, either personal or not, or in a mere Ghost God, whether Holy or unholy, we have no sort of faith. And we will here add, notwithstanding it would hardly seem to be necessary, that, as we understand the matter, the uncreated Father-and-Mother God or the eternal Elements, and what is known as created Nature or the vast infinitude of forms, high and low, great and small, which, by the action of such eternal Elements, are thereof and thereout being currently created, destroyed, re-created, and thus forever on in some form other in existence kept, are, in all essential respects, one and the same God, the difference being merely a thing of form and not of actual substance. Or, in still plainer terms, God we regard as being neither more nor less than the Sum of uncreated Elements and created things of them composed; and hence that suns, planets, vegetables, animals, etc., etc., are, each and all, composing fractions, not only of that grand Whole which Creation doth constitute and is, but also of that Power by whose action such grand Whole was into created existence pushed and ruled.—And such, we doubt not, is the Creator God that will be believed in and reverenced by coming generations of men;—a Deity possessed of both a *body* and a *spirit*, and not one that is all spirit and no body.

NOTE.—We have spoken of God the Creator as being our Mother as well as Father, for the reason that we believe we have a great common Mother as well as a great common Father. In other words, we have so spoken because, as we see it, the male or father principle and the female or mother principle do both, and both alike, have their seat in the nature of the eternal Elements of which organic creation, inanimate and animated, is ever currently composed. Without any tender mother, gentle nurse, or other loving female friend to watch over and care for poor Adam and Eve, what wonder that they should have gone sadly astray and tasted all manner of evil fruit? Not without the cheering presence and supporting aid of a Mother God could either plants or animals, high or low, ever have been pushed into being or multiplied in existence upon the face of the Earth by any amount of male Gods, no matter how great the number. Or, at least, such has come to be our religious as well as philosophic faith.

When we say that for sundry reasons we are led to think the aforesaid class of persons do inwardly believe as herein-before stated, we would not be understood as doubting the sincerity of their motives in claiming to believe otherwise, or as calling in question the benevolence of their designs in unremittingly endeavoring to inculcate and keep alive the idea of the existence of an actual personal Creator, and Governor of the universe. No, these inconsistencies and all others of a like character, we regard as being the legitimate fruits of their false early education; and hence things for which they are to be pitied and not blamed. But, then, we would be understood as confessing our inability to persuade ourself into the belief that, at very bottom they do think that any other inconceivably great, wise, and powerful Spirit Being created the worlds, and their movements in the fields of space doth regulate and govern, than is the *sum of all spirit substance*, thus personified. Not only this, but widely different as from early educational influences and the force of habit have come to be the settled forms of expression of this class of persons, when speaking of those things, we are not clear they are not in reality of the opinion, the same as are we, that spirit substance, notwithstanding by ancient usage personified and called by a great name, is, *per se*, just as devoid of thought, feeling, and intelligence, in the common acceptation of those terms, as are the material elements of which our physical eyes are composed, in their primary form, of ability to see. In other words, it seems to us, and we are by no means sure it does not seem much the same to them, that the material elements of which our physical eyes are composed, are, *per se*, just as devoid of ability to see, as are those which compose our ears or noses; and that the sensation called sight, is the legitimate result of certain functional acts performed by said material elements, when in proper organic form and consistency they are aggregated and arranged. It also seems to us, and possibly so to them, that said non-seeing, material elements, of which the eye is composed, would never be able to perform that peculiar kind of function which creates within us the sensation called sight, but for the supporting aid and stimulating presence of said material element's coeternal conjoint element, *immaterial substance.* It furthermore seems to us, and possibly so to them, that said *immaterial substance*, in the absence of the properly organized *material elements*, that is, in the absence of the physical eye, is not only just as devoid of sight, but just as incapable of performing the function which speaks into existence within us the act of seeing, as would be and is such *physical eye*, in said *immaterial substance's* absence. And of all thought, feeling, passion, and emotion which anywhere exists, and the organs, each and all, which speak these things into existence within the human tabernacle, the same. Or thus: Because, anciently, and when language was much less copious and perfect than now, men were in the habit of personifying almost every conceivable object, substance, and thing, and of dressing the same out in just such colors, and giving thereunto just such capacities and powers as fancy might suggest; and because, by a most bold figure of speech, some ancient somebody chanced to personify the class of elements, known as immaterial or spirit substance, and invest the same with all and singular the faculties and powers possessed by man, only in an infinitely superior degree; we cannot persuade ourself that the more sober, intelligent, and deeply reflecting portion of either Jews or Christians continue to believe, at very bottom, that said infinitely vast and widely distributed class of elements is a veritable, living, breathing, personal Being, possessing and possessed of an infinitely large, invisible head, body, and limbs to correspond; and hence of actual ability to see, hear, think, talk, etc. Indeed, we could almost as soon be persuaded that they inwardly continue to believe ~~that~~ old Father Time to be a veritable wretch of a personal being, going up and down in the Earth relentlessly swinging his ponderous scythe, *cutting down all both great and small*, just because duration, or lapse of years, is thus personified and pictured out in the olden hornbooks. But allowing, what must be conceded to be possible, that, at very bottom, they still continue thus to think and believe, then all we have to say is, that we feel quite certain they never would have arrived at any such anti-common sense conclusion, had it not anciently chanced to be so thought, hence written down, hence in the Bible placed, and hence most authoritatively impressed upon their brains in childhood, and all along, as a specially God-revealed verity. Be these things, however, as they may, we cannot doubt the two great, coeternal conjoint elements, *material and immaterial substance*, are so inseparably connected that, was either the one or the other to be struck from the roll of existence, not only would their great, *spirit-substance God*, but our much greater ONE, eternally be dead. In other words, was *spirit-substance* to be annihilated, then would material substance be dead for want of anything to unite with it and act upon it; and was *material substance* to be annihilated, then would spirit substance be dead for want of anything for it to unite itself with and to act upon; and hence, in either event, not only would their great, fractional, spirit-substance God be dead, that is, be powerless to produce any appreciable or living results, but our vastly greater WHOLE ONE, of the Sum of both classes of Elements composed. Not a complete and efficient *whole* is either sexual principle or class of elements alone, no matter how wide-spread or abundant the same may be.

We say, their great, fractional, spirit-substance God would be dead, etc., was material substance to be annihilated, because, notwithstanding it is conceded to be a thing that is possible, still we are most unwilling to think this class of men guilty of adoring a mere *spirit-nothing God*, or a God that is *wholly imaginary*. Or thus: If the Spirit God, in whom they believe and put their trust, is not composed of the *sum of all spirit-substance*, as by us assumed to be by them believed, or at least of some portion of such substance, then, by unavoidable consequence, he is not and cannot be composed of anything at all; consequently he must be and is a mere *spirit-nothing God*, or a Being that is made up entirely of *imaginary spirit-substance*, and not of such substance as has any existence in the broad realm of facts; and hence he must be and is *wholly an imaginary God*. We appeal, from the very nature of things, Must not this be so?

And now, for the purpose of enabling us to present our views upon certain points embraced within the scope of the foregoing subject in the clearest possible light, permit us to descend a little in the scale, and avail ourself of the beautifully illustrative and yet familiar example by our own beloved country, its government, etc., presented.

What, then, is that august Being, or great and mighty Power upon the Earth, which is known and designated by the name of Uncle Sam?—Manifestly enough, His Supreme, Republican Highness, Uncle Sam, is neither more nor less than the *sum* of the American people. Feeble, then, as is the individual power of the most potent American citizen, the *sum* of the power by the American people possessed doth legitimately constitute the *sum* of Uncle Sam's power; his residence being nowhere in particular because everywhere in general, from the broad Atlantic on the East to the Pacific on the West, and from the Gulf of Mexico on the South to the British possessions upon the North. All this is so plain that doubtless every American citizen understands, that each separate division of men called a State, doth legitimately constitute an important fraction of the United States, and hence that every individual citizen of every State, in all this vast Republic, is legitimately part and parcel of this great nation; is legitimately a component part of that *august being or great something*, known as Uncle Sam.

Happily, then, it is not necessary to enter into any labored argument to prove that Uncle Sam, whose existence is acknowledged the world over, and whose influence is felt in every sea and every land, is not, after all, a real individual or personal Being, possessing and possessed of a distinct corporeal body of colossal size, with a single head and duplicate limbs to correspond, (as to mere babes in knowledge upon such matters his great name and immense power would seem to indicate,) or that he is not a spirit Being, covering the major portion of all North America with his invisible personal presence, after the manner in which it is by many supposed that God doth fill and cover the entire universe. And since it is clear that His Supreme, Republican Highness, Uncle Sam, is not in reality a personal entity of colossal size, nor yet a spirit Being without body, form, or parts, but the *sum* of the American people; it must needs be reasonably plain that he has, for his composing elements, some forty millions of living, breathing, human beings, scattered over some three millions of square miles of territory, each possessing his own peculiar views, holding his own individual opinions, and managing his own private, personal affairs as to him seems best; but, for national purposes, firmly joined together upon much the same principle that are the different composing elements of the globe we inhabit; namely, by the spontaneous action of the joint and several natures existing in the different heads and hands of said composing elements, the American people. Hence, whenever any individual or set of individuals, anywhere within the geographical limits of this majestic Union of which they are a part, take upon themselves the responsibility of departing too widely from the general line of march which is spontaneously pursued by the majority, and duly chalked upon the statute book as being the sovereign will and pleasure of Uncle Sam by which all are to be guided, soon doth the appropriate, contiguous, superior fraction of the great *whole* in the form of District Court or other appropriate tribunal, aided by its ministerial corps, put forth the necessary power to bow them into order.

Just so, as seems to us, whenever a heavenly body, primary, secondary, or cometary, anywhere within the bounds of the universe, comes to be deviating too widely from the track prescribed by the general law of gravitation which pervades the whole, soon doth the appropriate, contiguous superior fraction in the form of circling planet or central Sun exert the necessary force to arrest the wanderer, and bring it back to place. And not only this, but as the government of the American States is not only a government of and by the people who constitute the nation, but a government which was created, put in operation, and kept in motion by the American people themselves; so this majestic Union is both a *self-created and a self-governing thing*. In other words, instead of this majestic Union being created or brought into existence, all at once and full-sized, out of nothing, by some pre-existent and hence extraneous Uncle Sam, who was greater and more potent than is its own vast and complicated *self*, its creation, from the very beginning until now, has been the result of the ceaseless joint and several workings, co-workings, and antagonist workings legitimately consequent upon the inherent nature of its different composing elements, the different individuals who compose the nation; the same in principle as was the Solar system, in our judgment, not created or brought into being, all at once and full-sized, out of nothing, by some extraneous Being or Power, greater and more potent than is its own vast *complex self*, but by natural process—extending back into the tide of old eternity beyond all human computation —legitimately consequent upon the eternal workings, co-workings, and antagonist workings of its different composing elements, the different kinds of Elementary Substance.

The more active, influential, and ambitious men in each of the thirteen olden, feeble, American Colonies, had no option in the matter, but were compelled by the nature that was in them and the force of circumstances by which they were surrounded, not only to hunger and thirst after becoming and being at the head of an American political organization, enjoying independence and wielding national sovereignity, but to feel their individual State weakness, and hence to fear the interference and oppression of other and more powerful States or political combinations of men. Wherefore, by virtue of these their own strong feelings and desires, aided by the force of surrounding circumstances, they were spontaneously moved, as by the irresistible force of attraction, to join themselves together into a common Union, offensive and defensive; and thus out of a few, weak, individual States, composed of comparatively a small number of feeble, individual men, holding different opinions, possessing different personal interests, and occupying only a fractional part of the eastern portion of the central division of North America, was spoken into being that infant political fabric which to-day stands out, not only in point of geographical size and numerical strength, but of national enterprise and power, the pride of every true American, and the wonder of the world.

And now, by way of concluding these illustrative remarks, we will take the liberty of propounding a few questions for the consideration of such of our readers as may be disposed to reflect thereupon.—1. Is it not the people, and not the soil they occupy, which, in a social, political, and theological point of view, constitute a town, a county, a state, an empire, and finally the world? 2. Admitting James Stokes to be an American citizen and a resident of the town of Hamburg, in the county of Livingston, and state of Michigan, Does it not follow, as a matter of course, that he is a composing fraction or component of said town, hence of said county, hence of said State, and hence of the United States of America? 3. And as such fraction of said town, hence of said county, hence of said State and hence of the United States, Does he not legitimately possess and carry about with him, in his own proper person wheresoever he goes, a corresponding fraction of the attributes and power of this American nation, which by mere figure of speech is personified and called Uncle Sam? 4. And hence is he not, by unavoidable consequence, a component part of the God of civil rule among men? 5. And wherefore is he not, by unavoidable consequence, a component part, not only of the God of civil rule among men, but of the world of human life; and not only of the world of human life, but of this old Earth from which his composing elements were taken, upon whose surface he resides as tenant, and into whose bosom he must soon return? 6. Infinitesimally small as comparatively he is, nevertheless, allowing the foregoing interrogatories to be answered in the affirmative, does it not, upon the whole, look rather reasonable, that he is also a component part of the universe itself, and hence of the universal God?

7. And should it be concluded that he must needs be and is a composing fraction, and hence a component part, of the universal God; then how is it possible to escape the further conclusion, that he legitimately possesses within himself, and so carries about with him wheresoever he goes, a corresponding fraction of the attributes and power of that august Being or grand Whole, of which he is thus a component part? 8. Laying aside the Bible, the Koran, and other kindred writings, Is there any evidence to be be found going to prove the existence of any kind, character, or quality of Supreme Eeing, Essence, or Power, great or small, material or immaterial, present or remote, except the one vast complex THING, the Universe itself? [a]

Because it is eminently proper for us, the people of the United States, in a suitable manner and at the proper times and places, to petition the different branches, departments, and officers of this vast government for such things as we ardently desire, and as it is within the province of the particular branch, department, or officer to grant, it does not follow that it would be wisdom in us to meet together every week, in our respective localities, and, upon our bended knees, essay to ask Uncle Sam, the great Personification of the entire governmental power of the nation, for those same things or any other. Indeed, would it not look a little shallow to see a man who is desirous of having the village, of which he is an active and influential resident, incorporated into a city, for example, go down upon his knees at home, or anywhere else, and essay to pour out his wishes to the great Personification of the American government, in substance as follows: O great, glorious, and forever blessed Uncle Sam! Be pleased to look down upon thy unworthy supplicant with favor, and grant, I beseech thee, unto our thriving village of H., a city charter? We appeal, Would it not? And yet in point of principle, and hence in point of fact, Wherein does it differ from offering up petitions, in the

a By the term Universe is here meant not only our Solar system, with all its different kinds and character of tenants, but every other similar system; and not only every such other system and its tenants, but every element in both primary and proximate form, in all that vast expanse or sea of elements called space.

same manner and form, unto God, the great Personification of the entire governmental power of the Universe, asking him to do things which belong not to His Supreme Highness to perform, and very possibly not to any of his different higher branches or more numerous inferior departments.

And finally, we appeal, Do not large numbers of men betray, at this present moment, quite as strong symptoms of being demented upon the subject of religion, by their systematically arranged practice of talking, praying, and singing to a merely imaginary personal God, as did the children of Israel, in the days of Moses, by their unquenchable desire to worship images, and bow themselves down before idols of their own silly fashioning?

Whether the ancient Romans were indebted to St. Paul for their favorite maxim, *Vox populi, vox dei*, or whether that great Apostle, from said adage, derived the notion that the God of civil rule and the *people* are one and the same Personage, it is needless to inquire, since certain it is that, in his celebrated Epistle to the saints at Rome, he inculcates the same sentiment, the language only being different. Let us compare and see.—"The people's voice is God's voice," says the Roman proverb.—"The powers that be, are ordained of God," saith Paul.—Rom., 13. 1. By the phrase, *The powers that be*, that Paul meant the civil authority possessed and exercised by the different officers of government is perfectly manifest; and yet no more so than it is that, by the phrase, *Are ordained of God*, he meant that the authority, with which the different officers of government are clothed, is ordained upon them, not by the heavens above, but by the God of civil rule among men; namely, by the *people* themselves. Wherefore, we feel warranted in saying that the ablest man among all the New Testament writers believed and, by fair implication, publicly taught and enforced the idea, that civil rulers, of every name and grade, derive their authority to exercise dominion over the governed, from the God known as the Will of the People; it not at all mattering whether that omnipotent will be positively proclaimed through the ballot-box, as is the practice in republics, or only tacitly expressed by their continued sufferance, as is the usage in monarchies.—Such is the New Testament authority upon this point, and we doubt not its correctness.—Nor can it be doubted, as we think, by any candid and reflecting man, that had that eminent Apostle chanced to have taken a few more such strides in the same direction, then, in so far at least as the Christian world is concerned, the mystery with which the character of God and his government had previously been veiled by Moses and others would have been mostly removed.

And now just three brief compound questions:—Is God really a personal Being; or is he only so by mere figure of speech?—Which? Is the Devil really a personal Being; or is he only so by mere figure of speech?—Which? Is Uncle Sam really a personal Being; or is he only so by mere figure of speech?—Which? Surely these are all questions which address themselves not to the imagination, but to our sober intelligence as men.

CHAPTER XIV.

GOD, HIS COMPOSITION, AND CHARACTER—*Continued.*

As from the united testimony of observation, experience, and reflection, we are compelled to regard some things as being certain, as we feel sure that not more than one of two or twenty different and conflicting views of the same subject can possibly be correct, and as our innate love of inquiry seems to be quite as deep-rooted and strong, as is the tendency in us to believe without evidence, (and the mere opinions of men, whether ancient or modern, and however dogmatically put forth, we can never regard as being either argument or evidence a disputed fact to prove,) so we are unable to believe any hypothesis, theory, or thing which to us doth seem incompatible with such facts and principles as we have become satisfied must be and are eternal verities.

With this brief explanation, we will at once proceed to state that, after long years of anxious thought upon the subject, we have at last become convinced by every form of inquiry and mode of reasoning known to us, that there must be and is *something* which is uncreated, and hence eternal; also that it must be and is this uncreated and eternal Something, be it whatsoever it may, which Parent Cause doth stand to all created forms and things, high and low, great and small, inanimate and animated, that are; also that not out of nothing nor all at once nor full-sized was existing creation ever spoken into being, but that the act or process whose result is creation is a work which is both constant and gradual; and hence a work which not only had its beginning away back in the tide of old eternity far beyond all human computation, but one which is still quite as vigorously being carried on as ever. Thus we have at last arrived at what to us doth seem to be a solid foundation upon which to stand, as well as a sort of touchstone by which to test the quality and determine the character, not only of the old Mosaic theory of God and creation, but of the numerous subordinate doctrines and parts of doctrines which have incidentally grown thereout.

Adopting the above, then, as our foundation and starting point, and we have no option, but are compelled to arrive at the following prime conclusions :—1. That it is Elementary Substance, in all its different forms and vast extent, which is that great, uncreated, and eternal something. 2. That it is the different elementary particles in the vast body of Elementary Substance contained, which, by gradual process legitimately consequent upon their undying natures and incessant workings, have aggregated, arranged, and cemented themselves into all the different worlds and systems of worlds, which now do or ever did exist; and not only into all these, but into all the infinite variety of inanimate furniture and animated tenants of every name and kind, that now have or ever had a place upon any of their surfaces. 3. That all this vast work of creation has been brought about legitimately, because all made to take place and be by the incessant action of the different particles of elementary substance, which, obedient to the law of their respective natures, have forever been unceasingly at work and doing the very things which they were compelled to do by virtue of their different, undying properties and powers. 4. That Elementary Substance is not only ITSELF the great, uncreated, and eternal Something, which out of certain fitting portions of its own vast Self has thus produced into being all created forms and things that are, but that, legitimately consequent upon its own undying properties and powers, it is the very Power which all creation moves and rules.

Such being the prime conclusions at which we are compelled to arrive from premises in which, as said, we have the utmost confidence, it follows, as a matter of course, that it must be impossible for us to believe or think we believe in any hypothesis, theory, or doctrine, however ancient its origin or however widely it may be received, which is irreconcilably at variance therewith. Moreover, from these said conclusions as data, we are irresistibly led to infer still further, that the vast infinitude of uncreated Elements, material and immaterial, and of created things which are of them composed, do legitimately constitute all the God there really is; and hence that the word God, in its very broadest literal sense, is but another name for Nature, or the Sum of all Elements and things that are, no matter in what form existing. And not only this, but that wherever, in all that vast expanse called space, there doth exist any kind or character of substance, material or immaterial, visible or invisible, simple or compound, in created form or in primary condition, there also doth legitimately reside a composing fraction of said great Something's mighty power and governmental rule. And not only both these, but that wherever substance of every name and kind and form doth end, there also doth that same great and eternal Something end, call it God, call it Nature, or by whatever name we may; the utmost limit of all Substance being said great Something's full bound; the sum of the numerous and different acts and operations which, in obedience to its undying nature, Substance All is compelled to perform, the total of said great Something's creative, governing, and destroying power.

Strange as it may seem, often as the word God is used in the Old Testament, it is nowhere defined therein; except that Moses tells the children of Israel in Deuteronomy 4th, when cautioning them against the sin of idolatry, that *the Lord their God is a consuming fire;* he having reference to *the Lord God whom they stood before in Horeb, when the mountain burned with fire unto the midst of heaven, with darkness, clouds, and thick darkness, and that spake to them out of the midst of the fire.* Such being the case, it can never be determined, with any degree of certainty, what idea the writers of that book intended to convey by the use of that high-sounding term; and hence it can never be positively known whether all who contributed to that volume meant the same thing when they made use thereof, be that thing whatsoever it may, or whether each, by its use, meant something more or less different from what was intended by every other. From a careful perusal of its pages, however, we are led to think, not only that no two of the writers meant precisely the same thing by its use, but that not a single one of the whole number had any very definite idea himself of the thing or things, upon which he was so liberally bestowing that appellation.

Long years thereafter, however, and when the New Testament was written, it seems to have been somewhat different, as he is therein declared to be *a Spirit;* to be *the Word;* to be *light;* to be *love.* In addition to this, and in imitation of Moses, Paul tells the Hebrews that "Our God is a consuming fire." Wherefore, in so far as this Testament is concerned, we are not left wholly to conjecture as to what its writers understood that word to mean, but are bound to infer and believe that, by its use, they meant some one or other of the aforesaid things, and perhaps all of them.

And finally, to come down to our own time, Mr. Webster defines God to be "The Supreme Being; to be Jehovah; to be the eternal and infinite Spirit, to be the Creator, and the Sovereign of the Universe." In other words, that great lexicographer has failed in his attempt at defining the word God; and failed for the reason that every appellation or phrase by him used in defining it is just as much involved in darkness and doubt, as is the one which is thereby sought to be explained.—To say that God is the Supreme Being; is Jehovah; and that Jehovah is the Supreme Being; is the eternal and infinite Spirit, and thus on, does not shed any light upon the composition, character, extent, or whereabouts of God, and hence is, in truth and in fact, just no definition at all. Of course, our definition of God may be defective,—may be wholly wrong; but, whether so or not, it is at least comprehensible; and hence it can be both understandingly attacked and understandingly defended.

Again, that Something is uncreated, and hence eternal,

doubtless every intelligent and sound-minded man will admit; also that it is this same Something, be it what it may, which PARENT-CAUSE doth stand to all created forms and things that are. Thus far, then, all may be regarded as one harmonious faith; and hence right here it is in the different answers given to the directly out-growing question, What is that uncreated and eternal Something which thus PARENT CAUSE doth stand to all created forms and things? that divergence begins. As already suggested, simply to say that it is God or that it is Nature does not shed any particular light upon the subject, consequently doth not satisfactorily answer the question, and hence amounts to little more than saying nothing.

How God came to be, or, in plain unfigurative language, how the ETERNAL ELEMENTS, one and all, material and immaterial, came to be in existence, and how of all their different undying properties and powers possessed, as a matter of course, can never be known or explained; but the fact that they are here, and in full possession of certain undying properties and powers which are forever active and at work, producing into existence results that are unto themselves legitimately correspondent, being perfectly obvious, it becomes the province of Observation, with her quick, clear eye, to note the variant results that are taking place around her, and of sober Reason to trace those results backward to their parent source, if she can.

Aside from the teachings of feeble instinct, narrow intention, spirit communications, so-called, and what is assumed to be divine revelation, Does not human knowledge consist in the number and amount of facts which have been discovered and brought to light by successive generations of men? And those same things being still left aside, Is there any way by which original facts can be derived to men, except through the three different channels, human observation, human experience, and human reason? Of course, after a fact is discovered by observation, learned by experience, or brought to light by process of reason from some other previously known fact as *datum*, it can then be transferred to others indefinitely on by mere words, but not before. Assuming these questions to be answered—the former in the affirmative, and the latter in the negative—we will next inquire, What do the three great teachers, Human observation, Human experience, and Human reason, say in reference to the great foundation question with which we started?

Do they not all unite in saying that not in a day, a week, or an age, was yon stately pine, for example, ushered into existence in its present form? Do they not all declare that it is not made of nothing, but of something, and not only of something, but of a large amount of appropriate somethings? Do they not all attest that was said ancient tree to be riven into splinters by lightning, kiln-dried, burnt to ashes, and these wide-scattered by the winds of heaven o'er field and forest, slope and plain, still not a single particle of its composing elements would be destroyed, or the nature of an atom, at very bottom, changed? In short, do they not all bear testimony that, in so far as they have ever been able to see and determine, it is of ELEMENTARY SUBSTANCE, and of nothing else, that all created forms and things are composed; and consequently that it is the form only of created things, whether high or whether low, whether great or whether small, and whether more durable or whether less durable, which is perishable, and not their composing elements? Perishable are all created forms and things; imperishable as the eternal God, their every composing element. Assuming all the last group of questions to be answered affirmatively, we will now submit the further and much broader one, How comes it to pass that, in the face of all the vast array of testimony which is offered by the three great and unimpeachable witnesses, Human observation, Human experience, and Human reason, the mass of enlightened human kind are, to-day, honestly of the opinion, that ELEMENTARY SUBSTANCE is not indestructible, hence not uncreated and eternal; and hence is not the THING which, by virtue of its own vast presence, inherent nature, and incessant workings, PARENT CAUSE doth stand to all created forms and things that are; and especially to all such created forms and things as are seen and known to be thereof wholly composed?—As seems to us, it is not because in the mass of the present generation of enlightened men there is a lack of brains, but because it chanced to enter into the imagination of certain of the ancient Fathers that, only two or three thousand years before they were born, ELEMENTARY SUBSTANCE, with all its different properties and powers, was spoken into existence all at once, out of nothing, in the complex form of full-grown worlds, and their respective furniture; and because, from that day down to the present hour, this same ancient, imaginary fact, as a specially God-revealed verity, has been so exclusively taught to every successive generation of children and youth, and so deeply impressed upon their young and tender brains, that it is almost impossible for any amount of after-observation, after-experience, and after-exercise of the reasoning powers to erase it therefrom.

But again, so closely allied and interwoven are cause and effect, everywhere; so perfect are the different adaptations and relations which, between effects and their parent causes, do everywhere exist; so dependent are the grades of things above upon those below by whose aid they have been pushed onward and upward, step by step, into their present, advanced state of being; and so slowly, silently, and systematically do all the different classes and varieties of things spring up, grow, and multiply around us, that it is no great wonder the ancient, semi-enlightened leaders of mankind inferred, that all this vast round of dependent harmonies must have been planned and brought into active existence by some pre-existent Being, of infinite wisdom, power, and skill possessed. And when it is considered that this same ancient idea has been carefully taught and religiously impressed upon the plastic brains of every succeeding generation of children by the preceding generation of parents and teachers, it not only ceases to be a matter of surprise that it has so long and generally prevailed, but becomes, instead, a marvel how men ever came so far to burst the fetters thus early imposed by education, strengthened by the sanctions of religion, and riveted by prejudice, as to be able to penetrate the darkness which has thus been brought to surround the naturally obscure subject of creation, etc., to the extent which they have. Thanks, however, to the law of progression, and hence to growing Reason, it has at last come to be seen by many of the more observing and thoughtful of the race, that the olden hypothetic answer by tyro Reason given to the ancient feeble inquiry, How came the world to be, and particularly the Earth, and all things thereupon? does not in the least clear up the original mystery, but simply diverts attention therefrom by merging it in another and a greater. In other words, Reason is, to-day, just as anxious to inquire and be informed who' it was, where his dwelling place, and what the composing elements of that supereternal and super omnipotent BEING that made this Spirit God of the ancients, and endowed him with the necessary wisdom, power, and skill to make out of nothing, all the different, substantial worlds, and systems of worlds which float in space, as was she, in her olden, feeble, and comparatively much less inquisitive estate, to know who made the Earth and Sun and Moon and man and beast; since she can no more comprehend, in her present superior state of development, how a greater and more potent Being or THING can rationally be supposed to be uncreated and eternal, than can she how a lesser and a feebler may;—can no more understand how a single, all-space-filling, Spirit God could self-exist, than can she how innumerable particles of elementary substance might. Indeed, she cannot quite as well see how such an unsubstantial Being could ever have made so many great and permanent realities out of stark naught, as she can; how ELEMENTARY SUBSTANCE, by virtue of its own undying properties and powers, might have managed to bring together certain fitting portions of its own vast SELF, and fashion them into that spherical body called the Earth, and which both observation and experience attest is made up of just such elements, and of nothing else.

Under such circumstances, what is to be done?—As seems to us just this: We must abandon the pursuit of light upon this subject, the same as upon every other, by plunging into deeper and still deeper darkness, and patiently wait and toil on after knowledge upon the giant subject of creation, the same as do we upon others, in the direction pointed out by the numberless veritable facts that are gratuitously furnished by this our goodly Mother Earth, and her composing elements.

Or, to present the idea in a little different form, impossible as it no doubt is for Reason in her present state of development satisfactorily to trace great Nature's operations backward and downward, step by step, through all created things that are to their composing elements, as in primary form, wide-scattered in the fields called space, originally they were; or to follow said elements from this same point onward and upward through all the different evolutions, forms of union, etc., which their own incessant workings caused them to undergo, perform, pass through, take on, assume, and occupy before they were finally arranged and moving, as to-day we see them, in the form of worlds and systems of worlds; nevertheless the idea, vast as it is, does not present to *her* patient, searching eye that same dark, unfathomable abyss, that does and forever must the theory which declares that not the things we see and know are here, nor yet their composing elements, are the great, uncreated, and eternal SOMETHING, but, instead, an invisible, unsubstantial Being, possessing and possessed of such incomprehensible wisdom, power, and skill as enabled him not only to plan, but also to execute, the doubly incomprehensible task of making all these stern realities out of just nothing at all.

As has been elsewhere said, it is not surprising that such of us as do not in the least allow ourselves to reason upon the subject of creation, etc., should continue on till stopped by death honestly *believing* just as in blank, confiding childhood we did, after having swallowed the dose so skillfully dropped into our open mouths by others' hand; and yet it is doubtful about there now being any very great number of really observing, thinking, reasoning men and women among us, who have not at least so far outgrown the impressions made in childhood upon their tender brains, as that, in relation to the old Mosaic theory of creation, they are compelled to entertain doubts quite as numerous and well-defined, as are all their remaining seeds of faith therein.

Who that is not blinded by prejudice cannot see, that as long as shall men continue firmly to believe that an extraneous, Spirit God made the worlds, and all things else out of naught, as long as shall they continue to believe that this same all-wise, all-powerful, and everywhere-present Being doth at all times reign in and rule over all created things that are, according to his sovereign will and pleasure, and as long as shall they continue to believe it to be part and parcel of his said sovereign will and pleasure, so to modify and vary his governmental action as specially to please, prosper, and otherwise upbuild such of his favorite, earthly friends as shall, with prayerful humility and faith, request him so to do, just so long will men continue to inveigh against growing reason as a carnal and unholy thing;—as a thing which is at war with the glory and government of God?—Who? And since it is certain that this olden view of God, creation, and his government, doth so completely embrace and cover the entire ground occupied by his created works, as not to leave exempt a single act or thing, great or small, present or remote, which is not made to take place and be pursuant to his said current, sovereign will and pleasure, instead of pursuant to the operation of fixed laws, deep in the nature of things themselves residing, therefore it cannot be otherwise than that such a belief has a direct tendency to dry up Reason at its very fountain.

What wonder is it then that the men of olden time who were much more exclusively indoctrinated into these views of God, his created works, and the government thereof, than are the tenants of the Earth to-day, should have thought within themselves that Reason was dangerous and infidel in its tendency, consequently that it ought to be restrained and its teachings put down by every available means, not excepting the dungeon and the stake? And especially what wonder, when is taken into consideration the fact that the semi-enlightened leaders of mankind, even in those days of mental darkness, had seen too much of patient, plodding Reason and her workings, not to understand that she never allows herself to jump at conclusions, but always endeavors to compare fact with fact, to the end that, from the ever truthful present, she may be able to read both the future and the past? Reasoning thus themselves whilst they were *her* decrying, they came to the conclusion, and no doubt legitimately, that inasmuch as unbiased Reason can never be brought to see how nothing could ever have been wrought and fashioned into something, but only how something might have been transformed into other and different somethings, therefore it would not do to let her have her own full way; lest, in some of her wanderings in search of facts and first principles, she might chance to go away back to the time when creation was not,—away back to the time when God, and God alone, (whatever that may be,) was all there was in the vast immensity called space; the which, if she should do, they felt quite sure it would be impossible for her, from such data, to draw any other conclusion than that the goodly worlds, and all things thereupon, inanimate and animated, must somehow have grown, been made, or come out of certain fitting portions of this same pre-existent and all-space-filling God; and consequently that they are to-day, each and all, the same as were they at the first, part and parcel of his and her own vast dualistic Parent Self.

Wherefore Reason was expelled from the ancient councils. And wherefore there are multitudes of well-meaning men upon the Earth to-day, who, notwithstanding convinced by their own observation and experience, that it is a thing impossible to make the teachings of sober Reason tally with their preconceived opinions, and thus aid them in their spread, never once suspect it is because their early borrowed faith is wrong; but, instead, unhesitatingly pronounce majestic Reason false, and worthy to be bound. In other words, the Christian world is full of men who see plainly enough the inference which untrammeled Reason would be compelled to draw from the premises, and yet they feel quite sure the inference must be wrong; and thus feel just because they were early taught and brought to believe that not out of fitting portions of his and her own vast, eternal Self did God create and fashion the worlds, and all things therein and upon, but out of blank nothing.

And now, for the purpose of showing as clearly as possible the blighting effects which such a theory of God, creation, and particularly of God's character and government, must have upon reason, and research into things natural, consequently upon the growth and spread of genuine knowledge among men, allow us to descend a little into particulars.

In the first place, then, it must be borne in mind that exercise, within the limits of abuse, is the natural parent of strength. Simply to remember and a thousand times repeat that a thing is thus and so, just because we have been told and taught it was, does not call into action our reasoning faculties, consequently doth not strengthen them. To become strong and ready reasoners, it is not necessary that we should exercise those mental organs which stand parent cause of our strong blind feelings, nor yet the moral and religious group, but it is necessary that we should exercise, and that vigorously, the organs of Causality and Comparison, these being the ones which speak reason into existence within the human tabernacle. Wherefore, to begin to quicken and unfold our reasoning powers, we must begin to inquire and pry into things; and to bring them up to the highest degree of activity and strength unto which they are capable of being brought, we must not only inquire into a few common-place things, but perseveringly endeavor to discover and trace the different causes, one and all, which produce into existence the different phenomena and things, high and low, great and small, by which we are surrounded.

Manifestly enough, then, the theory which makes the worlds to be in existence in the form, of the size, and in the places which they now are, not from any natural cause or chain of causes, but simply for the reason that, a few thousand years ago, it chanced to become and be the sovereign will and pleasure of an extraneous, Spirit God. to speak them into being all at once and full-sized, out of naught, does not furnish any data for Causality and Comparison to work upon, consequently not any for Reason to feed upon; and hence, instead of tending to excite those organs to action and foster them into growth and strength, it, in so far as the great foundation question of creation is concerned, compels them to wither and die for want of anything to do. Or thus: Inasmuch as to each and every inquiry which can be made in reference to the vastly interesting subject called creation, said theory admits of but one arbitrary answer, *It is the sovereign will and pleasure of Almighty God, whose judgments are unsearchable and ways past finding out that it should be so*, therefore, to that same extent, whether so intended or whether not, it deals to human Reason a most deadly blow. And since Reason, the purest, brightest jewel in the head of man, is thus excluded from this most inviting field of facts and principles, let us go a little further and see whether or not, by this same old theory, the different minor walks in nature are likewise barred against her patient researches.

It is not only universally understood that water falls upon the face of the Earth in the form of rain, but that the falling of water in this form is a thing indispensible to the growth of sustenance for both man and beast; and consequently it would seem to be both natural and holy that we should endeavor to acquaint ourselves with the causes, which so oft and opportunely do speak this inestimable blessing into active existence among us. But, then, as this ancient theory does not make water thus to descend from the operation of physical causes, deep in the nature of things themselves residing, consequently not from any cause of which our reasoning organs can take cognizance, but simply because it sometimes chances to become and be the sovereign will and pleasure of Almighty God to shower it down upon us, so here, also, is Reason hedged in by that same old, arbitrary theory. And so the blessed phenomenon of rain falling from heaven to water the thirsty ground and render it productive, just like creation, of which it is a part, furnishes no food for Reason to feed upon, no data for Causality and

Comparison to act upon, and hence, instead of fostering them into manly growth and strength, leaves them to dwindle, starve, and die of hateful inaction.

To prove that our most revered spiritual guides, the writers of the New Testament, understood the Mosaic theory of God, creation, and his government thereof as above interpreted, and consequently that they believed in their inmost souls, that water did not fall in the form of rain, because it was thereunto compelled by the natural operation of physical laws, but because it occasionally chanced to become and be God's sovereign will and pleasure that it should so fall; also that they understood it to be a uniform practice with Almighty God so to modify and vary his governmental action, as to make the same conform to the views and wishes of such of his different, earthly favorites as should, in a special manner, earnestly request him thus to do,—thereby making to a corresponding extent, not only the government of the world, but also of the universe, to depend upon the ever-varying views and wishes of these his said earthly favorites,—we will introduce the testimony of St. James.—This servant of God and of the Lord Jesus Christ, when writing to the twelve tribes that were scattered abroad, gave injunction as follows: "Is any sick among you? let him call for the elders of the church; and let them pray over him, anointing him with oil in the name of the Lord: and the prayer of faith shall save the sick, and the Lord shall raise him up; and if he have committed sins, they shall be forgiven him. Confess your faults one to another, and pray one for another, that ye may be healed. The effectual fervent prayer of a righteous man availeth much."—Whether the above apostolic teachings are in accordance with the workings of natural law or whether they are not it is needless here to inquire, since they are certainly ~~with~~ a medical system and the Bible medical system, and one which may not inaptly be styled The Prayer-Cure.

But to proceed:—For the threefold purpose of convincing the skeptical that there is such a thing as *effectual fervent prayer*, and of riveting the same firmly in the minds of the brotherhood, and of inducing them to have more frequent recourse to this mighty governmental lever, and hence be, to an extent greater than ever before, *themselves the power behind the throne*, which governs in both earth and heaven, this same witness goes on and cites them a precedent exactly in point; and this is it: "Elias was a man subject to like passions as we are, and he prayed earnestly that it might not rain; and it rained not on the Earth by the space of three years and six months. And he prayed again, [prayed that it might rain, meaning,] and the heaven gave rain, and the Earth brought forth her fruit."—James, 5. 14–18.

So now we appeal, according to the plain teachings of the Bible. Is not the fact established beyond a peradventure, that, at the special instance and request of a single human being, the inestimable blessing rain was withheld from the face of the whole Earth for the space of three and one-half, long, dry, and barren years? Also doth not said Bible testimony establish as firmly as can anything ever by Bible authority be established, that it is undying, part and parcel of God's current sovereign will and pleasure, so to modify and vary his govermental action, and hence the government itself, as to make it conform to the ever-varying will and pleasure of such of his earthly friends and favorites, as shall, in a special manner, earnestly request him so to do? And, finally, is not the inference from the language irresistible, that St. James, and all the other so-called divinely inspired, New Testament writers, believed, and would so have sworn upon the witness stand, had they been called upon to do it, that had not the man Elias *prayed again*, there would not any more rain have fallen upon the Earth during all the days of his natural life, and perhaps never; except that some subsequent favorite with the Lord had taken it into his head to neutralize such anti-rain petition, by offering up an equally *earnest* contrary one? We appeal, Is it not?

Save only the great and terrible drowning by the flood, there is not to be found in all the world's history, sacred and profane, any calamity, which in point of extent, duration, and terribleness, will at all compare with this that is said to have been brought upon the Earth, by the earnest prayer of a single human being called Elias. Were all the buildings, public and private, together with one-half the population of every kingdom, state, and country to be swept away by devouring flame, it would be a far less overwhelming calamity thatn a three-and-one-half-year's universal drought. In view of these facts, then, how very careful ought righteous men to be for what they pray! and especially how careful when they pray in *earnest.*

But still more; Does not the foregoing testimony establish the fact, that the different Bible writers honestly supposed it to be a part of God's current sovereign will and pleasure, so to modify and vary his govermental action, and hence the government itself, not only in reference to healing the sick and dispensing rain upon the earth, but in reference to every other branch and department of both earth and universe, as to make the same confoım with the ever-varying desires and needs of such of his earthly favorites as shall, in a special manner, earnestly request him so to do?—Beyond a doubt they felt just as certain that, at Joshua's special instance and request, the *Sun stood still in mid-heaven, and hasted not to go down about a whole day*, as they did that rain was withheld from falling upon the broad face of the flat, motionless Earth for the space of three years and six months, at the request of the man Elias. And thus on of all the numerous and different miraculous performances and things in the Bible recorded, and which they honestly supposed to have been made to take place and be, in manner and form therein set forth; it not at all mattering whether they supposed them to have been specially made to take place for the purpose of punishing some wicked Sodomite, towards whom or whose place of residence the Lord himself was personally angered, or whether directly in consequence of the earnest request of some one or other of his different earthly favorites.—Of course it will be understood as taken for granted, that all who believe the Bible to have been written by divine inspiration of a special character, and hence to be the word of Almighty God from beginning to end, have unfailing confidence in the correctness of the statements made, not only by Moses, and Joshua his immediate successor, but by St. James, and all the other so-called, specially God-inspired writers.

Not until men shall come to see and to feel that between such truths as are real, and such as are merely mental, or moral, there is not unfrequently a heaven-wide difference, and hence that it is possible to be very sincere and positive, and yet altogether wrong, can they be expected to live out in practice the advanced religious principle of refraining from speaking evil of such of their fellows as shall, upon some favorite dogma, chance to differ with them in opinion. And yet, kind reader, may we not indulge the hope that you will at least reflect upon the subjoined questions, before allowing yourself to heap calumny either upon us or our feeble opinions? 1. Do not wrong, narrow, and contracted views upon any subject, no matter what, tend to beget and foster into growth wrong, narrow, and contracted action thereupon? 2. By unavoidable consequence, do not the olden views of God, creation, and his government thereof, tend to beget, and foster into growth within the heads of such as are firm believers therein, a deep feeling, not of the necessity of close observation, careful study, and much thought, in order to store their minds with wisdom, but of strong faith in prayers and tears to God addressed therefor? 3. Is it possible for men to continue firmly to believe indefinitely on, that they are specially instructed in knowledge, guided in thought, assisted in action, and their mouths filled with words of wisdom from on High, without becoming more and more inclined, not only to fall into mental inactivity, but to look down with pity and contempt upon the teachings of human science and the knowledge gained therefrom? 4. And can it be otherwise than that such a belief must have a tendency to render its possessors more and more wise and great in their own conceit, (because wise and great, without study or care, far ahead of the dull teachings of observation, reason, and the natural sciences,) and hence wise and great quite beyond their neighbors who are not thus specially God-favored? 5. Do not these things, when all together taken and fairly considered, sufficiently explain why it was that anciently, and before the war against ignorance, superstition, and credulity was begun, there were so many men who, mistaking their senseless dreams, incoherent reveries, and the spontaneous promptings of their wakeful brains for facts past, facts present, and facts to come, poured directly into their heads by Almighty God as with a tunnel, honestly supposed they were possessed of the spirit of prophecy, consequently declared themselves to be in possession thereof; and hence, instead of being pitied and shunned as unfortunate monomaniacs, were listened to and honored, by a gaping, wondering world, as God-inspired prophets? Aye, and is not here also revealed the cause of there still being so many well-meaning men among us who, filled to overflowing with the fancy that they are God's specially chosen embassadors, presumptuously undertake to lead and dogmatically to teach, when, outside a certain, narrow, antiquated track, they are hardly qualified understandingly to follow?

As we have come to see it, the reason why there are not as many prophets and as great ones, in the world to-day, as there were in Old Testament times, is not because the spirit of prophecy is dead, nor yet because men cannot, now, quite as well and pertinently prophesy as ever they could, but because a more advanced world has ceased to give encouragement to the further production of the article, by ceasing longer to pin its faith upon the sleeves of such as would fain be its producers. Hence, should there ever again spring up as great a demand for prophecy as existed in the days when the Bible was written, soon, again, not only with the prophetic spirit, but with the words of prophecy, would large numbers of men be brimful and slopping over. In other words, wherever prophets, witches, fortune tellers, spiritual mediums, lecturers, school teachers, or any other kind and character of men, come to be in active demand by the taste, character, and condition of the people, there will soon spring up and flow in from abroad the requisite supply.

Before taking leave of this subject, permit us to suggest that, had some humble individual, only half a dozen centuries ago, dared venture to indulge the idea, and hence to have expressed the opinion, that the time would not unlikely come when the diameter of the Sun, the form and size of the Earth, the distances and dimensions of the planets, the character of the fixed stars, etc., would all cease to be hidden mysteries, and taught in the schools of every enlightened land, he would no more have been credited than should we now, were we to give it as ours, that the period will not unlikely arrive when men will quite as well understand the general character and operation of the different laws by which the worlds were gradually produced into being out of pre-existing elementary substance, material and immaterial, as do we to-day the character and action of those, which regulate their movements in the fields of space. And yet we just as confidently expect that such, in all due time, will come to be the case, as do we that men will continue to go on growing in knowledge, and increasing in ability to grasp facts, multiply arts, and augment the number and extent of the natural sciences, precisely the same as have they in the past.

O noble and exalted, but much abused, Reason! What wouldst thou not do for us, could we only be persuaded upon every subject to invoke thy friendly aid, instead of, upon certain fundamental questions of paramount importance, eternally spurning thee from us as an enemy!

CHAPTER XV.

NATURE'S LAWS AND JUDGMENT.

Allowing, as we claim and verily believe to be the fact, that God is not of Nature the Author, nor Nature of God the PARENT CAUSE but that they are both one; and consequently that the differently sounding terms, God, Nature, the Lord, great Nature, etc., are neither more nor less than so many different modes of expression the self-same thing to indicate, it follows that the laws of Nature are the laws of God, and sacred *every one*. Differ upon this point, however, as honestly men may, still it can hardly be doubted, we think, by the most firm believer in a God other than Nature and superior thereto, that the laws of Nature are quite important, potent, and universal.

If the laws of Nature are the laws of God, are God's laws, then their justice cannot be denied without also denying that their Author is just. And if they are not His laws, and hence may or may not be just, then, manifestly enough, has his existence long-since ceased to be a matter of any moment to the human family; since it is wholly pursuant to the operation of natural law that men are begotten, born, live, and die. In short, since there is not a human being anywhere upon the Earth, who has ever seen a single object, heard a single sound, smelled the faintest odor, tasted a solitary morsel, or, by sense of feeling, felt the slightest thing which is not both the creature and the subject of natural law, where is the wisdom and what the benefit of spending so much time in trying to teach, persuade, and scare mankind into the belief that, by such a code, it is not safe to live, and by such an one to die? Since it has never been proven and doubtless never will be that the laws of Nature are not the laws of God, and sacredly binding every one, Why should we be so very anxious to deceive ourselves and others into the pernicious belief that it is possible so to manage, and whip the Devil round the stump, as to commit sin without being obliged correspondingly to suffer?

To this it may not unlikely be objected in substance as follows: Some eighteen hundred years ago, God saw fit in his wisdom so far to amend his great natural code, as to enable men to escape the punishment due to their sins by the simple act of believing on Christ, his only begotton Son, who came upon the Earth in the form and appearance of a man, took upon himself the sins of the world, past, present, and prospective, and, in our stead, suffered their penalty, that we through him might live; that is, might be saved from the legitimate consequences of our numerous sins and iniquities. We say an objection of this kind may not unlikely be interposed, because it can hardly be doubted that many good and worthy men honestly believe, not only that the Bible teaches such a doctrine, but that every word therein contained is an eternal verity. And yet, with all due deference to the feelings and opinions of such, we must be permitted to think differently,—must be permitted to think that a thing is not any the more an eternal verity, because honestly believed to be a fact, or any the less a shallow falsehood, because found between the lids of the Bible, or any other book in artificial language penned. Or still more plainly, in so far as the commandments of Moses, the sayings of the prophets, and the teachings of Christ are affirmative of the laws organically enstamped upon man, in so far are they the commandments of the Power that made him; and in so far as they contravene the laws thus organically proclaimed, in just so far are they the mere misjudgments of those ancient men, and hence, as guides to human actions, are not worth the paper on which they stand recorded.

And here the question naturally arises, Upon whom are the commandments of Nature obligatory?—As seems to us they are obligatory upon such and only such as have received them; in other words, upon such and only such as have them enstamped upon their organisms by those different branches of the great Creator, known as hereditary causes, educational influences, the force of habit, or all these things combined. The man who is actually coarse-grained, low, and groveling, no matter how he came to be so, whether so born or whether so brought to be by education and the pressure of degrading influences, is no more commanded by the nature of which he is himself possessed, and hence no more by the Power that made him, to be delicate and high-toned in his desires, feelings, and conduct, than is a black man to be a white one, or a dwarf to pull down as much upon the scales as a giant;—not any more. By and through his own individual nature, be it high, be it low, and be it what it may, and not by and through the nature of Moses, or any other individual or set of individuals, ancient or modern, is every man commanded what to be, what to do, what to love, what to hate, etc. Indeed, as we have come to see it, one of the gravest errors of the old Mosaic system of religion, and also of the Christian, as for the most part it is taught and administered, is that, irrespective of the great natural difference in the organization, taste, temperaments, and mental balance of different individuals, (and no two even of the same class, whether high or low, can anywhere be found who are, in these respects or any other, exactly alike,) they issue unto all the same mandates, and require from all the same kind, character, and grade of obedience; whereout unavoidably grows, not charity, brotherly-love, and good-will one toward another, but unjust criticisms, accusations, counter accusations, etc.; which things not only greatly mar the beauties of those systems, but approximate quite nearly to paralyzing their usefulness. No man, Jew or Gentile, Turk or Christian, can any more reasonably be required or expected to exercise talents, whether secular or religious, of which he is not in possession, because some other man or set of men may chance to possess them, than can he to exercise ten, when in truth and in fact he has but one. All men have not the same organization, not the same mental balance, and not the same gifts either in quantity or kind, consequently they are not by the great Creative Power commanded to look all alike, think all alike, or practice all alike, and hence, thus do, they never did and never can: all which must needs be, upon the whole, both good and right, otherwise it would not, eternally, so have been and be. And wherefore, to all such arguments and objections as are herein before stated, we deem the following a sufficient answer:—

If the God who created the Earth, and all things therein and upon, had ever amended a single provision of natural law, or had ever annulled either conditionally or unconditionally a single clause thereof, relative to universal man, he would not, as seems to us, have intrusted its revelation and the chances of its spread to the narrow bounds of artificial language, upon scanty rolls of parchment written; but, in accordance with his ancient custom, would simultaneously therewith have issued undying proclamation to that effect throughout every sea and every land, by indelibly enstamping such amendment or annulment upon all the appropriate branches and departments of his created works; for, beyond a doubt with us, he speaks not to man or any other of his fractions, except by and through his works; and hence they are the whole of his OFFICIAL VOLUME.—

Legitimately consequent upon a command indelibly enstamped upon the organic structure of both man and beast, each doth multiply and replenish the Earth with his kind, and neither the one nor the other of them does it, because by the Bible so commanded to do. In other words, it was because the observing and philosophic Moses saw that such a commandment had organic existence in both man and beast, that induced him, for the enlightenment of the unthinking, to write it down as being the express commandment of God; and not because it was by him expected that his thus writing it down would add one jot or tittle to its binding force. And so of all God's commandments, since deep in the nature of things themselves they have their seat and binding force; and not at all upon mere human opinions, or the pages of any written book, for their existence or efficacy depend.

As fire uniformly continues to consume combustibles, as cold uniformly continues to freeze whatever is subjected to its chilly reign, and as men uniformly continue to be begotten, born, and nourished into growth and strength pursuant to the same old natural laws; so, pursuant to established order, life, to death, is ever compelled to give way, all our fond hopes and strong beliefs and fervent prayers to the contrary notwithstanding O Nature, blessed and lovely Nature! When will men come to know and appreciate thee as they ought? And when to understand that it only by rendering obedience to the laws which are written upon the pages of thy great and constantly growing, physical revelation, that they can be saved from sin, saved from sickness, and saved from a wicked, hence untimely, and hence the only death that ever was or ever will be to mankind a curse?

Again; since Nature's laws are permanently part and parcel of her own eternal Self, (because of all her numerous different properties and powers composed,) it needs must follow that a due proportion of these Her undying qualities, or eternal laws, are forever present and active, wherever and to the precise extent that any portion of her own vast Self exists, no matter how small may be the fraction, where its location, what its form, nor whence it came. Not only this, but the fact that Her laws are thus, forever, coextensively present and active with Herself, necessarily invests Her, and hence them, with all and singular those powers of omnipresence, omniscience, etc., which, from the blinding effects of early education and the force of habit, we have been wont to ascribe to an extrinsic, immaterial, Supreme Judge and Ruler of the World. In other words, the omniscience of Nature's laws grows out of their omnipresence; and their omnipresence, out of the fact of their being, everywhere and ever, part and parcel of Her own vast, universal Self. The laws of Nature being thus coequal, coactive, and coextensive with her own vast Self, they must of necessity be self-executive; and hence they must ever and everywhere render, not only the proper reward which is due to obedience, but the proper kind, character, and amount of punishment which is due to each and every act of disobedience, as well as meddling improperly with any portion of that universal Whole, of which such portion is a component part; be the thing thus, in any way, improperly meddled with, large or small, strong or weak, wholesome food or deadly poison.

This being how the matter stands out revealed to us, we are compelled to infer that Nature's judgment can be no other than a *general one*;—a general one not for the reason that at some particular time and place, in the distant future, she is going to try, judge, and execute judgment upon all men, of every generation, condition, and clime, for all past, present, and intermediate acts of obedience and disobedience to her numerous and, upon the whole, always good and salutary laws, but because it is everywhere constantly going on;—because her court is ever and everywhere open, and in active business-session eternally engaged; and so eternally engaged, because her universal laws, out of which it grows, are everywhere and ever actively alive; consequently are, at all times, and in all places, exerting their full force and effect; consequently are ever producing upon individuals, and hence upon universal, passing man, the same as upon all things else, their full quota of legitimately corresponding effects; and consequently are forever acting the part, not only of universal Judge, but of full Rewarder and final Executioner. And now, reader, for the purpose of enstamping this point upon your brain as indelibly as possible, suffer us to be a little tedious and relate a circumstance which, although quite simple, is nevertheless directly in point, and hence most strikingly illustrative of the subject.

In a neighboring town, a few years since, there resided a man who, believing that the properties and powers of *things* are not *things'* laws, hence that those laws are not permanently part and parcel of things themselves, consequently not equally fixed and irrevocable as are the things of which they are a part, and hence not self-executive, else believing that they were, (and which we cannot tell,) threw himself full upon the track, just as the ponderous train with lightning speed was bearing down upon him. Yea, and strange as the foregoing views may appear to such as are firm believers in a great and terrible judgment, at some distant future day, for present transgressions of law, consequently have never seriously thought upon the subject of a current general judgment, (which the necessity of any such great future one doth wholly supersede,) nevertheless, in this instance at least, they are proven to be in consonance with verity. For the stern gravity of that particular fraction of the great Ruler, which the iron horse doth constitute and is, did then and there, in full substance and effect, try, judge, and execute sentence of awful dismemberment and instant death, upon that frail organic structure which, up to that moment, had constituted him a living man. Thus was this individual, at that time, in that place, and not somewhere else nor long years thereafter, tried, judged, and executed for his said transgression of a law of Nature, or of God. But surely it cannot be necessary to multiply cases or vary examples to prove what reason, observation, and experience all unite in declaring to be both the universal rule and constant practice, throughout all vast Nature's infinitely diversified and never-ending round.

CHAPTER XVI.

MAN AND HIS DESTINY.

So intimately connected are the different links in great Nature's chain, that, in speaking upon other subjects, some things may have incidentally been said bearing more or less directly upon the question of the final destiny of individual man; nevertheless, upon that particular point, nothing has thus far been advanced. And now, before entering thereupon, we desire to say that, if we know ourself, we have an abhorrence to contending with our friends, neighbors, or anybody else, simply because they chance to differ with us in size, form, or opinion. We might, therefore, be disposed to pass this delicate question in silence, did we not take into consideration the fact that, whether for weal or whether for woe, we, too, have a through ticket in the great boat of human life; hence have, in common with every other individual that ever did, now does, or ever shall tread the Earth, an equal interest not only in enhancing the pleasures of the voyage, but in its safe arrival at its destined port, be that port personal eternal life to all, or be it to each, as an individual entity, and eternal sleep; and consequently that we have no right to shrink from its discussion.

As we have come to see it, then, there are in the human head quite a number of different mental organs, among which is one that is specially commissioned to create within us love of life, and hence desire to live; and another whose function it is to create within us the feeling or emotion called Hope. And since this latter mental organ, just like every other, is always, relatively, more or less large and active in the head of every individual, therefore, like every other, it always more or less helps to shape the views and mould the character of every human being. In other words, as the natural Voltaic battery or mental organ called Hope, whose function it is to create, and keep alive within us, the feeling or emotion which is also called Hope, is, just like every other mental organ, part and parcel of the human machine; so it, the same as every other, ever more or less helps to shape the course and stamp the character of the whole man, according to its relative size, activity, and power, as compared with the other organs in the same head. Moreover, whether aware of the fact or not, we do, each and all, just as unavoidably revolve around our respective dominant, mental organs, be they few or be they many, and be they which they may, as do the different secondary planets about their respective primaries. And of this the natural consequence is, that, when thinking of our own dissolution, (and no one is always thinking about this or any other one thing, except he be permanently insane,) we all have our hopes, more or less strong, not only that we shall live to a good old age, but on past death to all eternity; just the same as do we hope for a thousand other impossible things which it is within the compass of human nature strongly to desire to have take place, and hence to hope that they will. In short, such is man's organic structure and such his mental balance, that we all have our turns, more or less often and upon a scale larger or smaller, of soaring away upon the pinions of Hope in the same manner, and for the same general reason, that we have our turns of being wakeful, sleepy, talkative, taciturn, angry, etc. In the same manner, and for the same general reason, we all have our turns more or less often, and upon a scale larger or smaller, of feeling lonely in the midst of company, sober in the midst of jollity, angry without any just provocation, afraid when there is in reality no danger, and of hoping for things which have no foundation in fact, and consequently can never come to take place. All these mental acts, more or less often and upon a scale larger or smaller, we perform; and we perform them partly for the reason that the several organs in our heads, which stand parent cause thereto, are stone-blind, that is, do not possess either judgment or discretion, and partly because it not unfrequently happens that, for want of being duly exercised, they take on spontaneous action, the same as did the boy's mouth at school when *it whistled itself*

Again, notwithstanding we are all organized upon the same general plan, consequently are all human beings, still our different heads are no more all balanced alike than are our different faces all shaped alike; wherefore we have not all the same ruling organs, and hence do not all turn upon the same mental axis. On the contrary, Phrenology teaches, and observation attests its truthfulness, that some are so organized and balanced that, even in their most sober moments, feeling and emotion are their governing angels, intellect in their heads being quite subordinate, and hence only holding a slightly modifying commission therein; also that there are others whose mental balance is such, that, when not laboring under some undue excitement, intellect is naturally their guiding star, feeling and emotion acting the subordinate part. This latter class of persons, in their ordinarily cool and reflective moments, are able to look right over those mountains of causeless anger, groundless fears, and foundationless hopes with which, but a short time before, when laboring under some strong excitement or lost in reverie, their heads were filled, and see that they are merely the creation of their strong, blind organs of feeling, and consequently that, as guides to real truth, their testimony is of little value,—a thing which the former class of individuals can never do. We repeat, the former class of individuals can never do this, because, self-evidently, as seems to us, they are forever debarred from doing so by their uniformly ruling organs of feeling and emotion,—the very ones which create and keep alive those things within them. Indeed, it is just as certain that all men do not possess the same perspicacity, the same depth of thought, the same amount of intellectual power, as it is that they do not all possess the same bodily activity and muscular strength; and hence it is just as certain that said latter class are able to see, with their mind's eye, all around and far beyond the utmost stretch of the former's mental vision, as it is that the orbit of Jupiter lies all around and millions of miles outside old Earth's proud track.

We have not been thus particular in elucidating this point because we suppose it to be a new view of variant human nature, but because we wish to explain as clearly as possible how it is that some men are compelled to disbelieve in a continued personal existence after death, notwithstanding the blind organ of Hope, acting in concert with equally blind Vitativeness, doth more or less often, and with greater or less distinctness, create in their heads the pleasing emotion that they shall continue to live, not only to a good old age, but right on past death to all eternity. And here candor bids us confess that one of the best arguments we ever heard adduced in favor of the eternal personal-existence doctrine is based upon this very fact; namely, that all men, everywhere, do more or less strongly desire and hope thus, eternally on, to live. The *gist* of the argument may be briefly stated thus: Because universal man has in his head a mental organ, whose function it is to create within him deep love of life, consequently strong desire to live, also another whose function it is to create within him the emotion called Hope; and because this latter organ, when acting in concert with the former as its leader, legitimately creates within him the hope to live, not only to a good old age, but right on past death to all eternity; therefore it is inferred that he must and will so live, else were those organs made in vain.

That this argument appears quite plausible upon its face must be admitted; also that it would be unanswerable, but for the fact that the premises do not warrant the drawing of any such conclusion therefrom. We say, it would be unanswerable, but for the fact that the premises do not warrant the drawing of any such conclusion therefrom, because the sound-minded, middle-aged man does not live who will not find, upon carefully turning over in memory the pages of his past life, that this said Mr. Hope, so far from ever having proved himself a uniform truth-teller upon any subject, almost invariably stands convicted of being a gay and unscrupulous deceiver. Indeed, so plain is this, that no argument is needed to prove that not a middle-aged man, Jew or Gentile, Turk or Christian, bond or free, can anywhere be found who does not know from his own experience, that he has already buoyantly hoped for a thousand things which he has not yet realized, and which he is now just as certain he never can, as is he that the days of his youth, and hence of his youthful hopes, are forever past.

It has already been stated in effect, that the blind organ of Hope, when acting in concert with the equally blind organ Vitativeness as its leader, legitimately creates, within the heads of men, the hope that they shall continue to live personally, eternally on; and it was so stated because both Phrenology and experience prove, that the object or thing for which men hope is never determined by the organ of Hope, but always by the organ or combination of organs with which, as follower, it is blindly acting in concert. Thus, for instance, when acting with Acquisitiveness as its leader, it is not for life either long or short that an individual doth hope, but for wealth; when with Alimentiveness, then not for wealth, but something good to eat; and thus on. Wherefore, if the inference be correct, that, because all men do more or less ardently desire and hope to live, not only to a good old age, but right on past death to all eternity, therefore they must and will so live; then, manifestly enough, in pursuance of this same kind and character of logic, we are bound to infer, and hence to proclaim it aloud as a fact, that, because all men do more or less ardently desire and fondly hope to be great, rich, happy, and honored, therefore all men must and will be great, rich, etc.;—a conclusion so utterly at variance with both observation and experience, that it would seem that no one who is not desirous of being deceived would be in danger of being misled thereby. In short, it would seem as if the simple fact that all mankind do more or less ardently desire and fondly hope to live, here upon the Earth, not only for days, months, and years, but to a good old age; whereas, notwithstanding all these strong desires thus to live and fond hopes that they shall, full nineteen-twentieths of all these hopers are known to pass the gate of death, before the green old-age of sixty years is reached, ought of itself to be sufficient to prevent every candid and reflecting man from placing any particular confidence in the whisperings of such a flattering and deceitful guide. So much for the first and main branch of the argument which in substance declares, and effect, that, *because* universal man doth more or less ardently desire and fondly hope to exist personally on, past death to, all eternity, *therefore* he must and will so exist. Now for the second and minor branch which says, in substance and effect, that unless he is permitted thus on to live, then were those mental organs, which speak into existence within him such desire and hope, formed in vain.

It is admitted that the fact that all men have eyes, for example, furnishes unmistakable evidence that they were created to be used, and also of the existence of something in surrounding nature for them to see; but it is denied that the circumstance of man's being created a finite being, whereby he is denied the capacity of being able to see a thousandth part of the visible things which are in the world, or even of those particular places and objects which he is more or less desirous of seeing, furnishes any evidence that his eyes were formed in vain, or not for admirable ends. On the contrary, if the universality of the fact that the tendency in all men everywhere to perform the mental act of desiring to see is greatly in excess of their ability to perform the laborious and often impossible task of bringing themselves within eye-shot of all those innumerable, visible places and things which they are desirous of seeing, and hence of becoming ocularly acquainted therewith proves anything, it is, that, as a legitimate consequence of their desiring to see so very much, they will so bestir themselves as to come to see and understand a vast deal more than they otherwise would, and consequently be rendered correspondingly more wise and happy. Because the apple-tree, for example, in obedience to a law of its nature, performs the act of putting forth vastly more of blossoms than it is possible for it to bear of apples, it will not do to infer that the inherent tendency, in this kind of tree, to perform the act of putting forth such surplus, was created in vain.

Further, had universal man no such mental organ as Acquisitiveness, for example, he would no more love property, no more desire to possess wealth, no more exert himself to acquire it, and no more tax his ingenuity to devise ways and means to perpetuate its existence in the hands of his posterity after him, than does the dog that feeds upon the crumbs which fall from his table;—not any more. And had he no such mental organ as Vitativeness, he could no more perform the mental act of loving his life, or of desiring to live either longer or shorter, here or hereafter, than could he the act of seeing without eyes; and consequently he would no more love life, no more desire to live, and no more dread death, than does the oyster. Obviously enough, the effect of the existence of this organ, in the head of man, the same as in the head of animals below him, is to cause him to guard, protect, and prolong his bodily life as much as possible; and not to cause him to live a moment beyond such organ's death, or the death of that physical structure of which it is a part. Moreover, such is the frailty of man's organic structure, and such the multitude of surrounding agents competent to cripple and destroy him, that, but for the existence in his head of this said organ which prompts him to self-preservation, his destruction would steadily and unconcernedly go on, until, within a comparatively brief period, he would be blotted from the face of the Earth. Of this there cannot be a rational doubt. Wherefore, allowing it to be a fact, as we are compelled to think it is, that, of personal existence, the close of this bodily life is the final close, Is it not plain that this said mental organ, instead of being created in vain, is, to the human family, not only a blessing, but its savior?

Again, in addition to his other mental organs, man has in his head such an organ as Acquistiveness; and the consequence is he loves property, desires to accumulate it, is anxious to acquire a great deal, and studiously endeavors to guard against the possibility of its slipping away from him. And inasmuch as these acts, each and all, are normally performed or spoken into existence within him by his brain, therefore they afford him a species of pleasure; and therefore we have no right to infer that the organ, which thereunto parent cause doth stand, was made in vain;—have no right to infer it was made in vain, simply for the reason that, as a natural incentive to action, it causes him to wish for vastly more of wealth than he possesses the general ability to obtain or to manage. Upon the contrary, if the universality of the fact that such is the function of this organ as legitimately confers upon men, at all times and everywhere, vastly more capacity for desiring property and of wishing to possess it, than it does of skill and ability to acquire it, proves anything, it is, that, as a natural consequence of their thus desiring to acquire and possess immense wealth, they will be much more likely so to bestir themselves as to keep the wolf from their doors than they otherwise would, and hence be rendered correspondingly more comfortable and happy.—Because all men, everywhere, are desirous of possessing a great deal more property than they are able to get or ever do get, therefore all men, everywhere, must and will come to possess a great deal more property than they ever do come to possess; else was the mental organ which parent cause doth stand to such desire created in vain. Because all men, everywhere, are desirous of living, here in the flesh, to a good old age, therefore all men, everywhere, must and will continue to live, here in the flesh, to a good old age; (notwithstanding but few men, anywhere, thus long do live;) else was the mental organ which parent cause doth stand to such desire created in vain. And because all men, everywhere, are desirous of living personally on, in some form or other, past death to all eternity, therefore all men, everywhere, must and will, in some form, thus personally on continue to live; else was the mental organ which parent cause doth stand to such desire created in vain.—Strange logic, this!

But again; in addition to all his other mental organs, man

has in his head such an organ as Vitativeness; and the consequence is he not only loves his life, but desires to live as long as he can; and hence he endeavors to acquaint himself not only with the laws of his being, but with the character and qualities of things about him, to the end that he may be able so to adapt his action thereunto as to preserve his health and prolong his stay upon the Earth, until his physical machinery shall be fairly worn out, and he, in consequence, brought to die a strictly natural and hence unpainful death. Wherefore, manifestly enough, this said organ doth answer him a valuable purpose during all the days of his natural life; and wherefore, should it become worn out and die along with the rest of his physical organs, it would no more have been created in vain than were his eyes, his ears, or his nose, since every part of his proud, bodily structure is compelled to share the same fate.

And yet further: In addition to said organ of Vitativeness and all his other mental organs, man possesses one called Hope; the which, if he did not possess, he could no more perform the mental act of hoping for wealth, for success in his different undertakings, or for life either long or short, here or hereafter, than can he manifest mind without brains;—not any more. Hope, although not itself an executive organ, ever freely lends its aid to Vitativeness, Acquisitiveness, and such other organs and combinations of organs as desire its support. And of this, the consequence is, that man not only loves his life and desires to live, and live on, to a good old age, and yet still on past death to all eternity, but hopes he shall.

Wherefore, should this said hope-creating organ, the same as Vitativeness,—the love-of-life-creating organ, after having thus afforded him much good cheer during all the dark days of his natural life, finally become worn out and die along with the rest of his physical structure, it would no more have been made in vain than was his mouth, or any other of his numerous bodily organs which afford him pleasure so long as he lives, and which it is equally the mission of death to destroy, come whensoever it may. We say, should this said hope-creating organ become worn out and die along with the rest of his physical structure, etc., because the different organs, each and all, of which the brain is made ~~is made~~ up, are just as much physical things as are the heart and liver; consequently they are just as much subject to the operation of physical laws, hence must just as surely be blotted out by death, and hence, of the emotion called Hope, the same as of every other mental phenomenon, that must of necessity be the final close.

As sensation, thought, feeling, and emotion are, each and all, mere creatures of the brain, so we are alike indebted to that complex organ, not only for all the pleasures we enjoy, but for all the pains we suffer. And since normal action of the brain doth always afford a species of pleasure either higher or lower, it must therefore be more happifying, as well as more elevating in its consequences, to be busily engaged in tracing Nature's laws, unfolding her eternal facts, and endeavoring, as far forth as possible, to reduce them into practice, than it is or can be to be constantly meditating upon what some ancient somebody was led to think, and hence write down.

It is not denied that the emotion created in man by the organ of Hope is a pleasing one; but, then, it must be borne in memory that such is the complexity of the human structure that man is not all Hope, any more than is he all Acquisitiveness or Combativeness. In other words, it must be borne in memory that, in addition to Hope, he has numerous other mental organs, the normal exercise of each of which ever affords him its own proper kind and quality of pleasure. And whether right or whether wrong, we must be permitted to think that Intellect is the purest, brightest, and most substantial jewel in the head of man; consequently that the pleasures created and kept alive by the normal exercise of the intellectual organs are purer in quality, more exalted in character, hence more ennobling in their tendency, and hence more happifying in their effects, than are those which are created by Vitativeness, Hope, or any other of the blind mental organs. For others, of course, we cannot speak, but, as for ourself, we have no hesitation in believing that we derive more of real and abiding pleasure from the complex, mental act of endeavoring to read and understand human nature as it is, in other words, from the complex, mental act of canvassing, as far forth as possible, the different facts and circumstances which bear upon the origin, character, and final destiny of the animal called man, notwithstanding the testimony thus gained doth tend to diminish the possibility of deliberately indulging the hope of a future, personal existence beyond the grave, than would it be possible for us to derive from the simple act of blindly hoping that, beyond such bound, we shall thus live. Understand, it is not denied that we should be willing and more than willing—could we deem such a thing possible—not only to continue to maintain a conscious, spiritual, personal existence right on past death to all eternity, in the society of such of our beloved friends and acquaintances as have gone before, and those that must shortly follow, but to live this present, bodily life over, and over again, at least an hundred times from early youth to this our seventieth year, without ever tasting death at all, in the company of just such kind friends, neighbors, and acquaintances as now surround us. We repeat, we should be willing and more than willing to do either or both of these things, could we bring ourself to believe in the possibility thereof. As, however, we can no more believe in the possibility of the former than of the latter, for the reason that we are compelled to regard it as being directly at variance, not only with our own brief observation, but with the plain teachings of natural law; so we think we are not mistaken when we say that the absence, in our head, of an abiding hope of the former, doth no more leave an aching void therein, than does the absence of such a hope of the latter;—not any more.

In the spirits of the living, in animal magnetism, and in clairvoyance to a certain extent, we find no difficulty in believing, but in the spirits of the dead we have no sort of faith. Simply because we hear of many things being done that are claimed to be performed by the spirits of the departed, and for which things we are wholly unable to account, the same as we do of numerous things being performed by magic art which we are equally unable to explain, we are not prepared to believe they are not, one and all, somehow produced, or brought to take place and be, by the agency of individuals that are still alive and in the flesh, instead of by the spirits of the dead.

Because almost every one experiences more or less of those feelings which are called presentiments, because some few of such presentiments may chance to bear a faint resemblance, either fancied or real, to something which doth somewhere thereafter come to take place, and because this wide class of mental phenomena may be most easily accounted for by assuming that all such presentiments are just so many revelations to us made by the spirits of the departed, it does not follow that such assumption is a fact, or that any such things as ghosts, or spirits of the dead, ever had existence. Far from it!

As we see it, the way the so-called spirits of the dead do act toward us the part of guardian angels, ever hovering round us, is this: By the remembrance of the persons, character, etc., of the honored dead, we are ever more or less strongly inclined, not only to abstain from such practices and things as we know were to them abhorrent, but to imitate their virtues both by word and deed. And the more in-drawn, gloomy, and reflective the cast of mind, the more marked will be the effect produced upon the individual by the pale departure of near and dear friends.

Inasmuch, however, as we do not *know* that individual man will not continue to maintain a personal existence after he is physically dead, any more than do others *know* that he will thus continue to maintain it, so it may not be improper here to say that in case it shall turn out to be a fact that man is inherently possessed of such a nature, as renders him personally an immortal being, then, manifestly enough, as seems to us, such subsequent life will not depend upon any miraculous bodily resurrection, but be a disembodied continuance right on of this present life; and consequently that those who so live as to enjoy heaven now will continue to enjoy it then, and those who so demean themselves as to suffer hell now will continue to suffer hell then, except in so far as different individuals then, the same as now, shall, pursuant to the law of progression, make advancement or change their courses, and hence correspondingly alter their conditions.

And since we have thus plainly declared our want of faith in the personal existence of such as are physically dead, and this notwithstanding we are compelled to admit we do not *know* that they do not thus continue to exist, consequently may be in error upon this point; now, therefore, with a view to making all possible amends for the promulgation of these our honestly cherished views,—in case they shall turn out to be erroneous, and we unexpectedly find ourself in possession of a conscious, personal existence after that our body is no more,—we do hereby pledge ourself unto such of you, our friendly readers, as shall then be living here in the flesh, that we will make it our business to apprise you of the fact as speedily as may be; provided we can be permitted to do so, not in the awe-inspiring gloom of darkness, nor yet by aid and instrumentality of any stand-between ourself and you, whether he be friend or foe, but in some open and convincing manner in the cheerful light of day. And in case it shall be contrary to the rules and regulations of the spirit land for us to manifest ourself in such a way as we shall adjudge to be so plain and unmistakable, as to leave no room for you to doubt whether it be really we who are present, or whether some mere, living pretender to being in our confidence instead, then we shall deem it our duty to refrain from making any attempt at communicating with the bodily living tenants of Earth at all.

Remember this, our solemn pledge! also that it extends only to such as are friendly to the doctrines herein advocated. For, however much we may honor the persons and respect the motives of such as are honestly of the opinion that it is only by means of fiction on the back of fiction piled, that the world is to be enlightened, religionized, and saved, consequently would be quite willing to have us seem to put in our appearance, and humble confession make, whether we so continue to exist or not, in their veracity, and especially upon a point of this kind, we have not the same amount of faith.

But to return:—There are, perhaps, not many passages in the Bible which are oftener selected as the foundation of discourse upon funeral occasions, than is the simple question so anxiously asked by the disconsolate Job, "If a man die, shall he live again?"—Standing upon this brief interrogatory as their foundation, in the presence of the weeping living and silent dead, the ingenuity of a naturally kind-hearted and sympathizing clergy has been taxed to its utmost to prove from Nature's volume the correctness of the miraculous dogma of the resurrection of the body entire; consequently the personal existence of individual man in the distant future; and hence that said question must be answered in the affirmative. And probably one of the most taking arguments that has ever been drawn from natural revelation, upon such fitting occasion, in favor of the final resurrection of the body entire, and hence in support of an eternal, personal existence consequent thereupon, is based upon the fact that the vegetable kingdom is ever compelled to bow obedience to the annual changes of the seasons. The substance of the argument may be briefly stated thus:—

As in summer the forest is covered with leaves, as in fall they wither, die, and drop to the ground, leaving the trees naked and desolate during all the long and dreary rule of winter, and as, in spring they put forth buds, and again become clothed with verdure; So the man that yieldeth up the ghost to-day, and to-morrow crumbleth back into his native dust, there to remain during the cold and stilly reign of death, shall again come forth, in the great spring time of the resurrection, clothed with newness of life and immortality.

As this is not only a very pretty simile, but a beautifully illustrative argument to prove what it does prove, be it much, be it little, and be it what it may, so it may not be amiss, very briefly, to examine it. Between a large and flourishing tree covered with green foliage, and a man in his full health and strength, there exists a strong analogy; between its leaves which, from the chilly blasts of autumn, have become so withered and drooping as to be just ready to fall upon the ground, and a man tottering with the infirmities of age upon the brink of the grave, into which he is about to drop, the resemblance is most striking; but between a tree that is putting forth its buds in spring preparatory to expanding them slowly, but surely, into another full leafy covering, and a dead man suddenly rising from the grave and again assuming his former personal identity, there is not the slightest similarity. We say, between a tree that is putting forth buds in spring, etc., and a dead man suddenly rising from the grave, etc., there is not the slightest similarity, because, manifestly enough, it is not its former, dead, fallen, and partially decayed leaves which, in spring, are being rejuvenated, elevated in air, and reattached to their respective parent stems, and hence coming to clothe the tree suddenly in living green; but a new generation of them, so to speak, which are gradually being pushed into organic existence from inorganic elements, in precisely the same manner that was its former leafy covering only the spring before. Wherefore this argument, like all others that were ever drawn from nature to prove the correctness of that miraculous dogma, the resurrection of the body entire, and thereby the future personal existence of the same individual beyond the grave, is worse than a dead failure.

We say, this argument, like all others that were ever drawn from nature to prove the correctness of that miraculous dogma, the resurrection of the body entire, etc., is worse than a dead failure, because, if the comparison proves anything, it is, that dead men, or past generations of men, just like dead leaves, or past generations of leaves, so to speak, are never resurrected entire, but only little by little, as decomposition proceeds in the form of gas; consequently that subsequent generations of men, just like subsequent generations of leaves, are, ever, more or less composed of the self-same elements that were their long-since dead and decomposed predecessors; and hence, that it is the race of human beings that is immortal, the same as it is the race of leaves, so to speak, and not the different, dead, and decayed individuals of the race, any more than it is the different, dead, and rotten leaves of which the surface soil is composed;—the very doctrine which we are endeavoring to prove. Indeed, self-evidently, as seems to us, every attempt to prove from any portion of nature the existence of the unnatural, no matter when nor where nor by whom made, must not only fail of its object, but aid in establishing the diametrically opposing conditions of things, the same as doth the preceding comparison, and also Paul's celebrated grain-sowing one.[a] In other words, Is it not, in truth and in fact, just as absurd to attempt to prove from Nature the existence of miracles,—the existence of a state of things which is wholly unnatural, and hence with every act and principle of Nature's own vast Self at variance direct, as it would be to endeavor to prove from the almost infinite divisibility of matter, that matter is not divisible at all? We appeal, in truth and in fact, Is it not?

---

a First Corinthians, 15, 36—38.

CHAPTER XVII.

MAN AND HIS DESTINY—*Continued.*

Admitting the gift of life to be not only a blessing, but a great blessing, it does not follow that the Donor—whoever or whatever the same may be—is bound to bless us on and on therewith forever; and surely the termination by death of a blessing, which was thus gratuitously bestowed, cannot be construed into a curse. So plain is the principle here involved, that the poor tradesman, for example, would be pronounced either an ingrate or a fool, who should go grumbling around simply because a rich kinsman of his, unasked, had given him a dollar, instead of an eagle,—had given him for an indefinite period the free use of a shop and grounds suitable for carrying on his business, instead of executing a clear deed thereof to him and his heirs forever. What, then, becomes of the narrow, selfish and irreverent idea, that it is only a cruel mockery to be blessed with life at all, if we are not to continue to be blessed therewith right on past death to all eternity?

But admitting it to be among the things that are possible for human beings to continue to maintain a conscious, personal existence for a single moment after they are physically dead, and hence, by parity of reason, forever on, notwithstanding their composing elements are returned to gas, dissipated in air, and into numerous new, and different living combinations entered; and also admitting that they will and do thus live; still we are unable to see any ground upon which to base an argument or build a rational hope, that such after-life will be any more uniform in its character, any less checkered with difficulties, any less marred with disappointments and unsatisfied desires, hence any more a blessing, and hence a thing any more to be desired than is this present one, which the mass of endless-personal-existence believers so much affect to despise. Indeed, it would not seem possible, logically, to draw from the premises any other conclusion than this: As is this present life, so also will be the next; since both, and both alike, must be presumed to be the spontaneous gift of the same, great, wise, and self-consistent Author. Wherefore it is not surprising that the more sober and reflecting portion of endless-personal-existence believers are fast coming to the conclusion that the future life of man is simply a disembodied continuance of this present one; that heaven and hell are both of them conditions of being, and neither of them places; and hence that if we so demean ourselves whilst here in the flesh, as to create and carry about with us in our bosoms any particular species of heaven, we shall naturally and unavoidably continue to carry that same about with us when we shall have shuffled off this mortal coil; and if any species of hell, then that same in the unending future.

Further, admitting that the animal called man is to continue to maintain a conscious, personal existence in the distant future; admitting creation to be wholly a past and perfected work, as by Orthodoxy it is claimed to be, and hence that the more recent theory of progression is erroneous; also admitting the foregoing views of heaven and hell to be correct; (which in principle we must think they are, whether death is to man, the same as to the animals below him, the final wind up or not;) then it would seem impossible to escape the conclusion that each heaven-creating, hence heaven-deserving, and hence heaven-enjoying individual's heaven will forever be and remain the same thing, no less happifying, and no more ecstatic; and each hell-creating, hence hell-deserving, and hence hell-suffering individual's hell, forever be and remain the same, no worse, and no better; and consequently that no man's heaven, after the death of the body, will ever be to him a more blissfull reward than it was before that event, and no man's hell, a more baleful and excruciating punishment. Or thus: Admitting as above, and the conclusion seems to be irresistible, that for the good to die is simply for them to take leave of the body, and have the same kind, character, and amount of heaven which they themselves created and fostered into growth within their own bosoms, whilst here in the flesh, continued right on without intermission, diminution, or addition to all eternity; and for the bad to die is simply for them to take leave of the body, and have the same kind, character, and amount of hell which they themselves created and fostered into growth within their own bosoms, whilst in the flesh, continued right on without cessation, abatement, or increase forever.

Having thus admitted our concurrence in the principle involved in the more enlightened Christian idea, that heaven and hell are both of them conditions, and neither of them places, perhaps it may be well to go a little further and say that, according to our understanding, of the matter, the two above-named diametrically opposite conditions of being are not only more or less mixed up in the life of every individual, who long survives the infantile stage, but that both have their beginning, growth, and full maturity in the breast of individual man, whilst a living, breathing tenant of Earth, and at his physical death their final end.—Saints without blemish or sinners wholly bad there are none.

Aside from the seeming if not actual impossibility of the thing, (for that some things are impossible with the eternal God, as well as very many with that feeble, animated fraction of him, short-lived man, seems to us quite clear,) we can see no sort of necessity of any personal existence after death for the virtuous, in order that they may be rewarded with all the heaven to which they are justly entitled for being good and obedient; since, by unavoidable consequence, they not only currently enjoy all the heaven which they themselves create within their own bosoms, but are partakers in the joys of a great deal more that is therein created and kept alive by friends, neighbors, and associates. For, as we understand the matter, to obey the law is not to sin, —is to enjoy the fruits of obedience,—is to be happy,—is to be just as happy as we deserve to be, because just as happy as the nature that is in us will admit of our being rendered by our own virtuous thoughts, words, and deeds, and those of friends and associates. Nor can we any more see the necessity of an after-life for the vicious, in order that they may be punished with all the hell they justly deserve, and, in fact, with all that it would be beneficial to them or anybody else to have heaped upon their heads; since, by unavoidable consequence, they not only currently suffer all the hell which they themselves create within their own bosoms, but are made to taste the pains of a great deal more which is created and kept alive therein by associates, and other companions in sin. For, beyond a doubt with us, to disobey the law is to sin,—is to call down upon ourselves suffering, the legitimate fruit of disobedience,—is to be miserable, —is to be just as miserable as the nature that is in us will admit of our being rendered by our follies and iniquities, and those of our vicious companions. Or to present the idea in a little different form, inasmuch as both virtue and vice do naturally and unavoidably bring along with them their own rewards, and inasmuch as in the lives of even the most virtuous and happy adults, there doth exist more or less of vice, and consequently of that suffering condition called hell, and in the lives of even the most abandoned and miserable, more or less of virtue, and hence of that happy condition denominated heaven; therefore, by operation of natural law, each and all do suffer all of the former, and enjoy all the latter, which they create within their own bosom, in addition to sharing more or less largely in whatever of the one or the other condition is therein created and kept alive by friends, neighbors, and associates; and hence do suffer and enjoy all of each which they justly deserve. We say, in addition to the sharing more or less largely in whatever of the one or the other condition is created and kept alive by friends, neighbors, and associates, because, in a state of society, it is not supposed possible for the willing and obedient wholly to escape the ill effects of the wrong doings of the unwilling and disobedient; or of these latter to go wholly unblessed by the virtuous acts of the former.

As, by natural operation of the meteorological laws, the rain is made to descend upon, and bless, not only the just, but the unjust; so, by natural operation of the great social law, the consequences of men's acts, whether good or whether bad, are not confined wholly to themselves, but unavoidably more or less extend to and affect others. Nor is it supposed that all men are organized alike; that is, are all alike fine-grained and sensitive in their feelings; or that all are equally coarse-grained and obtuse. Neither is it inferred that all enjoy or suffer alike intensely for the same kind and character of acts; but only that each doth suffer and enjoy appropriately, because each through the medium of that organic nature of which he is himself possessed, and hence through the medium of that very nature, which, whether coarse or whether fine, and whether sensitive or whether obtuse, parent cause doth stand to all the different acts by him performed. In this way, as we have come to see it, by operation of natural law, the bad, or those in whom vice predominates over virtue, do unavoidably suffer all the hell and enjoy all the heaven which they justly deserve; and the good, or those in whom virtue is in the ascendency over vice, enjoy all the heaven and suffer all the hell which they justly merit, and, it is hardly necessary to add that, in a great Parent of injustice toward even the most erring of his children, or of special favoritism toward even the least faulty, we have no sort of faith.

And now, for the purpose of still further narrowing down the discussion between these our more enlightened, hence less bigoted and intolerant, and hence more widely social and happy Christian friends, and our humble self, we propose to go a step further and confess our faith in the doctrine of human probation, to the extent that we deem the same to be consonant to fact. It is admitted, then, that what will be the character of man to-morrow, for example, is to a greater or less extent immediately probationary or dependent upon the character he forms to-day, and hence mediately probationary or dependent upon that formed upon each preceding one of his life. Or, to make it more plain, suppose the life of an individual to be divided into the five popularly well-known periods; then the character, which such individual will possess in his childhood, may be said to be immediately probationary upon the character formed in infancy; the character which he will possess in youth, to be immediately probationary upon that formed in childhood, and hence mediately upon the one formed in infancy; his character in manhood, immediately upon that formed in youth, and hence mediately upon the one in the two preceding stages; and his character in old-age, immediately upon that formed in manhood, and hence mediately upon the one in each of the three preceding stages; and here, as we hold, with the close of ripe manhood's towering stage, does his probation come to an end

It must be obvious, we think, that, during the periods of both infancy and childhood, it is to parents, nurses, teachers, etc., that we are indebted for nearly all the so-called probation which is usually placed to our individual credit; for much of that to us, thus credited during youth, to parents, teachers, and associates; and for not a little of that in ripe manhood's stage, to companions and other circumstances not of our own choice or creation, and over which we have not unlimited control. Wherefore, as seems to us, it cannot fail to be seen by the more thoughtful and observing, that we do not individually come quite as near to being our own creators, quite as near to forming our own characters and shaping our own destinies as, in the heat of imagination and fullness of self-conceit, we are wont to claim.

But to return from this digression:—Why thus abruptly end the probationary period with the close of ripe manhood's stage?—Because, as we understand the law by which man's existence is regulated and governed, it is with the succeeding period of imbecility from tottering age that his personal existence doth come to a close; and because, in so far as we can see, there is no more evidence that the character formed, more properly outlived and lost, by an individual during the period of fading, dying, old age, is going to give shape to a subsequent stage of personal character after he is dead, than there is that his character in infancy was shaped by some fancied preceding stage of ethereal existence which he never had. In other words, as we are satisfied that birth is the beginning or first end of individual man's separate, personal existence in any form, so, in the absence of any evidence to the contrary, we are forced to the conclusion that death is the close or last end of that same existence; and hence that it is just as much a thing impossible for the closing stage of an individual's life, be that closing stage the period of old age, or whatever preceding one it may, to give shape to a subsequent stage which is never to follow, as it is for the first, or infantile stage, to have been probationary upon a preceding one which never had existence. Of course, it will be seen that we are here speaking of an individual as a distinct, personal entity, separate and apart from everybody else; and not of an individual as inseparably forming a part of that vast chain of human beings, past and to come, of which the present tenants of earth are but the connecting link.

That the race, without any special impropriety, may be considered immortal, we doubt not; consequently we have no difficulty in believing that very many members of the race who, for long ages past, have been corporally dead and buried, are living still; not personally, of course, but in and through us their lineal descendants now here, as well as in their other kind and character of works. In this way, doubtless, the character of the next generation is quite largely probationary, not only immediately upon the character and acts of the present one, but mediately upon the character and doings of all that have ever preceded it. Indeed, it is a part of our religious as well as philosophic faith, that Abraham, Moses, David, and very many more of our long-since departed sires, by and through the characters which they formed and lived out whilst here, do still continue to make their mark and stamp their likeness more or less distinctly, not only upon us their thus-far-remote descendants, who legitimately constitute the as-yet-latest edition of themselves, but upon all those with whom we their said latest edition do come into civil, social, or domestic contact. And thus on and still on, whereby are rendered immortal, not only individual men and women, but their characters; and not only their characters, but even their thoughts, feelings, and desires to the extent that they are spoken out in acts appropriate forever on to live.

Of course, we may be wrong, but then, as we have come to see it, there is not only vastly more of real truth, but of stimulant to great and noble actions, in this simple, unpretending view of man, the character of his probation, the nature of his immortality, and the means to be used by every one who is desirous of securing to himself a chance of being a sharer therein, than there is in that olden, opposing doctrine whose legitimate tendency is to limit inquiry, stint observation, cripple reason, forestall the judgment, narrow down the natural flow of the social feelings to a select few, and correspondingly to dry up the fountains of generous, manly, sympathy for the destitute and suffering outside that narrow circle, thereby rendering all who come within its influence, and especially its votaries, just as narrow minded, selfish, and intolerant, and hence unsocial and unhappy, as it is possible for the most constant appeals to self and self-love, coupled with the most thrilling descriptions of self-danger, and a narrow escape of darling self therefrom into a state of crowned and shining immortality, all wrought up in self, to make them. As self-love and fear do both have their origin in the blind, selfish sentiments, and not in the intellectual organs, nor yet the moral group, so science, observation, and experience all bear testimony, that notwithstanding the former is powerful to urge men on to the accomplishment of many narrow, selfish purposes, and the latter to restrain them from doing such things as they adjudge would be likely to result injuriously to self, or self-interest, still they are neither of them natural incentives to disinterested action, benevolent action, patriotic action, or, indeed, to acts which are truly great and noble of any kind. Hence, think of it as we may and continue to practice as we will, it is not by appeals made to either of these selfish sentiments, but only by developing the intellectual and moral departments of the human brain, that man can be dragged upward, and still upward, from his originally low, selfish, and savage estate, to a state of genuine manliness of aspiration, feeling, and of character.

Watchfulness, prudence, circumspection, etc., are all of them products of the normal action of the large mental organ called Cautiousness, and fear, dread, terror, etc., of its abnormal. Wherefore we should not, by appealing to men's strong, blind fears, use terror as a lever to pry them into embracing any theory or doctrine as unqualifiedly right, or into the rejection of any as absolutely wrong. In other words, when it is some real truth we are aiming to impress upon the brains of men, and not some nauseous dose of deception that we are desirous of cramming down their throats, it is to their sober judgments that we should address ourselves, and not to pallid fear.

In a philosophical point of view, between the deliberate practice of appealing to the strong, blind passion, fear, for the purpose of influencing men to believe and to act contrary to the dictates of their sober judgments, and persuasions made by tyrant lash and gloomy prison to effect the same object, What is the difference? Indeed, at this late day and age of the world, Is not the former course of action quite as unjustifiable, as was the latter in days of yore?—Between aspiring to be good for goodness' sake, and refraining from doing evil for fear of hell, the difference in effect is as broad as the firmament.

And now, for one moment, let us glance at the doctrine of human probation, as the same is, to-day, quite generally taught and believed. It is not only well known that some few individuals do hold on to the vital spark to a great age, but that they continue to cling thereto until they quite outlive their own personal characters as men, become infants the second time, and hence are destitute of any existing, personal character at all. If for such to die is simply for them to take leave of their earthly tabernacles and enter upon a future state of disembodied, personal existence, and if their personal characters in that future life are to depend upon the characters which they formed, outlived, and lost, whilst yet probationers in the flesh, then, manifestly enough, the future, personal existence of all this class of individuals must be a most empty and worthless affair. But, allowing, as may not unlikely be claimed by its advocates, that it is the character which is formed and manifested by such in ripe manhood's stage, and not the one in drooping age, that is probationary to the character which they are to possess and carry about with them in the unending future, still there doth remain another difficulty quite as great. For if imbecile old-age is to be set down as a sort of blank in life, or rather as a period thereof in which those individuals who attain thereto are not accountable to either God or man for what they say or do, but are simply hanging on to life upon their own account, What then is to be done with that other imbecile stage, first infancy? And what with all that innumerable multitude of human beings that survive it not; consequently have no childhood, hence no youth, and hence no manhood in which to be probationers, or form characters for eternity?

It is certain that vast numbers of the race die in infancy, very many in childhood, and more or less in every succeeding stage. If, therefore, the millions of human beings that die annually, during the first hour of their brief, infantile existence, do not form any personal characters, (which they manifestly do not,) if they are to continue to maintain a personal existence after they are dead, and if their characters in that future state of existence, are to depend upon those which they formed whilst probationers here in the flesh, then most assuredly they must forever be and remain as birth finds them, and death leaves them, characterless; or, at best, have only the character of puling infants, helpless and senseless to the very last degree. If, to all this class of individuals, death is not the final wind up, the same as it undoubtedly is to animals of lower order, then surely they must possess a sadly blank, future life, and hence be compelled to enjoy an equally void heaven, else to suffer a correspondingly vacant hell.

Manifestly enough, as seems to us, there is but one way of escaping the numerous difficulties with which error is constantly and upon all sides round beset; and that is to plant ourselves squarely upon facts and abide the consequences. And whether right or whether wrong, we can see no surer way of determining, upon any and all questions, what is fact and what is not, then to use freely our reasoning powers in connection with our physical senses, and accept the testimony thus obtained, be it what it may.

Be it understood by all, and especially by such of our readers as with us herein most widely differ, we do not state these our feeble views for the purpose of dividing the house of religious faith against itself and thereby destroying it, but because we are desirous of having it become a thing united and standing upon a living and constantly growing basis; and hence a thing which shall endure and bring forth the fruits, not of narrow, sectarian division and hatred, but of charity and universal good-will forever. In other words, we do not state them because we think them popular, nor yet for the reason that they were taught to us at some theological seminary on purpose that we might teach them to others, but because, upon as full an investigation of the subject as we are able to make, we are compelled to regard them as being really true; because we have an abiding faith that real truth can never long and permanently be brought to suffer loss by investigation, but will continue to go on gaining in growth and strength thereby; and because it is real truth, be it what it may, that we are desirous should speedily triumph, as triumph ultimately we feel sure it must and will. Or in still other words, as we regard free thought, free speech, and free discussion, as being the promoters of real truth, and lack of thought, restricted speech, and non-discussion, of error, so we feel it our duty to do what we can to speed the former, and destroy the latter. Real truth, like the diamond, will bear the light, bear handling, bear the severest scrutiny. Not so such truths as merely moral are. These, however seemingly beautiful in theory, and high-sounding in empty declamation and thoughtless song, just like the mock-diamond, must not be too closely viewed,—must not be too severely tested. And why must they not? Is it because they are too brilliant for human eyes to look upon; or because of an origin too sacred to be pried into by mortal man?—Neither. But because such is ever their shallow origin, and such their consequent lack of intrinsic worth, that they cannot bear the crucible,—can never long endure the scathing light of full and fair discussion. In a word, such truths not being by nature children of the light, it is only at a distance or in semi-darkness they possess the power to shine.

CHAPTER XVIII.

EDUCATION, MIND, BRAIN, ETC.

Upon that old, worn-out, and yet forever new subject, Education, we feel constrained to say that too much care cannot be bestowed upon the Common School; and especially in those countries where the will of the people, as expressed through the ballot-box, is the supreme power of the land. We say, especially in those countries where the will of the people, as expressed through the ballot-box, etc., because, in such, it is almost without exception within the walls of the District Schoolhouse that the laboring classes receive their education, in the popular acceptation of the term; and because it is the Heaven-born mission of those numerous and diversified classes, whether enlightened or unenlightened, polished or unpolished, to stand and be to the social fabric what the foundation is to the building—the support of the whole superstructure. Such being manifestly the case, it requires no argument to prove it to be the duty of all to try so to rear that rising generation of children, who are fast coming to possess the Earth with all its rich developed and undeveloped resources, as to make of them substantial men and women and not merely gilded automatons.—Between training up children in the way they should go by pursuasion, kindness, and the force of example, and merely restraining them from going in the way they should not by the use of the rod, the difference in effect is fearfully wide.

Because it is easier to put forth our hands and pluck the goodly fruit which others have toiled long and hard to bring to maturity, than it is to raise them for ourselves, because it is less laborious to read, remember, and thoughtlessly repeat what others have thought, observed, and written, than it is to think, observe, and originate for ourselves, it does not follow that verbal memory should be taxed to the verge of idiocy, at the expense of golden, but stifled and sleeping judgment. Great and numerous as have been the recent improvements in books, teachers, modes of instruction, school discipline, etc., we must think this non-thinking and consequently barren practice is still quite too generally mistaken for an expanding and ennobling process. Wherefore we would urge it upon all having the care of children and of youth, and especially upon those natural guardians and instructors, the fathers and mothers in the land, to strive diligently to cultivate in those that are fast coming to occupy their places, habits of industry, economy, and perseverance,—habits of observation, reflection, and thought,—habits of self-reliance and self-government; as well as that comparatively idle and easy one of reading, remembering, and parrot-like repeating, what others before them have thought and said and written. In short, both early and late, teach them the high and holy art of being useful to themselves and others by inuring them to the stern realities of living and of life, instead of dwarfing all that is inherently great and noble in their natures by loading down their memories with those numerous, formal, sickly moralities which must needs be forgotten, else unlearned, before truly wise they ever can become. Indeed, it would seem about time that people generally, and especially the leaders in Israel, should abandon the ancient idea of trying to save men, notwithstanding their numerous sins of omission and commission, by praying God to forgive the same; and turn their attention to teaching those said sinners, and particularly their comparatively unoffending offspring, what they must and what they must not do, would they save themselves from sin, hence from its bitter penalties; and hence from all necessity of that special salvation of which only the disobedient and law-breaking have need. Is it not manifestly better policy to lock the door of the stable whilst the horse is safely within, than it is to leave open the entrance to the spoiler, and then run ourselves to death in our zeal to recover the missing goods, arrest the thief, and bring him to punishment? In brief, Is it not a real truth, and one which is just as applicable to the mental man as the bodily one, That an ounce of saving preventive is ever worth a full pound of after-salvation or of cure?

We would not be understood as intimating that the teachers of the way and plan of salvation, as it is called, are not, as a class, sincere in their endeavors, nor that the mass of them do not honestly believe the bodily man to be one entity, and the mental man another and vastly more important one. On the contrary, it is our opinion that a large majority of the clergy honestly regard the mind as being not only an entity, but a personal entity; and not only a personal entity, but an entity which is wholly unphysical in its origin, unphysical in its nature, and unphysical in its action; and consequently an entity which is not dependent upon physical laws, physical causes, or physical means for its existence, manifestation, or support; and hence an entity that will never cease to be, but continue to go on manifesting the functions of thought, feeling, passion and emotion, reason and of knowledge, when all physical organs, laws, causes, and things shall have passed away. Nor can we doubt that the body of the clergy are just about as blindly dependent upon a few master spirits in the profession to do for them their theological seeing and thinking, as are the mass of the laity upon such body to do theirs. Far be it from us, therefore, to impute unto them any malintent for thus generally neglecting, as a thing not included in their high commission, to doctor the bodily man; that is, to give direction, activity, and power to the functional action of those numerous physical organs of which the man of clay is composed, notwithstanding it is upon these things that his education, as a physical being, must and doth forever depend. What! seriously think they are not acting according to the light they have? Think they are thus going about teaching and exhorting men with the corrupt intent of leading them astray to their hurt? We hope it is not in our nature to entertain of any considerable number of our fellow-men so ungenerous a thought; and yet, in reference to the real truthfulness of their teachings, as well as to the effect which they produce upon their followers, we are obliged with them quite widely to differ. For, as with them, so with us, we have no option, but are compelled to see according to the light we have,—are compelled to regard man as being not only animal in his instincts, and animal in his habits, but animal in his origin, and animal in his nature to the very bottom, and all the way through to his final end, the same as is the neighing steed; only that he is much more complex in his structure, vastly more perfect in his nervous department, and hence of vastly higher capacity and order. In other words, as man stands out revealed to us, he is neither more nor less than one greatly complicated and yet most perfect bundle of physical organs, possessing and possessed of just such capacities and powers, in kind, quality, and amount, as the action of those organs confer upon him, and no other. The brain, that hidden source of thought, feeling, passion and emotion, reason and of knowledge, is just as much part and parcel of his animal structure, and hence as much a physical thing, as is the skull that contains it, the blood that feeds it, or the heart which pumps its nutriment thereto; consequently it is no more subject to be operated upon by agencies or laws, not within great Nature's code embraced, than are the coats of his stomach or the linings of his intestines; and hence its education, or the education that is commonly denominated mental, must needs be just as much a natural and physical affair, as is that of his muscles, or any other part.

As it is the act of seeing which constitutes the thing called *sight*, so it is the act of thinking, feeling, etc., which constitute the thing called *mind*. In other words, as the brain of man, the same as that of every other animal, is a physical organ and governed in its action by physical laws, so the act of thinking in man is just as much a physical act, and hence just as much governed by physical laws, as is the act of thinking in the horse or any other animal. Such as are not determined to disbelieve this, but simply doubt its accuracy, let those watch carefully their own thoughts, feelings, and emotions; observe closely those of the insane as clothed in words they issue forth, or as in disjointed action they are spoken out; also let them compare the thoughts, feelings, ~~and emotions,~~ and emotions of great and good men in their dotage, with those of the same individuals when in their prime; and then if they are not more than half convinced that thoughts, feelings, and emotions are the very things which mind do constitute, consequently that mind is just as much the creature of that complex, physical organ, the brain, as is locomotion the creature of the muscular system, and hence that it is from beginning to end a physical act organically spoken into existence, we shall be a little surprised.

If it is desired to give the brain, or any particular organ or department thereof, strength, expertness, capacity of endurance, or tendency to quick and ready as well as long continued action, we must exercise it vigorously, being careful to keep within the limit of overtaxation or abuse. Of course, it is not claimed that, as a stimulant thereto, larger and yet larger weights should be placed upon it, the same as if it were a muscle that we were educating to carry heavy burdens, or that more and yet more of the Sun's strong rays should be let to fall upon it, the same as if it were an optic nerve; but that we should apply to it its own proper stimulant,—should tax and exercise it by compelling it oftener, quicker, longer, better, and more spontaneously to perform the act of producing within us the desired thoughts, feelings, or emotions, as the case may be, such being its proper function.

The thing commonly called *mind*, (and which was doubtless so called because it, the same as every other phenomenon, must needs have some name,) we do not regard as being an entity of any kind, but simply a compound act of the brain, the same, for a familiar illustrative example, as is the thing called jumping-the-rope, a compound act of the muscles. Jumping-the-rope! why, what is it but a compound act that is legitimately performed, or spoken into transitory existence, by certain contracting and expanding movements of that compound organ or department called the muscles? Surely this is all it is. And mind, when not spoken out in either words or action, what is it but a compound act which is legitimately performed, or spoken into a transitory existence within us, by certain undulatory movements of that compound organ or department called the brain? As it seems to us it is just this and nothing more. The fact is too well established to admit of doubt that, by pressing upon the brain, where a portion of the skull has been removed, consciousness becomes suspended, and the compound mental act, which constitutes what is called mind, at once becomes a non-existent thing, the same as does the compound muscular act called jumping the rope, the moment that motion in the appropriate muscles is brought to a stand, no matter from what cause. We say, the compound mental act, which constitutes what is called mind, at once becomes a non-existent thing, because it is abundantly proven that as long as the pressure upon the brain continues, and as often as repeated, so long and so often is the brain prevented from performing those peculiar undulatory movements which speak into existence, not only consciousness, but thought, feeling, emotion, etc.—the very things which mind do constitute and are. With these facts staring us in the face, How is it possible, rationally, to come to any other conclusion, than that the compound mental act which constitutes mind is no more a being or entity of any kind, and hence is no more a thing that is immortal, than is the compound muscular act which constitutes jumping-the-rope?—How? Properly speaking, then, the act performed by the brain and called mind can no more be the subject of educational training, than can the act performed by the muscles called jumping-the-rope;—not any more.

If we wish to become more alive and active mentally, it is the *brain*, the organ which speaks into existence within us the act known as mind, and not the mere act itself by the brain thus into existence spoken, which must be taught and habituated to greater activity by appropriately taxing and compelling it to perform, and accurately repeat, those same undulatory movements which mind do constitute; the same as must we by careful repetitions of the proper movements educate the *muscles* which speak into existence the act of jumping-the-rope, and not the mere act itself, would we become expert in the performance of that muscular feat.

If the thing called mind is not a being or entity of any kind,—is not in its primitive state of existence a homeless stranger, wandering up and down the immeasurable fields of ether and of atmospheric air in search of some vacant, puny infant born, into which to enter and a temporary habitation find, but is merely an act which is legitimately performed or spoken into existence by the brain, the same as is the thing called jumping-the-rope not a being or entity of any kind, but merely an act which is legitimately performed or spoken into existence by the muscles, then the question naturally arises, How comes it to pass, since all men have brains, that all have not the same amount of mother wit, or native capacity and talent? In other words, how happens it that, in almost every age and land, there are a few downright idiots, as well as another few who, though blessed with quite inferior educational advantages, are nevertheless not only a living law unto themselves, but stand boldly out as lights in the pathway of science, creators in the fields of art, and guides in the road to virtue and of happiness? Doubtless the noble science of Phrenology would explain the matter somewhat in this wise: It so happens for the reason that, pursuant to the operation of hereditary causes, there are some few individuals born, in almost every age and land, with such a quantity, quality, form, and location of brain, as merely fit it to perform those inferior grades of function which are common to animals of low order; whilst another few there are who are born with such a quantity, quality, form, and location of brain, as both fit and strongly predispose it, not only to be vigorous and active, but to perform those peculiar undulatory movements which create within the heads of its possessors, such thoughts, views, and opinions as, with a greater or a lesser portion of Nature and her undying laws, most beautifully accord; and hence, in just so far, it constitutes them intuitively strong in those certain directions, or natural geniuses upon those particular subjects. And as we know of no theory of mind, save this which makes the brain to be not only the organ by and through which it is manifested, but the thing which, speaks it into existence, that will satisfactorily account for one half of the different kinds of mental phenomena which are constantly being exhibited upon all sides round, so we must regard this circumstance as furnishing presumptive evidence at least, that this theory, and this alone, has its foundation in eternal verity.

"And have you any idea," inquires one, "that you will be able to bring others thus to think and believe?"—To this we answer: As we have come to see it, that is not a thing which is optional with either them or us, but wholly depends upon our being able so far to reach and operate upon the proper mental organs in their heads, as to cause such organs to execute those same undulatory movements which create and keep alive those ideas in ours. This done, and the same thoughts, views, feelings, and opinions will just as certainly be spoken into existence within their heads, as will the same human arm, or ten thousand different ones, always execute or speak into existence the same acts, whenever the same muscular contractions and expansions shall come to take place therein. In this way, it not unfrequently happens that such is the influence exerted by brains of a positive stamp upon such brains as are to them inferior, and of a negative order, as to cause these latter to vibrate in unison with the vibrations of these said former; and hence for the time being to produce, within the heads of this latter class of individuals, the same thoughts, feelings, etc., that have existence in the heads of the former class. In this way it happens, more or less often, that children are brought to feel and to think themselves guilty—and hence to confess that they are—of having committed some certain act which is now both honestly and forcibly, but quite injudiciously, being laid to their charge by parents, guardians, or teachers; the which act they not only never did commit, but perfectly well knew they never did, before coming to be thus charged therewith; and which act was by them unqualifiedly denied at the beginning, the same as it will be again, (if they are superlatively truthful children,) when from such overpowering influence, and its effects, they come to be freed. Yea, and it also sometimes happens that an individual of mature years, and one possessed of a brain of full average activity and power, but of impressible order, by being suspected, accused, reaccused, brought before the examining authorities, bound over for trial, and otherwise wrought upon, is at last brought to feel and to think that he must be guilty;—that he must be and is guilty of the crime which is thus wrongfully, but persistently and with crushing force, being laid to his charge. And wherefore, his brain being thus brought into this morbid and passively active condition, with reference to this one particular matter, he finally confesses himself guilty, notwithstanding, in truth and in fact, he is perfectly innocent. The sight of a mountain, or other object of interest from which we have been separated for years, at once brings to our recollection, as it is called, not only the name, but various incidents connected therewith; and it does this for the simple reason, that it again causes the same undulatory movements to take place in our brains, which did its presence at a former period of our lives. The man who is drunk remembers much better what he said and did a month ago, when last drunk before, than he does what he has since said and done whilst sober, and *vice versa*.—Corollary:—Like condition of the brain, no matter how brought about, is just as essential, not only to the existence of like mental capacity and power, but to the production of like thoughts, feelings, and emotions, as are like causes to the production of like effects of any other kind.—As a man becomes old and childish, more properly childlike, his brain becomes old and childlike; that is, it becomes lax and feeble like the brain of a child. The old man's brain has now become incapacitated to perform those same, strong, undulatory movements which it was wont to do when both he and it were in their prime; and hence is just fitted to perform such feeble, fickle ones as it did long years ago, when in age, as well as condition, he was a child before. And of this the consequence is, he fails to remember events which transpired whilst in the vigor of manhood, but remembers quite well such as occured when he was a child, notwithstanding so many more years have rolled between. Also the sudden recollection, or coming up in memory, as it is called, without any known exciting cause, of a thought, name, or circumstance long-since forgotten, What is it but the simple recurrence of that same wave or undulatory movement in the proper portion of the brain, which was present or taking place therein, when the thought, name, or other circumstance had existence there, long years before ?—As seems to us, it is just this, and nothing more. And thus on, of every kind, character, and grade of mental act or thing, commonly called recollection or memory, to the full chapter's end.

Such for ages has been the current of men's ideas, and hence such has come to be the genius of language to denote and convey them, that it is no easy matter to express clearly any thought which is measurably new, and especially is this the case of ideas upon subjects that are purely mental in their character ; that is, of such as have sole reference to the character and functions of the brain. This is a difficulty, however, over which it is of no use to mourn, notwithstanding greatly embarrassing, since, manifestly enough, naught, save time, patience, and perseverence, will ever work its cure. But the difficulty is upon us, and the consequence is, we not unfrequently find ourself obliged to use words in a way, which we deem, not only improper, but grossly absurd, in order to make ourself even partially understood. Thus, for instance, as we understand the matter, it is no more consonent to fact, and hence no more proper to say, *study* strengthens the mind, than it would be to say, *walking* strengthens the walking. And yet, when speaking upon some subject on which we desire to be as fully understood as possible, it becomes necessary to use such forms of expression as are in common use, and hence familiar to those addressed.

As seems to us, of the foregoing example, this would be the correct form of expression: Study strengthens the brain, and particularly that portion of it which is called into exercise by the act of studying, the same as does walking strengthen the muscles, and particularly that portion of them which is called into exercise by the act of walking; it being a law upon the human organism unalterably enstamped, that exercise, within the limit of abuse, strengthens every organ in the whole animal fabric.

Admitting the phenomenon called walking cannot be manifested without the presence and action of legs, it needs must follow, not only that legs are walking's organs, but that they are the organs which speak into existence the thing called walking, as well as manifest it. In the same manner, admitting the phenomenon called mind cannot be manifested without the presence and action of brains, it needs must follow, not only that the brain is mind's organ, but that it is the organ which speaks into existence the thing called mind, as well as manifests it. And admitting not only that the brain is mind's organ, but that it is a physical organ either simple or compound, it matters not which; then it needs must follow that the act of studying exercises the brain, and hence strengthens it, just the same, and for the same reason, that does the act of walking exercise the legs, and hence strengthen them; and consequently there is nothing more strange or unaccountable about the one than about the other. We say, admitting the above facts, and the case will so stand; and, as for ourself, we fully admit them. That the brain is the organ of all the mind that is in man, and hence of all the mind or mental action he ever manifests, seems to us just as clear as it does that the muscular system is the organ of all the motion that is in him, and hence of all the motion or muscular action he ever manifests. And wherefore, when from overstudying either children or men become languid and weary to a state of exhaustion, we must think it is not their so-called immortal minds that are *tired out*, and hence need rest, but their frail, mortal brains.

And yet once more we repeat, as we see it, the brain, notwithstanding within the dark and narrow confines of the skull locked up, is just as much a physical organ as are the muscles; and consequently that the act of thinking is just as much a physical act, or an act which is spoken into existence by the appropriate physical organ, as is the act of walking. In other words, for the reason that we are compelled to regard the act of walking, (which merely for example has been selected,) as not being an entity of any kind, but simply an act that is spoken into transitory existence by a certain portion of that complex, physical organ or department called the muscular system, for that same reason are we compelled to regard the act of feeling devotional, for another example, as not being an entity of any kind, but simply an act that is spoken into transitory existence, within the human head, by a certain portion of that complex, physical organ or department called the brain. And thus on of all the different acts by the human brain performed; and which acts, when altogether taken, the thing called mind do constitute and are.

Such being our well-settled views, it follows that we are compelled to think the compound act which is spoken into a transitory existence within us by that complex, physical organ or department called the brain, and which act is called mind, just like the compound act of walking which is spoken into a transitory existence by the proper portion of that complex organ or department called the muscles, is not an entity of any kind; consequently should never be spoken of as such,—should never be spoken of as a thing possessed of a permanent existence, but only as an act or passing performance of the brain; and hence the act of habituating the brain to reproduce in regular order certain undulatory movements, or the committing to memory, as it is usually called, of this, that, or the other lesson, can no more properly be called food for the minds of children or of men, than can the act of running of a foot-race be called food for the running;—not one bit more. And yet, as has been said above, and for reasons there stated, in the prosecution of this work, we not unfrequently find ourself obliged to speak in this same absurd manner.

As, however, time, patience, and persevering industry do make their impress upon all things human, so we not only hope, but confidently expect, that such will continue to be the progress of ideas, and hence such the corresponding changes in language to denote and convey them, that, for the most part, the adjective *mental*, and also the word *moral*, shall ultimately be driven into disuse by a qualifying epithet derived from the noun brain, in the form of *brenal* or *brainal*. And thus on, and still on, until the numerous difficulties in language by which that complex act of the brain called mind is at present surrounded shall all be removed.

As it is physical bread taken into the stomach and not exercise, which is the food of both brain and muscle, so this food they must both continue to have, else, of that complex, brenal act which constitutes mind, as well as the compound, muscular one which constitutes walking, there would soon be an end. We may be mistaken, but, then, we are unable to persuade ourself that the more thinking portion of our Christian friends are visionary enough seriously to suppose that there exists any such thing as human mind, in the wilderness islands of the ocean or the depths of the sea. And yet why should not mind have a dwelling in both these places, and especially in the crowded cabins of the numerous foundered ships, over which, and their unfortunate human freight, the dark blue waves have closed forever, provided it be an entity, and not a mere brenal act; and hence possesses the power to exist indefinitely on in the absence of living human brains to speak it into existence?—Why?

Of course, the man who is in good health, and surrounded by every pleasure which prosperity and the society of friends can afford, when he rises in the morning, wakeful and rested, cannot bear to think of taking leave of his friends that are clustered around him, stepping into a dark chamber, getting into bed, and sleeping all day. And why not?—Simply because to do so at that particular time, and under the then existing circumstances, is directly at variance with his fresh, wakeful, and highly social nature. In a few short hours, however, the gloom of night is sure to arrive, when, being weary from action, dull from the past day's wakefulness, and satiated with social pleasures, he gladly suspends his business, withdraws from his friends, divests himself of his clothing, gets into bed, closes his eyes, and falls into a profound sleep. Now, most assuredly, this living, breathing death, or state of unconsciousness even of his own existence, to which, under the pressure of these altered circumstances, he thus becomes a willing martyr, cannot be to him a thing unpleasant, so long as shall it thus uninterruptedly last; and hence could not be construed into a curse upon him, should it thus continue from dewey eve to balmy morn. And why not?—Simply because, as remarked above, at this particular moment, to take temporary leave of his business and friends, as well as of a state of conscious existence, is in full harmony with his present tired and satiated nature. Wherefore, by parity of reason, was this same profound sleep or type of death imperceptibly to lapse into death actual, and hence continue uninterruptedly on to all eternity, there could not be, to such individual, anything more monotonous, unpleasant, or dreadful in it, than there was in the first hour of that sweet, death-like repose, which was by him, the same as by us and everybody else, so fondly courted. And the fact that his friends, in obedience to a law which regulates and governs human nature in the living, would be compelled to mourn his departure, has nothing at all to do with the case; since the dead man, the only individual now in question, is passed entirely beyond the reach and operation of any such law. And hence, by the very plainest parity, much as we may be compelled to dislike the idea of dying, (by virtue of a certain law extending through and through all animated nature, and having reference to the protection and preservation of this present, bodily life, and not to any state of existence beyond the grave,) even when health is feeble, prospects gloomy, and friends stand coldly aloof, nevertheless, in all due time, when prostrate upon a bed of sickness we lie, or by the night of chilly age o'ertaken, our feelings will become so much altered that everything about us will seem to have undergone a change; and we in consequence find ourselves gradually becoming more and more weary of this toilsome, wakeful, conscious state of personal existence, and hence correspondingly more and more willing to exchange the same for death's kindly proffered everlasting sleep. In short, as certainly as do children dearly love to slide upon the ice in the cold and the snow, and as certainly as does a fit of sickness temporarily, and old-age permanently, quench out this desire, just so certainly, in all due time, will dread of death be compelled to depart from us, and desire to lay ourselves quietly down and be forever at rest take its place. Such, in our humble opinion, is the verdict which the dispassionate judgment of enlightened man, will ere long be compelled to pronounce, not only upon the benign institution, sleep, which, by its daily interposition, doth kindly relieve us about one-third of the time from a state of conscious existence, but upon that equally benign institution death, which, at the proper moment, doth kindly interpose, and so relieve us eternally therefrom.

That it is trying to a parent's feelings to stand by and see death's cold, destroying hand laid upon a son of culture and of promise, just as he is entering upon broad manhood's stage, we know by experience; and yet we must think there is more of pleasure in the lives of such as are thus early snatched away, in proportion to the perplexities and pains, than there is in the lives of those who longer live. And these are our reasons: Up to that period of life, care is measurably unknown. Up to that period, pleasures grow almost everywhere. Up to that period, hope, expectation, and confidence supremely reign. From and after that time, life assumes a much sterner aspect. From and after that time, cares, anxieties, and disappointments constantly do thicken.

CHAPTER XIX.

SOUL, SPIRIT, MIND, ETC.

Much as has been said and written about the immortal soul, the immortal spirit, and the immortal mind of man, we have never been able to obtain any very clear notion of what is meant by those high-sounding terms. Wherefore we will now take the liberty of inquiring, Do the different terms, immortal soul, immortal spirit, and immortal mind of man, all mean the same thing; or does each mean a different thing?—Which?

Allowing the two forms of expression, immortal soul, and immortal spirit, to mean the same thing, to mean a thing that is both spiritual and immortal, and the term immortal mind to mean something different; then the question presents itself, Is the soul of man an organized structure, and hence from bottom to top of spiritual organs composed; or is it an inorganic spirit something, and hence of organic structure, form, and parts devoid?—Which?

Allowing the soul of man to be an organized structure, and hence of spiritual organs composed; then the question arises, Is it governed in its form and limited in its extent, by the form and extent of the physical human fabric with which it is in companionship; or is it, in both form and extent, independent of its physical companion, the bodily man?—Which? And if it be an organized structure, and hence of spiritual organs composed, Does it see, hear, feel, think, etc., independently; that is, by means of its own appropriate, spirit organs; or is it indebted for all this class of capacities and powers to the existence and action of certain appropriate, physical organs, possessed and exercised by its physical mate, the bodily man?—Which? In other words, Is the soul of man possessed of spiritual hands, feet, eyes, ears, lungs, brain, tongue, etc.? And if so, does it see, hear, think, breathe, etc., by means of said spirit organs; or is it indebted for its ability to perform those different organic acts, either in whole or in part, to the existence and action of certain appropriate physical organs, possessed and exercised by the corporeal being called man?—Which?

Upon the other hand, allowing the soul of man to be an inorganic spirit something, whether existing within the narrow limits of its physical companion, the bodily man, or whether it exists in a state of diffusion, and hence occupies a more extensive field, How can it be supposed to see, hear, think, walk, etc.; since such things are none of them entities, but each and all mere acts or things which are spoken into a transitory existence by organic action; since organic action was never known to be performed without organs; and since inorganic substance, whether material or spiritual, and no matter how abundant, is not of organs of any kind possessed?—How?

Further, Did the soul of the man Tiberius Cesar, for example, eternally exist; or was it created when Tiberius was created?—Which? And if it eternally existed, Did it eternally exist in its full manhood's strength; or was it from all eternity up to the time when Tiberius was born, and began to wax great and strong, only of infantile size and strength possessed?—Which? Upon the other hand, if Tiberius' soul did not eternally exist, and hence was created an infant soul when he was created an infant man, and if his said *soul* was in possession of *mind*; then the question arises, Did both the infant soul of Tiberius and the mind of Tiberius' said infant soul grow with his growth, strengthen with his strength, sleep when he slept, awake when he awoke, etc.; or did one or both of them do any or all of these things independently of said physical Tiberius; or did they not do them at all?—How about these things?

Allowing the human mind to be an attribute of human beings; and not only of human beings an attribute, but a real entity; and not only a real entity, but a something which is immortal in fact, as well as in name; then the question presents itself, Is the mind an organized structure, and hence of incorporeal organs composed; or is it an incorporeal inorganic something, and hence of organic structure, form, and parts devoid?—Which? And if the mind of man is an incorporeal organized structure, Is it governed in its form and limited in its extent by the form and extent of the physical human fabric with which it is in companionship; or is it, in both form and extent, independent of its physical companion, the bodily man?—Which? In other words, Does the mind hear, see, think, etc., independently; that is, by means of its own appropriate incorporeal organs; or is it indebted for all this class of capacities and powers to the existence and action of certain appropriate physical organs, possessed and exercised by its physical mate, the bodily man?—Which? Upon the other hand, if the mind **is** an incorporeal inorganic something, whether existing within the narrow-limits of its physical companion's head, the head of man, or whether in a state of diffusion it exists, and hence occupies a much more extensive field, How can it be supposed to see, hear, think, etc.; since such things are none of them entities of any kind, but each and all mere acts or things which are spoken into transitory existence by organic action; since organic action was never known to be performed without organs; and since inorganic substance, whether material or immaterial, corporeal or incorporeal, is not of any organs possessed?—How?

Further, Did the mind of the man Pontius Pilate, for example, eternally exist; or was it created an infant *mind* when Pontius was created an infant *man?*—Which? If it eternally existed, then the question is, Did it eternally exist in its full manhood's strength; or was it from all eternity up to the time when Pontius was born, and began to grow and wax strong, only of infantile size and strength possessed?—Which? And if the mind of Pontius was created an infant when he was created an infant, Did it grow with his growth, strengthen with his strength, sleep when he slept, awake when he awoke, swoon when he swooned, fail with age when he with age did fail, etc.; or did it do any or all these things independently of said physical Pontius; or did it not do any of them at all?—How about these things?

With all the light which has been shed upon this subject by the much that has been said and sung and written about the immortal soul, the immortal spirit, and the immortal mind of man, How many persons out of every ten, upon the spur of the moment, will answer all the foregoing questions alike? How many out of that number, after a week's examination of the different authorities, and another week for reflection thereupon, will answer them alike? And how many be willing to abide by the logical consequences of each and every answer, which, at the fortnight's end, they themselves shall give?—How many?

Manifestly enough, to explain a mystery by a circumlocution which only tends to render the mystery still more dark and mysterious, doth not particulary benefit the learner, whether it does the teacher or not. Why, then, will not some one of the many teachers, who seem to understand these things, be kind enough to explain them briefly, straightforwardly, and without concealment or mystification; so that we common mortals, whom they equally concern, may come to have some faint idea, not only of what is meant by those high-sounding terms, but of the character and extent of the things wherein from the effect of early education and the force of habit we are wont to imagine, and hence to say, that we believe?—It is not the error that is clearly defined and plainly spoken out, which is seriously hindering, misleading or dangerous; but the one that is enveloped by the fogs of indirection, circumlocution, and uncertainty, as that by its advocates it can be made to mean anything or nothing, as the exigencies of the case shall seem to require. Such will-with-a-wisp errors, however grossly absurd, it is hardly possible to tree and expose.

Self-evidently, as seems to us, whatever is possessed of consciousness, or even of animated existence, except of very low order, must be possessed of an organized structure, and hence have body, form, and parts. And whatever is possessed of body, form and parts, must of necessity be finite in dimensions, finite in character, and finite in the strength of the functions which its different composing organs are competent to perform. Wherefore, for the reason that the eye can never perform the act of hearing, the ear the act of seeing, the heart the act of thinking, the liver the act of reasoning, or the kidneys the act of judging, for that same reason it must be impossible for inorganic substance, whether material or spiritual, and no matter how abundant or where existing, ever to perform, or speak into existence, a single one of the different organic acts which, when altogether taken, the thing called mind do constitute and are.

As we have come to see it, brain, and the complex phenomenon called mind, stand in the relation of cause and effect; the human mind being the legitimate effect of the existence and action of human brains; horse-mind, of the existence and action of horse-brains; goat-mind, of goat-brains; and thus on downward until the thing called mind becomes lost in instinct.—That mind exists in the absence of brains to speak it into existence, Who in this enlightened age is prepared to believe? And who that believes it is prepared to plant himself squarely upon the proposition, and, from the evidences afforded by Nature's volume, publicly maintain it over his own signature?—Who?—Because man has a much larger brain than has the horse; because the brain by him possessed differs widely in form from that possessed by the horse; because it is much more complex in its structure than is the brain of the horse; because his brain is much more vigorously exercised as well as much more highly cultivated than is the brain of that quadruped; and because, legitimately in consequence of all these advantages, the higher animal man possesses and manifests a much higher order of mind than does said lower animal; it will not do to infer that his mind is not, from beginning to end, a brenal production, the same as is that of the horse; and hence that its existence will not cease with the death of that noble brain which is its parent cause.

As the brain of the horse Dexter, for example, stands parent cause to the existence of all the mind by him possessed or manifested, be it little or be it much, and as the brain of said horse is clearly a thing that is mortal and not immortal, so the mind of said horse, the product of the existence and action of his said mortal brain, must also be mortal and not immortal. In like manner, since the brain of the man John Jenks, for example, stands parent cause to the existence of all the mind by him possessed or manifested, be it much or be it little, and as the brain of said John is clearly a thing which is mortal and not immortal; so the mind of said John, the product of the existence and action of his said mortal brain, must also be mortal and not immortal. In short, because the ancient Fathers who wrote the Bible were profoundly ignorant of the brain's character and function; because that great muscular pump, the heart, was by them supposed to be the parent of the affections, the source of thought, and seat of understanding; and because, in consequence of such ignorance and misjudgments, they were in the habit of speaking of mind just as if it was a real entity, instead of speaking of it as being a mere act that is spoken into transitory existence, within the head, by that complex organ the brain; it will not do for us, from a blind reverence for ancient men, ancient opinions, and ancient modes of thought, to repudiate the testimony of facts, and trample under foot, as worthless, the deductions of reason and the teachings of natural science.—Not in this way is progress ever made.—

The soul of man and the spirit of man, we regard as being one and the same thing,—as being neither more nor less than the life of man,—as being a thing which is spoken into being and maintained in existence in the same way that is the life, soul, or spirit, of the horse; namely, by organic action. The hour a man finally ceases to perform the organic act of breathing, that hour with him doth all organic action come to an end; and hence, from and after that time, he is just as devoid of the thing called life, soul, or spirit, as is the horse whose lungs have finally ceased to perform the act of inhaling the inspiring influence in atmospheric air contained. In other words, we have no option in the matter, but are compelled to think that organic structure, and what is called by the different names life, soul, or spirit, stand in the relation of cause and effect; human life, soul, or spirit, being the legitimate effect of the existence and action of certain vital organs, which are part and parcel of the organic structure of human beings; horse-life, soul, or spirit, of the existence and action of certain vital organs, which are part and parcel of horse-beings; and hence that the life, soul, or spirit, of a man, the same as that of the horse, is just as much a thing which is mortal, as is his organic structure, its parent cause. We say, life, soul, or spirit, is the legitimate effect of the existence and action of certain vital organs, etc., because both men and horses possess sundry organs which, although quite useful, are not essential to life; and hence death doth not necessarily result from their loss.

Of course it is easy, very easy, to scoff at the idea of comparing a man to a horse in any respect, or for any purpose; but then it fortunately so happens that scoffs and sneers are weightless arguments with men of brains, and especially with such as are sincere inquirers after real truth, whether it accords with ancient moral truth or not.

The stock of elements from which all created things are made, notwithstanding inconceivably vast in amount, is nevertheless not unlimited.

Of the amount of elements, in some form, there is never any variation; but, legitimately consequent upon the continuous acts of creation and destruction, their amount, in any particular form, is constantly varying.

There never was and never can be anything, great or small, material or immaterial, inanimate or animated, made out of nothing: that is a thing which is simply impossible.

There never was and never can be any such thing as a miracle, in the sense of that word as used by theologians; and yet, of marvels or things wonderful, there is no conceivable end.

Great as God is, he is just as absolutely limited in power and bound by law, as is the feeblest atom.

Much as the eternal God has done and is still doirg, he

never works, except by the use of means, and never, except by the use of just such means as are in existence at the time and ready to his hand.

Vast as creation is, God never made a single thing which is not a legitimate result of the means used in pushing it into existence in created form; and hence never a thing which is not, from beginning to end, the creature of law.—The foregoing propositions, whether correct or whether erroneous, would seem to be, each and all, as fully self-evident as any that can be named, which are not demonstrable.

From the erroneous assumption that, "With God, all things are possible," is drawn the equally erroneous conclusion that, notwithstanding it is an invariable custom with him nowadays to work in accordance with fixed laws, he was much in the habit of working contrary thereto in days of yore, and thus performing miracles. What! God work a part of the time in accordance with law, and thus produce into existence things that are natural, and a part of the time contrary to law, and thus perform miracles? Why, such a charge against the character of a God "With whom no variableness, neither shadow of turning," is simply libelous.

As the elements of which our physical bodies are composed do fall back of their own weight into the common stock whence they came, hence become the same as new, hence are again seized upon by Creative Process, and hence again by her used in building up such further created forms and things as are they appropriate to do, thus rendering creation's epoch one vast cycle; so, reasoning from analogy, it would seem to follow that the same thing must needs befall the elements of which our spiritual bodies are composed, provided any such bodies we really have. We say, provided any such bodies we really have, because if we have such bodies, just like a spirit God, they must needs be composed of something,—must needs be composed of spiritual substance; and, of that substance, the same as of material, there must undoubtedly be some limit, however vast may be the amount. If, therefore, human beings have spiritual bodies, as well as physical ones, and if their spiritual bodies, do not die, the same as do such physical ones, consequently the spiritual elements of which they are composed are not, in like manner, emptied back into the common stock whence they came, and hence are not and cannot be by Creative Process, in like manner, reused and re-reused indefinitely on; then, by unavoidable consequence, just as soon as shall the original stock of spiritual elements, by the creation of spiritual bodies, become exhausted, (and, at the rate human beings are being created, thus exhausted at some time they surely must be,) just so soon will the further creation of human beings be compelled to stop, or at least the further creation of them with spiritual bodies. Did not destruction follow at the heels of creation and pull down, creation would soon be compelled to cease building up for want of materials with which to do it. Not until the Sun and Moon and Earth and stars shall fall into decay can other worlds and systems of worlds be created thereout.

CHAPTER XX.

HOPE'S CHARACTER AND MISSION.

Hope has her proper kind and quality of pleasures, the same as does knowledge, for the reason that the act of hoping, just like the act of knowing, is the legitimate offspring of a brenal organ whose normal exercise doth speak it into pleasurable existence within us. Hope, too, the same as knowledge, has her proper sphere in which to operate, also her bounds which she can never pass: that sphere, the entire round of uncertainty; that bound, all knowledge whether actual or merely upon faith dependent; it being no more possible soberly to hope for what we know or even firmly believe can never happen, than it is for this same bright, but dark futurity-loving angel to feed upon the settled past. Or, to present the idea in a little different shape, the emotion called Hope, the same as the feeling of anger or fear, is a creature of the brain, the offspring of the proper brenal organ whose function it is to rear castles upon the sandy foundations of uncertainty, and to feast itself upon the glittering products of the unknown future.

Such being Hope's true character and mission, she is ever bound to fly the approach of stubborn facts, the same as is coward fear the awakening of manly courage, it being at the point where certainty ends and doubt commences, that she ever begins to flap her gilded wings. In other words, what we know or even firmly believe can never come to take place, we cannot possibly hope for; and, for what we know or firmly believe is certain to come to pass, not any more. Thus, for an assumed example, the hunter, who this evening shall have the misfortune to get benighted and lost in the wilderness, will no doubt impatiently wait and anxiously watch for the coming of to-morrow's light to help him out;

but, then, he cannot possibly hope the Sun will rise at midnight and give him light, for the reason that he knows full well it will not do it; and not a bit more that it will rise at the proper time to-morrow morning, since of the taking place of that event he feels equally certain.

Such is the nature of the human machine, and such the distribution of labor among the different organs of which it is composed, that neither actual knowledge nor unqualified belief is any more competent to excite to action the brenal organ called Hope, and thus cause it to create within us the emotion called by the same name, than is the sound of a drum or the odor of a flower to excite into action the optic nerve, and so cause it to create within us the sensation called sight;—not any more. Wherefore the fact that the best of us Christians do more or less indulge the hope that death may not be to us, as individual entities, an eternal sleep,—do more or less strongly hope and believe that in the end of the world when the "Sun shall be turned into darkness, and the Moon into blood," we shall be raised from death unto life, is conclusive evidence that we do none *know* that such will be the case, nor yet with our whole souls *believe* that it will. To this same effect taught the philosophic Paul some eighteen hundred years ago, when he said: "For we are saved by hope. But hope that is seen, is not hope: for what a man seeth, why doth he yet hope for?"—Rom., 8. 24.

Again, as of every other brenal organ, so of this particular one whose function it is to create within us the emotion called Hope, in different individuals it doth quite widely differ, not only in its actual size, activity, and power, but also in its relative, as compared with the other brenal organs in the same head. Widely different, therefore, as forever must be the strength of this emotion in different persons, in the same individual its relative influence is always proportionate to the relative strength of its organ, and the weakness of the evidence which stands opposed to the taking place of the desired thing upon the one hand, or in favor of its taking place upon the other, and no matter which. As, however, this is an important point, and as we are desirous of being clearly understood upon it, so we must be permitted to be a little prolix, and illustrate the same in manner following:—Upon a beautiful autumnal afternoon, a mother sent her little son a short distance to a spring upon the bank of the river, for a cup of water. With a willing heart and light step the little fellow started upon his mission, but, alas, he never returned! The delay made aroused the mother's fears, and in search of him she went. The father was hastily summoned from his toil of felling the trees of the forest, and he the search repeated. Soon were the few, hardy, neighboring settlers apprized of what was going on, and, ere the Sun's last rays had faded in the West, the rough, bushy, and deeply entangled margin of the old St. Lawrence, her adjacent wilds and deep blue waters had been as thoroughly searched as time and circumstances would permit, and yet of the missing child no trace was found. Night finally put an end to their efforts, and as the probabilities all seemed to point toward the fact of his having somehow fallen into the river, by whose strong current he had been borne onward and inward to a deep and watery grave; so filled with this belief, the sympathizing neighbors returned to their respective cabins, and soon, by them, of the sad incident, no more was thought or said. Not so, however, with those fond and sadly bereft parents, notwithstanding to the same painful conclusion they were intellectually compelled to yield an unwilling assent. No; for as Certainty had thus far failed to set her seal upon the fate of their darling boy and only child, so Hope, in them, still retained a sort of dreamy, spasmodic existence. We say, Hope, in them, still retained a sort of dreamy spasmodic existence, because, in spite of the convictions of their better judgment, for days, months, and even years were those fond parents more or less upon the watch for that darling form, and instinctively listening to catch the silvery accents of his call. Oft upon the long evenings of the ensuing winter, whilst seated before the large, open fire watching the curling smoke in its lazy and fantastic ascent, would instinctively spring up in memory, not only the name, but the image of their dear lost one. And often, before they were aware of it, would they be absorbed in conversation and speculation, not upon what was his probable fate, but upon what Hope whispered might possibly have happened to their darling boy. We say, upon what Hope whispered might possibly have happened, etc., for so deep and strong was their love for their missing child, consequently so ardent was the desire that he might somehow and somewhere be still living, that, upon such occasions, they were almost certain so to talk the matter over, and cook the thing up in their imaginations, as, for the time being, mutually to revive and strengthen each other's hopes up to a point bordering so close upon belief as to be near akin to faith, that their dear Herbert was not food for the fishes, but had been ruthlessly torn from them by the hand of some of the few straggling Indians that were occasionally known to pass up and down the stream, in their light canoes. In this way, strange and unaccountable as to the acerb old bachelor it may appear, time after time did those fond parents become so filled and temporarily carried away with this irrational, but comparatively pleasing idea, that, in fancy, they saw their unhappy, little, chieftain son, of only seven summers, throw down his tiny bow and arrows, run from the hated red men, thread his lone and tedious way through wood and thicket, across marsh and stream, to the home of his birth, all naked and worn, but safe and well.

And now, we appeal, when are taken into consideration all the circumstances of the case, Were not the anxieties, hopes, and feelings of those sadly bereft parents so perfectly natural, as not to need analysis or comment? And yet, in point of principle, wherein do they differ from the hopes and feelings by us indulged of a future, happy existence for ourselves and loved ones in some far-off, invisible world, when, in so far as it is possible for our surviving friends to see and determine by sense, we are as dead and cold as the clods of the valley? And not only the principle of the thing, but the means whereby those bereft parents, upon the long winter evenings, did thus mutually revive and strengthen in themselves such fond hopes, wherein do they essentially differ from those by us used at our interesting prayer meetings, and other religious gatherings of a like character; where, by alternately talking, singing, praying, and exhorting, we excite, cheer, and encourage each other on, until, for the time being, we become mutually wrought up to that peculiar pitch of excitement and hope ecstatic, which we are wont to call *The outpourings of God's spirit, getting our spiritual strength renewed, etc.?*—Of course, we may be wrong, but then, it really seems to us that, in all this class of cases, we, his feeble animated fractions, mistake effects, by ourselves legitimately produced, for the special interposition and influence of Almighty God.—

For the reason that those parents had in their heads such an organ as Philiprogenitiveness, for that reason was their innate love for their missing child both deep and strong; and hence, for that same reason, was their desire that he might live to cheer their pathway, bless their declining years, and solace them in death correspondingly deep and strong. They did not positively know that he was dead, wherefore they more or less fondly, but dreamily, hoped he was not,—hoped he had not fallen a prey to the remorseless waters; but was somewhere still alive, and they by him remembered. The breathing of those fond, dreamy hopes the one to the other was perfectly natural, and the repeatedly doing so not only tended to keep the feeling alive in each, but to strengthen the same in both. In like manner, for the reason that universal man has in his head such an organ as Vitativeness, for that reason is his innate love of life both deep and strong; and hence, for that same reason is his desire to live correspondingly deep-seated and powerful. He does not positively know that he will not somehow, in some form, and somewhere continue to maintain, on and on, a conscious, personal existence after that he is physically dead, decomposed, his elements resurrected in the form of gas, dissipated in air, and into millions of new and different created forms have entered; and hence he more or less indulges a sort of dreamy hope that he shall: And the breathing of this hope the one to another at the conference meeting, and upon other similar occasions, (for, during the mass of the time which is not thus specially dedicated to the service of the Lord, it would hardly be supposed from either speech or action, that any such idea had ever entered into the human head,) is not only natural, but legitimately tends to keep the same alive, and strengthen it in each and all. And the reason why upon the Sabbath-day, and occasionally at other times—when not with some more practical idea or pursuit absorbed—we are wont to assemble ourselves together, to the end that we may see each other and, by means of the different instrumentalities invented and used for that purpose, the more readily be brought to fall into this same magnetic condition, and hence into this same train of hopeful reflections, is partly because we are created social beings, and partly because the doing so doth temporarily relieve us from the monotonous round of thoughts, feelings, cares, and anxieties of every-day life, by calling into play a deeply rested class of our brenal organs which are panting for exercise. Or thus: Because we are organically commanded to be social beings, as well as organically commanded to love our lives, and hence to try to preserve them, therefore we do earnestly desire to live and enjoy the society of our friends, not only until we are old, quite old, but still on beyond the bounds of the grave. And hence by the aid of Hope, acting in concert with Vitativeness, the organ which creates within us love of life, we come to indulge in a sort of blind, dreamy belief, more or less strong, that we shall thus continue to live and enjoy; and so forget not the assembling of ourselves together, to the end that our strong social organs may be gratified by the congenial companionship thus periodically afforded, and our weak faith therein be renewed and strengthened. And finally, as we have come to see it, and as has been elsewhere said and repeated, love of life is neither more nor less than a physical feeling or act, which is spoken into existence within us by the proper brenal organ, the same as is love of children, of property, etc., by their respective, appropriate organs; and, of the strong desire which we feel to live, not only until we are old, very old, but on past death to all eternity, the same; and of the hope that we shall so live the very same. And thus on of our every wish, thought, feeling, and emotion, just as surely as is the brain the organ of mind.

We are not unmindful of the fact that the individual, in whose head the organ of Order, for example, is large and active, is prone to think and to feel that he should have been very miserable, had it been his fortune to have possessed that same disregard for method, that same slovenly nature and slip-shod turn of mind which are possessed and manifested by Mr. Careless. But, then, it must be borne in memory that this individual, had he been born and brought up a Mr. Careless, would then have been a Mr. Careless from sole to crown; and hence would all along have been compelled to regard his pet idea of "a place for everything, and everything in its place," as being all a matter of fuss and feathers. In like manner, to those who are so organized and balanced that hope in them is eternally springing up and running over like a fountain, (the same being a leading trait in their characters, because a ruling organ in their heads in point of activity,) it undoubtedly seems as if the world would be all a blank, but for its constantly cheering rays. And yet, because such persons by virtue of their organic structures and the force of habit are compelled to feel thus, and because it really seems to them as if the pleasures derived from observation, reason, and knowledge, can never come to equal those which, by the light of such observation, reason, and knowledge, must needs be curtailed, crowded out, and destroyed, it does not follow that these their said feelings and opinions are correct interpretations of the general workings of Nature's laws. Upon the contrary, this is manifestly a narrow, brenal error, and very similar to the one which children and youth commit when they fancy—as not unlikely we all have done—that the pleasures derived from sliding upon the ice, riding down hill, the merry party, the crowded ball-room, etc., can never be equalled, much less eclipsed, and finally crowded out of their heads to make room for joys more rational,—to make room for those solid and enduring pleasures that are ever incident to maturer years. We repeat, all this, although perfectly natural under certain circumstances and at a certain stage of life, is nevertheless a narrow, brenal error that is spoken into existence within us by the strong, blind organs of feeling and emotion; and hence it is an error which a more enlarged acquaintance with ourselves, with human nature, and the fountains from which legitimately flow the different tastes, capacities, and streams of human happiness, will enable us intellectually to see and correct. And thus on of all the different brenal organs and combinations of organs which parent cause do stand to all the different tastes, dispositions, and traits of character by man possessed and manifested, in any and all the different stages and conditions of life.

Although not a single human being now alive has ever tasted death, but only life, nevertheless are we not all intellectually convinced from the past history of the race as written in the grave-yards, that we too are mortal; and hence that, sooner or later, we also shall physically die? As every reflecting man must be presumed to be convinced of this, so every reflecting man must be presumed to know that this kind and character of teaching is directly calculated to preclude from rising up within him the fond Hope that, from the reign of physical death, he, his own dear self, may possibly escape. We repeat, every reflecting man must be presumed to know this; and yet who is prepared to say it is not both wise and proper thus to teach, and thus believe? And who to affirm that it is not, upon the whole, better and more happifying to any individual to understand the fact, even in reference to this most solemn of all earthly events, than it would be for such individual to go on deceiving himself and others with the Hope that he, and all such others as shall come to believe and practice as he does, will never physically die,—will never, personally, be blotted from the face of the Earth, the same as have uniformly been our fathers? And not only this, but so long as it is universally known that man's love of physical life is the strongest of all his loves, and his dread of physical death the deepest of all his dreads; and so long as it is admitted in both theory and practice, that it is better for every one to understand the fact that he must surely, physically, die, notwithstanding this is the very thing which above all others he would most gladly avoid, than it would be for him to go on from the cradle to the grave indulging the hope that, unlike his predecessors upon the Earth, he will never be compelled to yield up his physical life; How can it rationally be supposed that the tinsel pleasures afforded by the soaring angel Hope, upon this same subject or any other, do outweigh the sober, solid joys afforded by the practice of that patient perseverance in the investigation of facts, which doth ripen into knowledge, and which knowledge, by unavoidable consequence, must and doth have the effect, to an extent with itself correspondent, to clip her gilded wings?

Self-evidently, as seems to us, actual knowledge is always more enlightening in its tendency, hence always more elevating in its character, and hence always, upon the whole, more happifying in its effects, than is a mere hopeful belief in even the most honeyed fiction. Wherefore we are compelled to think that the pleasures afforded by the normal exercise of those brenal organs, whose function it is to fill us with light and knowledge of what actually is, and is to be, are always of a higher grade than those afforded by that class of blind organs, whose function it is, in wisdom's absence, to swell us with the unreal, and puff us up with windy conceptions of what is not, nor, indeed, ever can be. And wherefore we have no option in the matter, but are compelled to hold that the pleasures which flow from knowledge, or rather from the vigorous exercise of those brenal organs which lead thereto, and so bring us into its possession, are not only superior in quality, but also in kind, to those derived from the riotings of Hope in the broad fields of uncertainty.

But to return once more to those sadly bereft parents:—Who does not know that they were anxious to embrace the fact that their darling boy was drowned, if drowned he really was? And who not that it is in the nature of us all to be anxious to learn as speedily as possible, that the dearest friend we have in the world is dead, if dead he is? And yet it cannot but be manifest to all that such knowledge, the moment it is received, must have the effect to blot out forever the hope by us so fondly cherished of enjoying that friend's sweet society for long years to come.

Because every organ by man possessed is, upon the whole, good, and not absolutely bad, a single one; and because the normal exercise of every organ, within the limit of abuse, doth legitimately afford him a species of pleasure, either higher or lower; it must not be inferred that they are all alike good and noble, and hence that they are all equally exalted and happifying in their functions. Upon the contrary, as it is neither Vitativeness nor Hope, but the intellectual group, which first and foremost in the human temple stand, so the pleasures afforded by this class of brenal organs do legitimately constitute a superior order. Wherefore, whether reasoning from analogy or whether from facts, we must regard it as being unphilosophical to conclude that, when man shall come to know more of himself and more of Nature's legitimate workings, and consequently to understand not only that he must surely, physically, die, (the very thing he most doth fear and dread,) but that that event, come when it may, will be to him, as an individual entity, the final wind-up, he will any the less enjoy life, or be any the less useful and happy in consequence of such knowledge. Indeed, the inference would seem to be irresistible that, in this latter branch of the case, the same as in the former, the sober, solid joys which flow from knowledge, and the act of endeavoring to acquire, must outweigh the pleasures afforded by that Hope which it is Certainty's mission, upon any and all subjects, to blot out and forever destroy the moment it arrives. At any rate, in the enjoyment of such a faith, we have lived happily for years, and by it, much as we love to live, we are not afraid to die.

Moreover, unless we mistake human nature and the legitimate incentives to actions, great and noble, the settled conviction that our only chance of living on, after we are physically dead, resides in the posterity we shall leave and the works we shall have performed, would of itself almost work miracles;—would almost work miracles, not only by way of stimulating us, each and all, to try to do something worthy to be remembered by coming generations, but by impressing us with a more deep and lively sense of the duty we owe to ourselves, our children, and to society. And hence we must think that such a conviction would do more, in a few brief generations, toward unfolding and elevating both bodily and brenally that race of which we are a part, than is it possible for any amount of timorous hope, and narrow, selfish belief in a personal existence for darling self beyond the grave ever to do.

CHAPTER XXI.

"WHATEVER IS, IS RIGHT."

"All nature is but art, unknown to thee ;
All chance, direction which thou canst not see ;
All discord, harmony not understood ;
All partial evil, universal good.
And, spite of pride, in erring's spite,
One truth is clear,—WHATEVER IS, IS RIGHT."

Whatever is, must of necessity be right, for the reason that whatever is, is caused to be by Nature,—is made to take place and be by operation of natural law. Or, to state the proposition a little more fully, if it be a real truth, which we must think it is, that

"All are but parts of one stupendous whole,
Whose body Nature is, and God the soul,"

(God and Nature being only different names for the same thing,) then, manifestly enough, whatever doth come to have existence, no matter when nor where, must come to have it legitimately, because spoken into being pursuant to the workings of some branch or department of Nature ; consequently must be part and parcel of Nature herself; and hence must of necessity be, upon the whole, not only right, but *good and right.* In other words, if God, the Creator of all things, is, upon the whole, good and not bad; then, by unavoidable consequence, must all created things be, upon the whole, good and not bad. And if the Creator and Governor of the universe doth reign in and rule over all things, upon the whole, right and not wrong ; then, by unavoidable consequence, must all things operate, upon the whole, right and not wrong ; and so be themselves productive of results that are, upon the whole correspondingly right and not wrong. Or, in still other words, between God, the PARENT

TREE, and his created works, *the fruit*, there can never be supposed to exist the slightest discrepancy.—That like begets like, and not unlike, is a law which can never be controverted.

We are not unmindful that, to this view of things, an objection may not unlikely be urged somewhat as follows: If it be a fact that nature, God, and the Sum of all Substance, material and immaterial, in created and in primary form, are one and the same; consequently that the laws of Nature, or of God, by which the universe is sustained and governed, are neither more or less than the joint and several natures of things themselves, working on and working ever in just such a manner as they needs must work; consequently that all thinks ever did, now do, and forever will continue to work together in such a manner as currently to produce results which are, upon the whole, good and not evil; consequently that whatever is, is of Nature,—is of Nature's legitimate workings, or of some branch or department thereof, and hence must of necessity be, upon the whole, *right* and not *wrong*; then what is the use of making any effort to bring about a change in this, that, and the other thing, since everything is all good and right now? Or to state the objection as for the most part it is our fortune to hear it presented, "If you believe, as you affirm, that the state of things which currently exists, no matter what that state, where the place, nor how widely different from what at some other point of time it may have been, is, when taken in all its bearings and consequences present and remote, not only good and right, but is, in fact, the only state which, at that time, in that place, and under the circumstances then and there currently existing and operating as producing cause, could possibly have been; then why are you not content to sit still, look on, and rejoice over the old Mosaic account of creation, since that is a thing that *is* and for thousands of years *has been*, instead of thus endeavoring to overthrow it?"

And now, reader, before attempting to answer this objection, we must be permitted to state our position with regard to certain branches of creation a little more fully than has yet been done, to the end that whether right or whether wrong, whether we make a convert of you or whether we do not, you may be put into more full possession of what are our feeble views upon that underlying subject. As seems to us, then, this Earth is, to-day, a very different thing from what it once was,—is, as a whole and upon the whole, greatly in advance of what in its early and cometary stage it must have been; also that the change from a feeble embron body of eccentric order to one far more perfect has been the work of long and countless ages. In other words, we hold this our goodly Mother Earth to be, the same as the present cometary masses which sweep through space, one of Nature's legitimate offspring; and that she is indebted for her present advanced size, rotund form, and queenly appearance to what, for want of a more appropriate and expressive term, we shall call *progressive creation*. Moreover, from as full and impartial a survey of this wide field as we are able to make, we are compelled to regard it as being not only possible, but probable, that when the surface of this Earth, including its aqueous, aerial, and other external surroundings, became so far advanced in the scale of perfection as anywhere to offer, for the first time in its history, a fit, quiet place, the proper equable temperature, and suitable abundance of nutriment to support in being and foster into growth the lowest species of vegetable life, which ever had existence thereupon, then, and not till then, was that species, for the first time, spoken into organic existence upon its face, out of certain fitting, inorganic elements; and this not by miracle, nor yet by design, in the common acceptation of the term, but pursuant to the operation of natural law; in other words, by the combined presence and operation of a few, low, feeble, appropriate, and appropriately pedisposed vegetable-creative causes. In this way probably did vegetable creation begin; and thus on, and still on, has been the advance of our planet, and its adaptations to sustaining and fostering into growth vegetables of a higher, and yet higher grade, vegetable life ever keeping pace therewith; because, as already suggested, legitimately pushed up, step by step, thereby.

Or thus: As, for the first time in its history, vegetable life must have been pushed into being by the joint presence and operation of a few, low, and trifling vegetable-creative causes, so the character of that first species must needs have been correspondingly low and frivolous. And the more the surface of the Earth and its different vegetable-life-sustaining surroundings became advanced, the more predisposed vegetable-creative causes became advanced into ripe ones, consequently the more numerous, as well as correspondingly more complex and higher, legitimately became the acts or processes called creation; and thus continuously on.

Because, at a creative point of time, inconceivably far back in old eternity, predisposed vegetable-creative causes became advanced to such a state of ripeness as legitimately compelled the act or process of organic creation, out of certain fitting inorganic elements, to begin, and because, from that time onward, said process was constantly extending its domain and rising in character, we by no means think there was constantly being spoken into primitive existence a correspondingly increased and increasing number of new, different, and higher species of vegetables. Upon the contrary, as we see it, it is just as much an act of creation or an exertion of creative power to push a tiny, predisposed acorn, upon the hill-top, into a giant oak, as it is, in a warm, damp closet, to push the appropriate and appropriately predisposed inorganic elements into organic existence in that low form of vegetable life, known as mildew; or as it was, at the proper point of time in Earth's great history, to push into organized being, from the appropriate and appropriately predisposed inorganic elements, the first stem of that low plant which ever had existence upon its face. And besides we must regard it as being a much higher and more powerful creative act.

Thus it will be seen that, not by chance, according to our view, was the Earth clothed with her past, rich, vegetable garment or her present more beautifully variegated one, nor yet by sudden stretch of some mighty Power that, outside ALL SUBSTANCE, an independent existence had; but that as a natural consequence of Earth's gradual advancement, additional and higher vegetable-creative causes, one after another in regular succession and ascending scale, were constantly being pushed into a state of ripeness. In this way, not only was original creation imperatively commanded to proceed and speak into primitive existence other, and yet other, species of vegetables, but such low species as had already come into being were compelled to feel the stimulating effects of these same constantly increasing genial influences; and hence were legitimately being pushed upward and still upward, by slow gradation, (too slow to be by dull sense perceived, because quite too slow to make any appreciable alteration during the life of any single observer,) until, in process of time, more or less of these became so much improved in character and elevated in condition, as first to form a higher species of the same low order, then a lower species of an order higher, and thus on till now; the constantly increasing remains of each existing species, order, and class of vegetables furnishing fit aliment for the creation of others a little higher; whereby, by the joint and several action of propagative and progressive creation, the further original creation of vegetables was in no small degree superseded, without impairing the final, greatly multiplied result. And as it is not unlikely that the same first and lowest combination of vegetable-creative causes simultaneously arrived at maturity in many different localities, traversed by the same isothermal line, so it is not improbable that the same low form of vegetable life was spoken into original existence in as many different places at one and the same time. In other words, it is not unlikely that such was the case in places having the same mean temperature; because it cannot be supposed that the same combination of creative causes could simultaneously have come into ripe existence at the equator, and in the polar regions, on the mountains, and in the sheltered valleys; and consequently not, that the act or process of vegetable creation began at the same time all over the face of the globe.

And further, it is not supposed that the bottom varieties

of vegetables, be they few or be they many, from which all others by the joint and several action of propagative and progressive creation have been derived, ever awaited the slow process of propagating themselves in different lands and upon distant islands by means of roots or seeds, brought from some other locality, but, instead, it is believed that they were spoken into primitive existence in numerous different places, in one and the same way; namely, by means of the presence and operation of the same kind and character of ripe vegetable-creative causes. Hence, was an island, by volcanic action, now to spring up from the depths of the ocean, as in the world's vast history has more than once occurred, we doubt not that as soon as its form became settled, and its surface so far mollified and enlivened by Solar influence, gathering dew, descending shower, etc., as to render it a fit place for sustaining and fostering into growth any low species of vegetable life, so soon would that species there spring up; and that without the aid of man or beast, bird or insect, wind or wave to transport and strew the seed. And thus would creation, at that place, continue to go on and advance *pari passu* with advancing circumstances, until, not only mildew and the mosses would be there, but until, in the long lapse of ages, it would be covered with herb and flower, trees and fruits, similar in kind, character, and appearance to those common upon other isolated islands of similar size, soil, and temperature; because spoken into being, and pushed up creation's gradually ascending grade, by similar climatic and other creative causes.

Such being the views by us entertained, of course we see no insurmountable difficulty, but only harmony and beauty in the theory which proclaims, that when, in the progress of events, our globe, and its aforesaid aqueous and aerial surroundings, with the above-named vegetable kingdom added thereunto, had become so far advanced, elevated, and enlivened as to offer, for the first time in its vast history, a fit, quiet place, the proper equable temperature, and suitable abundance of the proper vegetable aliment to sustain and foster into growth the lowest form of animated existence, then, and not till then, was that said first and lowest form of animal spoken into being out of elements, which were but one degree elevated above the inorganic state; namely, out of vegetable substance; and all this not by miracle, nor yet by design, in the common acceptation of that term, but pursuant to the operation of natural law; feeble, and inanimate, but ripe animal-creative causes. And thus on of animal creation, the same in principle as of vegetable, until, by the joint and several action of original, propagative, and progressive creation, were pushed into being, out of fitting elements, all the numerous and different kinds and grades of animals that ever had existence upon this earthly ball.

For the purpose of elucidating the idea intended to be conveyed by the term propagative, and also progressive creation, perhaps we cannot, from all created nature, select a more universally familiar example than that presented by the common potato. As the potato, which to-day has a place upon the table of both prince and peasant, is a very different article, not only in quality, but in size and appearance, from what it was when its existence was first made known to the civilized world by the early explorers of the American wilds, so the question which presents itself is, What has produced this change?—As we understand the matter, the greatly improved condition presented by this invaluable tuber is in part the result of the numerous additions that have been made to the number of its different kinds or varieties by the simple act of propagating its original scanty ones, and partly the natural consequence of the greatly improved conditions which time and climatic circumstances, as well as a much more enlightened cultivation thereof, have thrown around certain superior kinds or varieties, thus by propagative creation obtained, and not because there has been a new creation of this kind of plant, or any special miracle wrought in its favor. Of course, it will be understood that what is true of this particular vegetable, in these respects, must needs be true in principle, not only of all other vegetables, but also of animals of every kind and grade, only that the degree may be more or less different.

As vegetables of every kind and grade are sustained in existence and advanced in growth by means of absorbing from air, earth, and water certain appropriate, inorganic aliment, so we must regard the vegetable kingdom as being wholly composed or made up of what was inorganic substance, up to the moment of its incorporation into the vegetable fabric. In other words, since the vegetable kingdom is a legitimate branch or composing fraction of the globe, (it being wholly made up of substances which, in their elementary estate, are purely inorganic and of the globe a part,) and since all animals derive their nourishment from vegetable substance, either directly by eating such substance themselves, else indirectly therefrom by eating the flesh of other animals, and which flesh, be it of beast or insect, fish or fowl, is neither more nor less than vegetable substance by such animal organisms elaborated and elevated; it cannot therefore be otherwise than that the entire animal kingdom, man included, is wholly made up of elements which, in their primitive or uncombined estate, were devoid of any recognized order of life, and which remained in that condition up to the moment when they were incorporated into the animal fabric; except in so far as they had previously become elevated and enlivened above the inorganic state, by having entered into the composition of that great half-way station legitimately existing between the two extreme domains, inorganic substance and animated nature, known as the vegetable kingdom. And moreover, as we understand the matter, vegetables and animals possess within themselves the elements of progress to a greater or less extent; and all such varieties, species, orders, and classes, both of vegetables and of animals, as lack this principle, that is, do not possess enough thereof to enable them to keep pace with Earth's advancement in the scale of perfection, or with the rising circumstances by which they come to be surrounded, are doomed to dwindle down and finally become extinct.

Having thus stated our feeble views, in this brief and general way, not only upon the subject of vegetable and animal creation, but of the causes which deep down in the nature of the eternal elements do underlie all action, and hence all progression, we will now endeavor to explain why it is that we are not content to sit still, look on, and rejoice over the old Mosaic account of creation, since that is a thing which we are not only compelled to regard as having been for a long time, upon the whole, good and right, but a thing which will continue to be such, just so long, and to just as wide an extent, as shall it continue to be an existing thing; that is, just so long, and to just as wide an extent, as shall it continue to be a thing by currently existing men believed; and not any longer or any more widely.

As we understand the matter, then, not by chance, nor yet by design, in the common acceptation of the term, but by Natural ordinance, there are not only many different things which have existence in the world, but many which act in opposition, more or less directly, the one against the other, whereby vastly more beneficial results are produced into being than could ever come to exist, were the action of one portion suspended, or did all act in the same direction. Hence, as a very humble composing fraction of the world of mankind, consequently of old Earth from which our composing elements were taken, and hence of that eternal Nature of which we are a part, it is not in our feeble, individual nature to be content to sit still, look on and rejoice over the old Mosaic account of creation, and consequently not in our power to do it; both which, in like manner, being things that are, we are compelled to regard them as being also, upon the whole, *good and right.* In other words, as we see it, it is not in the nature and consequently not within the power of any human being possessed of an active temperament and decided personal character to be content to sit still, look on, and rejoice at sight or sound of things which affect him not agreeably, but disagreeably;—to be content to sit still, look on, and rejoice at sight or sound of things which are not in harmony with his nature, but directly at variance therewith. And we put forth our slender efforts to arrest the onward progress, not only of this ancient doctrine, but of all such opinions, doctrines, and practices as are to us offensive, for the cardinal reason that such is human nature, everywhere and ever, that it is not within the power of any human being, possessed of strong feelings and a character of the positive stamp, to neglect to manifest, in some way, his disapproval of and opposition to whatever doctrine, practice, or thing his feelings detest, his moral sentiments disapprove, and his judgment condemns. We repeat, such is human nature, everywhere and ever, that it is impossible, under such circumstances, for the aforesaid stamp of man to neglect or refuse to put forth opposing efforts; and, to prove the correctness of the assertion, we offer in evidence the broad practice of universal man—with the single exception of the think-nothing, do-nothing, towstring order. Moreover men are not only organically commanded and hence compelled to manifest their disapprobation of and to put forth opposing efforts against such opinions and practices as are to them obnoxious, but, as might naturally be expected, and as observation and experience prove to be the fact, the character of the opposition manifested is ever in harmony with the character of the different individuals and associations of men who put it forth. If the strong, blind feelings predominate over the moral sentiments and intellect, (which in that class of persons but little removed above the brute creation they ever do,) then the opposition is sure to be of the harsh, denunciatory, and proscriptive order; and if the intellect over the feelings and moral sentiments bears rule, (as in men of highest grade it now quite largely does,—except when laboring under some undue excitement,) then not dictation or proscription, but persuasions and arguments, are the weapons used. And thus on it goes, the character of the opposition ever being found to vary according to the relative size, strength, and activity of the different brenal organs and groups of organs, which thereunto parent cause do stand;—all which being, as we are compelled to think, in strict accordance with human nature, consequently with that eternal Nature of which human nature is a part, therefore, notwithstanding unable to trace its bearing but a little way, we cannot for one moment doubt that so, upon the whole, it is good and right that it should be.

As when we give it as our opinion that all things, at all times, and everywhere, when taken in all their bearings and consequences present and remote, do work together for good and not for evil, we have just as direct reference to the acts and doings of those feeble, animated fractions of the universe called men, as to the influence exerted by that vast Orb about which old Earth and all things thereupon are constantly made to wheel; so, for the purpose of ridding the argument of all unnecessary incumbrances, we propose to drop from the account not only the influence exerted by those immense fractions, the Sun, Moon, and different planets all, but the effects produced by earthquakes, floods, in short, by all that class of physical agencies over which it has come to be generally admitted that man has no direction or control, and consequently about which, whether their workings are, upon the whole, productive of good or of evil, it must be alike useless to argue and impious to complain. We say, all that wide class of physical agencies over which it has now come to be generally admitted that man has no direction or control; because it was anciently quite generally supposed that the iniquities of human beings were the provoking cause of countries being deluged, cities being swallowed up by earthquakes, etc.; and because the idea is already to some extent extant, and not unlikely may take root and grow, that the fraction man has more or less to do with producing droughts, winds, and even tornadoes, by draining and deforesting the Earth's surface; and more or less with causing the rain to fall in showers, if not in torrents, by digging canals, growing timber, building railroads, etc.

This, then, is our narrower and more practical position: Whatever, at any time, or anywhere, doth come to have existence by human agency, must of necessity be, at that particular time, place, and extent, when taken in all its bearings and consequences, present and remote, both *good and right.* We say, whatever, at any time or anywhere, doth come to have existence by human agency, must of necessity be, at that particular time, place, and extent, when taken in all its bearings and consequences present and remote, both good and right, because we not only hold creation to be a continuous and progressive work, but that man, the highest and noblest animated branch of all terrestrial creation at least, is also progressive. Indeed, as we have come to see it, eternal sameness, no matter what the kind, never was and never will be in accordance with great Nature's course. Consequently we have no idea that the state of things which by human agency doth now exist in China, for example, and hence is, upon the whole, good and right there, would also be good and right here; or that the same state of things which by human agency existed among men three thousand years ago, for another example, and which state was, upon the whole, not only good and right then, but was, in fact, the only state which, by such human agency as then existed, could possibly have been brought to have existence, would also be good and right for men now. Upon the contrary, it is believed that man is to-day, as a whole and upon the whole, greatly in advance of what he was in the days of Moses; consequently that he has no option in the matter, but is legitimately compelled, by his advanced nature, to stand parent cause or creator to correspondingly advanced views, sentiments, desires, feelings, etc.; and hence to a correspondingly advanced state of things.

Three thousand years ago! why, only a little more than three short centuries since, proud England's reigning queen was in the habit of riding in state upon horseback, seated on a pillion behind her chamberlain, who engineered the train. Then, too, a common chimney was so rare a luxury in that boasted land of civilization and refinement, that a large share of the dwellings were warmed and the delicacies of the table prepared by fires kindled by the walls, the smoke being left to find its way out at the roof, doors, and windows as best it could.

Now, all this, notwithstanding quite improper in our fast age, was, at that day, not only good and right, but stately; and so good and right and stately for the reason that, at that time, coaches, steamboats, railroads, stoves, etc., were among the things not yet created; and not yet created because the proper kind and character of creative causes had not yet come into ripe existence within the heads of men, the gods whose province it is to speak these things into existence. In those good old bean-porridge days, too, there was not a newspaper published in all the British realm. To-day it is widely different, and to-day it is doubtless good and right that we the present tenants of Earth should be all bustle and activity, straining every nerve to make high or respective marks; and yet, before a single century shall have rolled away, it will be equally proper that we all quietly sleeping in our graves should be. And thus on of man and his doings to his latest posterity.

If the more favored of the race could only be persuaded calmly to consider the fact that, even at this late day and age of the world, human beings are not spoken into existence in the form of full-grown men and women, but are ushered into the world puny, helpless and ignorant to the very last degree; and if they would further reflect that the continued presence and operation of unfavorable circumstances are quite sufficient, in the brief period of a single generation, to ruin the health, derange the form, dwarf the size, and blast the brains of such infants as inherited from their parents organizations and life-powers which legitimately entitled them, under the kind care and guidance of favorable circumstances, to become and be models of physical perfection and giants in intellect; then, we think, they would find no great difficulty in becoming converts to the continuous and progressive theory of creation, the old six-day account thereof to the contrary notwithstanding.—Only a few thousand years ago, according to the Mosaic account, and Earth and Sun and Moon and stars were not. Only six days thereafter, and all were here as now; and creation a thing forever past.—Most singular philosophy!

The fact is, or at least, so it seems to us, the world ever belongs to those who are alive and upon it, and not to the honored dead, or the yet unborn. Every future generation of men, one after another in regular succession, the same as in the past, will become and be first a present generation and of the world possessed, then a past generation upon whose shoulders of observation, experience, research, and modes of thought the next succeeding present one will stand. Consequently, the civilized world over, the present revered opinions upon all such subjects as have not yet come to be accurately understood, the subject of creation among the rest, are certain to become outgrown and left behind just as soon as *per* force of advanced observation, experience, and reflection, this or any future generation of men shall come to be in possession of opinions thereupon, which are radically different; precisely the same as has the past popular and religious opinion, that this our Earth was the great primary and central thing in all creation, the Sun being supposed to be a body of quite inferior size and importance, whose business it was to rule the day upon the Earth, by imparting light and heat to the upper and only habitable side thereof, during a certain portion of the twenty-four hours,—the duty of taking charge of the night, upon the same side, devolving upon the Moon and stars.

As a matter of course, the grand idea which underlies the present scientific theory of the universe, and the movements of the different heavenly bodies, was, when first ushered into existence, all new and wrong to the then stupid and blindly superstitious mass of mankind who thought and believed by ancient proxy, they not yet having been sufficiently touched by live coals from the altar of human progression to see its force, or appreciate its beauty. Wherefore the then new and greatly advanced idea being a thing which, in so far as their *heads* were concerned, had not yet come into existence, consequently it was a thing which was not yet either good or right to them; and hence, with one accord, they pronounced it false, contrary to the Bible, and treasonable to God. And wherefore also, as was perfectly natural, they denounced, proscribed, and imprisoned its promulgator; which several acts, although very foolish, and notwithstanding a grievous wrong to the poor, suffering Galileo, had the effect to invest the new doctrine with a much deeper interest than would a quiet reception of its unostentatious announcement; consequently served to give thereunto a far more rapid and wide-spread circulation; hence tended to hasten the removal of ignorance and the consequent elevation of the race; and hence were, when taken in all their bearings and consequences present and remote, both good and right.—"The blood of the martyr is the seed" of progression as well as "of liberty."

And here, perhaps, it may be well to suggest that, in weighing great and complicated questions of this kind, it must not be forgotten that it is one of the inevitable incidents of the social state, even in times of profoundest national peace, that more or less frequently the liberty, and even the lives of individuals, have to be yielded up a sacrifice to appease popular indignation, promote the general quiet, and advance the public good. And who that has seriously reflected upon the subject is prepared to believe that the different inevitable incidents of the great, God-ordained social state, whether in time of war or whether in peace, are not, each and all, when taken in all their bearings and consequences present and remote, good and right? Obviously enough, the sanguinary struggle, for example, which gave us birth as a nation, was not a blessing to the hundreds and thousands of brave individuals whose mangled forms were laid cold in death upon the different battle-fields; and yet, when taken in all its bearings and consequences present and remote, who doubts that said revolutionary struggle has proved itself to have been a blessing to the human race, and especially to that particular portion thereof called the American people?—Who?

But to return:—Ignorant, superstitious, and set in their borrowed opinions as were the contemporaries of Galileo, still the more stubborn world did move and kept on moving, not only upon its axis and around the Sun, but onward and upward in the scale of perfection, and its feeble, short-sighted, self-willed tenants were compelled to bear it company, partake of its advanced nature, and drink in new and additional ideas; until, finally, the old, narrow, one-sided, and anti-common-sense notion of a flat, stand-still Earth, and revolving-about-it Sun, which for ages had been both the popular and religious opinion,—just because, by some ancient somebody, it had been proclaimed to be a God-revealed truth, and because, during all those long ages, it was a thing which filled and satisfied men's heads,—was compelled to give way to make room for another more in accordance with man's advanced brenal condition, and hence more in accordance with eternal fact.

Such being our well-settled views, it follows, as a matter of course, that we are unable to conceive of any clearer proof that the condition of things which, at any time or any where exists, and no matter what that condition nor what the extent thereof, is, upon the whole, good and right, than is contained in the fact that such condition, to such extent, doth then and there existence have; nor can we conceive of any surer evidence that some other imaginary state would not be, upon the whole, as good and right, at that particular time and place, than is presented by the fact that such other imaginary state doth not, then and there, existence have. In other words, we must think that every kind of condition which, at any time or anywhere, doth come to have existence by human agency, doth come to have it legitimately, because, then and there, pushed into existence and fostered into growth by a corresponding state of brenal development which it fills and satisfies; and that every kind of fancied condition which, at any given time or place, had not such existence, had it not for the reason that it was not legitimate,—had it not for the obvious reason that, with such a state of brenal development as then and there prevailed, it could not possibly coexist, much less have been spoken into existence and fostered into growth thereby.

And now, whether right or whether wrong, we trust it will be seen that we do not regard the harmony of the Universe as consisting either in inaction or eternal sameness of any kind, but, instead, are of the opinion that it ever legitimately grows out of that undying law which, being internally part and parcel of the eternal Elements themselves, imperatively commands everything in all created nature, high and low, great and small, inanimate and animated, to be ever active and exerting all the power it has. Wherefore, as a very humble fraction of universal active and progressive man, we have no option, but, just like Moses and every other comparatively bold and independent thinker that ever was or ever shall be, are compelled to put forth our feeble efforts to bring the opinions and practices of others to be in unison with our own. And wherefore, to the extent that this our weak endeavor shall exert an influence upon human thoughts and human actions, be that influence much or be it little, be it wide-spread or be it only to a few confined, and be it of long duration or only for a day, to that extent, and no further, does it become and be a *thing that is;* consequently, to that same extent, and no further, just like the old Mosaic account of creation, the sayings of the prophets, and the writings of every other man that ever wrote or ever shall write, it must of necessity be, upon the whole, a thing which is both *good and right.* And hence, to the extent that such endeavor shall have the effect to narrow down the existence of said Mosaic account, to that same extent it must needs be, upon the whole, both good and right that such olden account should be narrowed down,—should cease to be an existing thing; that is, should cease to be a thing by existing men believed, and hence unto them a moral truth.

And yet one thing further, Allowing our views of Deity, his composition, character, laws, mode of government, etc., to be erroneous, and that God is, as by orthodoxy claimed, a Spirit Being, unchangeable in his nature, and of infinite wisdom, goodness, and power possessed; also allowing that this Spirit Being, by virtue of a code of laws of his own supreme enactment, doth reign in and rule over all created things in Earth and heaven, according to his sovereign will and pleasure, What, then, is the irresistible conclusion to be drawn therefrom?—As seems to us, just this: In the plenitude of his wisdom, goodness, and power, he created all things good and not bad, right and not wrong; and, in the same plenitude, doth reign in and rule over all in a way that is consonant with his great, glorious, and eternal nature; hence in a way that is pleasing and not displeasing unto him; and hence in a way which is, upon the whole, both *good and right.* Indeed, we must confess ourself just as unable to see how any other conclusion can ever, rationally, be arrived at by such as firmly believe in the existence of an infinitely great, wise, good, and powerful Creator who, either by a fixed-law government or without, doth reign in and rule over all his works, according to his sovereign will and pleasure, as we are to see how it can ever, rationally, be concluded by anybody that the Sun is square, whilst all the while firmly believing it is round.

When from observation and reflection a man has become satisfied that any theory or doctrine, no matter what, is really true, he must of necessity be satisfied that all such other theories and doctrines as are incompatible therewith are false and imaginary. In other words, if certain things are really true, it follows, as a matter of course, that such other things as are incompatible therewith cannot also be, and hence that they are unworthy of any serious consideration. Thus, for instance, if the elements of which the numerous worlds and systems of worlds are composed are self-existent, and if such elements, in all their inconceivably vast amount, are not, in truth and in fact, a personal being, nor yet a composing fraction of such a being; then, by unavoidable consequence, there is not and cannot be any such thing as an all-space-filling personal God. If, consequent upon the nature of their composing elements, such is the permanently existing mutual relation between the Earth and Sun, as compels the former to circle around the latter and to revolve upon her axis in the manner which she does, then there is not and cannot be any necessity for the existence of a personal God, great or small, wise or simple, to superintend their movements or look after their welfare. If the soul or spirit of man, the same as that of the horse or any other animal, is not an entity of any kind, but simply organic function, or a thing that is spoken into existence and maintained therein by the presence and action of his bodily organs, then it is a thing which must of necessity be quite as transitory as is his physical structure, its parent cause; and

18

hence there can be no such things as ghosts or disembodied spirits, naked or clothed, stalking about among us either by day or by night. And thus on, not only of every known truth, but of every firmly-believed-to-be-one, and all such other things, whether few or many, as are incompatible with either the one or the other. And if the souls or spirits of men are really entities, and hence things which are capable of existing independently; that is, are capable of existing in the absence of living physical human beings to speak them into existence and maintain them therein; then, to the existence and multiplication of human spirits or soul entities, neither the multiplication of human beings nor, indeed, their presence or existence, is a thing essential; and hence, of such soul entities, there may be just as many and just as prolific, intelligent, and happy ones upon the uninhabited islands of the ocean as in the crowded city.

Or, to present the idea in little different form, no matter whether really true, or whether only morally so, to believe that a God of infinite wisdom, goodness and power *created all things* that are, would seem to be equivalent to believing that *all created things* are, upon the whole, good and right, and not wrong and evil, a *single one*.—Indeed, to believe as stated in the first instance must be equivalent to believing as stated in the second, because, of the former belief as postulate or premise, no matter whether correct or incorrect, the latter belief is a logical consequence from which there is no escape.—To believe that this, that, or the other created thing is not only relatively less good and right, but wholly wrong and evil, is equivalent to believing that the God who created them lacked the necessary wisdom to enable him to plan their creation aright; else the necessary goodness to induce him to desire so to plan it; else the necessary power to enable him to carry into execution the plan, which his infinite wisdom and goodness prompted him to conceive. To believe that a God of infinite wisdom, goodness and power doth reign in and rule over all created things that are, according to his sovereign will and pleasure, is equivalent to believing that he reigns in and rules over them in a way that is, upon the whole, good for them and pleasing unto him, and hence in a way which is, upon the whole, right and not wrong. And finally, to believe that this, that, or the other created thing doth operate and work, not only relatively less right, but wholly wrong, is equivalent to believing that the God who reigns in and rules over said thing lacks the necessary wisdom to enable him to determine in what manner it must needs be reigned in and ruled over, in order that it may be reigned in and ruled over aright; else the necessary goodness to induce him to desire thus, in and over it, to reign and rule; else the necessary power to enable him to carry into effect, in and over the same, the governmental plan which his infinite wisdom and goodness prompted him to devise.

Corollary :—Whatever is admitted to be planned by infinite wisdom, prompted by infinite goodness, and executed by infinite power, naught, save quite finite wisdom, else less finite folly, will ever attempt to impeach.

CHAPTER XXII.

COMPOUND CAUSES AND COMPOUND EFFECTS.

Notwithstanding by usage of language almost all causes and effects are represented as being single or simple, still it can hardly be doubted, we think, that almost every effect, which anywhere in nature doth ever come to take place, is a legitimate result not only of a compound cause, but of two or more compound causes; and not only of two or more compound causes, but of two or more which are more or less directly opposed the one to the other, in both character and action. Not for the simple reason that the rafters of a building are set sloping in opposite directions do they support the ponderous roof, but for the compound one that they are thus set in pairs, married at the top, and firmly secured against spreading at the bottom. Indeed, we must think that creation, as the same exists around us to-day, is quite as much indebted to the opposing action of heterogeneous forces, as it is to the joint action of such as are homogeneous. And, whether reasoning from analogy or whether from our own limited observation and experience, we are forced to the conclusion that, as in the physical world, so in what is called the moral, effects, of every name and kind, which are not actually simple, (and of such the number is believed to be small,) are produced into being and sustained in existence, not by the operation of any single or singly acting cause, however prominent or powerful, but by the aid and operation of a greater or lesser number of different causes, acting in opposition, more or less directly, one against another.

Compound causes, whether chemical, muscular, or brenal, not only produce compound results, but they produce results that are different from those which must needs be produced by the lone operation of any single cause among the whole number. Perhaps there are not a dozen laws upon any of the statute books, which had the sanction of the entire law-making body by which they were enacted; and probably not one which, in all respects, met the views of a single individual member, out of the whole number of those who sustained it by their votes upon its final passage. The laws which are annually passed by a congress of men selected as well from the different classes, as from the different localities, and hence representing the different interests of the country, are not only widely different from those which would be enacted by any single individual among the whole number, but are, upon the whole, much better adapted to guard, protect, and foster the diversified interests of the nation.

The correctness of the foregoing views being admitted, it follows that, with the single unimportant exception of effects which are purely simple, every act, institution, system, and thing, which is the product of human brains, is spoken into existence, or made to take place and be, not in a line of accordance with the character of the lone influence exerted by any one of the different causes, whether major or minor, which help produce it into being, but in a line which accords with the complex character of the combined influence exerted by the entire sum of producing causes. In other words, since each individual cause of the whole number, whether chemical, muscular, or brenal, doth ever modify, in a degree corresponding with its power, the result which would naturally follow from the lone action of every other cause; therefore the resultant effect, or final result, must necessarily accord, not with the lone influence exerted by any one of the different producing causes, but with the complex influence exerted by the whole combination of them.

As great and permanent results are seldom produced by trifling causes, whether simple or compound; as every change is not reform, and as almost every great and permanent change which ever comes to take place in the so-called moral world, as well as in the physical one, doth gradually come to take place therein; so the conclusion is irresistible that, for most of our reforms, social, political, and religious, we are just about as much indebted to the rigid conservative who acts as brake upon the wheels, as to the fiery radical who, with headlong speed, would fain propel the car. Or thus: Because different individuals and parties of men take opposite views of the same subject, consequently act, and act with spirit, in direct opposition, the one party against the other, and thus achieve a result at which neither party was aiming; it by no means follows that such result is not, upon the whole, a better one than could possibly have been brought about, had they all thought as did either party, and hence all pulled at the same end of the same rope. In a word, as it is only by being brought into sharp collision that flint and steel can be made to emit their strong sparks of light, so it is only by means of a thorough interchange of opinions, boldly and squarely proclaimed, that men can be brought to see their narrow pet errors, and hence driven into the embrace of broader and more correct views.

Wherefore let no man fold his arms in despair, because, in comparison with the great world of human life, he so nearly approaches to being a cipher, but rather let him arouse himself, and unremittingly put forth whatever of power he doth possess to bring the neighborhood in which he resides, the church of which he is a member, the state of which he is a citizen, the nation to which he belongs, and the world of mankind, of which he is a component part, to be what he is desirous that they should become; never once forgetting that, in proportion to the power he shall thus relatively exert, in that same proportion will he legitimately exert a moulding influence, not only upon the present generation of men, but, through them, upon the next succeeding one, and thus forever on.

CHAPTER XXIII.

THE DECALOGUE'S ORIGIN AND SCOPE.

Inasmuch as we Christians are wont to attach so much importance to those certain lines of Scripture called the Decalogue, and inasmuch as this importance is not thereunto attached on account of their substance, but because of the miraculous manner in which they are supposed to have been derived to us; so we propose very briefly to trace the history of those tables of stone, upon which are said to have been written "The words of the covenant, the ten commandments," and which tables the Israelites preserved with such jealous care; to the end that our readers may be enabled to see and judge for themselves whether, from Moses' own testimony—when in proper chronological order read and considered,—it was Almighty God who prepared those said tables, and who wrote upon them the writing that is said to have been written thereupon, or whether it was the man Moses who did both the one and the other.

According to Moses' showing, then, in Exodus 24. 12, it appears that God commanded him to come up into the mount, and be there: and he, God, would give unto him tables of stone, and a law and commandments which he had written; to the end that he, Moses, as his specially chosen servant and mouthpiece, might teach them. From the balance of the chapter it appears that Moses went up into the mount as by God he was commanded, and there remained forty days and forty nights. It further appears from the 18th verse of the 31st chapter, that God, after having made an end of communing with Moses upon the mount, gave unto him "Two tables of testimony, tables of stone, written with the finger of God." It also appears a little further on, in the 15th and 16th verses of the next chapter, that "Moses turned and went down from the mount, and the two tables of testimony were in his hand: the tables were written on both their sides; on the one side and on the other were they written. And the tables were the work of God, and the writing was the writing of God, graven upon the tables."

As from this account it is clear that Moses did, at that time, receive from the hands of the Almighty two tables of testimony, tables of stone, the writing upon which was the writing of God and graven thereon; it therefore becomes important to understand what became of those said tables, and of the writing which, according to said Mosaic account, God had written with his finger, and graven thereupon. As appears, then, from what immediately follows, the people, for whose special benefit and instruction all this had been done, became so very anxious, during Moses' said forty-days absence, to worship something which their eyes could see, (as plainly enough doth the history of this ancient people reveal the existence of their strong perceptive organs and weak reflectives,) that they made them a golden calf, and set it up as a god unto which to offer up offerings, and before which to bow down and worship. It further appears from what follows immediately thereafter, that, when Moses, upon his return journey, came near enough unto the camp to see the calf, and hear the impious singing with joy before it, his "Anger waxed hot, and he cast the tables out of his hands, and brake them beneath the mount. And he took the calf which they had made, and burnt it in the fire, and ground it to powder, and strewed it upon the water, and made the children of Israel to drink of it." And so, now, we appeal, according to Moses' own immediate showing, Were not the *two tables of testimony*, *tables of stone*, which he declares God gave him, and upon which he affirms that God had written with his *finger*, right here by him, Moses, destroyed; and that too without their ever having been published, or made public at all? And hence, right here, does not the full history of said demolished tables, together with the writing that was upon them, no matter what it might have been, come to an end?

So much for the two tables of stone upon which, according to Moses' account of the matter, God himself wrote; and so much for the writing which, according to his own statement made at the time, or at least upon the very heels of the transaction, never reached the people to whom it was addressed; and hence was never seen by mortal eyes, except his own and possibly by those of his right-hand man Joshua.

After the stern, summary, and terribly bloody measures adopted by Moses, upon his said angry return from the mount, had again restored tranquillity and order among that ignorant, superstitious, and rebellious people, it appears, however, from the testimony of this same witness, as recorded in the first four verses of the 34th chapter, of this same book, that, at the close of another interview between God and himself, the Lord said unto him, "Hew thee two tables of stone like unto the first: and I will write upon these tables the words that were in the first tables which thou brakest. And be ready in the morning, and come up in the morning unto mount Sinai, and present thyself there to me in the top of the mount. And no man shall come up with thee, neither let any man be seen throughout all the mount: neither let the flocks nor herds feed before that mount. And he hewed two tables of stone, like unto the first; and Moses rose up early in the morning, and went up into mount Sinai, as the Lord had commanded him, and took in his hand the two tables of stone." Now this quotation which begins the history, not only of the second set of tables, but of the ten commandments which were afterwards written thereupon, preserved and handed down from generation to generation, until, finally, they were copied upon paper, placed in a book called the Bible, and so brought down to us, makes it plain that Moses, and not God, hewed and prepared them. And not only this, but it establishes another important fact; namely, that Moses proved himself so handy at working upon stone, that these tables, by him thus made ready, were *like unto the first;* that is, were like unto the two, which, according to his statement, God himself, the great Master Workman, had previously been at the trouble of preparing for him, and which he, in his hot anger, broke.

Now, by just going back to the first part of this same quotation, it will be seen that Moses not only represents the Lord as commanding him to *hew two tables like unto the first two*, but as promising him that he, the Lord, would write upon them the words that were in the first tables which he, Moses, thus angrily cast from him and broke. We say, by thus going back it will be seen, that, according to Moses' statement of the matter, the Lord promised him that he would himself write upon said second tables the words that were in the first, because, in order to come at a right understanding of the case, it is necessary that a clear line of distinction be drawn between what Moses now and here says the Lord promised he would do upon those said tables, and what he subsequently and in another place tells us, that he himself, and not the Lord, did upon them. In other words, as the question which just now concerns us is, How did the words of the covenant, the ten commandments, get upon those second tables? so we will let the history, not of what Moses beforehand says was promised to be done upon them, after he should bring them up to the top of the mount, but of what he subsequently declares was done upon them, and by whom performed, after he got there with them and whilst he was yet there, speak for itself. Yea, and the very next thing we hear about those said tables, we hear from this same witness Moses in the 27th and 28th verses of the chapter last named, and which read as follows: "And the Lord said unto Moses, *write thou these words*: for after the tenor of these words I have made a covenant with thee, and with Israel. And he [Moses] was there with the Lord forty days and forty nights; he [Moses] did neither eat bread nor drink water. And he [Moses] wrote upon the tables the words of the covenant, *the ten commandments*."—And so, now, in all sincerity we ask, Is it not plain, from Moses' own testimony—when in proper chronological order read and considered,—that it was not the Lord, but the feeble fraction of the great HIM known as the man Moses, who both held said forty-days' fast, and who wrote upon those tables the words of that covenant, which was then and there called "The ten commandments;" and which commandments, together with the tables containing the same, were by him delivered unto the children of Israel, and by them so sacredly kept, preserved, and borne about with them wheresoever they went; and which were finally copied upon paper, inserted in the sacred volume, and so handed down to us?

And further, Is it not obvious that this Moses' first and freshest historic account of the origin of the ten commandments, and of the particular manner in which they found their way upon said tables of his own preparing, must be, as far as it goes, either really true or really false? And further still, admitting this his first and freshest historic statement of the matter to be true to the facts as they actually transpired, then can anything be plainer than that all subsequent statements in reference to this same transaction must be false to the extent that, in sense and substance, from such first, they do irreconcilably differ? We say this his first and freshest historic account of the way and manner in which the words of the covenant, the ten commandments, found their way upon said tables of stone of his own preparing, must be, as far as it goes, either really true or really false, because we find, upon examination, that it seems to have been quite customary with the Bible writers to repeat a thing over, and over again, just as if they supposed the oftener the history of a perfected transaction was written down and clinched with a *Thus-saith-the-Lord*, the more a fact and the less a fiction it become; and because we find this same Moses, some forty years thereafter and near the close of his eventful life, again attempting to travel over this same historic ground; when, from a failure of memory or some other cause, his iterated statement of the transaction so far varies from his first historic account thereof, and which was penned when the circumstances were yet fresh in his recollection, that he now, at this late day, makes the Lord, and not himself, to have been the person who executed the writing upon said second tables. And this is what he now and here at this late day says: "At that time [referring back to the time, now some forty years past, when the Lord instructed him, in 34th Exodus, to prepare said second set of tables] the Lord said unto me, Hew thee two tables of stone like unto the first, and come up unto me into the mount, and make thee an ark of wood. And I will write on the tables the words that were in the first tables which thou brakest, and thou shalt put them in the ark. And I made an ark of shittim-wood, and hewed two tables of stone like unto the first, and went up into the mount, having the two tables in mine hand. And he wrote on the tables, according to the first writing, the ten commandments, which the Lord spake unto you in the mount, out of the midst of the fire, in the day of the assembly: and the Lord gave them unto me. And I turned myself and came down from the mount, and put the tables in the ark which I had made; and there they be, as the Lord commanded me."—Deut., 10. 1-5.[a]

And now, since it is a fact which can never be gainsayed, that, from some cause or other, this ancient witness has, at these different periods of time, stated the matter so very differently that the one statement cannot be made to harmonize with the other, (except it be admitted that he and the Lord with whom he seemed to be upon such terms of intimacy, and in whose name he so oft and lengthily did speak, were one and the same person,) What is to be done? Shall we treat him just as we would any other man,—just as we would a cotemporary upon the Earth,—just as we would a fellow-townsman who, in giving in his evidence before us when sitting as a court, should thus contradict himself upon a most material point? In short, shall we apply to him the rigid rules of evidence; that is, treat him as a witness who

[a] NOTE.—No notice is here taken of what Moses says in the fourth, fifth, and ninth chapters of this same book of Deuteronomy which closes his voluminous testimony, and where, in his garrulous old age, he over, and over again, repeats the story of certain tables of stone, etc., for the reason that since he does not in either of the two first-named chapters inform us to which set of tables he refers, and as in the ninth he makes it clear that he there has reference to the first tables, which he himself so unceremoniously destroyed at the foot of the mount, and hence not us or anybody else concern, so it is but fair to presume, that in said fourth and fifth he had reference to the same; and especially is it not since in both these chapters the accounts given are, as far as they go, not only consistent with his account of said first tables, but are each in direct contradiction of the history of the second set, as given by himself almost simultaneously with his performing the act of writing upon them.—

stands before us self-impeached, and so reject his entire testimony; or shall we, in consideration of his being not only a very ancient witness, but the only witness there is or ever can be in the case, so far relax toward him the judicial rule as to receive his voluminous evidence, and, in so far as his statements shall be found to be in flat contradiction the one of another, adopt that statement as most likely to be consonant to fact, which was by him first made;—that statement which was made with both clearness and precision directly upon the heels of the transaction;—that statement which seems the least well-calculated to forward his own personal aims and interest, in a word, that statement which, upon the whole looks most reasonable? Although we cannot intellectually see any good reason why his evidence should not be subjected to the same rigid rules that should the evidence of a man of to-day, still, when we reflect that he is a very ancient witness; also that upon his lone testimony, whether trustworthy or whether untrustworthy, must forever rest the decision of this great question; also that, in spite of all that intellect can say or do, there doth ever legitimately exist in the heads of men a much stronger feeling of veneration for persons and things that are ancient, than for those which are modern, we are forced to concede the policy, if not the propriety, toward both him and his testimony, of relaxing the rule.

Acting, then, in accordance with such concession, we will now proceed to inquire, Situated as this most ancient witness was, at the head of that ignorant, superstitious, idolatrous, and rebellious people, and over whom he was anxiously endeavoring to exercise supreme governmental control, which, in all human probability, would be most likely to further his own personal aims, promote his own private interest, and crown with success his towering ambition, to have them believe that the Creator and Governor of the world was upon such terms of intimacy with their chief leader and ruler, as that he graciously condescended to gather his immense Self together upon the top of the mount, to the end that he might, with his own august finger, trace upon slabs of stone, for their special guidance and instruction, those said commandments which they were thus peremptorily required to remember and obey, and which commandments were so very adverse to their strong, blind feelings and boisterous practices; or to have them understand that they were simply positive requirements of their kindred fellow-mortal, the man Moses?—We may be wrong, of course, but then, judging from human nature as exhibited all around us; also from the way the people went a whoring after false gods, and worshiping idols during Moses' first forty-days absence from them, in spite of all that his sub-leaders and under-rulers could do to restrain them, we must think the former. And which, upon the whole, looks most reasonable, that it now took that same God, who, long years before, in six days created the heaven and the Earth, and all things therein and upon, forty days and forty nights to write upon said tables the few brief lines in the Decalogue contained; or that Moses so contrived and managed the thing, as that, in said space of time, he finally succeeded in scratching and graving them thereupon himself?—Why, since it was clearly within his power, in that length of time, to have done such a thing, (he having had, according to his own showing as will be remembered, some little practice in working upon stone,) since the inducements to do the thing were both numerous and strong, and since we can never presume in favor of a miracle to account for a phenomenon which the natural alone is quite sufficient to explain; so we have no option, but are compelled to decide that the latter does. We say, since it was clearly within his power, in that length of time, to have done such a thing, because, by counting the words contained in the Decalogue, as by him originally given in the 20th chapter of Exodus, it will be found to contain but three hundred and seventeen words, Italics included; and because any mere novice in the art of engraving upon stone would now be able to chisel the same thing legibly, thereupon, in less than forty hours. And we say, by counting the words contained in the Decalogue, as by him originally given in the 20th chapter of Exodus, because, as by him chronicled, long years thereafter, in 5th Deuteromony, said document will be found to have become expanded into three hundred and sixty-nine words, including Italics;—a phenomenon which, in so far as we now see, can never be accounted for, except in one or the other of the following ways: Either these words of the Lord, thus laboriously traced upon stone, possessed the faculty of self-multiplication; else Moses, pursuant to a law of human nature which is quite widely manifested, after this most ignorant and credulous people had become firmly established in the belief that whatsoever he said or did was sanctioned by the Lord, took upon himself the responsibility of making such additions and amendments thereto, as he adjudged expedient.

And now, since we have gotten to inquiring into the reasonableness of circumstances and things which are only incidentally connected with the subject, and hence only incidentally important, as well as into such as are fundamentally so, permit us to go a little further and ask, Why, in all human probability, did the cool, calculating Moses thus unceremoniously, and without consulting the views of the great Giver, break those first tables of stone which had cost him so much valuable time in waiting for them, and the Lord so much labor in preparing and writing upon them?—Well, as seems to us, it was because he wisely concluded, from the way the people were conducting themselves when he came within eye-shot of the camp with the broad tables in his hand, that they were not in a sufficiently calm, confiding, and submissive mood to welcome, with reverential awe, those tables with their stringent contents; and hence not in a mood that rendered it prudent to venture a trial of that grand experiment upon their credulity, upon the success of which so very much depended. And, as broken tables of stone, the same as dead men, tell no tales, so right here, at the foot of the mount, they were forthwith destroyed; and the experiment postponed until a more propitious time should arrive. And why did Moses, directly upon the heels of this transaction, cause some three thousand men of this

God's specially chosen people to be put to death?—See last paragraph but one of 32d Exodus.—Well, judging from the way politicians and office seekers, high and low, in this our day, do manage to work themselves into places of power and perpetuate themselves therein, we must think he caused it to be done because he adjudged, from what he then and there saw and heard, that the only way in which that people could ever be induced peaceably to submit to his high pretensions, and reverently to receive at his hands, as the act of God, such a set of laws as he was desirous of giving them, was by *relatively increasing* the number of the sons of Levi, who were ascertained to be with him to a man, by *actually diminishing* the number of such of the malcontents, as he knew were most actively opposed to him. We say, judging by the way the politicians and office seekers, high and low, in this our day, do manage to work themselves into places of power and perpetuate themselves therein, because, in point of principle Moses then and there did just what these men now and here do; only so widely different were the human elements with which he had to deal from those which they have to manage, that, necessarily, the character of the degree had to be correspondingly different. In other words, the same mild persuasives by which an intelligent populace may be influenced and led would fail to penetrate the intellects or reach the feelings of a people, sunk in the depths of ignorance and barbarism. Such a people, no matter in what age existing or in what country found, can only be brought to see, but by first being brought to feel; and, according to his own account of the bloody transaction, make them feel he did.

Again, when the Lord commanded Moses, in the 27th verse of the 34th chapter of Exodus, to write upon the second tables the words of the covenant, the ten commandments, Why did he not remind the Lord that only just now he had promised him, (as he could prove by just going back a few verses to the beginning of the chapter where it was duly recorded,) that He would write them for him, thereupon, Himself?—Well, as really seems to us, he was not deterred therefrom by his extreme modesty, but by the dimness of his recollection of the Lord's ever having promised him any such thing.

And, finally, Why was there not a man allowed to be seen *throughout all the mount*, during Moses' said second forty-days stay upon it? Also why were the flocks and herds prohibited from *feeding before it* at that particular time and no other?—Well, we must think it was not for fear that some one drawn thither by idle curiosity, or coming there in search of kine which were quietly feeding thereabouts, might chance to discover an invisible God, with his spirit finger, making letter after letter, word after word, and sentence after sentence leap into existence upon those slabs of stone; but to guard against the possibility of the visible man Moses being caught in the act of laboriously bending over them, with graving tool in hand.

But, allowing all these queries and conclusions to pass for naught, still it must be conceded by every intelligent and candid man, that all the evidence there is in the world, upon which to base the belief that the Lord ever performed the celebrated miracle of writing the Decalogue with his finger upon tables of stone, or anything else, is derived from this single human witness, Moses; whose testimony upon this very point is so contradictory that, by one of the plainest rules of evidence, he would be pronounced self-impeached, and his uncorroborated statements weightless, were only a man of to-day, instead of being a man of some three thousand years ago. This, we repeat, must be conceded by every intelligent and candid man; and yet, throughout all Christendom, such is the blinding effect of that early religious education which has been so deeply impressed upon the human brain, that we make no doubt there are scores of well-meaning persons right here among us, who, if called upon so to do, would unhesitatingly take the witness stand and swear, that they *know* it to be a God-revealed fact.—Nowhere is any portion of the Decalogue discovered traced upon stone by the finger of God; and, yet upon every rock and stratum under the whole heaven, is some portion of the world's vast history found written by the hand of Time

One thing more:—Whether right or whether wrong in the opinion that the ten commandments had their origin in the head of the man Moses who penned their lines for the special guidance, not of subsequent generations of enlightened men, but of that ignorant, superstitious, and stiff-necked people, whom he was endeavoring to lead and to rule, and in whose ears he caused them so oft to be sounded, we cannot be mistaken when we say that they were, each and all, designed to operate as a restraint or otherwise upon their strong blind feelings, selfish propensities, and moral sentiments, and not one of them to act as a check upon inquiry, or a restraint upon sober intellect.—The first two commandments read thus: "I am the Lord thy God, which have brought thee out of the land of Egypt, out of the house of bondage. Thou shalt have no other gods before me. Thou shalt not make unto thee any graven image, or any likeness of any thing that is in heaven above, or that is in the Earth beneath, or that is in the water under the earth: thou shalt not bow down thyself to them, nor serve them: for I the Lord thy God am a jealous God, visiting the iniquity of the fathers upon the children unto the third and fourth generation of them that hate me, and showing mercy unto thousands of them that love me, and keep my commandments."—Manifestly enough, these were both addressed to Veneration, and designed to act as a check upon that large and over-active organ, in the heads of the adult portion of the Israelitish people, and thus prevent them from bowing themselves down before all sorts of images, and worshiping, as gods, idols without number.

Commandment third:—"Thou shalt not take the name of the Lord thy God in vain: for the Lord will not hold him guiltless that taketh his name in vain."—This was evidently designed to operate as a check upon Combativeness, as that organ, when large and especially when diseased, is prone to create profanity of feeling, and hence to give itself vent in profanity of both speech and action.

Commandment fourth:—"Remember the Sabbath-day to

keep it holy. Six days shalt thou labor, and do all thy work: but the seventh day is the Sabbath of the Lord thy God: in it thou shalt not do any work, thou, nor thy son, nor thy daughter, thy man-servant, nor thy maid-servant, nor thy cattle, nor thy stranger that is within thy gates: for in six days the Lord made heaven and Earth, the sea and all that in them is, and rested the seventh day: wherefore the Lord blessed the Sabbath-day, and hallowed it."—This, the longest of all, was addressed to both Veneration and acquisitiveness, and designed, as well to foster habits of cleanliness, by setting apart every seventh day as a day of rest, as to prevent the heads of families, masters, etc., from working themselves, their children, servants, and cattle to death from a mere thirst for gain.

Commandment fifth:—"Honor thy father and thy mother; that thy days may be long upon the land which the Lord thy God giveth thee."—This was an appeal to the organ of Veneration, as the same existed in the juvenile portion of the Israelitish people, and designed to operate as a strengthening plaster thereto in the heads of the young, (that organ ever being much weaker in children and youth, than in adults,) and thus cause such juvenile portion to be more deferential and obedient to their parents who, from their greater knowledge and experience in the world, were much better judges of what was for the good and safety of this class ot persons, than were the children, the youths, and the maidens themselves.

Commandment sixth:—"Thou shalt not kill."—This was addressed to the organ of Destructiveness, which was manifestly large in the heads of that people; and designed to operate as a check thereupon, whenever it should be inclined to pursue its bent to kill and destroy beyond the bounds of safety to the lives of others.

Commandment seventh:—"Thou shalt not commit adultery."—This was addressed to the organ of Amativeness, and evidently designed to restrict sexual intercourse, among that ignorant, idolatrous, and sensual people, within the bounds of the proper marriage relation.

Commandment eighth:—"Thou shalt not steal."—This was a further appeal to Acquisitiveness, and intended to operate as an additional restraint upon that organ which, when over-large and active, not only prompts men to work themselves and those under them unreasonably, but to take without leave what does not belong to them.

Commandment ninth:—"Thou shalt not bear false witness against thy neighbor."—This was leveled directly at the organ of Secretiveness, and designed to operate as a check upon that cat-like individual who, when over-active and strong, was doubtless then, the same as now, not only quite prone to tattle and fib about his neighbors, but to swear falsely against them, the better to enable him to carry out some dark, nefarious plan.

Commandment tenth:—"Thou shalt not covet thy neighbor's house, thou shalt not covet thy neighbor's wife, nor his man-servant, nor his maid-servant, nor his ox, nor his ass, nor anything that is thy neighbor's."—This the last was yet another appeal to the organ of Acquisitiveness, and evidently designed to prevent the desires even, of that avaricious gentleman, from extending too far within the bounds of his neighbor's rightful possessions; as well as being a pretty sharp hint to Mr. Amativeness, that he must not look too long and wishfully upon the fair face and form of his neighbor's better half.

Having thus run through the Decalogue from beginning to end, and finding no such injunction; as, Pry not into things which are dark and mysterious, whether ancient or modern; Reason not, for it is carnal to do so; or Trust not to the guidance of reason, for its teachings are false and deceptive; so again we repeat, whether the ten commandments had their origin in the head of the great lawgiver Moses, who penned their lines, or whether they did not, it is certain they do not contain a word which can be tortured into conveying the idea that it is not eminently proper for all, young and old, male and female, bond and free, to use their eyes; and not one that it is not eminently proper for them to exercise their reasoning faculties to the fullest extent upon any and all subjects.—No; not one. A single additional suggestion to such of our readers as are firm believers not only in the divinely inspired character of Moses and his writings, but of the whole Bible, and we close.

Notwithstanding Moses' essays to go back to the creation of the world and give us, in chronological order, the history of Adam, of Eve, of Abraham, Isaac, Jacob, etc., all the way down through the long line of generations to the very day of his death, he nowhere teaches the immortality of individual man. Indeed, as we understand language, the Bible does not furnish the first particle of evidence that any such idea as a continued personal existence beyond the grave, in spiritual form or any other, had ever entered into the heads of either gods or men, until we are pretty well advanced in the pages of the last half of the Old Testament; and, for many pages more, the contrary doctrine is quite as distinctly shadowed forth as is this. Of all the numerous personal rewards that were promised by Moses for obedience, not one was promised to extend beyond the bounds of the grave; and not one of all the many personal punishments by him threatened for disobedience was threatened to extend a moment beyond the death and destruction of the bodily man. Whoever doubts this, let him carefully peruse the five foundation books of the Bible ascribed to Moses, and judge for himself.

Corollary:—Either Moses was not, in any special manner, inspired by God as to what he should say when, as a stimulant to virtue, he was penning his long list of promised rewards for acts of obedience, or when, as a check upon vice, his dread catalogue of threatened punishments for acts of disobedience; otherwise God, at that time, must have been totally ignorant of the fact that men, unlike other animals, do not actually die when to all appearance they seem to, but, instead, continue to live, in spirit form, personally on past their bodily death to all eternity.

Again; as from the language of the Bible, as well as from that of natural revelation, the inference is irresistible that, at the day and age when Moses wrote, God was not aware that men could be much more suitably rewarded for acts of obedience, as well as much more effectually punished for acts of disobedience, after they were physically dead and gone, than whilst they were yet bodily alive and here; so it is not surprising that he did not instruct that great law-giver to resort to the practice of appealing to their strong, blind fear of an endlessly-long and dreadful future hell for the punishment of sin, as a more effectual means of restraining their angry passions, and otherwise hawing them into civil, social, and religious order. No; in this respect, the olden teachings of both God and Moses are quite behind the times.

CHAPTER XXIV.

RELIGION PROFESSED AND RELIGION ACTUAL.

The cultivation of one brenal or organ or set of organs no more tends to give tone and direction to the action of another organ or set, than does the training of the muscles of the fingers by writing have a tendency to give tone and direction to the action of the toes in walking. There are doubtless many persons who intellectually know much better than they practice,—many who, in spite of themselves, do often perform acts and commit excesses which they are intellectually certain they had better not; and this because their brenal education when children instead of being general and harmonious was partial and inharmonious,—because whilst intellect and verbal memory in them were being carefully cultivated, their strong, blind organs of feeling, passion, and emotion, as things of little consequence, were neglected; thus increasing the tendency of the organs of intellect and of feeling to alternate in action, instead of habilitating them to work harmoniously together, under the guidance of the former.

As it is not the intellectual organs, but the selfish ones, the large strong organs of feeling, passion, and emotion which incline their possessors to selfishness, to selfish indulgence, and into other low practices to fall, so it is *these*, and not *those*, which in the majority of children and youth do most need to be looked after, educated, and disciplined. In other words, it cannot be doubted that the discipline, which this large class of blind organs do early receive in the nursery and the school-room, does more towards forming the characters of the mass of children, and hence toward shaping the destinies of the men and women into which they afterwards do grow, than does all the intellectual advancement they in either place receive. And herein it is, as we see it, that resides the chief merit which the Christian system of religion possesses over both the Jewish and Mohammedan, when taught and admitted in anything like its original purity. We say, herein it is that resides the chief merit which the Christian system of religion possesses over both the Jewish and Mohammedan, not because we think the teachings of Christ are more especially directed to the strong, blind organs of feeling and desire than are those of Moses and Mohammed, but because, unlike theirs, his do not pander to those organs in the human head; consequently do not tend to render them just so much the more strong and active, and hence their possessors just so much the more certain into low and sensual indulgencies to fall. Or thus: As the teachings of Christ, unlike those of Moses and Mohammed, were designed to operate as a restraint upon the pet passions and desires of men, and as they are kindly and persuasively put forth, therefore they do strongly tend so to modify and restrain the latitudinous cravings of the lower grade of brenal organs, as to bring them into subjection to the higher and more truly friendly and unselfish ones. For this reason it is, as we see it, that wherever the Christian system has come to be dominant, there are the rich and the poor, the strong and the weak, the male and the female found to be standing more nearly upon the same plane of civil, social, and religious equality than anywhere else.

But to return:—As it has already been stated, and the cause thereof very briefly explained, that there are many who know much better than they practice, so now we will say there are many who practice much better than they know; that is, much better than they intellectually know any good reason for doing as they do. And this comes to take place and be simply because their natural feelings and desires, unlike those of the former individuals, are much more evenly balanced, delicate, and truthful, than are their intellects cultivated and strong.

And now, to prevent, if possible, any misunderstanding in reference to our position touching to the Bible, we will here take occasion to say that we no more expect the numerous real truths of a practical character, which adorn the pages of that olden volume, will ever become outgrown and left behind, than we do that the numerous real truths of a practical character, which adorn the pages of the text-books on natural philosophy, astronomy, etc., will;—not any more. But, then, it is our opinion that the pages of the different scientific text-books of to-day are adorned with many more such truths, and blackened with much less of actual and misleading error, than are the pages of that ancient text-book of theology, called the Bible. In other words, for the reason that man has heretofore been a progressive being, for that reason has the Bible, that ancient text-book of theology, both Jewish and Christian, become mostly outgrown and left behind by the more thinking and intelligent religionists of both classes; nor have we any idea that the end of progression in theological science, or any other, has yet come.

And here, perhaps, it may be well to state distinctly what, in a general way, has already been said a number of times before; namely, that, with Christ's *general religious teachings*, we have but little fault to find; our principle objection to them being that they are too limited in amount and circumscribed in their breadth of sweep, to reach and cover all the different needs of very much more enlightened, hence greatly advanced and constantly advancing man. Wherefore, instead of wishing to cripple or destroy any of the really truthful and practical fruit-bearing doctrines that were taught by Christ, we are desirous of having added thereto, and of currently adding, all and singular the teachings of genuine science of every name and kind; to the end that both the theory and the practice of religion, no matter by what name called, may come to be so broad and deep as to take in all real truth, whenever and wheresoever found, and so *pure and undefiled* as to cover with its mantle of charity not only the *widows and the fatherless*, but every son and daughter of Adam that is in trouble or affliction, no matter what the form nor what the cause thereof. We say, with the *general religious teachings* of Christ, we have but little fault to find, because we can never consider the views or crotchets by him entertained and put forth in reference to his being in both a literal and a special sense the Son of God, etc., as forming any part of his general religious teachings; and also because there are a few of his teachings which, although of a general and religious character, are not only wholly impracticable, but erroneous. Thus, for example, Mark reports him as saying and doing thus: "And on the morrow, when they [Christ and his disciples] were come from Bethany, he [Christ] was hungry. And seeing a fig-tree afar off, having leaves, he came, if haply he might find anything thereon: and when he came to it, he found nothing but leaves: for the time of figs was not yet. And Jesus answered and said unto it, No man eat fruit of thee hereafter forever. And his disciples heard it."—Mark, 11. 12—14. In reference to this same subject-matter, Matthew reports him as saying and teaching as follows: "And when the disciples saw it, they marvelled, saying, How soon is the fig-tree withered away! Jesus answered and said unto them, Verily I say unto you, if ye have faith, and doubt not, ye shall not only do this which is done to the fig-tree, but also, if ye shall say unto this mountain, Be thou removed, and be thou cast into the sea; it shall be done."—Mat., 21. 20—21.

Now, plainly enough, it would not do for us to imitate this his strangely absurd teaching, and so destroy our fruit trees of any and all kinds, simply because we chanced to be hungry for fruit, and because upon our orchards we found nothing but leaves; and that at a time when, by natural ordinance, they were prohibited from having any fruit upon them. And equally plain must it be to every candid and reflecting man, that it is not within the bounds of the possible to remove a mountain either large or small, simply by saying unto it, Be thou removed, and be thou cast into the sea," or into any other place we might chance to prefer; and consequently that such teaching, notwithstanding put forth in a most plain and positive manner, is both erroneous and impracticable to the very last degree.

Moreover, Matthew reports Christ as saying and teaching thus: "Then came Peter to him, and said, Lord how oft shall my brother sin against me, and I forgive him? till seven times? Jesus saith unto him, I say not unto thee, until seven times: but, until seventy times seven."—Mat., 18. 21—22. Now, this teaching, however beautiful it may sound in theory, can never be lived out in practice; and for the plain reason that it is expressly forbidden by general human nature, as the same is organically enstamped upon man by the God that made him. Hence, talk it as we may, no man can endlessly forgive and keep on forgiving offenses committed and repeated against him by father, mother, sister, brother, or anybody else: nor would it be a virtue in him to do so, even if he could. There is not only a time to forgive offenses committed against us, but a time to cease forgiving them, and also a time to resent their repetition and punish therefor.

Again, in his celebrated sermon on the mount, Matthew reports Christ as exhorting and teaching as follows: "Behold the fowls of the air: for they sow not, neither do they reap, nor gather into barns; yet your heavenly Father feedeth them. Are ye not much better than they? Which of you by taking thought can add one cubit unto his stature? And why take ye thought for raiment? Consider the lilies of the field how they grow; they toil not, neither do they spin; and yet I say unto you, That even Solomon in all his glory was not arrayed like one of these. Wherefore, if God so clothe the grass of the field, which to-day is, and to-morrow is cast into the oven, shall he not much more clothe you, O ye of little faith? Therefore take no thought, saying, what shall we eat? or, What shall we drink? or, wherewithal shall we be clothed?"—Mat., 6. 26—31. Now it cannot but be obvious to every candid and reflecting reader of the above, that, was either the letter or the spirit of this teaching to be universally adopted and lived out in practice, it would inevitably bring poverty, starvation, and nakedness upon the whole human family, and that in comparatively a short period of time. Neither the luxuries nor the comforts nor the barest necessaries of life can ever long and permanently be enjoyed by man, without *much taking thought,* and also much labor and care; wherefore all such teachings as are thereunto adverse, no matter by whom put forth nor when, are both unwise and impracticable. But again; Mark reports Christ as commanding and teaching thus: "Afterward he appeared unto the eleven, as they sat at meat, and upbraided them with their unbelief, and hardness of heart, because they believed not them which had seen him after he was risen. And he said unto them, Go ye into all the world, and preach the gospel to every creature. He that believeth and is baptised, shall be saved; but he that believeth not, shall be damned. And these signs shall follow them that believe: in my name shall they cast out devils; they shall speak with new tongues; they shall take up serpents; and if they drink any deadly thing, it shall not hurt them; they shall lay hands upon the sick, and they shall recover."—Mark, 16. 14—18. Now this teaching, notwithstanding put forth in as clear and emphatic language as any doctrine he ever taught, is, nevertheless, wholly erroneous in both its letter and its spirit. No amount of mere belief or mere baptism or both can ever save men from the commission of sin, and never from its painful consequences. Neither are serpents and deadly drinks thus easily rendered innoxious, nor the sick in this manner to be cured, teach differently who may.

And yet again; John reports Christ as saying and teaching as follows: "Then the same day at evening, being the first day of the week, when the doors were shut where the disciples were assembled for fear of the Jews, came Jesus and stood in the midst, and saith unto them, Peace be unto you. And when he had so said, he shewed unto them his hands and his side. Then were the disciples glad when they saw the Lord. Then said Jesus unto them again, Peace be unto you: as my Father hath sent me, even so send I you. And when he had said this, he breathed on them, and saith unto them, Receive ye the Holy Ghost. Whosoever sins ye remit, they are remitted unto them; and whosoever sins ye retain, they are retained."—John, 20. 19—23. Now this idea, thus plainly taught by Christ, that his immediate disciples, and hence their successors to the ministry, have the power to remit or pardon sins, is not only directly at variance with fact, but fearfully misleading and dangerous in its consequences; so very much so that more than one-half the Christian world do still continue to believe this same sadly erroneous teaching, and their priests to be essaying to practice in accordance therewith; that is, essaying to pardon sins and granting indulgencies for their commission. But, of this, enough; since it is not our aim to mar the beautiful simplicity or detract from the transcendent merits of Christ's general religious teachings, when taken as a whole; but simply to show that he, just like all other great and good men, both ancient and modern, had his weaknesses and faults; hence, just like such, was liable to err both in judgment and practice; and consequently that it is both foolish and wrong, and not wise and religious, to attempt to defend or to follow such of his teachings as are either manifestly erroneous or wholly impracticable. In a word, as we see it, the true course to pursue, as well in matters of religion as in politics or anything else, is this: No matter by whom taught, nor when, whatever is both truthful and practical adopt, and whatever is either erroneous or impractical reject.

And here it may not be improper to say that, as a guide to human actions, the Golden rule, so-called, and thus called as well on account of its transparent simplicity and great worth, as because forever present with us, if we will but ask ourselves what it is that, under like circumstances, we would have others do to us, is none the less wise or eminently practical, because pronounced and taught by the heathen philosopher Confucius, more than five hundred years before Christ was born. Said rule, as thus early laid down by Confucius, reads as follows: "*Do unto another what you would he should do unto you; and do not unto another what you would not should be done unto you. Thou needest only this law alone; it is the foundation and principle of all the rest.*"—As taught by Christ it runs thus: "*All things whatsoever ye would that men should do to you, do ye even so to them: for this is the law and the prophets.* Thus parallel do the brains of men of like taste and character occasionally come to vibrate, not only at different periods of time, but in lands far remote.

Another suggestion: In this short sentence pronounced by Christ, we have his warrant for affirming that, in substance and effect, both the law and the prophets were proclaimed and taught by that Chinese heathen, long centuries before the Christian system, which is based thereupon, had its beginning.

And yet another: That Christ was largely indebted for the sweetness of his temper, the kindness of his feelings, and the character of his aspirations to the singularly joyous state of his mother's views, feelings, and aspirations, during the period of gestation, cannot be doubted. As to what were her views, and what the character of her feelings and aspirations, during that interesting period, Luke bears brief testimony as follows: "And Mary said, Behold the handmaid of the Lord, be it unto me according to thy word. And the angel departed from her. And Mary arose in those days, and went into the hill-country with haste, into a city of Juda, and entered into the house of Zacharias, and saluted Elizabeth. And it came to pass, that when Elizabeth heard the salutation of Mary, the babe leaped in her womb; and Elizabeth was filled with the Holy Ghost. And she spake out with a loud voice and said, Blessed art thou among women, and blessed is the fruit of thy womb. And whence is this to me, that the mother of my Lord should come to me? For lo, as soon as the voice of thy salutation sounded in mine ears, the babe leaped in my womb for joy. And blessed is she that believed; for there shall be a performance of those things which were told her from the Lord. And Mary said, *My soul doth magnify the Lord, and my spirit hath rejoiced in God my Savior. For he hath regarded the low estate of his handmaiden: for behold, from henceforth all generations shall call me blessed. For he that is mighty hath done to me great things; and holy is his name.*"—

Luke, I. 38–49. Wherefore, we repeat, it cannot be doubted that much of excellence was enstamped upon Christ by his young and joyous mother, whether he inherited any virtues from his putative Father or not.

And still another: The fact of its being impressed upon Christ in infancy, in childhood, and all along, that he was begotten by the Holy Ghost, and so was the Son of God, undoubtedly had much to do with making him the kind and character of man he was. In other words, his constantly laboring under the impression that he was begotten and born to greatness and goodness, and hence that great and good things were expected of him, had a strong natural tendency to create, and keep alive within him, both ardent desire and firm determination so to speak and to act as not to disappoint those high expectations.—High expectations and praises discreetly bestowed are much better calculated to elevate the character of children and promote them in the ways of virtue, than are low expectations and censure unsparingly applied.

Religious science, the same as the science of medicine or astronomy, should, as far forth as possible, be based upon the hard pan of facts, be they what they may, and discovered how and when they will; and not upon the quicksands of assumed miracles, or theoretic conjectures either ancient or modern. Yea, and here we cannot refrain from remarking that, so long as shall the avowed friends of the Christian system of religion presist in basing it, not only upon assumed miracles, but upon miracles unto which, were they genuine, not the slightest practical importance attaches, instead of upon its real merits,—instead of upon its actual workings in the broad fields of practice; in other words, in endeavoring to make its value to consist, not in the living out of the great human virtues which were taught by Christ and exemplified in his life, but in a mere, blind belief in his superhuman origin, divine nature, etc., just so long will they be obliged, not only to keep industriously hedging against the developments that are constantly being made by science, but to make further, and still further, concessions thereto;

until, finally, of such assumed foundation, there shall be nothing left. In order to be a Calvinist, in the very broadest sense of that term, it is not necessary for a man to believe, for an assumed illustrative example, that Mr. Calvin's father was a wizard and his mother a witch, just because he chanced to have the misfortune so to think and publicly to state at divers times and places, but only that his religious belief and practice should correspond with the distinctive *theological doctrines* taught by that eminent divine.

The mere name, " Christian," which was derived from the name of the individual called Christ, and which, according to Acts, 11. 26., was, for the first time, applied to his disciples at Antioch, some twenty years after his death, may not unlikely, in the long lapse of ages, die out and become forgotten; but the great human virtues by him so impressively taught as being essential to happiness, and which he so beautifully exemplified in his own daily practice, such as kindness, charity, brotherly love, etc., will continue to live and bless mankind so long as civilized man shall tenant the Earth.—It is not the name by which principles or a system of principles may chance to be called that renders them valuable, but the quality of the fruit which they are found to bear.

The heathen philosopher Confucius, who taught and exemplified in his life substantially the same great human virtues that were taught by Christ, some five hundred years later, was just as much a Christian practically, as was Paul or Peter. Or thus: Had the same religious principles and practices which were taught by Confucius, and five centuries thereafter by Christ, chanced to have been called Confucianism, after the name of that philosopher and leader, or Naturism, because of their general concurrence with Nature and her laws, instead of Christianity, after the name of Christ, they would not have been one jot less intrinsically valuable, and hence any less worthy of the world's approbation and esteem, than are they now. No; gold will be gold, and brass, brass, be they presented by whom they may and called by whatsoever name they will.

Among the different heathen nations of the world, there are doubtless many men who, notwithstanding they never heard the name of Christ, are quite as good Christians, in actual practice, as any of us.—In order to reap the full benefits of Mr. Graham's dietetic system, for example, and hence be, in all essential respects, a Grahamite, it is not necessary that a man should profess to be one, or even that he should be aware that any such man as Mr. Graham ever had birth; but only that, in the single matter of eating, his *practice* should coincide with the dietetic teachings of said Mr. Graham.

That there are many, very many, good Christians or practically religious men, among all the different religious sects, we are happy to believe; and yet we must be permitted to think that there are far more of such among what are called the world's people, than among the members of all the different sectarian churches put together.—Profession, however long and loud, is nothing; practice, however modest and unpretending, everything.

Nor can we resist the conclusion that the different agricultural classes from the nature of their employment, consequent habits, and modes of thought, are brought and kept in closer relation with God, his promises, commandments, and laws, than is any other large class of persons by their occupation, consequent habits, and modes of thinking; and hence that the average farmer and mere man of the world, so-called, whilst busily engaged in turning the soil, scattering the seed, tending his flocks, etc., doth more truly serve not only himself and his fellow-men, but his great Maker, than does the average man of any other class, notwithstanding a regular member of St. Paul's Church, for example, whose steeple he is sure is half a foot higher than any other in the town or county. Indeed, so close is the connection between the intelligent tiller of the soil, whether a professor of religion or not, and the God whom he is constantly invoking by the use of the plow and the harrow, the spade and the cultivator, the shovel and the hoe, etc., etc., to bless his labors, and supply him with bread to eat, to sell, to feed the wayfaring stranger, and give unto the neighboring poor, that there seems to be very little room fo. any mediator or other middle man to crowd himself in between them. Of course, with the ignorant and blindly superstitious husbandman, the case is somewhat different; and hence, upon such, the tax that is constantly being levied upon ignorance and credulity quite heavily falls.

Again, as it is a knowledge of God's facts which constitutes wisdom, and not blind faith in such things as may or may not have any real existence that does it, so it must be just as much our religious duty to search after knowledge by reading, by observation, by the use of our reasoning powers, and experiments carefully made, as it is to feed the hungry, clothe the naked, or be kind, charitable, and forgiving one toward another.—In his own proper day, that Dr. Franklin was a master electrician cannot be doubted; but then it is not to be supposed that he understood, and hence taught either directly or by fair implication, all of that sublime science which it is possible for subsequent generations of men, with their greatly superior advantages, ever to come to know. Just so Christ: although a most eminent religious teacher, in the day and age in which he lived, and that too by example as well as precept, still he could not have understood, and hence could not have taught, however desirous he might have been to do so, everything upon the great and important subject of religion, which is necessary to guide the steps and satisfy the yearnings of after generations of men; —of after generations of men who, by the aid of his said teachings, and their own observation and experience added thereto, have become greatly advanced in knowledge, civilization and refinement. As we have finally come to see it, whether right or whether wrong, just as certainly as is man a progressive and not a stand-still being, just so certainly must the system of religion by Christ introduced, and hence called the Christian system, be correspondingly progressive both in its theoretical teachings and practical workings, otherwise it must of necessity fail to meet and satisfy progressive man's much more numerous and farther advanced religious needs. Or thus: Self-evidently, as seems to us, no matter what may be the living science or system, by whom founded nor when, it can never remain stationary for many decades of centuries, so long as shall man continue to be a progressive animal.

Or, to state the matter a little differently still, to the leading of a religious life, it is not necessary that a man should believe, in substance and effect, that the God who created the world, and all things therein and upon, was so stern, self-willed, and unforgiving in his nature, that he would not consent to pardon or pass by unnoticed the offenses committed by us his children, against himself, his dignity, and laws;—is not necessary to believe that he, God, was so exceedingly good and perfect, that he could not and would not consent to look upon the sins committed by the frail human beings whom he, unasked, had made, with the least bit of allowance. Neither is it necessary to believe, in substance and effect, that the only Son he ever begat, in consequence of his being begotten in accordance with carnal usage, carried by a real flesh-and-blood woman the ordinary length of time, and then by her born into the world, was so little like his stern old Father, and so very like unto his amiable, young mother, that his heart did literally overflow with the milk, not of God-kindness, but of human kindness and other kindred virtues resident in the breast of man. And consequently that this his said Son was not only willing to forgive us our transgressions, but so exceedingly anxious that we should be forgiven them that, to enable his stern Father to do so without seemingly relenting or one jot to relax the rigor of his laws, he consented to take them all upon his own shoulders and suffer death therefor. Nor is it necessary to believe that after being thus put to death for our transgressions, and lying in the grave some three days and nights, he arose bodily therefrom as fully alive and well as ever. Nor yet is it necessary to believe that, because he is said thus to have arisen, therefore shall we, one and all, at some future day, in like manner and form arise. No; these are all mere speculative questions, and not things which, whether so or whether not so, can ever by anybody be reduced into practice; consequently they do not constitute any part of a practical religious life and character; and hence do not form any part of that religion which, entering into men's daily lives, goes down into all their dealings and doings both public and private,—the only kind that is really worth having

Real, practical religion, no matter by what name called, is not a mere Sunday garment to be worn at church, and then laid aside for the rest of the week, but a thing which marks men's deportment toward their kindred fellow-mortals of every age, class, and grade;—a thing which enters into the character of their goods, wares, and merchandize;—a thing which characterizes their treatment of all such inferior animals as, from either pleasure or profit, they keep about them. In a word, it is being good and kind and charitable and forgiving ourselves, and not simply believing that Christ was good and kind and charitable and forgiving, that makes us Christ-like, makes us practically religious, makes us happy.

CHAPTER XXV.

THE LABORER'S BREAST, VIRTUE'S SEAT.*

"Those who labor upon the earth," says the sage of Monticello, "are the chosen people of God, if he ever had a chosen people, whose breasts he has made the peculiar depository for substantial and genuine virtue. It is the focus in which he keeps alive that sacred fire which otherwise might escape from the face of the Earth. Corruption of morals in the mass of cultivators is a phenomenon of which no age or nation has furnished an example."

From this brief expose of human nature and its workings, we are led to infer that those who labor not upon the soil, or at anything else, but feed and fatten upon the toil of others, are the children of the Devil, if he ever had any children; it being in their heads that those unhallowed fires do have their origin, which consume the vitals of virtue, work corruption in the foundations of society, and cover the earth with pollution and wretchedness. Not only this, but, from the same brief text, we are led to conclude that not in the heads of the toiling millions of either section of the Union, but in the fertile brains of the planting aristocracy of the South, and the manufacturing aristocracy of the North,—aided respectively by their pampered political adjuncts and theological satellites,—were hatched into existence and fostered into growth those strangely antagonistic ideas and bitter sectional feelings which have ripened into that double attempt at revolution, that is now covering our fair land with the blood of her children, slain by each others' hand. We say, those strangely antagonistic ideas and bitter sectional feelings which have ripened into that double

*NOTE.—This written for a Lyceum Paper during the dark days of the Republic, in the fall of 1863.

attempt at revolution, etc., because it is no more clear to us that it was and is the design of the one aristocracy to create, out of certain territory covered by the national flag, a new confederacy of States, having negro-slavery for its chief corner-stone, than that it was and is the intention of the other to revolutionize such slavery, in its present legalized form, entirely out of the Union, without suffering an inch of territory to be withdrawn therefrom.

Be all this, however, as it may, it is certain that a revolution is upon us.—And yet, in the midst of all this gloom and darkness, we have an abiding faith that all things, everywhere and ever, do work together just as, from the force of currently existing circumstances, they needs must work; and hence that they do, at all times and everywhere, upon the whole, work together for good, and not for evil. Wherefore, let the end of this bloody, fratricidal strife, come when it will, the future *status* of the negro among us be decided as it may, and the map of America remain uuchanged or not, we cannot doubt but that all this destruction of life, all this waste of treasure, and these dreadful human sufferings, are just so many needful agencies of enlightenment to us, the American people, to open up the way to that higher grade of civilization and consequent enjoyment which, pursuant to the law of human progression, awaits us in the future. In other words, as we see it, such is human nature, the world over, and such the character of certain obstructions that do occasionally come to block the wheels of progression, individual, state, and national, that they can never be removed, except by the stern argument of brute force unsparingly applied. But for the fierce storms of one kind and another which have ever, occasionally, been taking place in Earth's atmospheric envelop, it would not have been that same pure and healthful thing which it now is; and but for the fierce storms of war which have ever, occasionally, been taking place among the habitants of Earth, men would not have been occupying that same high plane of intelligence, civilization, and social equality which they now are.

Corollary:—Reason as we may, when the weather is fair and no breakers in sight, the case now before us belongs to a class which can never be settled in accordance with the workings of natural law, and hence never in accordance with what is, upon the whole, for the best good not only of the contending parties themselves, but of the world of mankind, without ignoring for the time the gentle teachings of Christ, and falling back upon the stern example of the old Mosaic God.

CHAPTER XXVI.

FIXED-LAW REIGNS.

Admitting that man cannot so much as draw a breath, think a thought, or move a muscle, except he does it by aid operation of natural law, consequently that, from sole to crown, he is of Nature a legitimate part, it would then seem to follow that the different kinds and grades of results by him produced into being are, each and all, natural productions; and hence that, in a philosophical point of view, between the works of Nature and the so-called works of art, there is not any real difference. Or, to present the idea a little more at length, because it is a fact that but for the pre-creation upon this Earth, by natural process or somehow else, of that complex bundle of elements called man, there could never have been produced into being upon its face, any of the different kinds or grades of things which are of human origin, or a single one of all that infinite number and variety to whose production the labor of man, to a certain extent, is a thing essential, it no more follows that said productions are not from beginning to end the productions of Nature, or the legitimate results of the existence and operation of natural causes, than it does that the present vegetable and animal kingdoms are not; since it is certain that the compound element called water is an essential ingredient in the composition of every plant and animal under the whole heaven, and since it is also a fact that but for the pre-creation upon this globe, by natural process or somehow else, of said compound element called water, there could never have been produced into being upon its surface, any of the different kinds of vegetables or animals that are of aqueous origin, or a single one of all that infinite number and variety in whose composition water is both an essential requisite and the principal ingredient. Water, the same as every other element and thing, in a state of isolation, that is, in the absence of anything to act upon it or by it be acted upon, is powerless to produce results of any kind; and yet, existing not by itself, but in intimate connection with almost every other terrestrial element and thing, it legitimately becomes an agent of great power, and hence stands prime cause to the production of numberless different kinds of phenomena or results; and the same of all the different created agents, inanimate and animated, man included.

Again, admitting that, by the lone action of the natural agent water upon other substances, numberless different kinds of results are produced into being; admitting that, by the lone action of the natural agent atmospheric air upon other substances, numberless other different kinds of results are produced into being, each and all of which are essentially different from anything which ever was or ever can be brought into existence by the action of water or any other lone agent; admitting that, by the joint action of any two natural agents or creative causes, say atmospheric air and water, for example, there are yet other innumerable multitudes of different kinds of results pushed into existence, each and all of which are, in like manner, essentially different from anything which ever was or ever can be brought into being by the lone action of either element or cause, or by the joint action of any other two; also admitting the same thing to be true not only of atmospheric air and water, but of the joint action of every possible number of creative causes above the binary; also admitting that all these countless myriads of different created products, whether the result of the lone action of some one creative cause or of the joint action of ever so great a number, are, each and all, the production of Nature; and also that the complex bundle of elements called man, in obedience to the organic nature which is indelibly enstamped upon him, doth also join in and work along with those other innumerable creative causes, whereby are pushed into being yet still other innumerable kinds and character of things, each and all of which are, in like manner, essentially different from anything which could ever have been brought to take place and be, but for the influence legitimately exerted by the presence and action of man's inherent power; it would then seem to follow that the things, one and all, to which that child of Nature called man doth stand prime cause of their existence, precisely the same as those to which the natural production called water doth so stand, are natural productions; and hence that, in a philosophical point of view, between those things which are usually spoken of as natural productions, and the so-called works of art, there is not any real difference.

But again; inasmuch as water which is neither more nor less than one of Nature's inanimate fractions, in obedience to the law of its nature and the force of circumstances that bear upon it, doth legitimately exert power, descend from the clouds in torrents, and so washes or makes holes in the ground, for example; inasmuch as the electric fluid which is neither more nor less than another of Nature's inanimate fractions, in obedience to the law of its nature and the force of circumstances that bear upon it, doth legitimately exert power, leap from the clouds, and so tears or makes other holes in the ground; inasmuch as the fox which is neither more nor less than one of Nature's animated fractions, in obedience to the law of his nature and the force of circumstances that bear upon him, doth legitimately exert power, and so digs or makes still other holes in the ground; and as man who is neither more nor less than another of Nature's animated fractions, in obedience to the law of his nature and the force of circumstances that bear upon him, doth legitimately exert power, and so digs or makes yet still other holes in the ground; therefore is the conclusion irresistible that the holes made by either one of said animated fractions, no matter which, nor what the form or size of such holes, are, each and all, just as much the work of Nature herself as are those which are made by either one of said inanimate fractions; and hence that, notwithstanding the distinction which, by usage of language, is made to exist between those things in whose creation man is known to act a part, and such as, in their creation, he no sort of hand doth have, in a strictly philosophical point of view, there is no difference. That men, water, foxes, etc., do each make or produce into existence some things, and also unmake or destroy some, cannot be denied; How then can it be doubted that they are, each and all, composing fractions of that Power which all created things doth make and rule?

For the reason that the different acts which water, atmospheric air, and other inanimate agents perform, are natural acts, and the results by such action produced into being natural productions, for that same reason are the different acts which the fox, beaver, and other animated brute agents perform, natural acts, and the results by such action produced into being natural productions. And for the same reason that the different acts and productions of either of the above classes of agents are natural acts,—are the acts and works of Nature, (because performed by one of her composing fractions,) for that very same are the different acts by man performed natural acts, and the results produced into being by such action natural productions. In other words, for the broad reason that, throughout all vast Nature's realm, not blind chance, but fixed law, eternally doth reign, for that same broad reason is each and every act by man performed, the legitimate result of some natural, exciting cause; precisely the same as are all the different acts by inanimate or brute agents performed. When the inanimate agent water, for example, runs down hill, as in the form of brooks, rivers, etc., it is seen to do, it performs such action because it is thereunto compelled by the strong law of gravitation which is one of its undying attributes; and when it performs the act of running up hill, as in a portion of the siphon it is seen to do, it performs such action, not because it is in accordance with its nature thus to act, but because it is thereunto compelled by the presence and operation of a power which it is impotent to resist;—because it is thereunto compelled in direct opposition to its own inherent nature, by the pressure of the atmosphere upon the surface of the fountain in which the shorter arm of the siphon is immersed. In the same manner, when a condemned criminal, for another example, in consequence of receiving a government pardon, performs the act of walking out of that prison of which for years he has been an inmate, he performs it because he is thereunto compelled by the promptings of his own inherent nature; and when such a criminal walks into that dark and gloomy cell where, pursuant to legal sentence, he expects to end his days, he performs such action not because he is thereunto prompted by his own inherent nature, but because he is thereunto compelled by the presence and operation of circumstances which are too strong to be by him resisted; and thus on to the full chapter's end.

But, to present the idea in still another form, allowing existing creation to be the legitimate result of the presence and operation of certain creative causes, deep in the nature of the undying ELEMENTS eternally residing, and not the production of a vast six-day miracle as was anciently supposed, then it needs must follow that, throughout all vast Nature's realm, fixed-law eternally doth reign; consequently that great Nature, or the mighty God, (if that name any more appropriate shall be deemed,) is, at all times and in all places, limited in his power and governed in his action thereby; consequently that all his different composing fractions, inanimate and animated, man included, are, in like manner, limited and governed; and consequently that, from the mighty God himself all the way down to his feeblest elementary fraction, law-existing and law-limited agency is all the agency there really is. As soon as by aid and operation of the appropriate simple, pre-existing creative causes, the more important compound, inanimate elements or agents, such as water, atmospheric air, etc., were ushered into existence, so soon did such compound agents, each and all, become so many additional compound creative causes to the pushing into existence of such other additional created things, and hence additional creative causes, as were the legitimate result of the spontaneous action of their several inherent natures; and consequently just such different kinds and character of things, inanimate and animated, as could not by any possibility, before that time, have been brought into being. In the same manner, as soon as by aid and operation of the proper kinds and qualities of pre-existing, natural creative causes, the different bottom kinds of animated structures were ushered into being, so soon did such animated structures, each and all, legitimately become so many additional created things, and hence additional creative causes to the pushing into existence of yet such other additional things, as, by virtue of their several inherent natures and the force of surrounding circumstances, they needs must. And thus forever on; every additional created thing, high and low, great and small, inanimate and animated, man included, standing and being, as soon as into existence brought, an additional creative cause to the pushing into being of yet still others; whereby and wherefore, of newly created things, and hence of additional creative causes, the end is not yet nor soon likely to be. Or, at least, this is how it seems to us.

Simply for the reason that, a few short centries ago, the causes which produce the rainbow, the rising and falling of the waters in the form of tides, the eclipses of the Sun, the occultation of the stars, etc., were wholly unknown, it would not have been wise, in the men of those days, to have inferred that these phenomena where not, each and all, produced into being by operation of natural law. In like manner, simply because, in almost every branch and department of animate nature, there are constantly taking place a great variety of things, the precise causes whereof are not yet understood, it will not do to infer that these things are not, each and all, from beginning to end, the legitimate results of the existence and operation of proper natural causes. And simply for the reason that man, the highest and most complicated of all known branches of animated nature, is constantly feeling impressions, thinking thoughts, and performing acts, the precise causes whereof he is unable to see or to trace, it cannot be a mark of wisdom in him to infer that he is not, from bottom to top and all the way through, the creature of natural law, the same as is every other animal and thing;—cannot be a mark of wisdom in him to infer that he thus doth feel, think, and act independently, not only of hereditary and educational influences, but of the influence which is ever legitimately exerted upon him by the numberless different circumstances and things, inanimate, and animated, by which, from life's earliest dawn to its final close, he is constantly surrounded. And, finally, because there are some circumstances and phenomena which, from the very nature of things, can never be *known*, but only more or less strongly inferred and believed from the light which other circumstances and things do shed upon them, it cannot be a mark of wisdom in any set of men, no matter what their profession nor what their standing, pompously to assume to know all about them; and surely not of modesty to go about dogmatically teaching such impiously assumed knowledge, as God-revealed verity.—As from premises which are in accordance with real truth not a single false conclusion can logically be drawn, so whoever has abiding faith in any theory or doctrine, no matter what, need have no fears that its logical consequences will lead him upon ground where it is not safe to stand.

Agreeably to our understanding of the matter, the leading points in the olden theory of God, his government, the creation of man, etc., as to-day they are generally taught and professed to be believed, may be briefly stated thus: God is a personal Being that is all-wise, all-good, all-powerful, free to think, speak, and do as he pleases, and is not accountable for anything he may think, say, or do. Man is a personal being that is exceedingly weak in knowledge, all-bad and wrong from bottom to top, very nearly powerless, free to think, speak, and do as he pleases; and yet, for everything which he may please to think, say, or do, he is accountable to that God who took upon himself the responsibility of thrusting the poor, feeble creature into existence without his knowledge or consent; and in whose power it was to have made him to think, say, and do precisely as he wanted that he should.—Of the obvious logical consequences of such a theory we shall say nothing, but simply commend them to the consideration of its numerous friends and admirers.

According to our view of God, his government, the creation of man, etc., and which has already been quite fully explained, the Creator and Governor of the universe is, by unavoidable consequence, just as much compelled by the law of his nature, that is, by the different undying properties and powers inherent in his several composing elements, to create whatsoever he doth create, to destroy whatsoever he doth destroy, and, in short, to do, in all respects, just as he does, as is water, one of his composing fractions, by the law of its nature, to run down hill, when not therefrom prevented by some one or other of his different composing fractions. We say, as much as is water, one of his composing fractions, by the law of its nature, to run down hill, etc., because, obviously enough, neither water nor any other of great Nature's different composing fractions is great Nature's SUM;—is the Creator and Governor of the universe;—is the mighty God himself. Wherefore, notwithstanding it, the same as every other of his fractions, doth forever possess and exert a *pro rata* share of great Nature's vast power, unlike great Nature's SUM, it doth not possess, in its comparatively brief, fractional self, *all the power there is;* and wherefore, in its action, notwithstanding the strength of its own inherent nature, it is ever legitimately compelled not only to bow obedience to the commands of such other of great Nature's fractions as are to it superior, but more or less to feel the influence of such as are thereunto inferior. And, of all of great Nature's different fractions, man included, the same.

And yet a little plainer still: By unavoidable consequence, according to our view, great Nature, the eternal Elements, or the mighty law-governed God, could no more help creating the world when he did, where he did, and as he did, than could the world help being by him created when it was, where it was, and as it was; could no more help creating man when he did, where he did, and as he did, than could man help being created by him when he was, where he was, and as he was; and can no more help reigning in and ruling over man in the manner that he does, than can man help being, by him, thus reigned in and ruled over. And thus on, not only of all the different acts and things by God,—Nature, or the Sum of all Substance performed, but all those by His, Her, or Its different composing fractions of every name and kind. In a word, not chance, nor choicc, nor yet design, in the common acceptation of that term, but fixed-law, (which is but another name for the undying nature in Elementary Substance resident,) in all things, and everywhere, eternally doth reign. Or whether right or whether wrong, and be the logical consequences what they may, this is how the matter stands out revealed to us.

CHAPTER XXVII.

HOW GOD TALKED WITH MOSES.

Strange as the views by us put forth of God, his commandments, heaven, hell, etc., may appear to many, we think we are not mistaken when we say that some of their leading features are more or less distinctly shadowed forth in the teachings of both the old and New Testaments.

Thus, when John says, "He that loveth not, knoweth not God; for God is love:" we do not understand him to mean that the Creator and Governor of the universe is wholly composed of that attractive and attracting principle which performs so important a part therein, but only that as love or attraction is an essential element in the nature of the eternal HIM, therefore, in whose breast this same principle doth not exist in a highly developed and active state, he lives not in the enjoyment of the smiles of Heaven.—First Epistle of John, 4. 8.

Christ, when speaking to the Pharisees about the kingdom of God, is reported by Luke as teaching as follows: "The kingdom of God cometh not with observation: neither shall men say, Lo here! or, Lo there! for behold, the kingdom of God is within you."—Luke, 17. 20—21.

To the same effect taught Paul when writing to the saints at Rome; and this is his language: "Let not then your good be evil spoken of: for the kingdom of God is not meat and drink, but righteousness, and peace, and joy in the Holy Ghost."—Romans, 14. 16—17.

And when addressing the church at Corinth, Paul tells the living, breathing members thereof that they are the temple of God; and these are his words: "Know ye not that ye are the temple of God, and that the spirit of God dwelleth in you? If any man defile the temple of God, him shall

21

God destroy: for the temple of God is holy, which temple ye are."—First Corinthians, 3. 16–17. And subsequently, when writing to this same church and the saints in Achaia, he enforces the same idea thus: "And what agreement hath the temple of God with idols? for ye are the temple of the living God; as God hath said, I will dwell in them, and walk in them; and I will be their God, and they shall be my people."—Second Corinthians, 6. 16.

In reference to the commandments of God being organically enstamped, or ingrained into man's nature, and hence part and parcel of man himself, hear what Paul parenthetically says in his celebrated epistle to the Romans, second chapter, thirteenth, fourteenth, and fifteenth verses: "For not the hearers of the law are just before God, but the doers of the law shall be justified. For when the Gentiles, which have not the law, [the written law, meaning,] do by nature the things contained in the law, these not having the law are a law unto themselves. Which shew the work of the law written in their hearts, their conscience also bearing witness, and their thoughts the meanwhile accusing, or else excusing one another."

As, however, this is little else than an extract borrowed from Moses, so let us turn to the writings of that great lawgiver and see what it is that he himself doth say upon the subject.

"And thou shalt return and obey the voice of the Lord, and do all his commandments which I command thee this day. And the Lord thy God will make thee plenteous in every work of thine hand, in the fruit of thy body, and in the fruit of thy cattle, and in the fruit of thy land, for good: for the Lord will again rejoice over thee for good, as he rejoiced over thy fathers: if thou shalt hearken unto the voice of the Lord thy God, to keep his commandments and statutes which are written in this book of the law, and if thou turn unto the Lord thy God with all thine heart and with all thy soul.

"For this commandment which I command thee this day, is not hidden from thee, neither is it far off. It is not in heaven, that thou shouldst say, Who shall go up for us to heaven, and bring it unto us, that we may hear it, and do it? Neither is it beyond the sea, that thou shouldst say, Who shall go over the sea for us, and bring it unto us, that we may hear it, and do it? But the word is very nigh unto thee, in thy mouth, and in thy heart, that thou mayst do it."—Deut., 30. 8—14.

When we come to extend our mind's eye over the five books of history and of the law that were written by Moses, also to take into consideration the object for which those books were written, the circumstances under which they were penned, and the character of that people to whom, for immediate effect, they were addressed; we find ourselves compelled to interpret the singularly mystical language in which he clothes his different historic narrations, and the peculiar stereotyped forms of expression by him used in issuing unto them his orders, and giving them his commandments, to mean, in plain common prase, just about this: As your leader and chief ruler, I, Moses, have made nature, and particularly that branch thereof which the creature man doth constitute, my great study, to the end that I might thereby discover what human nature is, what its normal condition doth enjoin and what it doth prohibit; never for a moment doubting that, of all created nature, inanimate and animated, God is the Author. And, in consideration of your present deplorably low and ignorant estate, whatsoever thing I thus find to be a law of any branch or department of created nature, I feel myself warranted in declaring that same unto you, for your edification and guidance, as being the express commandment of the Lord.

In this way, by and through the natural language of his created works, and in no other, has God talked with me from time to time and I with him. In this way, by and through the emphatic language of their constant practice, and in no other, has he told me that, in and by the act of creating man, beast, fish, fowl, and insect, he commanded them, each and all, to be fruitful and multiply, and replenish the Earth.

In this same way also have I been enabled to see and to read in human actions all around me, not only the strong natural desire, but the ability, of the animal called man to dominate over the beasts of the field, the fowls of the air, etc. And having thus myself, by observation, experience, and the deductions of reason, come to be in possession of numerous important facts and circumstances which have the force of laws or commandments, I have not hesitated to omit all unnecessary explanation and to declare the same unto you, for your edification and guidance, as being the commandments of God to man and beast expressly given at the time of their creation. And thus on of all the numerous and different revelations to me made; and which revelations, as your teacher and leader, I have, from time to time with all due solemnity, and as the occasion seemed to require, proclaimed unto you as being either the past doings or the present declarations of the Lord, according to the nature of the case.

Modern illustrative example:—"Charlie, dear, hang up your little stockings in the corner; for just as like as not Santa Claus, with his great, big pack, will come down the chimney and fill them with something nice. Santa Claus loves good little boys that mind their mothers."—Thus spoke a fond and pious mother to her little son upon a Christmas, some thirty years ago. Quick as thought, little Charlie's half-closed eyes were wide open, and sparkling like diamonds. As, however, his mother did not seem to be particularly communicative just then, he presently put away his shoes in their accustomed place, hung his little blue stockings upon a nail in the chimney corner, and went to bed, there to dream of Santa Claus and candy.

Early next morning Charlie jumped out of bed, ran to his stockings, found one stuffed with candy and raisins, and in the other a nice, little, yellow-covered primer, in which was contained the Westminster Catechism. By turns he laughed, by turns looked admiringly upon his treasures, and by turns he wondered how old Santa managed to get upon the top of the house, work himself down the chimney, etc.

Of course, his numerous sage inquiries were all answered, but whether the answers filled him with light, or whether they still further added to the darkness by which he was already surrounded, may be regarded as a little uncertain.

"Why Charlie," cried a fond, pious mother, only two days thereafter, to a little boy who had somehow managed to wriggle himself into a closet of goodies, "come right out here in one minute, or the great, big bugbears will bite you! Don't you remember what lots of nice things Santa Claus brought you for being a good boy, and minding your mother?" And, strange to tell! about this time mount Sinai seemed to be all on fire and quaking at its very base!—Or rather, about this time, a sort of low, scraping, scratching noise was heard upon the wall, somewhere in the vicinity of his mother's large easy chair. Charlie heard the noise, and notwithstanding he was a little doubtful, still he was so far mystified as more than half-way to fear and also to believe it was a bugbear coming after him; and so, with the air of a culprit, he quite hastily put in his appearance behind his mother's big chair, in which she was comfortably seated rocking the baby.

Now, that Charlie has since grown into a great and learned man, we know; but whether or not he still continues to put the same construction upon his mother's said mystical language and feigned manner, and hence to regard the teachings of said yellow-covered primer with the same superstitious reverence that, in those days of timorous, childish ignorance, he did, we have not heard him say. But then, from certain indications, we strongly suspect he has long-since come to understand not only who was the mysterious personage called Santa Claus, but the true character of that said bugbear which he was sure he heard, and, by the eye of faith, almost saw, and of which he was thus afraid.—It may be well enough thus to create for ourselves a little mirth at the expense of the ignorance and inexperience of our children when small; but, then, we must insist that it would not only be unwise, but absolutely wrong for us, (we knowing better,) both early and late, and all along, and in every conceivable way, to do all in our power to prevent them from ever outgrowing such fabulous teachings upon any and all subjects. Encourage inquiry in every one, young and old, and not endeavor to smother and prevent it in anybody, should be the motto of all; and especially of such as are acting the part of leaders and teachers.

That Moses reasoned correctly when he inferred that, of every branch and department of created nature, God was the Author, consequently that the bottom laws which regulate and govern the actions of the animal creation, man included, are all ingrained, and hence that they are the commandments of the Lord, *every one*, as seems to us, cannot reasonably be doubted. And yet, when he took it upon himself by his authoritative manner, mystic phraseology, and dark proceedings, so far to mislead that ignorant, superstitious, and credulous people over whom he was acting in the threefold capacity of teacher, supreme lawgiver, and chief executive officer, as to cause them to think and verily to believe, that not by natural process, which they should try to learn and imitate, did he come to be in possession of his knowledge of what are and what are not God's commandments, but that the Lord graciously condescended to reveal them unto him in a personal and miraculous manner upon the top of the quaking and fiery mount; to the end that he, in God's stead, and as his specially chosen servant and mouthpiece, might declare the same unto them, we must think he committed an error, the ultimate consequences of which he little dreampt of.

And what are some of those ultimate consequences?—Why, by thus assuming to speak authoritatively, and as God's specially chosen servant and mouthpiece, instead of only in the capacity of an industrious historian, profound philosopher, and able statesman, he was not only the means of temporarily deceiving that most ignorant, superstitious, and credulous people in reference to the matter, but of permanently misleading a large and worthy portion of the world of mankind from quite an early day, down to this present hour. In short, by so doing he was the means of enstamping the seal of superstitiously believed-to-be verity, not only upon his numerous sound opinions in said five books contained, but also upon his numerous misjudgments therein recorded; and not only upon both these, but upon all his numerous, political ordinances and ceremonial religious requirements that were instituted and proclaimed for present effect; thus conferring upon all he said and all he did, no matter for what purpose said or with what object done, a sort of immaculate immortality.

In the same way that God talked with Moses, in that same way doth he talk with men now; every carefully made observation or experiment being a question propounded directly to God, and the result thereby obtained, his emphatic answer; call it prophecy, divine revelation, or by whatever name we may. Or, at least, such has come to be our well-settled opinion.

But again; it is no more clear to us that the different fountains that are in the world stand immediate cause to the creation of the different streams that are therein, than it is that the different kinds and character of men that have lived upon the Earth have stood immediate cause to the creation of all the different kinds and character of Deities that were ever believed in and worshiped. Wherefore we must think it about time that the God which was created by Moses for the special benefit of the children of Israel, a people who, without preparation or fitness, had been suddenly elevated from a condition of the most abject slavery to that of freedmen, and who were unquestionably the most ignorant, superstitious, idolatrous, and vindictive people known to historic record, should be made to give place to a Deity that is more in accordance with that high order of intelligence, civilization, and refinement, at which the leading nations of the world are now arrived.

Judging of Moses' character and designs from the character of his writings and the things which he did, we are led to conclude, not only that he was a shrewd observer of men and things, but that by his strong personal ambition and active philanthropic spirit, he was led and ruled. Wherefore we must think that he was much more intent upon devising some plan whereby he might successfully restrain, manage, and elevate, in the scale of humanity, that hitherto ignorant and down-trodden people, whom he had been so largely instrumental in freeing from bondage, and towards whom it was his ambition to act the part of sole law-giver, prime leader, and chief ruler, than he was of making such vast improvements in civil polity, and deep discoveries in natural science, as to cause himself to be looked up to and reverenced by remotest posterity as the father of statesmanship, and of philosophy the founder. Not only this, but, from the character of his writings and the things which he did, we are led to infer that, at the very time when he conceived the bold idea of creating the kind and character of God which he did, he was far more desirous of creating such a mythical Deity as would so completely fill, satisfy, and confound the heads of that ignorant, superstitious, and idolatrous people, as to compel them to look up thereto with profoundest awe, and thus cause them to cease bowing themselves down before idols of brass, or any other god of their own foolish making, than he was of creating such an one as would be likely to command the respect and receive the homage of enlightened generations of men for thousands of years thereafter. In other words, because the shrewd, aspiring Moses, for the purpose of obtaining the strongest possible influence over that proverbially ignorant, rebellious, and stiff-necked people whom, as has been said, he was so largely instrumental in freeing from bondage, and hence of bringing into a condition where they were without law to restrain them, precedent to guide them, or government to protect them, was induced to resort to the bold expedient, not only of claiming to hold communion directly and specially with God, but of speaking to them in his great name, and as by his express authority, whenever it became necessary for him to give unto them such laws and dictate to them such practices as he adjudged were best suited to their then ignorant and savage condition, we can see no good reason for believing it to have been his wish that such, without alteration or amendment, should continue to be the law and the practice, even among this peculiar and peculiarly situated people, for a single day after the circumstances which then rendered such laws and practices necessary should have passed away. Upon the contrary, in our judgment, the evidences are both numerous and strong, that he expected, that even this most ignorant and degraded of all people would gradually improve in manners and morals,—would gradually make advancement in knowledge, civilization, and refinement; and hence that, sooner or later, they would outgrow the necessity of having everything sent home to their superstitious fears and riveted thereupon with a *Thus saith the Lord*;—would outgrow the necessity of all such fabulous teachings and high-handed measures to restrain their angry passions, deter them from worshiping idols, and keep them within the bounds of common decency and order.

CHAPTER XXVIII.

DESIGN.

Because man, the masterpiece of all creation, by virtue of his composing elements and peculiar organization, possesses a certain faculty called Design, as well as numerous other capacities and powers; and because everything in nature, with which he has come to be acquainted, seems to bear upon it the marks of having been formed and placed where it is with reference to its filling the place it does, and which place, had it not been filled, would have left a break in creation's chain that would have been destructive of the general strength and harmony; therefore it is inferred by numerous brains of the first order, that existing creation cannot be the existing result of those numberless, undying causes which, inherently residing in the nature of vast creation's composing elements, have forever been at work and doing the things which, by virtue of their undying natures, they were legitimately compelled to do; and hence been forever at work producing into being, here, there, and everywhere, just such results as, between which and their parent causes, there ever legitimately exists that perfect order of mutual adaptation and relation which is the parent of harmony and of Design the very essence; but that it must be and is the perfected work of a pre-existent Being, greater and more potent, than are all these his created works together put. And yet, strange to say, by the same strong brains that it is concluded that these countless myriads of created harmonies, inanimate and animated, could not have been in existence, had they not been made and placed here by a pre-existent and hence extrinsic Maker, greater and more potent than are all created things, their composing elements included,—by those very same it is also concluded that this said greater and more powerful extraneous Being, not at all *himself* a MAKER needs must have. How such diametrically opposite conclusions, drawn premises precisely the same in character, may strike others we know not, but, to us, the case seems to present the most perfect example of straining at a gnat and swallowing a camel, humps and all, of any to be met with in the history of enlightened man. Just think of it! At the same time that it is gravely concluded that the vast amount of elements, which are known to be in existence in the form of worlds and systems of worlds, cannot possibly be self-existent; hence cannot possibly be eternal; and hence cannot possibly be of active, creative, and destroying power eternally possessed;—at that very same it is just as gravely concluded that the infinitely vast amount of elements, which are supposed to exist in the form of an infinitely great, extraneous, personal Spirit God, can be and are self-existent;—can be and are eternal;—can be and are, of active, creative, governing, and destroying power, eternally possessed.

And why is it that so many men of good natural abilities, excellent learning, and undoubted piety, draw such very different conclusions from premises which, in point of principle, are exactly alike, the degree only being different?—As we have come to see it, it is simply because they are so prejudiced and blinded by their early religious education as to be incapable of seeing clearly or reasoning dispassionately upon this subject. Wherefore, for the reason that they are unable to see how, during a long past eternity, the particles of elementary SUBSTANCE which, from their indestructibility, proclaim themselves eternal, and, from their active natures, are known to be forever at work exerting all their power, could have managed to work themselves into all the different worlds and systems of worlds which are seen to be floating in that illimitable ocean of elements called space,—for that same reason they do not seem to have any difficulty in seeing how an extraneous, pre-existent, unsubstantial Spirit Being, greater and more potent than are all these together put, could in full existence be without a MAKER, and, out of stark naught, make all these mighty and substantial things. As certainly as would these men have been pagans and not Christians, had they chanced to have been born in a pagan land, brought up under pagan institutions, and, from early childhood, been educated in the pagan religion and no other, just so certain is it that their early education upon this subject stands parent cause to these particular preconceived opinions thereupon, which have grown with their growth and strengthened with their strength until, finally, they have come to be in relation thereto their settled opinions and established modes of thought. And not only this, but as certain as does their early education upon this subject stand parent cause to their present, settled opinions and established modes of thought thereupon, just so certain has that same education been the cause of producing in their brains, to a corresponding extent, the permanent habit of vibrating in just such a manner as shall speak into existence within their heads, that same set of narrow and discordant ideas which were so indelibly enstamped upon them whilst they were yet pliant and soft.

Of course, it is not claimed that the power of habit is omnipotent; but only that, inasmuch as all habits derive their power to dominate over men, to the extent they ever come to possess it, directly from the brain and not from the bones or muscles; therefore, by unavoidable consequence, this particular brenal habit, in these men, (just like the one which, by virtue of early education, doth take root, grow, and gather strength in the brain of the pagan; until, in spite of all his general good sense upon other subjects, a pagan in belief, a pagan in his manner of reasoning, and a pagan in practice he unalterably becomes,) is altogether too deep-rooted and strong to allow them to see clearly or reason dispassionately upon this subject.

Nor are we unmindful that there are brenal habits of different kinds; consequently, that it not unfrequently happens that the minds of men upon various subjects are brought to run, as it were, in a groove,—are brought to revolve around some strange idea as its centre; and hence that it is possible it may be by virtue of an overwhelming habit into which our brain has somehow fallen, that we are compelled to think and believe upon this subject in the manner which we do. But, then, when we reflect that the old Mosaic theory of God, creation, etc., was most thoroughly pricked into the brains of these men, during the susceptible periods of infancy, childhood, and youth; also that our present opinions thereupon were not thus manufactured and stamped upon our brain by others' hand; we are irresistibly led to conclude that, in reference to this particular subject at least, upon which so many moulding influences are brought to bear, it is much more probable that their brains do still retain those same particular habits and modes of thought which were so deeply impressed upon them whilst they were yet blank sheets, than it is that ours has been able since its arrival at maturity, not only to burst the shackles imposed upon it by a like, early orthodox education, but to perform the feat of creating unto itself a different habit sufficiently strong to cause it to speak into existence within us a set of ideas in reference thereto, which are widely different in many respects from anything we ever happened to hear advanced,—except that such ideas are the legitimate outgrowth of a careful study of natural revelation.

But again; because all animals of importance with which we have come to be acquainted are ushered into being and pushed up creation's gradually ascending grade, step by step, into their ripe estate, by the aid and operation of light, for example, as one of their fractional parent causes; and because such fractional parent cause has enstamped its likeness or left its creational impress upon all such animals in the form of an organ whose special function it is to take cognizance of its said stimulating parent cause, and so afford them pleasure; and also because, between the thus legitimately created effect, the eye, and its special, parent cause, light, there is seen to exist that same perfect order of mutual adaptation and relation which, throughout universal Nature, doth everywhere exist between effects and their parent causes; it has therefore, by very many worthy men, been hastily concluded that these said mutual adaptations and relations could not have existed, had not a pre-existing planning Mind been careful, when he created the thing called light, to enstamp upon it just such properties as would render it agreeable to that feeble and then uncreated thing called the eye; and which it was determined should not be created until the next day. Obviously enough, the moment the ancient supposition is adopted that creation is a perfected work which, at a certain time, a few thousand years back, was brought into being all at once and full-sized, out of naught, just as it now is, from and after that moment there is no way left for accounting for the numberless different adaptations and relations which are seen to exist between creation's different parts, but by ascribing the whole matter directly to the action of some inconceivably great, wise, powerful, pre-existent, and hence extraneous Being. But, then, since it is certain that such ancient assumption is at variance not only with observation, but also with experience, and not only with both these, but with the plain deductions of reason drawn from them as data, it follows that such ancient assumption cannot be an eternal verity.

We say, since it is certain that such ancient assumption is at variance not only with observation, but also with experience, and not only with both these, but with the plain deductions of reason drawn from them as data, because not a single vegetable, animal, or thing, in all creation, did we ever see thus spring up, all at once, full-grown and great, either out of nothing or from appropriate elements, but, upon the contrary, always by gradual process from very small beginnings. In other words, as all created things, small and great, with whose rise and progress we have come to be acquainted, do gradually come up by growth or accretion of some sort, out of pre-existing elements, from very small beginnings, (if not from beginnings, quite beyond the reach of human sense to discover,) so it is perfectly logical to conclude that all other created things, the worlds included, came into being and obtained their present forms and size, in the same way. And since not a single created thing was ever known to spring up, all at once and full-sized, out of nothing, or even out of pre-existing elements; it must therefore be wholly illogical to conclude that the worlds were ever thus produced into being. Wherefore, instead of blindly assuming that creation was ever thus, all at once, sprung into being the grand harmonious-whole which to-day it is seen to be, we have, as seems to us, the best reasons for believing that, for countless ages and by gradual process, the same thing in principle, which, from life's earliest dawn to its final close, we all around us see, has been steadily going on; each created thing, as soon as into being brought, standing parent cause to the creation of some other as its legitimate effect; and said effect, as soon as into creation sprung, standing parent cause to the creation of yet another legitimate result; and thus on till now; every effect occupying the two-fold position of a legitimate result with reference to its own proper parent cause, and of parent cause with reference to the effect which, in turn, it doth itself produce; whereby, by the operation not only of single causes, but also of compound ones, the number and variety of created effects, and hence of creative causes, have long since become infinite, and are still increasing. And wherefore, as creation as are effects, by unavoidable consequence, forever true to their parent causes from beginning to end, bottom to top, and all the way through, just so certain are all the beautiful adaptations and relations, which effects are seen to bear and have to their parent causes, part and parcel of said effects themselves. Or, to present the idea in a little different dress, as certainly as doth a parent cause push into existence an effect, no matter what the kind, just so certainly must it, by unavoidable consequence, push into existence, *pari passu* therewith, all and singular those beautiful adaptations and relations which such effect doth bear and have to its said parent cause. And since such adaptations and relations must of necessity be correspondent to their producing causes, and since what is true, in this respect, of one parent cause and the effect by it produced, must needs be true of all parent causes and the effects by them produced, so this is all the premeditation that is requisite and all the Design that is needed to insure between the countless myriads of different parent causes and their effects, of which creation is ever currently composed, that general and particular harmony which everywhere, in all vast Nature's realm, doth constantly prevail.

Or in yet another dress; the properties of Substance, in all its vast infinitude and numberless different forms, being fixed and immutable, no amount of desire or design can ever change the nature of the feeblest atom, or one jot alter its mode of operation. Hence not a single act can ever be performed, or a single phenomenon or thing produced into existence, except it be done in accordance with the rulings of some branch or department of natural law, no matter what may be the thing designed to be accomplished, nor who the designer. In a word, as we see it, it is the undying nature of the Elements themselves, or the inside God, so to speak, that all things creates and moves and rules, just as He, She, or It needs must; call the same fixed-law, foreordination, predestination, design, chance, or by whatever name we may.

Instead of going back, then, to the days of Moses for light, and adopting the supposititious theory that the Earth was made and perfected upon the very day on which creation first began, and that the blind fishes, within the Mammoth Cave, were created therein just four days thereafter, and therein created without eyes, because it was foreseen by their Maker that there would never be any light in that place for them to see; we are compelled to infer that the Earth, in crude form, was created a long time before said cavern had existence beneath its crust. And not only this, but that, at some time thereafter, certain fishes which had been pushed into being by the aid of light, as one of the fractional creative causes unto which they were indebted for their existence, and which were consequently in possession of eyes to see and enjoy its sparkling beauty, unfortunately found their way into its dark, subterranean waters; where, for want of the cheering presence and supporting aid of that said special eye-creative cause, light, their orbs of vision, from non-use, gradually became more and more feeble; and thus on, with every succeeding generation of fishes brought into being therein, until, finally, upon the principle that like begets like and nothing begets nothing, from the organization of their remote progeny, light's special organ was dropped. This we regard as being an uncreating process; and one which, we doubt not, if brought continuously to bear upon the animal called man for only a few hundred, brief generations, would add yet another link to the chain of evidence going to prove that neither creation nor uncreation is the work of a week, a year, or an age.

No matter when or where operating, the same kind and character of causes, whether creative or uncreative, ever produce the same kind and character of effects. Hence the reason why within the same isothermal lines, upon the Eastern continent and upon the Western, upon the spacious islands of the Atlantic and of the Pacific, the same general kind and character of indigenous plants and animals are found. And hence, also, the reason why, in a few brief generations, the same breeds of cattle, horses, sheep, etc., may be, here, there, and everywhere, so much improved, simply by improving the creative causes that do bear upon them; namely, their food, treatment, and general surroundings.

Plainly enough, as seems to us, had the creative causes inherent in the elements of ancient Mother Earth been different from what they were, then a correspondingly different flora and fauna would have been here; and no extraneous Spirit God could have prevented it, much less have spoken into being such as now exist, in opposition thereto. And had the character of that great vivifying agent, Solar light, been different, then organs composed not only of correspondingly different elements, but of correspondingly different form, size, etc., to take cognizance thereof; hence a correspondingly different set of adaptations and relations would have existed all around and all the way through; consequently just as perfect harmony would have prevailed as now; and hence equally as strong evidence of Design would have been everywhere manifest.

And now, may we not indulge the hope that our readers will do us the favor and themselves the justice to consider candidly the different evidences by creation presented, and then answer, unto themselves, the following questions:—Do you believe that, at the end of a million of years, the progeny of a pair of those eyeless fishes would also be blind, were said pair to be now taken from their dark abode and placed in a sunny pond where not a fish exists, and where, during such full period, said pair and their progeny should have sole occupancy? And should you be forced to the conclusion that such progeny, at the expiration of that comparatively brief period in the world's vast history, would be in possession of eyes, such as other fishes have, then, the further question, To what god, other than the inanimate and yet animating rays of Sol, would you ascribe their creation?—Of course, it is hardly necessary to say that we regard the so-called rudimental eyes, observable in the heads of those fishes, as being neither more nor less than the feeble and constantly fading remains of what were perfect orbs of vision in the heads of their foreparents, at the time of their falling into this dark abode.

Day after day the Sun looks down upon the Earth and, by slow gradation, from appropriate elements, into being speaks, not only the feeble plant, the gorgeous flower, the perfect fruit, and stately tree, but, by aid and operation of these legitimate effects, as so many additional creative causes, all that vast variety of animals which, but for the pre-creation and hence pre-existence of the vegetable kingdom, could ne'er have here a being had. And surely the eye of man never beheld anything more divinely bright than is the kingly visage of its father Sol; and never anything more transcendently beautiful than is the queenly face of Mother Earth, when in her rich summer livery clad.

CHAPTER XXIX.

FACTS VERSUS FICTION.

As we have come to see it, the more widely observant and thinking men of the clerical profession do not, at very bottom, so much differ with us as to the origin of the book called the Bible or the truthfulness of its different pages, as they do in reference to what is and what is not, upon the whole, for the best good of mankind that they should be taught and brought to believe. In other words, whilst they are honestly of the opinion that, upon the great and important subject of religion, it is, upon the whole, better for all, and especially for the lower classes in society, to be taught and brought to believe a certain kind and quality of fiction, than it is that they should be instructed in the genuine facts, we are just as honestly led to conclude that, when taken in all its bearings and consequences present and remote, the teachings ot facts upon that subject, the same as upon every other great and important one, must necessarily tend to enlighten, elevate, and bless, all the different classes and grades of men to a greater extent, than does or can the continual teaching of any kind or character of fiction; and consequently that sober facts a great deal more, and cunningly contrived fictions a great deal less, had better be studied, taught and believed. We repeat, as we have come to see it, the more widely observant and thinking portion of the clergy, although quite too wise and prudent openly to avow or even privately admit—outside their own narrow fraternity—any such unpopular belief as would be the one that, upon the great and important subject of religion, fiction is better than fact, do nevertheless believe, at very bottom, that it would be an injury to society, and especially to the lower classes, to be instructed in the facts in reference thereto;

and consequently that it must needs be and is a benefit to them to be taught and brought to believe a certain class of fictions instead. Nor can we for one moment doubt that these men believe it to be their duty, in order to render their doses of deception more palpatable, and hence more certain to go down, to christen them with the fair name of Fact; and not only believe it to be their duty thus to christen them, but to maintain in the most solemn and asseverative manner, that they are not administering mere religious fictions, but God-revealed verities. Of course, it is not supposed that there are any among these who are seriously afraid that knowledge upon this subject, or any other great and important one, will ever mislead or injure them, but only that it would be bad, very bad, for their neighbors and others. Such men, notwithstanding entirely sincere in their course of action, can never be supposed to be worshipers of real Truth, for the reason that they are not in love with her for her own dear sake; and they can never be expected to fall in love with her for her own sake, so long as they do honestly think it is not through the agency of fact, but of fiction, alias pious falsehood, that the world is to be enlightened, elevated, and from dire destruction saved.

Allowing the real issue between these our much respected Christian friends and our humble self to be correctly stated; also allowing that, unlike the mass of their kindred fellow-mortals, they are not more influenced in their religious opinions, and guided in their action thereupon, by those particular habits and modes of thought which are impressed upon them during the susceptible periods of infancy, childhood, and youth, not only by parents and teachers, but by the general tone of that society by which they were surrounded, than they are by the unbiased teachings of sober intellect; then it would seem that all which is necessary to induce them to cease teaching unto others, as specially God-revealed verities, such things as they are quite well satisfied, within themselves, are merely gospel fictions of man's own invention, is to convince their judgments that, upon the whole, it would be better, as far forth as possible, to teach them the unadulterated facts.—A gigantic religious system with its hundreds of thousands of churches, teachers, and other appliances to keep the tiger knowledge chained; in other words, to keep men in ignorance upon the subject of religion, to the end that they may be kept from becoming vicious and unmanageable; and a gigantic school system running parallel therewith to disseminate knowledge upon all other great and important subjects, to the end that men may be rendered wiser, and consequently better! Where speech, as well as thought, is free, how a house, thus strangely divided against itself, can be expected to stand and to prosper we are wholly at a loss to discover.

From the little light we have, we are forced to the conclusion that there is no such thing as absolute evil in the world, but only an infinite variety of things which are, when taken in all their bearings and consequences present and remote, more or less good, *every one.* Doubtless great Nature, or the eternal God, just like his created works which are part and parcel of him, is, upon the whole, good, but not perfect. Indeed, in so far as it is possible to see and discover, there is no such thing as absolute perfection in anything or anywhere. That great and good men are the highest animated fractions of God of which we have any reliable knowledge will hardly be denied; and yet the very best man in the world is not wholly devoid of faults and weeknesses, nor the very worst, of some good and redeeming qualities.

Such being our views, we needs must think, not only that all the vast variety of facts, which are in the world are, upon the whole, more or less good and profitable to man, but that all the vast variety of fictions are. But whether right or whether wrong herein, it is certain that some things are far better than others from beginning to end, bottom to top, and all the way through. Thus, for a plain example, a beautiful prairie is a much higher grade of good, than is an impenetrable swamp; and yet we do not feel authorized to pronounce even this absolutely bad, but only relatively so, or a greatly inferior grade of good; since, being clearly a thing that is, it must needs be presumed to be one of the legitimate results of Nature's workings, and hence to reflect a certain portion of the character and attributes of its blessed Author. And then, again, there are some things which, although radically different in both character and kind, are nevertheless not only manifestly good and profitable to man, but good and profitable to an extent so nearly equal, that it requires some little observation and reflection to determine which of the two is the more so. And such is the case, in our judgment, not with any kind or character of fiction in perpetuity, when compared with fact, but with certain kinds of fiction temporarily, when with the proper kind of factscompared.

Or, to present the idea a little more clearly, self-evidently, as seems to us, of all the numerous and different kinds of fact that are in the world, those are to man the most valuable which are, upon the whole, to him the most useful; and, of all the numerous and different kinds of fiction, those are the best which the most strongly savor of such superior class of facts, and hence are temporarily made to serve as so many indexes or guides to lead men onward and upward in the scale of knowledge, to the more or less complete discovery and comprehension of the facts themselves towards which they point. In like manner, of all the vast variety of facts that are in the world, those are of the smallest value to man, which are, upon the whole, the least useful to him; and, of all the vast variety of fictions, those are lowest in grade which the least do tend to lead men onward and upward in the scale of knowledge, toward the discovery or better comprehension of any kind or quality of facts. This much being assumed as admitted, also that the character of every intervening fact and intervening fiction must necessarily reside somewhere between their two extremes, we will next endeavor to define our position a little more fully, in reference to that creature of the imagination called Fiction.

As we have come to see it, Fiction, Parable, and Fable do none of them derive their value from the circumstance of their being received and treasured up in memory as sober realities, but all, and all alike, from the compound fact of their not being so received, and yet being so framed as to have the effect to arrest attention, quicken thought, and stimulate inquiry; and hence the effect to lead men on to the embrace of those certain facts and principles, toward which they are thus significantly made to point, but which quite beyond their scanty words and narrow limits lie. It cannot be doubted that the brief old fable of *The Belly and the Members*, for example, has made its salutary impress upon many a youthful brain; and yet it is difficult to see how the brightest boy in the world would be rendered any the more wiser or better by committing that old story to memory and regularly repeating it himself, or having it sounded in his ears from the pulpit, every Sunday for the next forty years; provided he should be so unfortunate, during all that length of time, as to mistake it for a literal fact. And, of all the numerous so-call miracles and other religious fictions which are being dogmatically taught, not only to children, but also to men, for the purpose of so far stifling inquiry and forestalling their judgments as to cause them to embrace the shadow instead of the substance, the same.—Fictions, fables, etc., just like bank-notes, are only valuable when significant of something which has inherent worth.

But, notwithstanding the radical difference which exists between fact and fiction, and notwithstanding the inherent supremacy of the former over the latter, it cannot be denied that it is frequently better modestly to teach for a season, unto the young, the ignorant, and inexperienced, such fictions as are more simple and easy of comprehension than are the facts toward which they are so unerringly made to point as that they must necessarily, more or less serve to arrest their attention, quicken their thoughts, and stimulate them to inquiry, and hence more or less tend to lead them onward and upward to a more full and correct understanding of the facts of which they are symbolic, than it would be to attempt, in the very first instance, to teach them such facts as it would be quite difficult and perhaps impossible for them to grasp and follow up, without some such preliminary aid. And hence, for this reason, if for no other, as soon as by the use of any set of fictions, no matter what kind nor how appropriate as stepping-stones, any class of learners, young or old, weak or wise, shall be brought to see and measurably to understand the facts toward which they point, just so soon should their use, as a means of instruction to that class of learners, be discontinued, and the facts themselves be presented and commented upon instead.

And now we appeal, How can it reasonably be supposed to have a tendency to enlighten, elevate, and bless any human being, young or old, ignorant or wise, dogmatically to teach and, in the most authoritative manner possible, to enforce it upon him that those certain religious fictions, which so oft and eloquently are being sounded in his ears, are not mere fictions used for the purpose of enabling him the more readily to see and comprehend the facts of which they are symbolic, but are, instead, *themselves those facts;*—are themselves a class of facts so awfully grand, that it is a sin against God and his own soul to doubt for one moment their divine reality? Among all the numerous and different instrumentalities that were ever invented for the promotion of good among men, Does not a falsehood rank quite low down in the scale, if not at the very bottom? And no matter by whom taught or whom believed, Are not such fictions as not at all of facts do savor, and not toward the discovery or elucidation of any fact do tend, unto falsehood quite nearly allied? Before the bar of Reason and of Common Sense, Is it not wholly unjustifiable for any man or set of men deliberately to invent and go about teaching downright falsehoods unto anybody, young or old, weak or wise? And no matter where nor by whom the thing is done, Is it not almost as unjustifiable deliberately to invent and go about teaching a class of fictions which are so dark and mysterious, and so very little of fact do savor, that, whether so intended or not, they are almost certain to be mistaken and swallowed by the young and immature, for sober realities from beginning to end, as it would be deliberately to invent and go about teaching downright falsehoods, for eternal verities? If the ill effects of wrong actions are in no way modified or arrested by the good intentions of the actor, if it is a greater sin against our fellow-men to deceive them upon a subject of vital importance than it is upon one which is of little or no consequence, and if religion is a subject of vital importance to universal man; then, by unavoidable, must it not be a much greater crime against an anxiously inquiring and implicitly trusting people, to go deliberately about endeavoring to deceive them in reference thereto, than it would be, in the same systematically arranged manner, to the same wide extent, and for the same liberal compensation drawn from the same confiding source, to go about among them dealing out false statements upon the subject of politics, finance, or any other of only ordinary interest and importance?

Admitting the eternal God to be the SUM of all SUBSTANCE and THINGS that are, corporeal and incorporeal, in created and in primary form, then is not the inference irresistible, not only that every human being is a composing fraction of the great HIM, but that every wrong committed against any individual is a wrong committed against God, because against one of his component parts? Or admitting God to be wholly an extrinsic Spirit Being, as by Orthodoxy he is represented, and also admitting him to be the common Parent of us all; then does it not just as clearly follow that the ignorant, paying taught, each and all, are just as much his children as are the learned and salaried teachers? And consequently does it not follow, as night the setting Sun, that a wrong committed against any individual or branch of God's family, whether high or whether low, is a wrong committed against Him and his supremacy; provided that, in the welfare of his children, whose very hairs are all said to be numbered, he takes any sort of interest? Whether viewed from the one stand-point, then, or whether from the other, the conclusion seems to be irresistible that it is just as much a sin against God, for a man to say or do such things as are injurious only to himself, as it is for him to say or do those which are to the same extent injurious unto some other individual of equal weight and importance, but not at all so to himself; the rule being, among us His children, or fractions of equal value, as increases the number injured, so increases in magnitude the offence which does it. By the same plain line of reasoning, it must be a serious crime against God for any set of men to make it the study and business of their lives to discover, not the best method to be adopted for enlightening their kindred fellow-mortals upon the subject of religion, (more properly upon the relation which they bear to their great Maker,) but the surest way of so far stifling inquiry, and forestalling the judgment of the present generation of children, consequently of the men into which they shall ripen, and hence through these of those which are to follow, as to continue endlessly on, in reference to this vitally important subject, all the impeding errors of the dingy past.

CHAPTER XXX.

HEALTH, SICKNESS, AND DOTAGE.

Much as we admire the patient industry and self-sacrifice of medical men generally, and unwilling as we should be to say anything which would seem to imply a distrust of the sincerity of their faith in their respective curative theories, still we must be permitted to think that the most successful practitioners are those who have learned by experience to use *placebo* remedies a great deal more and powerful remedies a great deal less, thus leaving it with nature in the system to do the curing, whilst their particular medical theory gets the praise and they the emoluments. Moreover, that most ancient of teachers, Experience, has abundantly proved that those are not the best nurses who most fussy are, and who, during all the live-long night, on tip-toe at the patient's elbow stand with lighted lamp to see if they cannot help him of something either that he does or that he does not want, but those who, without confusion or ado, keep everything about the sick room looking as cheerful and life-like as possible, and at the same time exclude, beyond the reach of eye or ear, everything which it is found annoys the sufferer.

Whether right or whether wrong, such is our confidence in great Nature, hence such in that particular branch of her within the human system resident, that, casualties aside, we have abiding faith that nature in us, through the medium and instrumentality of our animal structures and their composing elements, is so related and adapted to those other and older portions of great Nature by which we are surrounded, and by whose workings we have been pushed onward and upward, step by step, into our present exalted state of animated existence, as that it doth amount to full ability in her vested to keep and maintain the human species, the same as the undomesticated animals of the brute creation, in uninterrupted health from the cradle to the grave; and consequently that she would do this very thing for us, but for the numerous sins which are committed against her. Nor is this all, but hereout grows the strong assurance we feel that it is this same branch of great Nature within the human system resident, which, by virtue of the tendency she is constantly imparting unto its every organ normal action to perform, doth stand parent cause to all the good health we ever enjoy; and consequently that she is the only angel which has power so far to blot out transgressions committed against her as to erase their sad consequences from the system, and thus abnormal action into normal again to change.

This eternal bathing, half-bathing, washing, and water-soaking, because a very little sick, or because not content with being merely well, seems to us to be just about as injudicious as does that everlasting dabbling with some one or other of the thousand-and-one nostrums in the shape of anodynes and cordials, balms and balsams, oils and ointments, pills and plasters, salves and syrups, etc., etc., which for the same foolish reason is constantly going on. Of course, it is not claimed that either the one or the other of these pernicious practices is taught or sanctioned by the particular system out of which, as a monstrous excrescence, it has incidentally grown. Upon the contrary, it is cheerfully admitted that infant Hydropathy no more inculcates or upholds such aquatic folly, than does ancient Allopathy the ridiculous practice of making a patent apothecary shop of ourselves;—not any more.

Notwithstanding we have abiding faith in human progression, and hence confidently expect that men will yet come to understand the laws of health and causes of sickness much better than they now do, still we are unable to conclude that the time will ever arrive when there will be a perfect health millennium. Casualties and overpowering circumstances all aside, more or less sinners, or transgressors against the laws of life and health, there will doubtless ever continue to be; and, as a necessary consequence, more or less of sickness, transgression's bitter penalty. And as we cannot persuade ourself into the belief that full-grown men and women will ever spring up in a day, but will always continue to be, much the same as now, the product of time and care; so we have no hope that the healing art will ever arrive at such a state of perfection as to possess a medicine capable of so incorporating itself with fiber and tissue, as to cause nearly half the human fabric to slough itself off in a single day, and thus entirely supersede nature's olden remedy, fever-fire, the Augean stable to cleanse.

And here, perhaps, it may be well to state a little more distinctly what, in the course of these pages, has indirectly and in a general way been said a number of times before; namely, that we owe the mass of our strength of head and of heart, of digestive and evacuating powers, in short, of our every organ, muscle, and fiber, not to their having been eternally rocked in the cradle of ease and inaction, but to the hard service which from time to time, by the force of circumstances, they have been compelled to perform, inside the limits of overtaxation or abuse. But whether right or whether wrong in this, it can hardly be doubted, we think, that there is located in the human head an organ whose special function it is, not only to create within us the feeling called combativeness, more properly resistiveness, but to distribute and keep alive in every nook and corner of the system this same elastic principle, or tendency to put forth resistive efforts, extraordinary, and even most extraordinary, whenever sufficiently irritated or crowded upon by some obnoxious intruder. It is to this resistive principle that we are indebted not only for our ability to stay the influx of morbific elements into the system, when thereunto exposed, but to expel them therefrom when, from being overtaxed with labor in some other direction, they have been suffered to enter and measurably to become domiciled. Indeed, it is this principle within the system resident, which fights the system's battles, and wins for her the victory over intruders of every name and kind, to the extent that victory over them is ever by her won.

In this land of boasted light and knowledge, there are doubtless thousands upon thousands of poor, deluded, slaving, suffering, worshipers of mammon who, from year's end to year's end, do not know what it is to be rested, and consequently are never actually down-sick, because never well enough to be. Not well enough to be actually down-sick! not enough of snap and elasticity left in their constantly worn and jaded systems, to enable them to rally and make a determined effort to free themselves of the accumulated impurities of years which, like a mill-stone, are weighing them down, or nobly perish in the attempt. Half-dead, half-alive, bowed down with cares, anxieties, and watchings, they really are, as they do often say, but just able to drag their legs along. In fact, their whole frames from head to foot have come to be in the passive condition of an old and constantly running sore, which has become so inured to being a sink of corruption and open crater that it has not only lost all desire to close its mouth and be healed, but begins to delight in bathing its face with such impurities, as the more healthy parts of the system spurn from them with loathing and disgust. In a word, the nature that is in us is always very much like us. Wherefore the nature that is in any man may be as effectually broken and cowed into submission by the accumulated seeds of disease, in the shape of morbific elements creeping into the system when jaded and worn by too much labor, or in the form of medicines, when too long and regularly swallowed, as by the accumulated use of tyrant lash upon the back applied; when, as a matter of course, she is no longer her former free and elastic self, but the now cringing and abject slave. In other words, as by the long-continued use of tobacco, for example, it ceases to be nauseous, becomes pleasant, and finally to be intensely hankered after, so, by being for a long time tired or sick, no matter from what cause, the system gradually becomes inured to that particular condition of things, and hence correspondingly indisposed to make a single effort to bring about a change of programme. In this way, doubtless, do agues, fevers, and many other diseases, come to be, in the course of time, more a matter of habit into which nature in the system has fallen, than of anything else.

Eating too soon after rising in the morning, or before the blood has become properly aerated by the inhalation of fresh air, is no doubt a bad practice, especially for such as sleep in illy ventilated apartments; and that dormitory which, to a person who has taken an hour's exercise in the open air, still retains a close, disagreeable smell, is too confined. Indeed, no sleeping room or other apartment that is much occupied is properly ventilated, which has not at least two air-holes; one in or near the ceiling overhead, for the escape of rarefied air, and one at or near the floor, to let out the impure air expired from the lungs; and especially is this a fact in regard to rooms in which, during their occupancy, no fire is kept burning.

Whether it is more conducive to health and longevity to lie with head to the North, or whether it is not, we are unprepared to say; but we do incline to the opinion that it would be better for all, and especially for the sick, the old, and infirm, to lie upon beds having a regular inclination upward, from foot to head, of some several degrees, instead of upon such as are abrubtly elevated at the head by means of bolster and pillows. This we infer partly from our own observation and experience upon the subject; partly from the fact that, in both the upper and lower portions of the system, the circulation of the blood is ever more or less effected by its own inherent gravity; partly from the circumstance that the beasts of the field and fowls of the air whose habit it is, during their waking hours, to keep their heads above the level of the mass of their bodies, likewise to keep some certain portion of their bodies in a position more elevated than are certain other portions, the heart being regarded as the central point, do also, for the most part of the time when sleeping, more or less nearly approximate to maintaining in the same relative position, not only their heads, but every other great and important portion; and partly from the further fact that, in nineteen cases out of twenty, men are instinctively led to place themselves in such inclined position, when laying themselves down to rest in the shade upon ground that is not inconveniently sloping, and which is quite perceptibly so. But, for the purpose of rendering this point as clear as possible, permit us to present the case in the following exaggerated form: Allowing man's natural as well as habitual posture to be, by day, that of general uprightness, with his feet downward, What would probably be the effect upon his health and longevity, was he to ignore this fact, and so, regardless of the influence exerted by gravity upon the circulation and distribution of his bodily fluids, nightly betake himself to the repose of sleep in a position nearly vertical, but with his head downward?

As man is undoubtedly a living, breathing, feeding, moving, organic structure, the same as are the beasts of the forest, fowls of the air, and fish of the sea; so, as seems to us, had he always been as obedient to the laws of nature, as the same were organically impressed upon him and ingrained into him by the causes unto which he owes his creation, as have been and still are the undomesticated animals in their native homes, to the laws upon their organisms in the same way enstamped, he would be no more subject to sickness, pain, and distress, than are they. And as, beyond a question, not a few of the diseases which, to-day, afflict mankind, are the legitimate creation of those vast piles of medicines which have been taken into that citadel of vitality, the stomach, to cure some real or imaginary ail, located no matter where; and as, from generation to generation, there has been transmitted down to us by hereditary descent, a more or less strong predisposition to be afflicted by those same diseases which were thus superinduced upon our ancestors; and as it is not possible for nature in the system, in the brief space of time allotted to a single generation of men, wholly to eradicate the taint; it therefore becomes necessary, in order fully to regenerate and save the race therefrom, that both the repentance and the works done meet for repentance should be about as general, thorough, and chronical, as have been the sins which thereunto parent cause have stood and stand. Wherefore let no man falter in his efforts to know and obey the laws of life and health, simply because, by reason of his thus vitiated nature, he ever finds himself more or less strongly tempted to do the unnatural deeds of his fathers: or turn infidel to the faith that his sicknesses are all of them brought upon him either by his own sins, or those of his ancestors, just because, for a few brief years, he has been practicing repentence of former personal or ancestral follies, by living out a life of obedience and self-reformation, and yet doth not find himself wholly freed the seeds of disease; and hence from a predisposition to pain and sickness.

Since it is undoubtedly a fact that nature in the system can never vigorously prosecute a multiplicity of actions, whether normal or abnormal, muscular or brenal, at one and the same time, it therefore becomes necessary when hard sick, if we desire to be speedily and thoroughly healed, not only to abstain from labor with our hands and labor with our brains, but to keep ourselves in all respects as quiet and comfortable as we can. And as the weather in this region of country is never steady and seldom very warm, so let the hard sick, if possible, have the benefit not only of the invigorating effects of sunlight, falling into the room through the windows, but of a constant open fire. If this cannot be, then do not for an hour deprive them of the less genial warmth of a stove-fire, always remembering that there is a wide difference between warm air and impure air; also that, with the same amount of external openings, a room with a brisk fire in it will not only be twice as quickly and twice as thoroughly cleared of such impurities as may chance to be therein, but twice as well supplied with pure air from without, as will be one in which no fire is kept burning. It is not folly merely, but a species of madness to assume and act upon the assumption, that a person, when hard sick, is as able to resist the effects of dampness, ward off cold, endure draughts of air, etc., as would be that same individual or almost anybody else when well, though compelled to occupy, day after day, the same place. Wherefore, if it be the intention to do all that can consistently be done to save the man that is hard sick from unnecessary suffering, and perhaps death, let him occupy not some pentup back-bedroom without fire, and almost without light or air, but the most commodious and cheerful room in the house. Also let the location of his bed be such as to give him the benefit of pure, warm air, without having his head, or any other great and important portion, exposed to a draught, even should he chance to become and remain wholly uncovered; ever remembering that such air is much better adapted to relieve the skin of its constantly accumulating load of impurities than are piles of quilts and coverlets, besides being less burdensome and in no danger of getting kicked off. In this way, without the trouble of water baths or even of spongings, may the sick man's stock of comforts be augmented, the chances of his taking cold diminished, and the nurse relieved from not a little unnecessary labor and care. Nor should the feelings of a person who is well, and perhaps heated by exercise in waiting upon the sick, be the standard by which to regulate the temperature of the sick-room, but the feelings of the sufferer, if rational; and if not, then let it be done by a thermometer indicating some seventy or eighty degrees, Fahrenheit, when hanging against the wall on a level with the body of the sufferer. For, as already intimated, by thus maintaining the air in the room at a uniformly high and comfortable temperature, the patient can be permitted to lie almost naked; and so enjoy, practically, not only the luxury of a constant air-bath, but its purifying and healing effects. Beyond these things, which not at all disturb the patient's quiet or tax his strength, do as circumstances shall currently seem to demand, always being careful not to neutralize the healing efforts of nature in the system by doing too much. For, be assured, the best physician in the world is always at hand and ready to administer to our necessities, be they great or be they small, if we will only possess our souls in patience and let her; and that physician is *nature in the system.*

As a rule, the way to insure continuous good health is continuously to take good care of ourselves when well; and the way to get well when sick is to abstain from those practices and things which brought disease upon us, provided we know what they are. In case we do not know this and are quite ill, then our safest course is to call in a physician in whom we have confidence, and scrupulously obey his orders. And if, from any cause, this cannot consistently be done, then our next best course is to abstain from labor, both muscular and brenal, eat little, lay ourselves quietly by in a warm comfortable place, and trust to said physician, nature in the system, aided by time and a little nursing, to effect our cure. One of the crying wants of the age is more good nurses of the sick. And we can think of no surer way of obtaining and continuing the needed supply of this class of persons, than by elevating that hitherto low, inconstant, and ill-requited service into a profession, next in dignity, as it is in importance, to that of prescribing physician. Or whether right or whether wrong, this is how we see these things.

And here, in this connection, we will take occasion to say, that a well man and a sick man are two very different things consequently do give out very different manifestations; that is, do feel, think, and act very differently. This being universally well known, our readers will not deem it surprising, and especially not after what has been said, that now, when we are well, we have no notion of sending for a physician. Of course, they will not. And so let us go a step further, and see whether it ought to be considered any more remarkable, if, should we be taken hard sick, (which we by no means intend to be,) then not we, the well man, with his usual strength of body and of brain about him, but the sick man, the mere shadow and mockery of the well, in his then weak, fidgety, and childlike condition both of body and of brain, should hear sounds, see visions, dream dreams, be haunted with specters, seized with fear and trembling and a dreadful looking forward to death, judgment, and an eternity to come; and hence should call in not only a doctor of physic, but one of divinity also. Under the pressure of circumstances thus widely different, such somersets of feeling, opinion, and action are perfectly natural; consequently ought not to excite surprise; and hence should never be sought after and seized upon as trophy evidence of former error. Perfectly natural?—Why, yes; just as natural as it is unfortunate and foolish for the constitutionally robust to be eternally sick from August to Lent, and Lent to August. Perfectly natural?—Why, yes; because, as in health, so in sickness, the brenal man is but a composing fraction of the general physical one. It would therefore be just as reasonable and quite as proper to herald abroad the fact, to an eager, gaping, wondering world, that this, that, or the other noted prodigy of muscular strength and gymnastic feats was formerly in error, when he verily thought he could perform such wonders, just because now, when prostrated by sickness, or when by chilly and shriveling age o'ertaken, his muscles, the father of his strength, are as unequal to the task of putting forth the necessary power to perform his accustomed exploits, as are those of the puling infant. What! an old and worn out brain; a sick and disordered brain; a brain shorn of its power by reason of disease, preying upon its natural supporting aids below, expected to canvass facts, sift evidence, weigh arguments, and coin conclusions which are to outweigh and overturn the opinions by the same brain carefully formed and deliberately put forth, when it was not only itself in full health and strength, but faithfully backed and supported by a sound and vigorous system beneath?—It is folly, nay, worse, it is madness to expect it! As by common consent of mankind, insane men, men prostrated by sickness, and men in their dotage, the same as little children, are not held responsible for what they either say or do; so, because these same individuals, under the pressure of such circumstances, may chance to say and do some very silly things, we have no right to infer, and proclaim it abroad to the world, that the opinions entertained by such insane persons when rational, such sick persons when well, and such dotards when in their prime, were not sound. In reference to this matter there still seems to be lingering among us a lamentable want of clear understanding, else of fairness and candor.—By natural ordinance, it is the silly, talkative, little child, and not the half-grown boy, much less the full-grown man, that is *father* to the dotard.

CHAPTER XXXI.

HUMAN NATURE RELIGION'S SEAT.

Did love of dominion have its origin in the Bible; or is it a thing deep in human nature resident? Did religion have its origin in the Bible; or is it also a thing deep in human nature resident?

As human nature must needs be coextensive with universal man, so the inference is unavoidable that wherever upon the face of the globe the higher animal called shall come to exist, no matter how low the race, there also will dominion or government of some kind come to exist. And, of religion, the same. In other words, Religion of some kind is always found to exist wherever man is found to reside; and it is thus universally found, not because the Bible into all the world has gone and introduced it, (for not one-fourth of its present occupants are aware of the existence of any such book,) but because, as already suggested, it has its seat deep down in human nature itself. Or, in still other words, inasmuch as the Bible cannot be the cause of man's being a religious animal in those parts of the world where its teachings are wholly unknown, and inasmuch as it is a broad historic fact that wherever man is found to reside, there also is some form of religious faith and practice found to exist, therefore is the conclusion irresistible that the Bible is not the cause of man's being a religious animal anywhere.

Again, the Bible cannot be the cause of religion among men; for, clearly enough, long before its pages were written, deep down in the nature of man resided, not only that same strong love of dominion which stood parent cause to all the numerous and different governments which had existence prior to the appearance of that book, but that same unquenchable desire to pay homage to such personages, whether real or imaginary, as they adjudged to be their superiors, and be themselves looked up to and reverenced by such as they their inferiors deemed. Wherefore, so far from the Bible standing parent cause to the existence of the strong, innate, religious feeling and desire that is in man, it is this innate desire which stands parent cause to the existence of all the numerous and different religions that anywhere existence have. In other words, the broad history of man, which reveals the existence of not less than a thousand different religions in the world, fully justifies the conclusion that the book called the Bible, with all its religious teachings, the same as the book called the Koran and other religious standards, with their respective teachings, is a legitimate outgrowth of that same religious nature, which deep down in universal man inherently resides, instead of its being, of that nature in any human being, the producing cause. Viewed in the light of these facts, the only question of importance upon which the more intelligent adherents to the old stand-still religion of the Bible, and the advocates of a constantly growing and progressive religion, based upon currently advancing human nature, can reasonably be supposed to differ, is the following:

At this late day and age of the world, and especially in this most free, enlightened, and highly Christian land, Are the ancient inelastic religious teachings, upon the different pages of the Bible standing, as a whole and upon the whole, still in advance of the spontaneous religious promptings of the more enlightened and better portion of the people; or have they, as a whole and upon the whole, become by them outgrown and left behind? If, as a whole and upon the whole, of this class of persons, its religious teachings are still in advance, then it is plain that not even here has that venerable book ceased to be an instrument of religious elevation, whether it has of advancement in light and knowledge upon other subjects or not. Upon the contrary, if, by this class of persons, these said teachings have, as a whole and upon the whole, become so far outgrown that they are no longer competent to fill and satisfy the yearnings of their higher religious nature, then, as seems to us, it is clear that the time has arrived when they should be made to give place to a set of teachings which are thus competent; never for one moment doubting but what these latter, by proper care and simplification, will prove quite as efficient in dragging upward those laggards that are still below, as have been and would continue to be the highly parabolic former. Because, by the semi-enlightened inhabitants of the world at the day and age when the Bible was written, its dark and mysterious teachings were regarded as being a mine of thought and a mass of beauty, it does not follow that the men of to-day are bound to regard them in that same light.

So long as shall the Bible continue to be made the rule of human faith and the measure of its practice, so long must it, in some way, be brought to harmonize with the lights of Science. And as it is daily becoming more and more difficult to bend growing science, which is naturally unyielding, so as to make it with all the different Bible crooks conform; so the question to be settled is, How can such a reconciliation best be brought about and maintained?

Unless we greatly err, there is but just one way of doing it; and that is by so far currently straightening the crooked parts and passages in that volume found, as that, at all times, its teachings shall be made to accord with those of fair Science, be they what they may.—Men are fast losing their admiration for miracles, and becoming the lovers of sober fact.

CHAPTER XXXII.

DIFFERENT RELIGIONS AND DIFFERENT SECTS.

As religion, in its very broadest sense, has its foundation in the nature of universal man, so do all the different kinds and grades of religion have their foundation in the nature of the different kinds and grades of men. Not only this, but every sect, into which the different kinds and grades of religionists do anywhere form themselves, has its foundation seat, not in the heavens above, but in the peculiar nature of that class of individuals who, from a similarity of tastes, inclinations, etc., are led to band themselves together to compose it. Such being the case, it follows that the class of persons who are by nature, and hence in practice, the most stern, unchangeable, uncharitable, and unforgiving, knot themselves together into a sect of the strictest kind, whilst those less stern, less unchangeable, less uncharitable, and more forgiving, unite and form a sect correspondingly more liberal; and thus on. Wherefore the round-headed, hence excitable, and hence unstable class of persons, whether numerous or not, will ever be found to gravitate toward that sect whose articles of faith are most loose and general, whose discipline makes most allowance for its members to err without impairing their standing in the church, and whose modes of worship are least uniform and particular. And wherefore that sect whose faith and rules of practice comport most nearly with the tastes, inclinations, and habits of the most numerous class of individuals, is certain to take the lead in point of numbers, whether it does in point of intelligence and refinement, or not.

When, therefore, we come to take into consideration the great diversity of tastes, capacities and talents that exist among men; also to reflect that ministers to be of any particular service to their flocks must not be too much above them,—must at least in appearance, if not in fact, quite nearly be standing upon the same plane of intelligence, morals, etc., with those they are endeavoring to teach and to lead; we are forced to the conclusion that the leading managers of the sect called Methodists do manifest much practical good sense in ordaining, and sending forth into the field as ministers, men not only of high, but of low grade of character and intelligence, the better to reach and influence not only the higher, but the lower grades of human beings. By this practice of ordaining, and sending forth as teachers, *all kinds of men among all kinds of men*, instead of only *a certain kind among all the different kinds*, they do much toward relieving their ministers, each and all, from the necessity of having to resort to the hypocritical and demoralizing practice of becoming *all things to all men*, without impairing the beneficial results which Paul in so doing was aiming to secure.

We say, by this practice of ordaining, etc., they do much toward relieving their ministers, each and all, from the necessity of having to resort, etc., without impairing the beneficial results which Paul in so doing was aiming to secure, because as certainly as does that which comes frcm the heart of the speaker more readily reach and affect the heart of hearer, than does that which not thus from the heart, but only from the cunning hypocritical head doth come; just so certainly will those ministers who are low in the scale of intelligence, and hence do themselves believe, at very bottom, the things which they preach, gain more converts among that class of persons who are yet a little lower than themselves, than will those whose ignorance is feigned, whose sympathies are not genuine, and whose teachings, instead of being in accordance with their honest convictions, are, for the most part, just so many fictions conjured up and put forth to meet the occasion.—To effect the greatest amount of good with any given force, the right man in the right place is just what is needed.—That it is not the higher, but the lower grades of men, who most need to have thrown around them the restraining influence of church-membership, church pride, church-watching, etc., not only to keep them from crime, but within the bounds of common decency and order, is a fact which it is as unwise as unsafe to attempt to ignore. And surely it will not be contended that churches, either high or low, can ever anywhere be formed without members; or that they can ever anywhere be formed, except they be made up of such materials as do at the time exist in the locality.

Truly, "they that be whole need not a physician, but they that are sick." Wherefore let us all who are so fortunate as to be well,—so fortunate as to be, by nature, a law unto ourselves, remember that we are God-appointed guardians over such as are not. And wherefore let us take these our less favored fellow-mortals of every caste, color, and condition, just as we find them and, by all proper appliances, try to elevate them,—try to render them wiser and better, as well for our own sake as for theirs; since, more or less mixed up with them, we unavoidably are, and hence, more or less debased by their presence and downward-dragging influence, whilst low they shall remain, we unavoidably must be. In other words, let us try and be at least selfishly wise, if we cannot be benevolently so.

And here, in this connection, we will take occasion to say that, according to our interpretation of the signs of the times, the day is not far distant when numerous Naturists, or persons whose religious views are substantially the same as ours, will become tired of courting concealment, each by himself in some out-of-the-way corner, and commence the work of organizing themselves into a society or order, having for its object the discovery of real truth, its more rapid spread, and the enjoyment of its blessings; for its bond of union, similarity of taste, of feeling, of interest, and general good-will; for its motto, Progression; and the "Golden Rule" as the basis of its creed. This done, and they will begin to hold up their heads like men who are not ashamed of the faith that is in them. This done, and many, very many, who are not even suspected of having a leaning toward

Naturism, will rush to its embrace. Yea, this done, and such will soon come to be the numbers of the order as to enable its members, here, there, and yonder, to begin the work of erecting suitable buildings in which to meet for consultation, for meditation, for amusement, for the hearing of lectures, for mutual improvement by a free interchange of opinions, for concerting measures of relief for the neighboring poor, and all such other social, charitable, and religious purposes as may be deemed proper.

Without organization, there can be little concert of action; and without concert of action but little of moment can ever be achieved. Or thus: Just as long as men are content to hide their light "under a bushel," that is, to remain silent and inactive, or to speak and act only separately, no matter how great may be their numbers, what their form of faith, nor how unimpeachable their characters, just so long must they be content to be despised for their weakness. Yea, and just as soon as they become tired of this state of things—tired of being mere ciphers, take upon themselves a name, organize themselves into a body thereunder, and hence come to act in concert, just so soon do they become a power in the land commanding the respect of their enemies. In a word, the time has come and now is, when Naturists in religion may take their place at the head, where they properly belong; or remain at the foot, just as they please.—The Lord ever helps such, and such only, as look boldly up, step manfully forward, and help themselves.

The great religious rule that was first laid down by Confucius, as we have every reason to believe, and of which that philosopher declared, "Thou needest only this law alone; it is the foundation and principle of all the rest:"—The great religious rule of which, some five centuries thereafter, Christ emphatically said, "This is the law and the prophets;" and which rule has long since come to be called "golden," because of its beautiful simplicity and great intrinsic worth, What is it, and what its real import? Let us briefly examine it and see. "All things whatsoever ye would that men should do to you, do ye even so to them: for this is the law and the prophets;" [for this is the sum and substance of the teachings of both the law and the prophets, meaning.] Such is the brief letter of that invaluable rule, as worded by Christ; and this we regard as being its sober import: Before thou, O man! whosoever thou art, shalt say or do any thing that will necessarily affect thy fellow-beings, one or more, ask thyself this one plain question:—What is that, under like circumstances, thou wouldst have such individual or individuals say of thee or thine, or do unto thee or thine? And whatsoever, unto such question shall be thine own candid answer, that say thou of them or theirs, or do unto them or theirs, as the case may be; and whatsoever thou wouldst not have them say of thee or thine, or do unto thee or thine, that say not thou of them or theirs, nor do unto them or theirs.—Such, as we understand the matter, is a fair interpretation of the rule and nothing more.

And now, who cannot see that, in and by the act of laying down this rule, Christ just as good as said, (as far forth as it was possible for him to do so,) unto every son and daughter of Adam present and to come, and no matter how differently organized, educated, or circumstanced, Be thou thyself, and for thyself, from thine own feelings and the light which thou hast, the candid judge as to what, under the circumstances, it is right and proper that thou shouldst say and do? Yea, and who not that this is neither more nor less than letting currently existing and advancing man, with all his variant tastes, temperaments, and different degrees of development, be the currently existing and advanced judge as to what, under the circumstances, it is right and proper for him to say and do; instead of laying down to all men, of every clime, age, capacity, and condition, one and the same inflexible rule therefor?

Between a sliding scale, or a rule thus adapted to every kind, character, and condition of men, and every kind, character, and grade of circumstances, and a fixed standard adapted only to a single class of men, a single kind of conditions, and a single set of circumstances, the difference is heaven-wide, or, at least, such seems to have been the judgment of Christ in the premises, and we cannot for one moment doubt its correctness. It must therefore be a sad mistake to attempt to measure everybody else by ourselves;—a sad mistake to suffer ourselves to feel vexed, not to say angry, because a naturally thoughtless and careless neighbor, for example, leaves out upon the ground in the storm some favorite tool he has borrowed of us, when we see and know that that is precisely the kind of care he takes of his own tools; hence is precisely the kind of care which to him doth seem proper; and hence, unto him and for him, is all good and right.

When men, no matter who nor of what class or grade, treat others and others' things, whilst in their employ or possession, just as they treat themselves and their own things, they are evidently doing as they would be done by;—are evidently obeying the great foundation rule laid down by Christ;—are evidently doing what to them doth seem to be proper; no matter how widely different may be the teachings of Moses, the prophets, or the views of any other kind and character of men, whether ancient or modern. Or, at least, this is unquestionably the view which Christ took of the matter when laying down said rule; and who, upon a careful survey of the matter, is prepared to say that he was not eminently right? It is plain that Christ had faith in his fellow-men,—had faith in the integrity of variant human nature, whether the old Mosaic God had or not. In a word, no man lives up to the letter of the "golden rule," and certainly not to its spirit, who lets Moses, the prophets, the priests, or anybody else decide for him, as to what is his duty to his fellow-men; but only he who, regardless of all opinions, ancient or modern, *does by others* as he himself adjudges that, under like circumstances, he would have others *do by him*. Or thus: As men are far from being all alike in looks, taste, feeling, or judgment, and as they will doubtless thus forever continue to be; so it must be exceedingly difficult, if not impossible, for any one to be a Christian in either feeling or action, who, in his intercourse with his fellow-men, fails to take into consideration this great God-ordained fact.

And here we will take the liberty of adding that, as we have finally come to see it, within the letter of this brief rule of the heathen Confucius, and also of the man Christ, resides the spirit not only of all that is important in the *law and the prophets*, but the substance of all Christ's practical religious teachings. And not only this, but that, in truth and in fact, of all that is of any practical value in the Christian system of religion, not only is said rule the foundation, but of broader and more advanced Naturism, it is also the rock. And wherefore, sadly as in our daily walk and conversation we fall short of coming up thereto, it is upon this rock that with unwavering faith we have been striving to stand and endeavoring to grow in religious breadth and stature, for the last quarter of a century; or ever since our narrow escape from the quicksands of that general infidelity into which, for a time during middle-age, we felt ourselves sinking.

And yet one thing more: We cannot but regard it as being a mistake in our brother Naturists to allow themselves to speak disrespectfully, not to say sneeringly, of Christ as a man, simply for the reason that he had the misfortune to be early taught, and hence brought to believe, that, instead of being a mere flesh-and-blood being and of human origin, he was the Son of God and equal with the Father;—a mistake in them not to give a hearty welcome to any and all of that good man's religious teachings which are manifestly in accordance with high-toned human nature, and hence consonant to a religious state of society which it is most desirable should come to exist, simply for the reason that, just like every other man, of many things he was entirely ignorant, and in reference to some others greatly mistaken; or because, by his particular friends and admirers, he is believed in and idolized altogether too much. And no less a mistake must it be in our Christian friends to suffer themselves to speak disrespectfully, not to say contemptuously, of such of Nature's teachings as are manifestly in accordance with fact, and hence with eternal verity, simply for the reason that they were not understood by either Moses or Christ, and hence not by them taught or attempted to be; or because, by the particular friends and admirers of Nature and her laws, certain of her teachings may be indiscreetly lauded, or thrust into ridiculous prominence. In short, let our Christian friends pursue whatever course they may, it cannot be wisdom in us Naturists to make the gap between them and us any wider than are we compelled to do, by a paramount regard for what we know to be real truth, or at least have every reason for believing to be such;—cannot be wisdom in us to reject from our religious fabric a single stick of sound timber, simply because it was recommended by Christ, or its use commanded by Moses.—No; not with broad Naturism is any such narrow, fanatical course consistent.

CHAPTER XXXIII.*

BRIEF REMARKS UPON NUMEROUS SUBJECTS.

DISCRETION A PRIMARY VIRTUE.

As a rule, men are in duty bound to speak the truth, as they at the time understand it to be; in certain cases, however, they are not only at liberty not to tell the truth, as they believe the same to be, but to prevaricate, and even to state what they know to be false. As, for a too familiar example, when one is being perseveringly questioned by some inquisitive busy-body in the guise of a friend, as to things which do not concern him; and where the answers, if truthful, would be powerless to do good, and only potent to work mischief. Men are in duty bound to be prudent toward themselves as well as just toward others;—are in duty bound so to speak and so to act as not unnecessarily to injure themselves, or be the cause of dissentions which give no promise of yielding any compensating benefits.

DEATH A PURIFIER.

No matter how good or how great, all men whilst living are seen to be human beings, are known to be imperfect, have many warm friends, and many bitter enemies; and hence they are not unfrequently applauded and condemned for the self-same acts. In passing through the gate of death,

*Note.—As this volume is wholly composed, as its title imports, of selections made from a mass of fragmentary writings, extending over a term of full twenty years; so, when reading this chapter, it would be well to understand that nearly every piece herein is really supplemental to something which has already been said in some one or other of the preceding chapters,—all of them having been written and closed up, a long time before any portion of this one was penned.

however, they become purged of nearly all their faults, without losing a single one of all their many virtues; by lying in their graves a number of years, they become perfect; and, by lying therein for long centuries, veritable saints.—Such is the influence of veneration upon intellect and memory.

FOLLY NOT CONFINED TO YOUTH.

The fact is, and all of us who have lived to be old ought to know it, we can no more see, feel, act, or desire to act as legitimately do the young, than can we wear their fresh and joyous looks upon our wrinkled brows; nor can they any more, before the proper time arrives, see, feel, act, or desire to act as legitimately do we, than can they, before such time, shriveled and cadaverous looks put on. Wherefore, would we be loved whilst living and remembered with pleasure when dead, by that young and rising generation which is fast coming to possess the Earth, we must not eternally be harping upon their childish indiscretions and youthful faults; but remember that, of all these things in them, the same as has it in us, time will work a perfect cure. It is no more a sin to be young, than it is to be middle-aged or old; and hence it is no more wicked for the young to possess and manifest the feelings that are incident to youth, than it is for the middle-aged or old to possess and manifest such as are incident to persons of their respective years; not any more. That the boys with their guns, the girls with their dolls, and the youths and the maidens, in the merry dance, are just as appropriately and acceptably worshiping God, as are the middle-aged and old with their solemn faces, long prayers, and numerous sacraments, as seems to us, cannot rationally be doubted. In a word, it is that religion which makes people feel more cheerful and happy, whether young or old, and not that which renders them fearful, gloomy, and despondent, that is valuable unto them, and hence pleasing unto God.

KINDNESS AND CHARITY VS. SEVERITY.

As the world has no use for any more devils, severity, or hell than it has already gotten within its borders, and as there is great need of more kindness, charity, and forbearance among men; so it would be well for us all to cultivate these things, within ourselves and others, a great deal more, and those a great deal less. Yea, and as long as men will persist in believing and teaching that "the heart [the heart of man] is deceitful above all things, and desperately wicked," just so long should they remember, when preaching its abominations, that their hearts are but the hearts of men; consequently that these their denunciations against that particular organ must necessarily partake to the fill of this same great wickedness; and so try and let their heads learn charity, forbearance, and good-will, if their hearts will not.

MAN AN ANIMAL.

Of such as are disposed to ridicule the idea of man's being animal in his origin, and hence an animal in fact throughout every stage of his existence to his final end, only of superior order, we would like to inquire—And what is it that you would have others believe concerning their origin, nature, and final destiny, provided yours was the right to enforce upon them your desires in that regard? Would you, in reference to these fundamental questions, permit them to rely upon the testimony of their Creator, as the same stands out revealed to them upon the human organism enstamped; or would you, instead, have them believe the honeyed whisperings of their strong self-love, unchecked by the lights of reason, observation, and experience?—To become truly wise, as seems to us, it is not with our fond imaginings, because flattering to our vanity, but with real truth, be it whatsoever it may, that we must be supremely in love.

NAKED GHOSTS.

It would seem that men must have a gigantic capacity for believing to be able to believe that all the different articles of apparel by people worn are possessed of souls, and hence able to put in their appearance upon the bodies of the ghosts of their former wearers, the same as they did when by them being worn whilst yet in the flesh, and moving about among us. We say, men must have a gigantic capacity for believing to be able to believe that all the different articles of apparel by people worn are possessed of souls, etc., because, unless such inanimate articles do possess souls, then must the ghosts of departed men and women always present themselves in a state of nudity; provided always that, outside the disordered imaginations of the beholders, they ever present themselves at all.

MIND.

By the term "mind," we do not mean, as has already been said and repeated, an entity of any kind, but simply a certain complex act which is spoken into existence within the human tabernacle by the brain, and by nothing else; the same as, by the term "digestion," is not meant an entity or something which independently of the stomach doth anywhere exist, but simply that certain complex act which is spoken into existence within the human tabernacle by the stomach, and by nothing else. And here let us add that, notwithstanding the much which is still believed and taught to the contrary, mind has never yet been even presumptively proven to be spoken into existence, or maintained therein, by any organ, except the brain, and never in any way or anywhere, except by the action of the brain; else are we wholly mistaken as to what doth constitute presumptive evidence of a fact in natural science.

THE HIGHEST GRADE OF RELIGION.

That some men are so organized and balanced as to delight in tumult, broils, and blood cannot be doubted,—cannot be doubted that they would, at almost any time, rather see two dogs, bulls, or men fight than to eat. Such persons, of course, the same as the kind-hearted philanthropist, are compelled to derive their pleasures from just such organs and balance of organs as they possess; and they cannot by any possibility derive them from any other. Wherefore, notwithstanding it must be conceded that such do enjoy a sort of pleasure, still it cannot be denied, as we think, that the kingdom of heaven which they create, enjoy, and carry about with them, in their bosoms, is of quite a low grade. Indeed, in our judgment, those are the highest grade of religious men, and hence do currently enjoy the highest grade of heavenly kingdom, whose pleasures are derived not from making or seeing the meanest thing that is miserable, but from seeing and trying to make every human being, and every needful creature about them, comfortable and happy. Or whether right or whether wrong, such are our notions of the highest grade of religious sentiment and feeling; and hence such our notions of the highest grade of a religious God.

MAN OF GOD A PART.

Impious as may seem the idea to many, that individual man is a composing fraction of that Power which reigns in and rules over all things, in earth and heaven; nevertheless we must think a similar idea, if not the very same. was struggling for birth in Paul's brain, at the time he was penning the following sentence: "There is one body, and one Spirit, even as ye are called in one hope of your calling; one Lord, one faith, one baptism, one God and Father of all, who is above all, and through all, and in you all." Eph., 4. 4—6. We say, we must think a similar idea, if not the very same, was struggling for birth in Paul's brain, etc.; for, obviously enough, had he extended the sentence a very little further, by adding thereunto its plain, brief corollary, *And of whom ye are each a part*, he would then have covered the entire ground, not only by fair implication, but in express terms.

LIFE.

As we have finally come to see it, not only is organic action organic life, but the life which, in Nature's great laboratory, doth underlie this, and that parent cause thereunto doth stand, is electric life. Hence certain elements which in their primary estate are purely inorganic, consequently only of electric life possessed, legitimately become and are, when by electrical agency elevated and arranged in certain organic order, vegetable life; and when thereafter in a certain other and more complex organic order, animal life; and when in that particular organic form and order which constitutes them a perfect living eye, for example, then those heretofore inorganic and sightless elements legitimately become possessed of the faculty or power of creating within us, by the aid of the brain, the sensation called sight; that is, they are then capable of performing that peculiar kind and character of organic function which constitutes what is known as the act of seeing. And thus on of all the numerous and different nervous, muscular, and brenal faculties possessed and manifested, not only by animals of low order, but by man, the most complicated of all known organic structures, and hence the highest of all known animated beings. In a word, it would seem from numerous indexes, that the existence of that immaterial something, known as the electric fluid, must be coextensive with all material substance; and also that, between the two, there is a strong mutual affinity.

MIRACLES OR SUPERHUMAN ACTS.

That much practice, added to strong natural talent in the same direction, has a tendency to make perfect, and hence has enabled certain individuals in all ages of the world to perform many strange and apparently unnatural things, is not denied; but that Moses, Joshua, or anybody else ever performed a miracle, that is, an act which was not from beginning to end in strict accordance with some branch or department of natural law, we are wholly unprepared to believe. What! human beings perform acts which are superhuman? Beings who owe their very existence to the operation of natural causes, consequently are themselves from sole to crown of Nature a part, perform acts which are wholly unnatural,—acts which, with her eternal laws, are at variance direct? As seems to us, no such phenomenon ever did or ever can occur.

MAN-WORSHIP.

Allowing God to be, as by us claimed, the Sum of all Created things and uncreated Elements that anywhere exist, and hence that Earth, man, beast, and all things else, are of him a legitimate part; it needs must follow that in point of knowledge, within the bounds of this our mundane sphere at least, the fraction man doth stand pre-eminently at the head; and hence that, aside from the acts and doings of the animal called man, there is naught of power, in all this portion of the universe at least, that is exerted by design or wielded by discretion, in the common acceptation of those terms, except the little that is put forth under the guidance of the feeble brenal light by dumb brutes possessed. Not only this, but if the foregoing views are correct, much as the idea of man-worship is ridiculed by some, we do none of us greatly err when, obedient to the mixed nature that is in us, we up to men of superior wisdom, goodness, and power, as unto gods, with reverential awe do look. Nor are such of the lords of creation as believe in their truthfulness acting inconsistently when, in obedience to the mixed nature that is organically enstamped upon them, they adore, as angels, the more lovely and exalted of the gentler sex; since, obviously enough, in such case, save what of the angelic within the pale of blessed humanity resides, *angels* there are none.

"ALL HAVE ONE BREATH."

As has been elsewhere said and repeated, we must think that animal life is neither a created nor uncreated entity, but simply organic function and death its total absence. Or, to be a little more explicit, organic action, or function performed by animal organs, is the very thing which animal life doth constitute; and hence is the only thing which, from any animal, high or low, must needs step out to leave it dead. Wherefore, as with the horse he rides, so with the animal called man who rides him, the duration of that organic action which his life doth constitute can never one moment exceed in duration the organic structure which speaks it into existence.

Who doubts that the life of a horse is organic life ?—Probably no one. What warrant, then, have we for doubting it in the case of man ?

Is it because man dearly loves his life ?—So evidently does the horse and numerous other animals to him inferior.

Is it because he manifests intelligence, foresees consequences, and lays up in store for the morrow ?—All these things are performed by the bee, the beaver, and sundry other animals of quite inferior order, only upon a scale less grand.

But man has a *will and the power of choice.* Very well, and has not a horse the same? Does he not often declare by his acts, that he does not choose to be caught, and therefore will not be ? And does he not upon such occasions manifest foresight, as well as power of choice, by keeping out in the body of the field, instead of suffering himself to be worked into a corner ? Yea, and does he not reveal quite enough of determination of purpose when, by his acts, he most unmistakably declares that he has gone far enough, and so will not budge another inch ? We repeat, Does not the horse manifest all these things, the same as does the superior animal called man, only in an inferior quality and degree ?

Again, if human life is a real entity and not organic function, and if the life of the horse is organic function and not an entity, then how happens it that both men and horses are not only multiplied into being in the same way, but nursed, kept alive, and growing by the same kind and character of means; namely, by taking food into the stomach, inhaling atmospheric air, etc. ?

Of course, we do not pretend to *know* that the life of man is not a real entity, or that he does not possess existence independently of organic action, both endlessly before he is born and after he is physically dead; nor do we *know* that the life of a horse is not also such an entity. Just what we intend to affirm is, that, in so far as we are able to see and to judge, the evidences all seem to be against it; and consequently it is no more possible for us to believe it than it is to plant ourself upon nothing, and there stand. In a word, as, in a philosophical point of view, we are unable to see any difference between the life or spirit of a man, and the life or spirit of a horse, so we are unable to believe there is any;—are unable to believe there is any, for the reason that, think differently who may, actual belief, whether wise or foolish, is never a matter of choice, but always a thing of necessity.

"And moreover I saw under the Sun the place of judgment, that wickedness was there; and the place of righteousness, that iniquity was there. I said in mine heart, God shall judge the righteous and the wicked: for there is a time there for every purpose and for every work. I said in mine heart concerning the estate of the sons of men, that God might manifest them, and that they might see that they themselves are beasts. For that which befalleth the sons of men befalleth beasts; even one thing befalleth them: as the one dieth, so dieth the other; yea, they have all one breath; so that a man hath no pre-eminence above a beast: for all is vanity. All go unto one place; all are of the dust, and all turn to dust again. Who knoweth the spirit of man that goeth upward, and the spirit of the beast that goeth downward to the Earth? Wherefore I perceive that there is nothing better, than that a man should rejoice in his own works; for that is his portion: for who shall bring him to see what shall be after him?"

Such were the views entertained upon this subject by the ancient Preacher.—Last paragraph of third chapter of Ecclesiastes.

POPULAR OPINION EVER CHANGING.

In a land where no man is born with a gold spoon in his mouth and none with a spade in his hand, but where the avenues to learning, wealth, and honor are equally open to all, it is natural that men should come to think and to speak with a freedom that is unknown in the olden aristocratic countries of the world. Wherefore it should not be forgotten by any member of that great debating club, into which the people of such a country are certain to resolve themselves, that, notwithstanding it may be his fortune to be standing upon a pinacle of social respectability and honor to-day, he is liable, by a change in public sentiment and feeling, to be found occupying a very different position to-morrow. From the same high gallows which a proud and insolent Haman may to-day be erecting for the suppression of some humble Mordecai, who cannot find it in his heart to pay homage either unto him or his opinions, it is possible that he himself may ere long be left to dangle.

MAN THE CREATURE OF CIRCUMSTANCES.

As the nature which an infant possesses at birth is the creature of hereditary causes over which it had no control, and as the nature which an individual possesses in manhood is that same infantile nature, strengthened by time, developed by education, and moulded by circumstances; so, in truth and in fact, these are the branches of the great Creator which, by their joint and several action, have made him the kind and character of man he is. And consequently, it is upon these said branches, or creative causes, and not upon the individual himself, the mere effect, that must rest the responsibility, not only for his being the kind and character of man he is, but for his doing and desiring to do as he does,—if responsibility therefor anywhere doth rest. In childhood, from hereditary causes, educational influences, etc., we are led to desire and determine to pursue a certain course of action through life, but, by the presence and operation of various unforeseen circumstances that come to surround us in youth, we are deterred therefrom, and compelled to pursue some other; by the pressure of yet some other circumstances which unexpectedly come to surround us in early manhood, we are again compelled to change our course for yet another; and thus on all through our lives, not in a broad, smooth sea of independence of surrounding things do we sail, but in the narrow, jagged channel of circumstances which urge us on and direct our course. Instead of an individual's creation being begun and ended at birth, or upon any other particular day, it is from the date of his death backward, and still backward, through a long line of ancestors and ancestral influences that the period of his full creation legitimately extends. And not only this, but, from the cradle to the grave, (ancestry and ancestral influences being all left aside,) circumstances and things apparently trivial have much more to do with moulding the character and shaping the destinies of men, and hence in currently making them the kind and character of persons they currently are, than do any of the greatly superior branches or departments of the Creator and Governor of the Universe.—Of an endless chain, not the present link, nor yet the next preceding one, is the end.

INSPIRATION.

Much as has been said, sung, and written upon the subject, we can see no good reason for believing that the men of olden time were any more specially inspired, or taught of God, than are the men of to-day, knowledge then, the same as now, being, as we think, the product of human brains; and hence limited in kind, character, and extent by the capacity of that organ to speak it into existence within the human tabernacle. To the extent that Moses, St. Paul, Mr. Volney, or any other writer, ancient or modern, correctly interprets the laws of Nature and lays bare their mode of operation, to that extent doth such writer proclaim eternal verity; and hence to that extent is he taught of God by natural process, but not by him specially instructed, or made wise by miracle.

Allowing the men of to-day to be more enlightened, than were the men of olden time; in other words, admitting that, by the aid of all the arts and sciences which have been brought to light since the days when the Bible was written, and all the vast array of schools and other educational machinery which have since been put in operation to promote their spread, the present tenants of Earth have come to know more of great Nature, more of her laws, and more of their modes of operation to produce results, than did the ancients, or any intervening generation of men; it would then seem to follow and that quite plainly, that the men of to-day are just so much the more specially inspired, or taught of God, instead of less or none at all; consequently that their inferences, opinions, and statements are just so much the more likely to be in accordance with eternal fact; and hence that they should be correspondingly more sought after, examined, and believed.—Not with the ancients did wisdom die; neither will it with this generation.

As no man is capable of drinking in all of Nature, so no man is ever inspired by Nature's Sum; and as almost every man is capable of drinking in some small portion of Nature, so almost every man is by some small fraction of her vast Self inspired. The man does not live who is capable of delivering a masterly extemporaneous address, to an audience that is wholly composed of gaping fools; and yet men of only fair ability, not unfrequently become eminently inspired, when addressing congenial audiences of highly intellectual and silently attentive heads. The traveler derives inspiration from lakes and rivers; the geologist from rocks and stones; the botanist from leaves and flowers; the speaker from his hearers; and thus on. In short, from the cradle to the grave, we are all of us more or less inspired in our thoughts, feelings, and sentiments, and hence moulded in our characters, by the character of the different circumstances and things by which we are surrounded. And such, we cannot doubt, is all the divine inspiration there really is, ever was, or ever will be.

FIRST PRINCIPLES THE BEST GUIDE.

Not only do the views and opinions of different individuals of equal eminence in the same profession quite widely differ, but also those of the same individual, at different periods of time. Hence the man who plants himself upon the opinions of the Christian Fathers, the framers of the Constitution, or, indeed, upon precedent of any kind, can thereby prove almost anything he chooses. With first principles, it is not so. Wherefore, it is *these* a great deal more, and *those* a great deal less, that should be consulted by both divines and statesmen, would they advance themselves and us in wisdom's pleasant ways, instead of perpetuating, in both us and them, the errors of the past.

CREATION CONTINUOUS AND PROGRESSIVE.

Notwithstanding from the force of habit and the usage of language we are frequently led to speak of creation as being a thing which at some time had a beginning; nevertheless it is our opinion, not only that the elements, of which all created forms and things are composed, are eternal, but that creation, in some form, has eternally existed. Of course, it is not thought that the same worlds, and other minor forms and things which, to-day, do constitute creation's sum, eternally existed, or that they will endlessly continue to be, but only that the complex act or process, whose result is creation, is eternal; and hence that, of created things in some form and stage of maturity, there was never a vacancy and will never come an end.

Or thus: Of creation, which we regard as being both a continuous and progressive work, destruction is a preparatory process, and hence a branch. Simple comparative illustrations.—Preparatory to constructing a substantial edifice from the materials of which an old, tumble-down, stone castle is composed, such castle has first to be razed to its foundation. Preparatory to raising a crop of wheat from a field of growing clover, the clover has first to be plowed under, and there left to die and to rot. Preparatory to rendering steel intensely hard, it has first to be heated until quite soft. Indeed, so closely do creation and destruction follow at each other's heels, that the elements which compose the food we eat, the clothes we wear, and even those of which we are ourselves made up, have all been used before; —have all been possessed of organic life either vegetable or animal, and that not unlikely a thousand times before. In fine, it can hardly be doubted, as seems to us, that, throughout all past eternity, like elementary particles or creative causes have been constantly at work, producing into existence and also destroying, over and over again, like created forms, things, or effects, great and small, inanimate and animated; and not any more that they will continue on repeating and re-repeating these same acts throughout all eternity to come.

ALL MEN BRETHREN.

As all men have the same common parents; namely, Mother Earth and Father Sol; and as all men belong to the same common church; namely, the great church of humanity; so all men are not only brethren, but doubly such. And not only this, but inasmuch as every man is a priest by divine right; that is, was born one; therefore no man has need of being ordained by any of the so-called successors of the apostles, or other set of his fellow beings, to enable him to exercise his natural, and hence divine right of performing priestly labors, whenever and wherever his services may be acceptable, and he disposed to render them. Or thus: As Father Adam must be supposed to have been endowed with the right to offer up his own sacrifices and carry his own soul to market; so his descendants, one and all, must be supposed to inherit the same right equally with Aaron, the apostles, or any other set of men descended from the same common ancestor. Of course, it is not claimed that all are alike qualified either by inclination or ability, to execute this or any other right in the same skillful and impressive manner, or with the same infinitude of measured ceremoniousness; but only that such is every man's right by inheritance, if he chooses to exercise it.

CONSCIENCE.

It must ever be remembered that conscience, in order to be a promoter of real good and a guide to any high grade of happiness, must be enlightened; that is, it must be governed in its decisions, not by the blind feelings, however active and strong, but by the teachings of sober intellect. That the Jew, the Turk, and the Christian are alike conscientious in their religious beliefs and practices cannot rationally be doubted, and yet it is hardly supposable that they are all alike really good and happy; that is, that they are all good and happy in the same high degree. That the restless, energetic, and impulsive Paul was acting just as conscientiously, when going about persecuting the saints, as when, only a few days thereafter, he was journeying from place to place preaching the gospel of Christ, no sane man will deny; and yet, that the pleasures he derived from thus trying to injure the pure and the innocent were of a much lower grade than those derived from trying to comfort, elevate, and bless his fellow-men,—than those derived from trying to lift them out of the slough of sin and consequent suffering, we have his own emphatic testimony.

SELF-HELP THE BEST HELP.

All past observation and experience bear testimony, that those who, by dint of their own persevering efforts, manage to work themselves up to some ardently desired summit, no matter how high nor what its kind, do almost invariably prove themselves equal to the task of sustaining themselves there; whilst those who have to be coaxed up, dragged up, and every conceivable means used to get them up, are almost certain, when they come to be left to themselves, to topple, fall, and ultimately sink back into their original nothingness. And what is true of individuals, in these respects, must needs be true of classes, nations, and even races; since it is of individuals, and of nothing else, that these are all made up.

FEELINGS STRONG, INTELLECTS WEAK.

No matter how highly social the individual nor how well bred, it is impossible for a man, in whom intellect is weak and the organs of feeling and emotion strong, ever long to discuss a question with anyone holding opposite views, without becoming more or less angry or, in milder phrase, excited; and hence becoming more or less piquant and censorious. For this, of course, he is to be commiserated and not blamed; unless, indeed, it can be shown that he is to blame for being organized and balanced in the way he is. Nor is it possible for men possessed of strong and highly cultivated intellects, but of still stronger feelings and emotions, long to discuss a question, whereon they are evidently getting the worst of the argument, without so far forgetting their dignity and losing their self-command as to be guilty of violating the proprieties of debate. Of this, the halls of Congress furnish some notable examples.

Ambitious and keenly sensitive as are the organs of feeling and emotion, they can neither see nor reason.

CONVERSATION AND WORKS.

That some persons exhibit much more of method and talent in their conversation than in their works, and others much more of these in their works than in their conversation must be manifest to all; and yet who will explain the cause thereof, either upon the supposition of the brain's being a single organ, or upon the one which makes mind to be a real entity, consequently to be a thing which exists and acts independently of the brain, and hence a thing whose existence and action will not cease with the death of that physical organ? Agreeably to our understanding of the matter, the thing may be briefly explained thus:

As mind is not a real entity, but merely organic function, and as the brain is not a simple but a complex organ; so in the heads of some persons, either from hereditary causes, the force of habit, or the influence of both combined, the intellectual organs ever readily join in and work along with the organ of Language, but not along with those which are executive in their character and functions; and hence they are able to manifest considerable intellectual ability in their conversation, although but little in their works. And then there is another class in whose heads, from the same cause or causes, the intellectual organs ever readily join in and work along with those which are executive in their character, but not with that of Language; wherefore it cannot otherwise be than that these should be able to exhibit much more of intellectual ability in their works, than in their conversation.—Corollary :—It is folly and not wisdom to undertake to judge of a man's capacity for business, from his conversational powers; or of his ability to entertain an audience by his conversation, from the appearance of his farm, the variety of his manufactures, or the beauty of his other kind and character of works.

NATURAL ORDER.

The funeral sermon of the man whose long and eventful life has finally come to a close, from age, may be preached in an hour, and yet not in an hour, a day, or a year did his decease come to take place, but gradually, beginning back at that point in his existence where his second childhood began. When such a person dies, be the individual our own dear father, mother, or other near relative, it is not possible for us to experience that same deep feeling of grief which we ever do when a near and dear friend in the prime of life, by fell disease, is stricken down; and why not? As seems to us, it is because gradual death from age is a natural institution, and hence a blessed one; whereas sudden death in the fullness of life, from disease, being an abnormal or superinduced event, therefore it is an event which is at variance with natural Order, and consequently one with which nature's pulse in our bosoms can never beat in unison. Wintry days in the season of winter being perfectly natural, therefore, at that time, they are not particularly annoying; but, was so unnatural an event to take place as the dropping down upon us of a late December day, in early August, we should doubtless find it exceedingly unpleasant.

HOW IT IS DONE.

As the vast infinitude of pebbles, with which old ocean's shore is lined, do none of them possess the power spontaneously to stir, but are ever made to move and rub one against another by the action of the waves, whereby each is brought to act upon and affect the other, and whereby they are, one and all, just as effectually rounded and smoothed as if each possessed the power, not only of spontaneously stirring, but of thus abrading and polishing its own surface; so it is not upon himself, however great and powerful he may be, that a man's influence is exerted, but upon his neighbors and associates, they in return doing the same thing upon him. Yea, and in this way is society just as effectually enlightened, civilized, and elevated in the scale of humanity, as if each individual member thereof possessed the power of acting directly upon and affecting himself;—as if each individual member thereof possessed the power to make himself,—possessed the power to mould his own character,—possessed the power to lift himself from the ground by pulling at his boot straps, the same as can he thus elevate any of his neighbors by pulling at theirs.

THE SHEEP A GOOD SHEEP—THE WOLF A GOOD WOLF.

As all the different kinds and grades of animals, the same as plants, must be presumed to have been spoken into being just as they now are, by a pre-existent and hence extraneous God, else to have been sprung into existence low down, and so pushed up creation's gradually ascending grade into their present state of being, by operation of natural causes, deep in the nature of the undying elements eternally residing; therefore every kind and grade of animal, as well as vegetable, must be presumed to be, upon the whole, more or less good, and not absolutely bad, a single one. Indeed, take whichever view of the case we will, the conclusion seems to be irresistible that kites, hawks and wolves, the same as the sheep, cow and horse, are, each and all, part and parcel of Nature's grand harmonious Whole; and hence that they, each and all, are acting properly and not improperly, when they live out in practice the nature that is organically enstamped upon them.

Simply because we are unable to see the precise beneficial use which a thing subserves in the great natural economy, it will not do to infer that it doth not subserve any.

OBEDIENCE REWARDED, SIN PUNISHED.

To the extent that a man is prosperous and happy, to that extent is he righteous and not wicked; or more properly, to that extent is he an obeyer and not a breaker of the laws upon which the particular kind of success and happiness by him enjoyed depends. In like manner, to the extent a man is unprosperous and unhappy, to that extent is he disobedient, and hence sinful; no matter what may be his standing among his fellow-men, nor whether his disobedience is the result of ignorance or of deliberate intent. In other words, a man may live in constant violation of one set of laws, consequently be, in so far, an awfully wicked wretch; and yet be a scrupulous observer of some other set, say those upon which life and health are dependent, for example, and hence be, in reference to these, righteous and not wicked. Wherefore, notwithstanding all his transgressions in other directions, he is entitled to reap the rewards of obedience, in the direction and to the extent that he is obedient; and wherefore, instead of being prematurely cut off by death from disease, he is almost certain to be healthy and live to a good old age. Plainly as by the aids of natural science these things have come to be seen by a large class of persons now upon the Earth, it is evident that Job was not sufficiently inspired to understand them; otherwise he would not have inquired with such great fear and trembling, "Wherefore do the wicked live, become old, yea, are mighty in power?" Job, 21. 7.

INTELLIGENCE THE GUARDIAN OF LIBERTY.

As not religion of any kind, but intelligence is the natural guardian of liberty, so it is much to the schoolmaster and little to the priest that we are indebted for the enjoyment of that inestimable blessing. Notwithstanding the much, however, that has already been done by the schoolmaster, that there is still lingering among us much of unreasoning religion, much of stolid ignorance, blind superstition, arrogant bigotry, and rank intolerance cannot be denied; and yet, so long as shall speech remain free, the press untrammelled by law, and the natural sciences be taught, the old bloody scenes of religious persecution can never be re-enacted by Catholicism, Protestantism, or any other religious ism. No; never!

EARLY-MADE IMPRESSIONS LASTING.

"Train up a child in the way he should go; and when he is old he will not depart from it:"—Thus saith the great Proverbialist. By the same plain rule, teach children erroneously, that is, impress upon their young and tender brains as facts, things that are dark and fabulous, and they will continue to believe those same when grown up to manhood. And not only this, but should they be fortunate enough, during ripe manhood's stage, to outgrow such erroneous teachings, in their declining years, and *pari passu* with the sagging back of their brains into the lax and feeble condition of childhood, will they sag back into those same opinions that were thus early impressed upon them. Everywhere and ever, like causes, whether chemical, muscular, or brenal, produce like effects.

For the reason, then, that it is so very difficult to erase early-made impressions, or eradicate such opinions and practices as are gained in childhood, whether correct or whether erroneous, for that reason ought children never be taught dogmatically; that is, be told and retold authoritatively, that things are thus and so absolutely; but instead, that such and such things appear to be facts or are believed to be so, and upon such and such evidence, or for such and such reasons; thus leaving the door of after-inquiry thereinto, for themselves, widely ajar. In short, in educating children, the aim should primarily be to awaken a spirit of inquiry, and beget in them habits of thought and reflection, instead of a passive tendency to believe, remember, thoughtlessly repeat, and re-repeat, whatsoever may be unqualifiedly affirmed by their superiors in age, fame, or condition.

WHERE THE BLAME OR RESPONSIBILITY?

As God undoubtedly created that American animal called the skunk, and organically enstamped upon him all and singular his peculiar characteristics, so the poor feeble thing is no more to blame or responsible for being a skunk, and hence for smelling thus disgustingly skunky, than is God for having created him thus, or are we for disliking his company because he doth so smell;—not any more.—No man, high or low, weak or wise, is organically commanded, and hence required, to be what he never was and cannot be, or to do what he never did nor ever can do. In other words, no man is organically commanded, and hence required, to love what to him is decidedly hateful, or to hate what to him is especially lovely; and hence, talk it as we may, no man is to blame or responsible for not doing either the one thing or the other. Who or what then is to blame or responsible for all this; provided blame, or responsibility therefor, anywhere there be?

ALL LIKE ADAM, AND ADAM LIKE HIS MAKER.

"In Adam's fall we sinned all." In other words, our forefathers, the Adams from whom we descended, being imperfect, they transmitted to us their imperfections as well as good qualities; we the same to our children, and thus forever on. Or, in still other words, as not perfection nor absolute imperfection but imperfect goodness is an attribute of all created things, so it needs must have been an attribute of that Power which Adam and all things else created. And hence, theorize as we may and sing it as we will, it is "upon this line" that, in actual practice, the great battle of life has got to be fought out.

HOW MANY MORAL TRUTHS ORIGINATE.

It sometimes happens that what was known to be a falsehood, when first stated, comes to be to the utterer by its oft repetition a moral truth; and hence becomes a thing unto which he would be able conscientiously to make oath. And it is doubtless no uncommon occurrence for things that are wholly imaginary, but seemingly possible, to become transformed into moral certainties by the same process; and especially in the heads of such as are by nature, and hence in practice, greatly given to wondering and hankering after the wonderful.

With some, the more strange and unnatural the tale, the more readily it is swallowed; with others, the more miraculous upon its face the story, no matter what nor by whom told, the stronger must ever be the supporting evidence to create in their brains that peculiar undulatory movement which faith therein doth constitute.

A BEGINNING PRESUPPOSES AN END.

When there is no possible way of escaping the conclusion that a certain existing thing, no matter what, never had a beginning, but endlessly existed, it may doubtless be inferred, and that legitimately, that it will never come to an end; but how it can be inferred by men of brains that a thing is going to exist endlessly on, when they are compelled to admit it had a beginning, and hence has not endlessly been, we are at a loss to discover. Or thus: What better evidence can be required to prove that a thing will endlessly continue to exist, than the fact that it has endlessly been in existence? And what better, that a thing will not thus endlessly continue to be, than the fact that it had a beginning, and hence has not thus endlessly been? As seems to us, none.

Corollary:—The primitive idea intended to be denoted and conveyed by the word *immortal*, when applied to mind or any other created function or thing, has no foundation in the realms of fact; and hence is merely a moral truth, or a thing that is wholly imaginary.

BY WHAT POWER RULED.

As all the different parts of a thing are not only equal to the thing's sum, but are the thing *itself*, so all the different properties and powers of all the different elements of which a thing is composed must not only be equal to the sum of its properties and powers, but must be themselves such sum. It cannot therefore be unreasonable to suppose that, by the same undying properties and powers which now hold together in globular form, the various elements of which the Sun, Moon, Earth, and other planets are composed, by those very same were their composing elements brought into contact, arranged in proper order, located in their appropriate places, and there in harmonious union joined. Nor is it rash to presume that, by the same undying properties and powers which to-day retain in their respective orbital places, the different bodies of which our Solar system is composed, by those very same were those heavenly bodies, one after another, arrested in their wanderings in the fields of space, brought into their said respective places, and there, revolving in harmonious union, commanded to remain. When it shall finally come to be admitted, no matter how reluctantly, that the elements of which all created things are composed are not evanescent but eternal, it will also have to be admitted that their different properties and powers are likewise eternal. And when these two basilar facts shall be conceded, not of any hypothetic Spirit or Being, outside vast creation's limits placed, but of the different composing fractions of that great complex Something which ever within creation's bounds doth legitimately reside, (because all creation it doth constitute and is,) will men enquire, and seek for light and rules by which to discover and unlock, all such of creation's present mysteries as are not beyond the utmost reach of human comprehension.

Yon grand luminary that rules the day, imparting light and heat and life unto more worlds than this, what is it but a vast infinitude of particles of elementary substance, brought together by the law of attraction, which is part and parcel of their undying nature, and there, by such law, fast bound in *Sol?* And in what resides *Sol's* power to hold and guide the mighty spheres in their vast journeys through fields of space, but in this same undying nature of his composing elements;—but in the undying nature of just such elementary particles as, in their primary form and uncombined estate, no human eye could see nor human touch perceive.

CAUSES ARE EFFECTS AND EFFECTS CAUSES.

As there is never an effect without an appropriate cause, and as every effect, as soon as into existence pushed, itself becomes an appropriate cause to the pushing into existence of some other effect, and thus forever on; so the conclusion would seem to be irresistible that the thoughts, feelings, and acts of men, the same as the thoughts, feelings, and acts of the brute creation, the revolutions of the seasons, changes in the weather, and every other kindred act and thing, are all of them effects; and hence are, in some appropriate way, all caused, or brought to take place and be, by the operation of natural law. Of course, it is not concluded that all the vast variety of causes, simple and compound, by whose operation these numberless results are produced into being, stand clearly out revealed, or that all the innumerable effects by them produced are directly backward traceable to their respective causes; but only that cause and effect, through all created things, great and small, inanimate and animated, their parallel courses eternally do run; and hence that fixed law, in man and beast, and all things else, and everywhere, eternally bears rule.

DIFFERENT TEACHINGS PRODUCE DIFFERENT EFFECTS.

To teach men such things as are only morally true,—such things as merely have existence within the human head, no matter how great may be the number of the heads in which residing or what the class, is to darken their understandings,—is to sink them still lower in the depths of ignorance,—(they, poor deluded souls, all the while fancying themselves to be growing in wisdom,—) is to curse them. To teach men such things as are really true,—such as are consonant to fact, no matter how unpopular or greatly ridiculed the same may be, is to enlighten their understandings,—is to elevate them in the scale of intelligence,—is to bless them.

Ignorance of God's facts, "is really the curse of God;" and Knowledge of what actually was and is and is to be, and not of what Moses, the prophets, or any body else may chance to have thought and believed, "the wing wherewith we fly to heaven."

IDEAS BETTER THAN WORDS.

Far be it from us to speak disparagingly of a thorough classical education; and yet, since life at best is short, we must think it would be well as a general thing, to spend more time in gathering facts and augmenting the stock of ideas, and less in learning to express a smaller number in more languages than one. It is of ideas, clear and practical, and not of words, the mere signs by which ideas are denoted and expressed, that knowledge doth chiefly consist.

THOUGHTS, FEELINGS, ETC., CAUSED.

Not the human brain nor any other created thing is seemingly more fickle and uncertain in its action, than is the wind, and yet who seriously supposes the air doth ever stir, except it be commanded so to do by some appropriate exciting cause;—except it be commanded and empowered so to do by the operation of natural laws, deep in the nature of the elements themselves residing?—Who? And just as surely as is the air governed in all its movements by the operation of fixed laws, whereby winds of every kind, character, and grade, are all of them appropriately caused, or brought to have existence upon the Earth's surface; just so certainly, as seems to us, is the human brain governed in all its movements by the operation of fixed laws; whereby thoughts, feelings, emotions, etc., of every kind, character, and grade, are, in like manner, all of them appropriately caused, or brought to have existence within the human head.

LIFE AND DEATH BOTH BLESSINGS.

As neither life nor death, in our judgment, is a real enity, and as of the former the latter is believed to be an inevitable consequence; so we must think it would be wisdom in every one to try to adapt his course of action unto the conditions upon which health, longevity, and protracted usefulness are made to depend, as that of him it may be said, when from age he is ultimately compelled to lay himself down everlastingly to rest, By the gift of life, thou wast blessed; by faithfully discharging the duties of life, thou wast blessed; and finally, when no longer able to bear life's burdens or enjoy its pleasures, thou wast blessed by death.

CHRISTIANS.

It is no evidence that a man is a Christian, that is, that he doth shape his life in acccrdance with the teachings of Christ, because he makes a public profession of religion; and none that a man doth not thus shape it, because he does not seek either to bridge over his past errors or add to his present popularity and standing, by placing himself in connection with some popular church. Indeed, the fact that a man doth steadfastly resist the temptation of endeavoring to obtain for himself a public certificate of good character, by uniting himself with some popular sect, society, or order, we must regard as being evidence in his favor rather than against him. Of course, it is not thought that a man who was honest and upright before he joined a church will not continue to be so afterwards; but only that bad men, after uniting themselves with a church and thus making a public profession of being good and pure, will bear quite as close watching as before coming to be thus backed and supported.

WHAT IS BEST IS WHAT WILL BE.

It cannot be doubted that men do more or less desire and hope to live, personally on, to all eternity; and not a bit more that they do often desire and hope for things they can never have, and which things, had they not been denied them, would have been their undoing. If, upon the whole, it is for man's good that, in some form or condition, he should personally continue to live right on past death, to all eternity, then doubtless he will; and if, upon the whole, it is not for his good that he should thus continue to live, then most undoubtedly will death be to him, as an individual entity, the final close. A Creator that is, upon the whole, good and just, will do what is, upon the whole, for the best good of all his created works, be the same whatsoever it may. Or, at least, so it seems to us, and we are by no means sorry that it does.

CHRIST AND HIS DOINGS.

It would be well for all candid inquirers after real truth to remember that there is no evidence, whatsoever, that Christ ever wrote a single word of what is contained in the New Testament, the chart of that religious system which from him derived its name. Indeed, all we know or ever can know about Christ, his teachings, sayings, and doings, we gain from the declarations of men of quite low estate, and who, from their own account of the matter, cannot be supposed to be wholly disinterested witnesses; else from mere heresay testimony of a more or less roundabout and exaggerated character, and hence from testimony that is still less reliable. And not only this, but allowing all the recorded statements of such as were either eye-witnesses to Christ's doings or ear-witnesses of his teachings and sayings to be strictly correct, and also admitting all the vast amount of hearsay evidence in reference to this same subject matter, and upon the pages of the New Testament standing, to be really true; still, of formal ceremonies, stringent creeds, narrow articles of faith, and other trammelling church machinery, Christ is not the author.

SIN AND CONFESSION.

Allowing that God is not in reality a personal being, either great or small, but simply the Sum of all Substance personified, material, spiritual, and mixed, it follows that it is a thing impossible for us to sin against him as a Whole, or, indeed, against any of his different component parts, except only that comparatively insignificant branch, known as animated nature or the animated kingdom. This being admitted,—and it must be unreasonable to suppose that we can sin against the Sun, the Moon, the stars, or any other of his inanimate fractions, whether great or small, present or remote,—it follows that, with the exception of wrongs done to brutes, or at least something that is possessed of animated existence, and hence of the low sense of feeling, it is only against himself and his fellow-men that a man can perpetrate wrong,—can do iniquity,—can commit sin of any kind. And such being admitted to be the case, it is perfectly obvious, not only of what particular branch of the great eternal Whole it is that forgiveness for sin should be asked, but also unto what individuals of such branch, as far forth as possible, amends therefor should be made. Yea, and such being conceded to be the fact, it is plain that there are certain sins which are of such a nature, instance adultery, incest, etc., that, wrong as it is to commit them, it is a still greater sin to confess them;—a still greater sin to confess them for the reason that confessing cannot possibly undo or heal any thing, and it is more widely damaging in its consequences. Wherefore, manifestly enough, as seems to us, in reference to all this class of cases, the true course to pursue is to remain silent, and "go," and be sure and "sin no more."

ACTS BOTH CAUSES AND EFFECTS.

Notwithstanding thoughts rank first and foremost among the elements of which the thing called mind is constituted, and notwithstanding thoughts are merely brenal acts, hence are, in and of themselves, just as feeble and transitory in character, as are the pulsations of the heart; yet, as stimulants to muscular action, as well as to further action by the brain, they may stand exciting cause to the pronouncing of words and the performance of acts whose consequences shall be as enduring as the granite hills. Thus, for example, the simple, lucky thought, suggested by the boiling of a tea-kettle, (for thoughts it must be remembered are all of them caused, and hence are themselves effects as well as causes,) that steam might be so confined, liberated, and applied to machinery as to constitute a motive power, was undoubtedly the exciting cause which prompted the Marquis of Worcester, Savary, Newcomen, and others to experiment thereupon, to the end that they might ascertain whether such thought or idea was correct; that is, whether it was a real truth, and hence a thing of value to the world, or whether it was only a moral truth, and hence a thing entirely worthless. And so this simple thought, this simple exciting cause, has stood bottom cause to the harnessing of that power, and bringing its use to such a state of perfection as largely to work a revolution in the industries of the world. Yea, and the still further improvements therein, unto which this same simple thought, this same single exciting cause, is destined to stand bottom cause to the working out, who can forecast?—Causes which, in and for themselves, are as feeble and transitory as a breath of air or an undulation of the brain, may lead to results at which the world shall stand aghast; whilst those as potent and enduring as the mighty waters which precipitate themselves over the falls of Niagara, may remain wholly barren of any noteworthy results.

THE EVITABLE AND INEVITABLE.

Whether God is, upon the whole, good, or whethet he is not, or whether his created works, like himself, are, upon the whole, good, or whether they are not, it is certain that both he and they are as they are. Wherefore, to the extent that we his feeble fractions are obviously unable to work any change in either him or his works, it must be more happifying, as well as becoming, to take a cheerful view of things as they currently exist;—must be more happifying, as well as becoming, to conclude that, whether they are or whether they are not, upon the whole, all good and right, they are, at least, quite as nearly so as we should be likely to make them, was ours the privilege to run the universal machine;—must be more happifying, as well as becoming, than it is to go grieving, grumbling, and growling about because it is so hot or because so cold, because it is so wet or because so dry, etc. Not in being displeased and disheartened with what is and cannot be helped doth the kingdom of heaven consist, but in accepting the inevitable in humble submission, and trying therewith to be content. In other words, such things, whether high or whether low, whether great or whether small, as do not suit us, and as we have the power to alter or to modify, it is weak and unmanly to sit still, mourn over and grumble about, but manly and religious to grapple with, and do all that we can to mould them to our liking; and such as do not please us, but which we are obviously powerless to ameliorate or one jot to change, it is alike weak, unmanly, irreligious, and irreverent to grieve over or wage war against.

Sad, dyspeptic, grumbling, growling, vinegar-faced sinners exist in plenty both in the church and out; but sour, peevish, cross-grained, fault-finding, unhappy saints, Who ever saw any?—Gloomy, discontented, and unhappy saints; cheerful, contented, and happy sinners; strange things, these! Not in mere profession, however sincere, nor yet in hanging down the head like a bulrush, and grievously complaining of everybody and thing about us, high and low, great and small, doth religion consist; but in reverencing and yielding cheerful obedience to all such currently existing powers, laws, and commandments as it is obviously impossible for us to alter or evade. In a word, professor or non-professor, to love and obey is to be religious,—is to be reverent,—is to be dutiful,—is to be happy; to hate and disobey is to be irreligious,—is to be irreverent,—is to be undutiful,—is to be a miserable sinner. Or, at least, such are our views in reference to the matter.

EFFECTS MISTAKEN FOR THEIR CAUSES.

So close is the connection between certain effects and their parent causes, that there is no little danger of mistaking the former for the latter, and hence being seriously misled. Thus, for an assumed example, a sound and healthy man of unexceptionable habits, but of impressible order, meets a friend in the streets, at a time when the cholera is claiming its victims in that vicinity, and, among other things, is told in substance, that he looks bad—looks as if he was going to be sick—looks as if he might have the cholera hanging about him. The next day, in about the same place, he meets another friend, and, among other things, is told in substance, that he does not look at all well—looks as if he was going to have a hard fit of sickness—looks as if he might have the cholera, unless he took the very best of care of himself. The day after, and near the same spot, he meets yet another of his friends, and one in whose opinions he places great confidence; and, the usual greetings being over, is told in substance, that he looks ill—looks hollow-eyed and bad—looks almost exactly as Mr. B. did just before coming down with the cholera: adding, as a clincher, "Poor fellow! how much he suffered from fear of that terrible disease and then had to die with it at last." And thus on, as often as once or twice a day, and always in nearly the same place, is he met and told substantially the same thing by some one or other of his numerous friends; until, finally, sure enough, he is attacked by that fell disease and carried off thereby.

And now the question is, What caused that rugged man, thus to have the cholera, and hence to die therewith? Did the repeated remarks, thus made to him by his said friends about his looking ill—looking so hollow-eyed and bad—looking so very much like a cholera subject, so work upon and effect his mind, as finally to bring his physical system into such a diseased condition as to invite the cholera's attack? Or did such remarks so operate upon and effect his brain, the seat and centre of the nervous system, and the organ unto which, through the agency of the ear, they were specially addressed, as to cause it to vibrate in such a manner as to speak into existence within him, more and more frequently and distinctly, the sadly depressing thoughts of cholera, of its premonitory symptoms, terrible agonies, the fear of having it, and dread of dying therewith; until, finally, that organ became so far diseased, in consequence of such monotonous and painful vibratory action, as to cause it not only to keep said depressing thoughts, feelings, etc., constantly alive and revolving within his head, but so far to affect the balance of his bodily organs, (of which the brain, no matter what may chance to be its tone or condition, is ever the ruling center,) as finally to generate within him, or superinduce upon him, that most fearful malady?—As we see it, the latter is just as certainly the fact, as is it that complex physical organ called the brain, which speaks into existence within us the complex brenal act called mind, and not such act which speaks into existence our brains. And so of all the numerous ills of which mind or imagination usually has the credit of being the producing cause.

When a man becomes unsound of mind, either partially or wholly, it is because his brain has become either partially or wholly diseased; and hence it is unto such diseased organ which causes him to think, speak, and act thus strangely, and not to the mere acts by it produced or spoken into existence, that remedies should be addressed.

CHAPTER XXXIV.

QUESTIONS AND EXPLANATIONS.

QUESTION TO CHRISTIAN FRIENDS.

To the generally received opinion, whether sound or unsound, that, inside the prohibitions of positive law, men have a right to do with their surplus means as they may see fit, we shall offer no objection; and yet we must be permitted to ask our good Christian friends, one and all, and particularly such of them as reside in the larger towns and cities, this one plain question: Do you not candidly think it would be, upon the whole, more Christian, and hence, upon the whole, more happifying both to youselves and others, to build equally substantial, roomy, and comfortable, but far less magnificent and costly churches, in which to assemble and sing the praises of the meek and lowly Jesus, and expend the money thus saved in erecting neat little cottages for the free occupancy of the neighboring sick, lame, blind, and other unfortunate poor, such as Christ when here was wont to pity and to bless?

ANOTHER.

Why in all probability was it that the men who wrote the Bible,—the men who were essaying to lay down a chart of rules for the guidance of all coming generations,—the very men of old who had so much to say about the *mind*, did not lisp a syllable about that crowning part of man, the *brain*, upon whose presence and action mind is dependent not only for manifestation, but also for existence within the human tabernacle? Was it because of the brain's non-importance in the animal structure, as compared with the heart, liver, kidneys, and other oft-mentioned organs? Or was it because, with the aid of all the divine inspiration which, at that day and age of the world, was vouchsafed to man, they were as profoundly ignorant of the brain's nature and use in the animal economy, as was Nicodemus of the new birth?—Which?

Into such ancient darkness, Must it not be a poor place for advanced moderns to be peering in search of light?

AND ANOTHER.

Whether God is really a personal Being or whether he is only so by mere figure of speech, of what use can it be to pray him to bless us for Christ's sake, for Paul's sake, or any other great and good man's sake, ancient or modern, living or dead? In other words, if it be a fact, (which it undoubtedly is,) that "whatsoever a man soweth," whether it be the seed of blessings or of curses, "that shall he also reap;" How, then, can it otherwise be than that, if we would ourselves be blessed, it is we ourselves, and not somebody else, who must be obedient, must be good?

AND YET ANOTHER.

If God really is a Spirit, really is an omnipresent Being, really is a Being that fills all the vast immensity of space with his personal presence, How can he reasonably be supposed capable of withdrawing his personal presence from the wicked, for a single moment, or of bestowing, at any time, a double portion thereof upon the righteous, no matter where congregated? In other words, How can a personal God withdraw himself from a locality and still be and remain therein? And still be and remain in every locality he certainly must, if he really is continuously omnipresent and not merely spasmodically so. In short, How can an omnipresent personal God, either in a special or a general way, ever visit any place, ever go anywhere; since he is already there and all the time there, being always everywhere?—How?

QUESTION TO BIBLISTS.

What great good can result from men's believing the Bible to have been conceived and written by Almighty God, instead of by men who were subject to like passions, prejudices, and misjudgments with ourselves?—The obvious ill effects of such a belief is this: It operates as a check upon inquiry into the propriety of its commands, and the truthfulness of its statements, and so hinders progress.

QUESTION TO CLERICAL FRIENDS.

When you come to look back upon the past and also forward into the future, Are you not more than half inclined to think that, by preaching less of incomprehensible theology and more of plain common sense, you would gain more hearers, make more converts, and hence achieve not only a greater amount of good, but good of a higher grade?—Of course, it requires not a little of both will-power, and exertion, to get out of a deep ancient rut; but, then, the thing is sometimes done, and well doth it pay.

QUESTION TO FRIENDLY READERS.

"A wonderful and horrible thing is committed in the land; the prophets prophesy falsely, and the priests bear rule by their means; and my people love to have it so: and what will ye do in the end thereof?"—Such is the testimony of the Weeping prophet not only against his brother prophets, but also against both the priests and the people; and that, too, at the very time when it is claimed, that the spirit of the Lord in the shape of the spirit of prophecy was most abundantly being poured out upon the children of men.—Jeremiah 5. 30, 31.—And what think ye, friendly readers, Is not the thing still running in much the same old groove?

QUESTION TO EVERYBODY.

Is the sexual distinction in the human race, the same as in the lower animals, a God-created distinction, calculated to perpetuate and bless it, and consequently is the race, irrespective of such distinction, one grand, indivisible, and God-created whole; or is it a mere dualistic system of which the male sex is the Sun, and the female its solitary attendant planet? In other words, are the two sexes coeval and coequal, because each alike essential to the continuance and well-being of the other, and hence of the race; or is man, because not more than half woman, the fountain source of all the light and heat that are in the social system? And does woman, because not more than half man, only shine by borrowed rays, only possess just such and just so many wants, rights, and interests as the great masculine Sun may see fit to smile down upon her?

Do not all past observation and experience bear testimony that it is the weak and the timid who need the assistance of that outgrowth of the ballot-box, the law's strong arm, to shield them from the rapacity of the bold and the strong; and not the strong and the bold, to save them from being plucked and trodden under foot by weakness and timidity?

Thanks to the law of progression, the time-honored maxim that *the king can do no wrong to his subjects* has long since become outgrown and left behind, upon this side the Water; and thanks to that same ever onward-moving principle, the one that *husbands, fathers, and brothers can do none to their wives, daughters, and sisters* is fast falling into disrepute, and is certain ere long to become a thing of the past.

QUESTION TO SPIRITUALISTS.

How can a thing which is so very ethereal that it cannot be seen at all be any better seen in the night than in the day-time? Why do ghosts, goblins, and spirits "love darkness rather than light," or prefer singularly constructed cabinets to fair open rooms? And how are they any more able to go rapping and thumping about, without feet or hands, than to sit down quietly by our sides and speak to us in plain English without throat or tongue?

THE POSITION WE OCCUPY.

Not with religion, whether Jewish or Christian, Catholic or Protestant, are we at war; but only with what to us doth seem to be ignorance, superstition, bigotry, intolerance, and error, no matter what may be their different guises or multifarious forms. Or thus: With all such teachers of religion, whether Jew or Turk, Catholic or Protestant, as are faithfully trying to teach all of real truth, as they do honestly believe it to be, which they think their readers or hearers will be able to comprehend, and hence be benefited thereby, are we in full sympathy; but not with such pretended religious teachers, whoever they may be, as are studiously endeavoring to perpetuate and thicken the fogs of ancient ignorance, the better to enable them to bleed the people's pockets and lead them by the nose.—Sincerity, however erroneous, is always to be tolerated and respected; insincerity, ever to be reprobated.

WHEREIN WE HAVE MOST ERRED.

That the views which we have at last come to entertain, and which are herein thus briefly and feebly set forth, are somewhat radical, must be admitted; and yet, when is fairly taken into ~~the~~ consideration the legitimately trammelling effects of early education upon the action of the human brain, we cannot resist the conclusion that we have erred twice in hugging too closely the shore of the narrow sea of conservatism, where we have once by having launched out too far into the broad ocean of radicalism. Yea, and such in our humble judgment, will be the decision of the next generation of men.

Of early made impressions and youthful modes of thought, however narrow and erroneous, it is no easy matter to disabuse one's self, seek to do so who may.

CHAPTER XXXV.

LOOSE THOUGHTS—FOR WHAT THEY MAY BE WORTH.

CURSED OR BLESSED?—WHICH?

By a line of argument not easily proven fallacious, if fallacious it be, the worm that is blotted out, as a worm-entity, by being swallowed by a robin, is, by such act, as a whole and upon the whole, elevated in the scale of existence, consequently is, as a whole and upon the whole, thereby blessed; and for the following reasons: By natural process of digestion, absorption, assimilation, and incorporation, a portion of the worm's composing elements, consequently a portion of the worm itself, is thus brought to become and be part and parcel of that familiar songster; and consequently, to an extent corresponding with the amount which such incorporated worm-elements bear to the entire bird, it is thus brought to have a share in the sweets of robin-life. By the same line of argument, the worm is still further up the ladder of existence pushed, consequently still further blessed, when the bird which the worm now helps compose is eaten by a man; since, by still further process of digestion, absorption, etc., a portion of the robin's composing elements, consequently a portion of the elements of which the late worm was composed, now becomes incorporated into the human fabric. In this way, by the aid of the robin that swallowed the worm and the further aid of the man who, at the proper point of time, ate the robin, to an extent corresponding with the amount which said late worm's composing elements in the form of bird-flesh thus by the man eaten, and hence incorporated into the human fabric, bear to the entire man which they now help compose, in the joys of human life the feeble creeping thing is brought to have a share.

Or thus: Could a million of worms be instantly killed and, by some elaborating process, transformed, within a few hours, into a beautiful redbreast, Would they not be thereby elevated in the scale of existence, and hence, as a whole and upon the whole, blessed by the change? And if, as a whole and upon the whole, they would be thereby blessed and not cursed, then why is not each and every worm that is swallowed by a robin, and hence by process of digestion, absorption, etc., brought to become and be a composing fraction of a redbreast, in like manner blessed?

Admitting life of every kind and grade to be, upon the whole, a blessing, consequently that inanimate substance is blessed by every kind and character of creative cause, which elevates and enlivens it into animated existence, and the higher the form of such existence, the greater the blessing; also admitting the foregoing stray thoughts to be in accordance with the rulings of natural law, (which it would seem they must be, unless Nature is with herself inconsistent,) then, obviously enough, is their field of application inconceivably vast. In short, Is that great law of Nature, which irresistibly inclines superior animals to kill and eat such inferior ones as are to them both palatable and nutritious, founded upon the broad principle of general benevolence, and hence is it, upon the whole, a blessing not only to those eating superiors, but also to the inferiors thus eaten; or is it based upon the narrow principle of special favoritism to such superior animals, at the expense of the well-being of such inferior ones in point of power, if not in kind?—Which?

MEATS AND DRINKS.

In so far as has yet been determined by analysis, the two compound substances, nitric acid and atmospheric air, are composed of the same elements in kind, differing only in proportions; and yet the one is fatal to animal life, whilst the other is essential to sustain it. With the exception of atmospheric air, water is the most plentiful of all known compounds and composed, in so far as is yet known, of the two gases or elements called oxygen and hydrogen; the former being prime supporter of combustion, the latter one of the most inflammable of all known substances, and yet the two when existing together in the form of water will neither burn nor support combustion, but are, when in that state of union joined, flame's most effectual extinguisher.

From the foregoing facts, which are selected merely as examples, it would seem to follow that it is no evidence that a stable chemical compound, no matter what, is deleterious to life and health, just because some one or more of its different composing elements may chance to be; also that compounded substances are much more dependent, not only for their powers to nourish the system, but to destroy it, upon the strength of the union which exists between their different composing elements, than they are upon the nature of those elements when separately existing. In a word, the foregoing facts would seem to indicate that various articles, used as food and drink, would quite soon destroy us, were our stomachs capable of annulling the strong mutual affinity which binds in union their different composing elements; and thus setting each at liberty to prey upon our organic tissues, instead of each being compelled to hold fast its gripe, so to speak, upon the other. The same amount of saleratus, for example, that may be swallowed with impunity, when held in chemical union by and with a pint of hard cider, might injure and perhaps kill a man, if taken into the stomach by itself alone. Or should a very small pocket knife, for a clumsy but analogous example, be accidentally swallowed, when shut, it would not be likely to produce any very disastrous effects either to the stomach or bowels, for the reason that the dangerous element, the blade, however keen and sharp-pointed, is then locked, as it were, in a chemical embrace by the handle, too strong to be by the digestive powers overcome; and yet, was the blade of the same knife, when detached from the handle, to find its way into the stomach, the case would not unlikely be different.

POSSIBLE ORIGIN OF PRAIRIES.

No matter how spacious or how rich may be the inclosure, if kept constantly overstocked with cows, horses, and sheep, for example, the cows would all be compelled to suffer, starve, and die, before the sheep would be greatly pinched by hunger. Herefrom we are led to infer that it is at least possible, that the mastodon, which, from his enormous size, must have required a large amount of food to sustain him in health and strength, and whose capacious jaws were capable of craunching, as browse, shrubs, limbs and even the bodies of small trees, had something to do with deforesting those vast tracts of country in the West, known as plains and prairies, before he finally succumbed to starvation and so became extinct.

That those huge animals once roamed that wide region is certain. Wherefore it would seem to be certain that there must once have existed, in that locality, plenty of something for them to eat besides grass and such other small herbage as the buffalo, deer, etc., were much better calculated to grasp and subsist upon; and especially during the long cold months of winter. By a plain natural law, as seems to us, no sooner did that vast region become overstocked with the mastodon, buffalo, deer, and other herbivorous animals, than the further multiplication of trees, and hence the further renewing of the forests, became a thing impossible; since, in such case, not a seedling or sprout could long escape the voracious jaws of some one or other of those vegetable consumers. Thus, in process of time, the trees then existing, large and small, one after another, would be compelled by age, if nothing else, to pass away; and, as a necessary consequence, the animals requiring the largest amount of coarse vegetable food to sustain them in existence would be obliged to dwindle down and finally become extinct. The forests being thus once destroyed, the red man with his fires would be amply sufficient to keep trees from ever again growing, and multiplying themselves into forests, upon so much of that vast region as was both dry and exposed to the sweep of that devouring element.

That herbivorous animals had being before vegetable creation came into existence, or that the mastodon, elephant, buffalo, and other giant vegetable eaters ever, anywhere, became abundant before, in such locality, trees had time to shoot up their strong boles, stretch out their spreading limbs, and mantle the rich dry soil with their luxuriant foliage, it is unphilosophic to conclude.

That many of the fine marsh-meadows upon the small streams, in Michigan at least, are largely indebted for their creation to the industry of the beaver, doth seem to be evidenced both by the remains of their dams and the undecomposed bodies of the tamarack, black-ash, soft-maple, and other swamp-timber, found imbedded in the mucky soil of those meadows from one to three feet beneath the surface. By damming a creek at some point near its egress from a swamp, and thus overflowing the same, the beavers were enabled to live upon the bark of the trees, during the severe months of winter, until, by them and the water, the timber was finally all killed out, and they, in consequence, compelled to seek some other locality.

The timber being thus all killed out in a swamp of the proper natural soil and dryness, it is not unlikely that time and the grasses, aided by the Indian with flame and his ponies, were the creative causes which did the rest.

"THE BLOODY CHASM."

It was not so much from strong love of the institution of negro slavery as from deep hatred of the Yankees and Yankee traits of character, that caused the South to rebel against the Union; neither was it so much from strong love of the Union as from deep hatred of the Johnnies and Johnny traits of character, that caused the North to press the war so fiercely against the rebellion. Wherefore, as seems to us, the only way in which we can ever reasonably expect to become and be a united and happy people is by becoming more assimilated in taste and character, by means of a liberal flow of emigration from the less fertile and more populous North, to the more fertile and less populous South. In other words, it is only by intermingling as neighbors upon the same soil, that the Johnnies will ever become sufficiently Yankeefied and the Yankees sufficiently Johnnyfied to enable them to stand harmoniously together upon the same common platform of American sentiment and feeling, and hence to constitute, in truth and in fact, a united People.—The snake has only been "scotched, not killed."

STEAM.

As one of the constituents of water is prime supporter of combustion and the other exceedingly inflammable, so may it not be possible that this fluid may be heated to such a degree, when confined in strong boilers, as to cause a divorce to take place between its composing elements, and thus brought to produce results that are not properly chargeable to steam?

CHAPTER XXXVI.

SUGGESTIONS AND CONCLUSION.

HOW TO KEEP TIRE TIGHT.

By keeping the wheels of wagons and other heavy vehicles well covered with paint, (lead paints the best,) the tire will remain tight upon them until they are worn out; and when from neglect to keep them thus covered the tires have become loose, all that is necessary to render them tight again is to repaint the wheels thoroughly and, after the paint has become dry, give them a good soaking in water. In both cases, of course, it is taken for granted that the wheels were all right in the beginning; that is, that they were well put together, the timber thoroughly seasoned, and the tires properly fitted and set upon them. And in the latter case, or when shrunken wheels are being repainted for the purpose of retightening the tire upon them, it is further assumed that they are still sound and reasonably perfect.

As upon every part of a wheel, except the fellies, a good coat of paint will remain reasonably perfect for a long time; as it is this part of a wheel which much the most needs to be kept coated with paint, in order to keep the tire tight thereon; and as it is only from the sides of the fellies that it soon becomes worn off; so, in the majority of cases, it is only this small part which needs be repainted to keep the tire from ever getting loose, or to render the same tight again when it has already become so. Hence, allowing the tires upon all the wheels of a wagon to be loose, any man who is competent to drive a team can manage to daub over this small amount of plain surface with paint, in less time than he can drive to a smith's, get the tire reset, and come home again; and fifty cents will more than cover the expense of paint and oil with which to do it.

And this, as we understand, is the rationale of the thing: Neither air nor moisture is capable of penetrating iron, or passing through a good coat of paint. In other words, so long as wood is kept perfectly covered by either iron or paint, it cannot materially shrink or swell. Or, to be still more explicit, by covering a wheel with paint upon which the tire has become loose,—the same having been originally well fitted and set,—the air is excluded from the entire surface of the fellies, with the exception of their outer edge directly under the tire, which cannot of course be reached with the brush; and by soaking the wheel in water after the paint has become dry, the outer, or unpainted edge of the fellies, under such loose-fitting tire, will readily absorb moisture and keep on absorbing it, until they become so much swolen as again to fill the tire perfectly full; when, as a matter of course, no more moisture can enter and none that has already entered make its escape.[a]

If the farmers of America would all adopt and pursue this course, it would doubtless add to the length of life of this class of vehicles at least one fifth; and hence, in addition to the hundreds of thousands of dollars which would annually be saved to their pockets, it would work a saving to the country, in the shape of valuable timber, of an amount equal to one fifth part of all the vast quantity that is now being consumed in their construction, and which timber is daily becoming more and more in demand for other useful purposes.

Irrespective of the improvement in the looks, that it is good policy to keep the wheels of buggies and other light carriages well covered with paint cannot be doubted; and yet, owing to the small amount of wood which has come to be used in the construction of this class of wheels, it may

---

a We prefer this method to that of swelling the wheels before painting them, or to soaking them in oil for the purpose of retightening the tire.

not always be possible, by the use of paint, to keep the tires permanently tight upon them, or again to render them so, when once they have become loose.

WHEN TO CUT STADDLES.

Experience seems to prove that, in a majority of seasons in this latitude, trees, staddles, etc., which are cut late in August or forepart of September, will not sprout much; those late in September or forepart of October, less yet; and those late in October or forepart of November, least of all. The reason we suppose to be this: To trees, shrubs, and other perennials, Spring is the season of activity and preparation for labor; Summer the season of labor and growth; Fall the time for maturing and hardening the growth which the labor of Summer has added; and Winter a season of rest. Hence, by severing the bodies of trees, etc., from their roots at the time when the roots, from having parted with their juices to add new growth and bring the same to maturity, are in a state of greatest exhaustion, Winter, their natural season of rest and recuperation, becomes converted into one of suffering and death.

Timber cut in June, or when the bark peels freely, is not only less liable to become worm-eaten, but will outlast, either in the weather or out, that cut at any other season of the year.

HINT TO PARENTS.

For children to grow up healthy, happy, clear-headed, and strong, it is necessary that they should be sent to bed early, and there let to lie until they spontaneously wake up all over and all the way through. Indeed, it is better, not only for the young, but for the middle-aged, and even the old, to cultivate the habit of going to bed an hour before sunset,—if that be necessary, in order to secure sleep enough by morning,—than, by remaining up late, to fall into the habit of lying in bed an hour after sunrise.

Children that are habitually early retirers and good sleepers are not apt to become nervous, seldom get sick, and rarely make bad men. In a word, it is only whilst resting, whether sleeping or not, that old men recuperate and children grow.

A WORD TO BROTHER AUTHORS.

Have patience, think more, write less, publish less yet, and your works will longer live.

CONCLUSION.

And now, kind readers, one and all, a single assuring word before the final parting: Whether right or whether wrong, and whether acceptably or whether not, less blind faith and more investigation, less religion in empty forms and more in substance, less love toward God in mere words and more in action, are the things for which, in and through the act of penning these humble pages, we have sincerely prayed.

LIST OF ERRORS.

Page 7, line 26, the words "the faculty of" left out between "of" and "so."

Page 17, line 16, the word "influenced" should be "uninfluenced."

Page 21, line 29, the last "*those*" should be "*these*."

Page 23, line 9, the word "men" should be "then."

Page 29, line 15, the word "engraved" should be "ingrained."

Page 67, line 21, the word "him" left out between "treated" and "with."

Page 69, line 1, the word "On" should be "In."

Page 93, line 3, the word "some" should be "seven."

Page 109, line 3, for "It is not," read "Is it not."

Page 139, line 11, the word "those" should be "whose."

Page 149, line 29, the word "and" should be "not."

Page 155, lines 27 and 28, the word "intention" should be "intuition."

Page 164, line 33, the word "with" should be "both."

Page 166, line 6, the word "that" should be "than."

Page 170, line 16, the word "they" should be "then."

Page 182, line 7, the word "declares" should stand between "which" and "in," instead of following the word "substance."

Page 200, line 25, the word "wrought" should be "wrapt."

Page 241, line 14, the word "thinks" should be "things."

Page 243, line 12, the word "creative" should be "certain."

Page 246, line 6, between the words "law;" and "feeble" are left out the words, "in other words, by the combined presence and operation of a few."

Page 255, line 35, the word "internally" should be "inherently."

Page 280, line 4, the word "admitted" should be "administered."

Page 287, line 34, the word "more" should be "mere."

Page 290, line 8, the word "or" should be "of."

Page 319, line 22, the word "creation" should be "certain."

Page 324, line 36, the word "as" should be "are."

Page 327, line 16, the word "so-call" should be "so-called."

Page 331, line 14, the word "think" left out after the word "him."

Page 378, line 1, the word "so" left out between "try" and "to."

Page 380, line 2, the word "animated" should be "animal."

Page 381, line 4, the word "Newcomer" should be "Newcomen."

Page 383, line 30, the word "into" should be "unto"

www.ingramcontent.com/pod-product-compliance
Lightning Source LLC
LaVergne TN
LVHW011159110826
845150LV00006B/1262

* 9 7 8 1 4 2 5 5 4 5 7 8 9 *